Dendi Kartini Tinumbang

December 2003

Richard Wright
and
Racial Discourse

Richard Wright
and
Racial Discourse

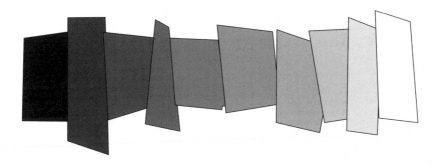

Yoshinobu Hakutani

University of Missouri Press
Columbia and London

Library of Congress Cataloging-in-Publication Data

Hakutani, Yoshinobu, 1935–
    Richard Wright and racial discourse / Yoshinobu Hakutani.
        p.   cm.
    ISBN 0-8262-1059-7 (alk. paper)
    1. Wright, Richard, 1908–1960—Criticism and interpretation.   2. Wright,
Richard, 1908–1960—Political and social views.   3. Literature and society—
United States—History—20th century.   4. Afro-Americans in literature.
5. Race relations in literature.   6. Racism in literature.   I. Title.
PS3545.R815Z666   1996
813'.52–dc20   96-10184
                                                                                CIP

∞ This paper meets the requirements of the
American National Standard for Permanence of Paper
for Printed Library Materials, Z39.48, 1984.

Designer: Leslie Forbes
Typesetter: BOOKCOMP
Printer and binder: Thomson-Shore, Inc.
Typefaces: Rotis Semi Sans and Palatino

To Michiko

Contents

Preface

This book is intended as a sort of revisit to *Native Son* and *Black Boy*, Wright's most celebrated fiction and nonfiction, and as an examination of his less known and less analyzed work, such as *Black Power, The Color Curtain*, and *Pagan Spain*. Because Wright's ideas often reflect those of writers in other cultures, a close study of his work in light of the diversity of other cultures as well as in comparison with the works of other cultures will provide insight not only into his own work, but into American culture in general.

In reconsidering Wright's fiction not merely as racial discourse but more significantly as the product of diverse cultures, I have discussed *Native Son* in comparison with Twain's *Pudd'nhead Wilson* and in contrast with Dreiser's *An American Tragedy*. In considering *The Outsider*, critics generally have considered Wright's philosophy in it nihilistic and imitative of French existentialism, but a comparison of the novel with Camus's *L'Étranger* reveals that Wright's novel is less nihilistic than widely believed and that it subtly expresses American idealism. Although Cross Damon professes to be a nihilist, as does Meursault, this African American is not indifferent to human existence, as is Meursault. Wright's hero, unlike Camus's, is an American idealist; he seeks love, friendship, marriage, success, freedom. *The Man Who Lived Underground* is also known as an existentialist work, but a rereading suggests that Wright was influenced by French existentialism, as well as by Zen philosophy, in which some French writers were interested in the 1940s. Like Emerson, Wright in this parable is emphasizing one's independence from God's power and influence. For Wright, an individual must achieve enlightenment by himself or herself even at the risk of losing sight of God, and this is akin to Zen doctrine. When *The Long Dream*, Wright's last novel written in exile in France, appeared in 1958, two years before his death, it encountered largely hostile reviews in America. A reevaluation of the novel, however, shows that Wright's final effort in fiction, concentrated on problems of miscegenation, thrives upon a dialectics between conservatism and liberalism; the South and the North; Clintonville, Mississippi, and Paris; America and Europe.

Wright's works of nonfiction, such as *Black Power*, *The Color Curtain*, and *Pagan Spain*, have not interested the New Critics. These "travel books," however, functioning as a collective body and as a distinctive genre, reflect the diversity in Wright's racial, cultural, economic, and political ideas in the context of his American, African American, European, Pan-African, and Asian experiences. Whereas Wright is primarily concerned with European colonialism in *Black Power*, and with problems of religion and with Catholicism in particular in *Pagan Spain*, he takes pains to develop his ideas on all these issues in *The Color Curtain*. As a result, *The Color Curtain*, based on his experience in attending an international, multicultural conference held outside the Western world for the first time, has become an important discourse on race and culture in postmodern American literature. Interestingly enough, Wright's discussion of racial and cultural problems in Asia and Africa does echo his view on such issues in America as expressed in *The Outsider*. The achievement of independent vision that Wright considers a crucial duty for the new Asians and Africans is what characterizes African Americans. This independent, double vision is what enables the nonwhite people of the world to acquire the basic ideas of democracy and freedom from the West but reject the inhuman aspects of capitalism: greed and materialism.

Finally, based on my recently completed edition of Wright's *This Other World: Projections in the Haiku Manner*, a selection of 817 out of the estimated four thousand unpublished haiku, I have concluded this book with a chapter on Wright's poetics, commenting on Wright's haiku in light of Japanese poetics. My objective was to determine Wright's conformity to, as well as his deviation from, the salient characteristics of the genre. To my surprise, not only did Wright follow Japanese aesthetics, but his well-wrought haiku also reflect the spirit of nature. In subject matter, Japanese haiku do not treat physical love, war, beasts, earthquakes, floods, and the like. Although Wright's prose work does convey eroticism, sensationalism, myth, evil, hatred, and prejudice, his haiku seem to shun such sentiments and emotions altogether. The most important philosophical tradition by which classic Japanese haiku was influenced is that of Zen. Zen practice calls for the austerity of the mind: one should not allow one's individuality to control action. Zen does not recognize the existence of good and evil, for both are but the creation of man's will rather than the spirit of nature. Traditionally haiku has little division between the perceiver and the perceived, spirit and matter, man and nature. Wright's best haiku, then, adhere to this tradition, and I have not interpreted them as modernist poems.

Acknowledgments

T his book owes much to many people and sources, including previous writers on Wright, as acknowledged in the notes and bibliography. I would like to thank, in particular, Robert Butler, Jerry W. Ward Jr., Robert Tener, and anonymous readers for the University of Missouri Press who have read part or whole of the manuscript and offered useful suggestions.

For the study of Wright's unpublished haiku, my chief obligations are to Mrs. Ellen Wright, who suggested in her letter to my colleague Robert Tener back in 1986 that he and I might work with her in the selection of the haiku and write an introduction and notes; to Julia Wright, whom I met along with Mrs. Wright at the African American Writers and Europe conference in February 1992; and to Patricia C. Willis, Curator of American Literature at the Beinecke Rare Book and Manuscript Library, Yale University, who kindly permitted my wife and me to work with these manuscripts. The 817 unpublished haiku in Wright's "This Other World: Projections in the Haiku Manner," edited by me and Robert Tener, will be published in the near future. I have commented on 55 of the haiku in the final chapter of my book.

In the course of my work, the Kent State University Research Council has provided a research leave and several grants-in-aid.

The following journals published my essays on Wright, which I have used in modified form in this book: "*Native Son* and *An American Tragedy:* Two Different Interpretations of Crime and Guilt," *Centennial Review;* "Creation of the Self in Richard Wright's *Black Boy*," *Black American Literature Forum* (now *African American Review*); "Richard Wright's Experiment in Naturalism and Satire: *Lawd Today*," *Studies in American Fiction;* "Richard Wright's *The Outsider* and Albert Camus's *The Stranger*," "Racial Oppression and Alienation in Richard Wright's 'Down by the Riverside' and 'Long Black Song,' " and "Richard Wright's *The Man Who Lived Underground,* Nihilism, and Zen," *Mississippi Quarterly.*

Above all, I owe my wife this book. Her struggle has been greater than mine.

Richard Wright
and
Racial Discourse

Introduction

1

In discussing the importance of Richard Wright, Irving Howe wrote in 1963, "The day *Native Son* appeared, American culture was changed forever." It would appear, from the intensive commentary in the more than half a century since Wright published *Native Son*, that the significance of his writings comes not so much from his technique and style as from the particular impact his ideas and attitudes have made on American life. His fiction, on which Wright established his permanent reputation, must be analyzed not merely as works of art but as racial discourse. To assess his achievement in such terms would require a broad study, not only of his technique of writing, but also of the social and cultural backgrounds of his fiction. His early critics' first consideration was that of race. They were unanimous in the view that if Wright had not been African American his fiction would not have been so significant. As his vision of the world extended beyond the United States, his quest for solutions expanded from problems of race to those of politics and economics in the emerging Third World. Finally, his long exile in France gave his national and international concerns a universal dimension, and this worldview is closely reflected in his later fiction. Thus Wright's development was marked by an ability to respond to the social and intellectual currents of his time.

Wright was a remarkably resilient thinker and writer. His successes are beyond dispute, his failures understandable. He has fascinated not only literary critics, but also philosophers, psychologists, sociologists, and historians. Although many of his fictional works failed to satisfy the rigid standards of the New Criticism, his evolution as a novelist has excited readers the world over. Michel Fabre is right in speculating that toward the end of his life Wright "was once again going through a period of ideological change which, had its course been completed, might have caused him to start writing in a new vein. It is highly probable that the civil rights and Black Power movements would have given him a second wind, had he lived another five years."

Needless to say, Wright's literary reputation was firmly established by his early works. *Uncle Tom's Children, Native Son,* and *Black Boy* alone have made him the greatest African American writer and accorded him the label of a major American novelist. His emergence as an African American writer was a phenomenon, as *Black Boy* clearly demonstrates, for not only did he endure racial oppression and lack of freedom in the South and the North, but he triumphed over them. His successful transformation of that experience into enduring writing has been recognized by readers of different races. Before Wright, African American writers primarily addressed themselves to an African American audience. If African Americans had written for a white audience, they would have been expected to present stereotyped pictures of African Americans. Exceptions like W. E. B. Du Bois and Charles W. Chesnutt went largely unheeded, because African Americans, as Wright said, "possessed deep-seated resistance against the Negro problem being presented, even verbally, in all its hideous dullness, in all the totality of its meaning." It was, therefore, somewhat miraculous that both black and white Americans believed what they read in *Native Son* and *Black Boy,* in which Wright destroys the white myth of the patient, humorous, subservient black man.

Some readers, notably James Baldwin, regarded Wright as a protest novelist, while some critics went so far as to attribute Wright's wide appeal to the sensationalism in his fiction. One cannot deny the terrifying suspense Bigger Thomas's actions generate, but Baldwin accused Wright of distorting the otherwise complex African American character. Other readers have disagreed: Robert Bone, a white critic, arguing that Bigger is one of the black people's "roles," felt that Wright did not simplify the complexity of black life. Although many of Wright's fictional works appear to be protest literature, they poignantly dramatize the themes of alienation, fear, and guilt that had not successfully been treated by Wright's predecessors.

It has generally been taken for granted that Wright was schooled in the tradition of American literary naturalism. In *Black Boy,* Wright tells us how he was inspired by Theodore Dreiser's *Jennie Gerhardt* and *Sister Carrie:* "It would have been impossible for me to have told anyone what I derived from these novels, for it was nothing less than a sense of life itself. All my life had shaped me for the realism, the naturalism of the modern novels, and I could not read enough of them." Such testimony, however, indicates only Wright's youthful taste in books; it hardly proves that he became a doctrinaire naturalist in his writing. Indeed, to what extent he is part of American naturalism has become one of the central questions about Wright's work. In *Native Son*, for instance, does he subscribe to the novel's implicit assumption that American social conditions are directly responsible for the degradation of African Americans? Recent criticism has modified or refuted the naturalistic reading, suggesting that Wright went beyond naturalism. The pessimistic determinism often associated with literary naturalism had taught the young Wright the meaning of racial oppression. A victim of oppression himself, Wright by necessity directed his energy toward rebellion. While he escaped the pessimistic outlook of naturalism, his respect for the philosophy helped him develop his own individualism and endow his characters with self-determination. Self-pity and rage alone would not have impressed modern readers. As Wright moved beyond anger and protest, he developed a new concern for character and literary discipline, seeking a deeper involvement in the world of philosophy and discourse. Naturalism taught him how to determine the position of human beings in the world; existentialism taught him how to liberate them from the strictures imposed on them.

Wright's affinity with Dreiser can be explained in another way. That Wright made no distinction between realism and naturalism in reading Dreiser's novels suggests a predilection for the fiction that mirrors social reality, the writing that not only expresses the sentiments of the socially oppressed but also thrives upon the unalloyed feelings of individuals. Wright might have had the same impression of the Dreiserian novel as did Louis Auchincloss, his contemporary, who wrote in his introduction to *Sister Carrie:* "How is it that such a bad writer could have been such a great one? . . . I suggest that there may be two answers: one, that urban life in America in the first two decades of our century corresponded to Dreiser's concept of it as a jungle, and, two, that he liked jungles, or at least that he liked the spectacle of ferocity, the drama of the struggle for survival. Perhaps what I am saying is that he liked life in the raw—or life in the raw as he conceived it."

The assessment of a writer's achievement cannot be complete without considering his influences upon other writers. Black literary history clearly indicates that after the publication of *Native Son* and *Black Boy,* quaintness and idealized folksiness disappeared from African American literature. Instead, writers like Chester Himes and William Gardner Smith wrote on the agonizing effects of the urban ghetto environment. During the forties emerged many examples of the so-called problem novel: Wright's influence can be detected in such works as Chester Himes's *If He Hollers Let Him Go*, William Gardner Smith's *Last of the Conquerors*, Ann Petry's *The Street*, Willard Motley's *Knock on Any Door*, and Willard Savoy's *Alien Land*, to mention a few. In the fifties African American literature came to occupy a permanent place in contemporary American literature. Despite disclaimers to the contrary by the authors themselves, Ralph Ellison's *Invisible Man* (1952) and James Baldwin's *Notes of a Native Son* (1955) as racial discourses would not have enjoyed the critical acclaim they did without the road Wright had paved a decade earlier. Like Wright, Ellison was deeply involved with the problem of race, but with the help of his creative imagination he succeeded in making what is racial and regional into what is universal. Likewise, Baldwin, with the sharpest rhetorical skills of any African American writer, described his work as a concern with "the depthless alienation from oneself and one's people—this is the sum of the American experience."

The magnitude of Wright's achievement and importance is indicated by the numerous biographical studies, a dozen of them book length, published since the forties. Constance Webb's *Richard Wright: A Biography* (1968) is a long, passionate account by a personal friend of Wright's. Despite Webb's access to Ellen Wright's notes, letters, and other original materials, the book lacks the coherence and chronology critics need. Although it provides useful information, it falls far short of a definitive biography of a major novelist, such as Mark Shorer's *Sinclair Lewis: An American Life* or W. A. Swanberg's *Dreiser*. John A. Williams's *The Most Native of Sons: A Biography of Richard Wright* (1970), though dismissed by Michel Fabre as a juvenile book, provides an intimate account of the psychological makeup of an African American novelist by an African American novelist. Although Williams persuasively demonstrates that the central theme of Wright's work is race, he hypothesizes that Wright would have established his reputation earlier and more easily had he not been an African American. Fabre's *The Unfinished Quest of Richard Wright* (1973) ranks with the biographies of Lewis and Dreiser mentioned above for its scope and organization, the only difference being that, despite Fabre's intention to exclude criticism, he does not do so in many parts of his book. The reason for this treatment can be explained partly by his statement of principle: "Literature and politics were two equally indispensable tools in the service of humanism. This is why I insist upon judging Wright's work as a whole, not separating his writing from its ideological framework, and not making a split, only artificially justified by his exile, in the unfolding of his career."

The earliest book-length critical study was attempted by Edward Margolies: *The Art of Richard Wright* (1969). Unlike those critics who regard Wright as a proletarian writer, Margolies successfully demonstrates Wright's themes of fear and alienation, though he admits that Wright "seldom achieved his fullest measure of artistic promise." Far from a critical study, *The Example of Richard Wright* by Dan McCall (1969) attempts to show the link between the author's personality and work, but McCall is surely handicapped by his failure to use all the biographical data available to him. In *Richard Wright: An Introduction to the Man and His Works* (1970), Russell C. Brignano organizes his study not by the chronology of Wright's writing, but by a focus on Wright's themes and topics. One of Brignano's unique contributions to Wright criticism is his attempt to discuss Marxism. Brignano argues, as does Fabre in his biography, that Wright was essentially a humanist and thus naturally collided with Communist Party doctrine. In *The Emergence of Richard Wright* (1972), Keneth Kinnamon explains convincingly that Wright faced more formidable obstacles in his youth than any other American writer. Kinnamon accounts for Wright's extraordinary accomplishment with well-annotated evidence. Referring to the emotional depravity the young Wright felt in his fanatically religious family and racially prejudiced community, as well as the occasional release he felt in reading fiction, Kinnamon carefully demonstrates how Wright converted his anger into creativity. Robert Bone's *Richard Wright* attempts to explain Wright's attraction to existentialism by noting his "tendency to make a virtue out of rootlessness, to conceive of the human condition as a kind of cosmic exile."

The positive effect of Wright's early life on his creativity is well summarized by Houston A. Baker Jr. in "Racial Wisdom and Richard Wright's *Native Son*," originally published in his book *Long Black Song* (1972). Baker maintains that Wright criticism has been hampered by tenets of New Criticism that overemphasize analysis of the work itself at the expense of examining the creator's life. It was Wright's fight for survival in early life, Baker points out, that contributed to the success of his early works. This phenomenon, Baker argues, continued after Wright had left the South and even the United States. On the other hand, Saunders Redding, a noted African American critic and writer, observes in his essay "The Alien Land of Richard Wright," included in Herbert Hill's collection *Soon, One Morning* (1963), that in describing his experience in Europe and Africa, Wright "turns precious and arty; honesty deserts him; dedication wilts; passion chills."

Among the studies focusing on Wright's relations to the Communist Party, John A. Williams's biography, mentioned earlier, is the most perceptive and sympathetic in its discussion of Wright's youth. As an African American novelist, Williams appreciates the strong attraction Communist politics had for the young Wright in the depth of the Depression. The most comprehensive history of Wright's association with the Communist Party is provided by Daniel Aaron in "Richard Wright and the Communist Party" (1971). Aaron traces Wright's connection with the actual or would-be Communist world from the early thirties: his initial involvement with the Chicago John Reed Club in 1932, then his membership in the American Communist Party, which concluded with the end of his literary apprenticeship, by 1940. Aaron's survey contains many facts of interest; for instance, the chairman of the first national conference for the John Reed Club held in Chicago in 1932 was a man named Jan Wittenber, the model for Jan Erlone in *Native Son*. The policy of black self-determination, to which Wright must have been attracted, was maintained between 1928 and 1934, but played down during the Popular Front period (1934–1939). As Aaron points out, by the midthirties Wright legitimately felt that "the Party oversimplified Black Experience." It would be difficult to determine exactly how Wright felt about black self-determination or the Black Republic at that time, but Aaron believes the Marxist lawyer's statement on African Americans in *Native Son* may provide an important clue: "They are not simply twelve million people; in reality, they constitute a separate nation, stunted, stripped, and held captive within this nation." Wright's growing disenchantment with the Communist Party is also suggested by his making fools of Jan and Mary, the insensitive Communists in the novel. Wright left the party, Aaron concludes, because he was unable to reconcile black nationalism, in which he had faith, with Marxist universalism, to which he paid lip service.

As for the literary tradition Wright followed, most critics view him as a naturalist writer. In his review of *Lawd Today*, "Dreiser to Farrell to Wright" (1963), Granville Hicks maintains that Dreiser influenced James Farrell, who in turn influenced Wright. Michel Fabre, however, argues in "Richard Wright: Beyond Naturalism?" (1975) that Wright, far from being deterministic and concerned with detail, sought intensity of feeling. Wright, Fabre says, is akin to Frank Norris, who viewed naturalism as a type of romanticism; reality must be twisted from the ordinary. Fabre bases his argument on "Blueprint for Negro Writing," in which Wright contends: "The presentation of their lives should be simple, yes; but all the complexity, the strangeness, the magic, the wonder of life that plays like a bright sheen over the most sordid existence should be there. To borrow a phrase from the Russians, it should have a *complex simplicity.*"

Discussion of Wright's relations with his literary contemporaries has focused on James Baldwin, who is well known to have regarded Wright as his mentor, but soon rebelled against him. In "Everybody's Protest Novel" (1949) Baldwin calls Bigger Thomas a descendant of Uncle Tom. In "Many Thousands Gone" (1951) Baldwin asserts that *Native Son* "suggested a revolution of racial conflict that was merely the liberal dream of good will in which blacks would obliterate their personalities and become as whites." Michel Fabre maintains in *The Unfinished Quest of Richard Wright* that although Baldwin was helped by his mentor, he was afraid the American public would not recognize his originality and, "therefore, leaned over backwards to assert their differences." To Baldwin, Wright's treatment of the problem of race seems to be directed toward the fictional but realistic presentation of his rage. Although sympathetic to the rage, Baldwin sees a basic flaw in Wright's technique, contending that the novelist must analyze raw emotion and transform it into an identifiable human experience. Hence there is a fundamental difference between the two novelists in dealing with fictional material: while Baldwin is interested in refining social reality for his purposes, Wright is bent on presenting racial experience as what Auchincloss calls "life in the raw." Baldwin cannot approve of Wright's use of violence, which he regards as "gratuitous and compulsive because the root of the violence is never examined. The root is rage."

Critics, however, attribute the difference between Wright and Baldwin to differences in their personalities and in their ideas of humanity. In "Wright, the Protest Novel, and Baldwin's Faith" (1974), Kichung Kim advances the theory that the difference between the African American novelists arises from two different concepts of man. Kim posits that the weakness Baldwin sees in Wright and other protest writers "is not so much that they had failed to give a faithful account of the actual conditions of man but rather that they had failed to be steadfast in their devotion . . . to what man might and ought to be. Such a man . . . will not only survive oppression but will be strengthened by it." Fred L. Standley, in his essay " ' . . . Farther and Farther Apart': Richard Wright and James Baldwin" (1982), examines their relationship in four major aspects: Wright as Baldwin's "spiritual father," Baldwin's betrayal of friendship, their concepts of "protest literature," and their interpretations of Bigger Thomas. Relying on a precise chronology of the events that occurred between them, Standley offers well-annotated evidence that their attitudes toward each other came from "the deep and irreconcilable differences" in their philosophies of life and theories of literature.

Interestingly enough, the controversy over the Wright-Baldwin relationship has involved other African American writers. In recent decades Baldwin's audience of American readers has displeased African American militants; Eldridge Cleaver in *Soul on Ice* (1968) called Baldwin one of the "Stepin Fetchits" of our age. Cleaver attacked Baldwin personally, claiming that his criticism of *Native Son* stems from an envy of Wright's masculinity. Cleaver furthermore despises Baldwin's work because in it he finds "the most grueling, agonizing, total hatred of the blacks, particularly of himself, and the most shameful, fanatical, fawning, sycophantic love of the whites that one can find in the writings of any black American writer of note in our time." Amiri Baraka, another militant writer, predictably shares this point of view. In *Home: Social Essays* (1966), Baraka accuses Baldwin of failure to become involved in the racial struggle: "Men like Baldwin and [Peter] Abrahams want to live free from such 'ugly' things as 'the racial struggle' because (they imply) they simply cannot stand what it does to men."

Baldwin and Baraka believe in two fundamentally different principles of love and hate. Baldwin, discovering that hatred has the power to destroy, has invested his absolute faith in the redemptive role of black people in American society through love; Baraka, observing that hatred of white people is the natural result of being black in America, has sanctioned hatred as the only reasonable reaction to racial oppression. Baraka is also critical of Wright's treatment of race in his fiction. Wright's fiction, as well as African American literature in general, has become a white literature written in imitation of "the useless, ugly inelegance of the stunted middle-class mind." As long as the African American writer refuses to look around him and "tell it like it is," Baraka warned in *Saturday Review* (1963), "he will be just another dead, mediocre writer.

Wright, Baldwin, and Ellison can be compared to Maugham, not to Joyce or Melville."

Baraka's disparaging remarks about Wright's achievement notwithstanding, the general estimate of Wright's work by white writers and critics is higher than that of any other black writer. As a writer and reader, Gerald Green in "Back to Bigger" (1966) claims that what really excites the modern sensibility is well-constructed social fiction like *Native Son*. For Green, Wright's novel, more than anything else, informs the reader what it means to be black in America. Richard Wright's Bigger Thomas, Green confesses, "still has the power to scare me silly. . . . Baldwin has never frightened me the slightest." Green concludes this general essay by mourning "what a falling off, from Richard Wright, say, to LeRoy Jones, from Sean O'Casey to Edward Albee." Donald B. Gibson, in "Richard Wright: Aspects of His Afro-American Literary Relations" (1982), argues that Wright differs from other African American novelists chiefly in the endowment of his characters with power. Another difference is his adherence to both naturalism and Marxism; while Wright is aware of the forces that control human behavior, he believes that life can be changed by people. Racism in Charles Chesnutt and Paul Dunbar, as Gibson shows, differs from that in Wright, who views discrimination not merely on the basis of race, but also on the basis of political, economic, and social considerations.

2

Wright criticism in the eighties and early nineties has been devoted to a rigorous reappraisal of Wright's life and work. Addison Gayle's *Richard Wright: Ordeal of a Native Son* (1980), based on documents obtained under the Freedom of Information Act, clarifies new information relating to actions by and against Wright on the part of the investigative agencies of the U.S. government. Gayle's work reveals, in particular, the long-suspected harassment Wright suffered from the FBI, CIA, and State Department. In the course of reading the material on Wright's Communist affiliation, Gayle discovered that the FBI in Paris had tried to make "the Baldwin-Wright literary controversy into a political one and pit one black writer against the other." Gayle also discovered that Wright's sudden break with the Communist Party in 1958 was triggered by his personal altercation with Benjamin Davis Jr., one of the most influential party intellectuals. Most important of all, Gayle became convinced that Wright's death by heart attack was largely caused by "the constant pressure and tension-ridden situations induced by the ordeal to which his government subjected him." Another major work on Wright's life, Margaret Walker's *Richard Wright: Daemonic Genius* (1988), focuses on Wright's intellectual development and, in particular, on the development from his segregated existence in the Deep South to his cosmopolitan living buoyed up with a universal worldview. Because Walker, an African American writer herself, experienced a similar ordeal and was personally acquainted with Wright, her memoir and impressions of him are of especial value. Walker calls Wright "a great intellectual, and his mind developed in a profound manner using a brain that was like a machine in perpetual motion." Small wonder the American government was paranoid about Wright.

Recent critical studies have focused on Wright's artistry and rhetoric. Joyce Ann Joyce's *Richard Wright's Art of Tragedy* (1986) cogently demonstrates that though the power of *Native Son* derives from the fierce battle Bigger Thomas wages against racist society, the impact of the tragedy on the reader comes directly from its language. Instead of monolithically characterizing Bigger as a victim of his racist environment, Wright, as Joyce shows, amply succeeds in portraying him in terms of dialectical images and ideas. Eugene E. Miller's *Voices of a Native Son: The Poetics of Richard Wright* (1990), rather than exploring the genesis of Wright's fiction in literary naturalism, examines the sources of Wright's literary theory in other traditions. As noted earlier, the serious limitation James Baldwin saw in Bigger's character is not Wright's use of Bigger as a symbol, but the absence of the social and human relations that underlie that symbol. What Baldwin failed to discover behind the symbol, Miller tries to fill in by exploring African American religiosity, folklore, and music. As Robert Butler's *Native Son: The Emergence of a New Black Hero* (1991) indicates, Wright criticism continues to pay special attention to *Native Son*. Butler carefully accounts for the many interrelated literary traditions underlying the novel. He has provided far more detail than have previous critics in explicating the setting, structure, characterization, point of view, tone, and theme of this epoch-making novel.

Recent critics also have paid attention to Wright's narrative technique in particular. In *Self-Discovery and Authority in Afro-American Narrative* (1987), Valerie Smith provides a lucid demonstration for Wright's portrayal of alienation and creativity achieved through language. Barbara Johnson, on the other hand, approaches Wright's narrative style and structure from the vantage points of feminism. In "The Re(a)d and the Black" (1988), she advances her argument that *Native Son* is marred by Wright's inability to describe either the black woman's voice or her story. While previous commentaries on the novel have cursorily been concerned with the overwhelming irony that Bigger is executed not because of his rape and brutal murder of a black woman, but because of his accidental killing of a white woman, Johnson's interpretation is based on a solid analysis of history and culture. Wright was surely handicapped, as Johnson notes, because of "overdetermination" and "underdetermination" in American writing: "it is because the 'rape' plot about white women or the 'idealization' plot about Indian women is so overdetermined that the plot about black women remains muffled beyond recognition."

Recent Wright criticism has also been concerned with *Black Boy*, perhaps one of the finest autobiographies American culture has produced. In "Sociology of an Existence: Wright and the Chicago School" (1985), Carla Cappetti, comparing Wright's autobiography to the findings by the Chicago School of Urban Sociology, concludes that social reality in the city is constructed by an opposition of "individual" and "primary groups, community, culture." Cappetti thus reads Wright's autobiographical persona as "condemned to travel from bondage to bondage forever, never to reach freedom." The point is understandable if it reflects only the ending of *American Hunger*, but it is mistaken if based on the last words of *Black Boy*. There Wright intimates that he has discovered an indelible connection to the legacy of American realism spearheaded by Dreiser and Mencken. Abdul R. JanMohamed's "Negating the Negation as a Form of Affirmation in Minority Discourse: The Construction of Richard Wright as Subject" (1987) defines *Black Boy* as Wright's dialectics, in which "not only does racist society negate Wright, but he too must negate himself, at least in public." Hence, black people in racist society, like slaves, can become the object of white culture but not its subject. JanMohamed shows Wright's transcendence of racism through forms of "dissembling"—for example, through reading literature and producing his own.

Both Janice Thaddeus and Herbert Leibowitz have closely examined *Black Boy* in comparison with *American Hunger*. In "The Metamorphosis of *Black Boy*" (1985), Thaddeus, tracing the publication history of *Black*

Boy, points out that the autobiography, as published, contains "the hesitancy in the final pages, the conditional verbs, the haltered rhetoric, the
mention of luck" rather than "a note of triumph" and "moment of truth."
Despite the fact that the final six pages of *Black Boy* were transferred from
American Hunger to generate Wright's feelings of hope and optimism,
Thaddeus argues that, when read together, both books underscore a
sense of isolation and bewilderment, "a sadness and disarray" in his
world. Thaddeus, however, overemphasizes Wright's lack of conviction
and sense of isolation, for *Black Boy* does end on a hopeful note and even
the ending of *American Hunger* does retain a ray of hope, however faint it
may be. In " 'Arise, Ye Pris'ners of Starvation': Richard Wright's *Black Boy*
and *American Hunger*" (1993), Leibowitz, also comparing *Black Boy* and
American Hunger, follows previous critics: he laments a lack of sparks
in *American Hunger,* the second half of the autobiography. But what
he ignores in his comparison is a juxtaposition of the character of the
young Wright in *Black Boy* to that of Ross in *American Hunger.* Wright's
treatment of the Ross episode, Leibowitz argues, suffers from Wright's
having "fallen into a sentimental trance." Clearly Wright is sympathetic
toward Ross and rightly critical of the Communist Party, but for his
autobiography Wright used Ross's demise as a foil to dramatize his
own self-creation. Ross in *American Hunger* is a sign of self-destruction
just as the young Wright is that of self-creation.

Although recent Wright criticism has been devoted to readings of
Native Son and *Black Boy,* it has not neglected such novels as *Lawd Today*
and *The Outsider.* William Burrison's "Another Look at *Lawd Today:*
Wright's Tricky Apprenticeship" (1986) explains Wright's skillful use
of African American trickster folklore. Burrison takes issue with Nick
Aaron Ford, who criticized Wright's creation of shallow, stereotyped
African Americans such as Jake, Bob, Al, Slim, Lil, Duke, Doc, and the
like. But Burrison regards Big Boy, Fred Daniels, and Bigger Thomas
as similarly "unflattering stereotypes." Few readers, perhaps save for
Ku Klux Klanners, would call Fred Daniels and Bigger Thomas "unflattering stereotypes"; both characters will go down in literary history as
modernist heroes of American tragedy. In "Christian Existentialism in
Richard Wright's *The Outsider*" (1982), Claudia C. Tate shows an affinity
between Kierkegaard's philosophy as expressed in *The Concept of Dread*
and Cross Damon's. Tate maintains that Wright's heroes—Silas, Bigger,
Fred, and Cross—all follow the pattern of spiritual redemption achieved
by Kierkegaard's dialectical psychology. Cross's "inverted wisdom" is

reminiscent of *The Sickness into Death* in light of Kierkegaard's use of the opposite image of salvation: spiritual wretchedness to be converted to spiritual redemption.

Recent studies have also dealt with *12 Million Black Voices* and *The Color Curtain*, two of the seldom analyzed nonfictions. In *Workings of the Spirit: The Poetics of Afro-American Women's Writing* (1991), Houston A. Baker Jr. analyzes *12 Million Black Voices* on the basis of American history and slavery and shows a distinction between African American male and female roles. Baker sees Wright's African American men as collaborators of northern machine culture and his African American women as domestics. Wright's historiography of black people, Baker explains, derives from "scientific socialism"; consequently, the woman, as domestic, is not "a productive force of Western modernism." Wright like Ellison, Baker persuasively argues, misreads machines as a sign of modernism. John M. Reilly's "Richard Wright and the Art of Non-Fiction: Stepping Out on the Stage of the World" (1986) incisively shows that in *The Color Curtain* Wright uses his own experience as an oppressed minority in advising the Third World elites on political modernism. The dynamics of will, represented in his autobiography, becomes a model for the political will of the Third World. Wright's philosophy in *The Color Curtain*, then, can be called political existentialism.

3

Now that Arnold Rampersad's edition (1991), *Richard Wright: Early Works* and *Richard Wright: Later Works,* has been completed, critics are anxious to compare the originally published versions of Wright's major works with the manuscript versions. Rampersad's contribution to Wright's criticism is enormous since this new edition, which has restored many passages deleted or revised, sheds new light on the works' sexual, racial, or political implications.

Even before Rampersad's edition was available, Keneth Kinnamon was the first to reexamine the publication history of *Native Son*. In "How *Native Son* Was Born" (1990) he reads the characterization of Bigger at the end of the novel as that of a man "left in existential solitude as the simple, monosyllabic concluding sentences sound the knell of that fate which inexorably follows his fear and flight." Kinnamon shows with precision how Wright revised that ending. It is also to Kinnamon's credit that Edward Aswell's hand in Wright's revision on sexual and political material is judiciously analyzed and evaluated. Not only did the editor's taste in literary style affect the Harper edition, but the negative impact *Native Son* would possibly have had on the American literary public in 1940 was also on the minds of author and editor. It was in 1963 that the late Irving Howe made the prophetic statement, as noted earlier: "The day *Native Son* appeared, American culture was changed forever." "The change," as Kinnamon says, "was not basic or profound, but it was real." Today, not only are we grateful to Aswell for being instrumental in bringing out such a book, as Kinnamon suggests, but also America, history will record, is forever indebted to Wright for writing it.

A reading of Rampersad's edition, incorporated into my discussions in this book, suggests that changes between the Harper edition and the original manuscript have to do not only with a type of censorship imposed on the Harper edition but also with a desire on Wright's part to make improvements on the style and structure of his novel. The Harper edition of *Native Son*, for example, cut out the masturbation scene obviously not to offend its readers. Wright, on the other hand, replaced the manuscript version of a dialogue between Bigger and Jack, which indicates their acquaintance with Communism, with a published version in which they are presented as naive, uneducated African American boys. In the Harper edition, then, Wright intended to underscore Bigger's dramatic growth and sophistication in world affairs at the end of the novel.

Some of the changes made in *The Outsider* also have to do with deletion of vulgar and sexually graphic expressions, but other changes concern Wright's intentions about character and ideology. Most of the cuts suggest that this novel, as originally conceived, was not as avowedly existentialist as critics have characterized the Harper edition as being. A new reading of the manuscript suggests that Wright's original intention was not to portray Cross Damon as a black man in name only but to create an African American, a genuine product of American society and culture.

While previous criticism has vigorously analyzed Wright's work in terms of American naturalism and European existentialism, it has become obvious that his fiction, nonfiction, and poetry are all buttressed by diverse cultural backgrounds. Even within American culture one cannot help recognizing the diverse strands of tradition and development that have influenced any writer's creative vision. It is commonplace to say that Wright's major phase as a novelist is reminiscent of the tradition of American naturalism, for Wright acknowledges in *Black Boy* that he was deeply influenced by "the realism, the naturalism of the modern novel" in America. In 1941, contrasting Dreiser to Dickens, Wright stated in the *New York Herald Tribune:* "I never could get into Dickens. He reeks with sentimentality. Theodore Dreiser, though, is the greatest writer this country has ever produced. His *Jennie Gerhardt* is the greatest novel." As late as 1955, when Wright lived in exile in Paris, he said in an interview in *L'Express:* "Of American writers, Theodore Dreiser first revealed to me the nature of American life, and for that service, I place him at the pinnacle of American literature." One can see Wright's kinship with Dreiser by placing side by side *Black Boy* and *Dawn, Native Son* and *An American Tragedy, The Long Dream* and *Jennie Gerhardt.* What Wright learned from Dreiser, son of a German immigrant, was the portrayal of American life by an outsider, as Wright was. Indeed, Dreiser was the first American writer who gave his culture a new horizon, and his work served Wright as a model of minority discourse.

But even American naturalism is not a monolithic tradition, and American society in the twentieth century has increasingly been pluralistic. It may be time to reexamine the tradition of American naturalism in regard to Wright. For one thing, he was not himself overly concerned with the usefulness of such a term as *naturalism* since he does not distinguish naturalism from realism. That is, Wright's work, particularly his early books such as *Uncle Tom's Children, Native Son, 12 Million Black Voices,* and *Black Boy,* is best analyzed not in terms of a doctrinaire literary philosophy such as naturalism or existentialism, but in the light of each book's historical and cultural backgrounds.

In comparison with the works of other major African American writers such as Langston Hughes, Zora Neale Hurston, Ralph Ellison, James Baldwin, and Toni Morrison, Wright's work is to a larger degree grounded in a cross-cultural or multicultural vision of life. In *The Outsider,* for instance, Cross Damon is told by his prosecuting attorney that for an African American to succeed in the white world requires a double vision, an ability to see the self both as an insider and as an outsider. Such an outlook upon life not only for African Americans but for all human beings, a vision of global interrelatedness, pervades Wright's later work beginning with *The Outsider.* His life in France and his travels in Spain, as well as his journeys into Africa and Asia, intensified this multicultural vision of life. At the end of his life, as his four thousand haiku well indicate, not only was he genuinely a humanist, but he also acquired Zen philosophy.

The advent of deconstructionism, the new historicism, and feminist, psychoanalytic, and cultural criticisms now enables us to gauge the relationships between Wright's work and its complex backgrounds. Such new approaches also help us discard overly artificial distinctions between fiction and nonfiction, novel and autobiography. To reassess Wright's work, one must also discard old distinctions among literature, history, and social sciences, as well as blurring other boundaries. *Native Son*, for example, can be read as an authentic historical document, just as *Black Boy* can be appreciated as a novel. Novels like *Native Son* and *The Long Dream* thrive on materials traditionally regarded as nonfictional and journalistic. Yet it is these materials that make the novels more accurate readings of American culture and history. In short, Wright's fiction, based upon history, in turn enlightens that history.

What buttresses Wright's work is his unique discourse on race and culture. As Wright modeled his portrayal of life on that of an American realist like Dreiser, he also was profoundly influenced by Dostoyevsky. In 1941, a Mexican editor asked Wright, "What literary influences do you recognize in your work?" Wright said, "The writers I like most and the ones the critics have pointed out to me as possible influences are Dreiser, Conrad, Sherwood Anderson, Maupassant, Flaubert, Chekhov, Joyce, Henry James, Stephen Crane, Gorky, and especially, Dostoevsky." As late as 1955, Wright told *L'Express:* "The books that have influenced me would make a long list. I'll be selective. Foremost among all the writers who have influenced me in my attitude toward the psychological state of modern man is Dostoevsky."

Wright's affinity to Dostoyevsky can be seen by comparing *Native Son* to *Crime and Punishment*. In both novels, the author's consciousness is conveyed in a dialectic discourse: it has a tendency to express itself in a variety of voices rather than a single voice. Just as Raskolnikov is not Dostoyevsky's mouthpiece, Wright takes pains to create a distinct voice for Bigger Thomas. In such a narrative, the protagonist does not abstract from his own experience and speak of himself in vague, general terms merely as a man. As the story unfolds, his voice becomes uniformly specific and individualistic. A change in his voice thus reflects a change in the way he exists in the world as an individual whose struggles, however representative they may be, are always, ultimately, personal.

Wright's discourse in nonfiction also bears some resemblance to Dostoyevsky's dialectic narrative. Both writers use the narrator's consciousness as a battleground for other people's voices. In *Crime and Punishment*, Raskolnikov's consciousness provides a forum for a diversity of voices engaged in complex interactions, just as the young Wright in *Black Boy* hears various voices of black and white people pitted against one another. There is, however, a fundamental difference between the two books in the development of discourse. In Dostoyevsky's dialectic narrative, opposing values and beliefs genuinely counterpoint one another. In such a dialogue, primarily based on philosophical grounds, opposing views enlighten each other and often result in synthesis. It is, therefore, unnecessary for the author to privilege a single point of view that expresses his moral or philosophical position. In *Black Boy*, on the other hand, Wright creates multiple points of view (radical, conservative, religious) representing different groups of black people, as well as multiple points of view (Ku Klux Klan, conservative, liberal) representing different groups of white people. In addition, Wright creates a silent voice that accounts for facts of history, and slavery in particular. In place of dialogue and synthesis, Wright creates in *Black Boy* a distinct, independent voice to express universal humanism, a conviction that prevails over any other point of view.

Wright's own consciousness varies from book to book. As late as 1954, when *Black Power* came out, he was still sympathetic toward Marxism. Throughout his career he was a capitalist as writing provided him with a livelihood. When he traveled in Africa he was taken up with what he called "the African primal outlook upon life," as at the Bandung conference he was impressed by the coexistence of multiculturalism and modernism in Asia, a piece of history that in turn provided him with a sign of progress for race relations in America. In his journey to Spain he discovered the paganism and superhumanism that underlie that culture. At the end of his life, he was fascinated by haiku and Zen. As a novelist he followed the tradition of American realism, but at the same time he tried to be a modernist like Joyce and Faulkner. All in all, Wright's fiction, as well as his neglected nonfiction, constitutes not merely a well-made narrative but also a postmodern discourse on race and culture unparalleled in world literature.

1

Lawd Today, an Apprentice Novel

awd Today, completed by 1935 and released posthumously in 1963, is an anomaly in Richard Wright's canon since it was written first but published last. It has puzzled critics since its publication, eliciting a variety of responses. Granville Hicks, in a review entitled "Dreiser to Farrell to Wright," affectionately defended *Lawd Today,* calling it less powerful than *Native Son* or *Black Boy* but uniquely interesting. What interested Hicks in this novel is that, though Wright was an avowed Communist at the time of its composition, he did not make a Communist out of Jake Jackson, its protagonist. Jake even despises Communism, but he also refuses to become a victim of capitalism. Sympathetic critics have considered Wright's delineation of Jake superb, or at least as good as that of any other character in his best fiction: Jake is uneducated, frustrated, but alive.

James Baldwin had earlier assailed Wright's treatment of Bigger Thomas in *Native Son.* He believed that Wright's characterization of Bigger is marred by a paucity of feeling the protagonist has for his fellow human beings. For Baldwin, though Wright records black anger as no writer before him had done, the expression of anger is also the overwhelming limitation of *Native Son.* What is sacrificed, according to Baldwin, is a necessary dimension to the novel: "the relationship that Negroes bear to one another, that depth of involvement and unspoken recognition of shared experience which creates a way of life." Baldwin further argued: "What the novel reflects—and at no point interprets—is the isolation of the Negro within his own group and the resulting fury of impatient scorn. It is this which creates its climate of anarchy and unmotivated and unapprehended disaster." But

Baldwin came around and said that "his great forte, it now seems to me, was an ability to convey inward states by means of externals."[1] Although this response specifically refers to "The Man Who Lived Underground," Baldwin also seems to have in mind Cross Damon in *The Outsider* (1953), whose prototype is Jake Jackson: Cross begins as an uneducated frustrated worker in the Chicago post office exactly as Jake does. In general, those opposed to naturalism in modern fiction were not appreciative of *Lawd Today*. Nick Aaron Ford, a black critic, could not even believe that it was written by Richard Wright. Objecting to Wright's concept as well as his technique, Ford deplored the book's melodramatic and disjointed pattern "with a multitude of hackneyed episodes." Lewis Gannett wrote that the novel lacks the tension of *Native Son* because of the monotonously overdrawn dialogue and the absence of overtones.[2]

Aside from Ford, no one has really objected to Wright's theme and content. *Lawd Today* is a black writer's painfully direct and honest discourse on a racial victim. To some readers, it is an interesting treatment of the antihero; to others, it is a satire on mechanized urban society, a realistic rendition of black life in Chicago's South Side in the Depression years, in which Wright was intimately involved. Michel Fabre's biography of Wright shows that the details of Wright's experience in Chicago as a postal worker closely correspond to those in the novel.[3]

If *Lawd Today* is regarded as a failure, the flaw must be found in its form and technique. Externally the book resembles James Joyce's *Ulysses*, which Wright had read.[4] The action is restricted to the classical unity of time and place; all the significant events of the protagonist's life occur in the same place and within twenty-four hours. Both Jake Jackson and Leopold Bloom are psychologically and sexually estranged from their wives; both have self-doubts and are socially frustrated. They suffer various nightmares and fantasies, go to bars with their friends, and meet prostitutes. But there are obvious differences: Jake is a black man in white America, while Bloom is a Jew in Catholic Ireland. Jake

1. Baldwin, *Notes of a Native Son*, 27–28, and *Nobody Knows My Name*, 150.
2. Ford, "The Fire Next Time? A Critical Survey of Belles Lettres by and about Negroes Published in 1963"; Gannett, "*Lawd Today* by Richard Wright."
3. See Edward Margolies, *The Art of Richard Wright*, 90–92; Keneth Kinnamon, "The Pastoral Impulse in Richard Wright" and "*Lawd Today*: Richard Wright's Apprentice Novel"; Michel Fabre, *The Unfinished Quest of Richard Wright*, 78–79.
4. Fabre, *Unfinished Quest*, 111.

tries to air his frustration through physical violence; Bloom has an inward, brooding personality. The most important difference is that of style and technique. Joyce's parodies of English authors and his use of interior monologues, free association, question-and-answer dialogues, and classical allusions are well blended in describing Bloom's world. Wright's use of radio broadcasts, card games, historical references, and his parodies of political systems are all interesting in themselves but may not be well suited for the one-dimensional characterization of Jake Jackson.

Unlike Bloom, Jake is not merely the protagonist but the only character whose actions constitute the action of the novel. The book is divided into three parts—"Commonplace," "Squirrel Cage," and "Rats' Alley"—each corresponding chronologically to the three periods in Jake's typical day. This might be compared to Wright's division of *Native Son* into "Fear," "Flight," and "Fate," but his theme basically differs between the two novels. Both novels are naturalistic in terms of philosophy: Jake and Bigger are largely victims of environment. In both Wright tries to show that their actions are the inevitable products of the circumstances and implies that one must blame society, not the individuals.

In terms of technique, however, the novels are not equally naturalistic. Although both are filled with realistic detail and documentation, Wright does not weave metaphor into *Native Son* as consciously and as much as he does into *Lawd Today*. While *Native Son* contains no specific literary allusions, some critics have noted Wright's conscious effort to create artistic images. James Nagel, for instance, observes that the novel is not only a solid sociological study of the black man's life in the United States, but also a work of art that "transcends the limitations of sociological prose." The most significant artistic element is Wright's use of the imagery of blindness.[5] The allusiveness of the section titles in *Lawd Today*— "Commonplace," "Squirrel Cage," "Rats' Alley"—is further intensified by the epigraphs appropriate to Wright's purpose: Van Wyck Brooks's *America's Coming-of-Age*, Waldo Frank's *Our America*, and T. S. Eliot's *The Waste Land*, respectively. On the other hand, the titles in *Native Son*— "Fear," "Flight," "Fate"—are not only devoid of metaphor but free from any allusions to specific literary texts.

5. See Nagel, "Images of 'Vision' in *Native Son*."

Wright's method in *Lawd Today* is twofold. On the one hand, he has adopted social determinism, a version of literary naturalism, to account for Jake's behavior; on the other, he has accumulated documentary details characteristic of a naturalistic style, but his scenes are imparted with gratuitous metaphors and images. Not that there is a disharmony between a given scene and its metaphorical allusion; indeed, each scene is carefully constructed to evoke an appropriate vision. Jake and his three black friends must put in eight boring hours through the night, sorting letters at the main post office in Chicago, "a squirrel cage." The brothel Jake and his friends visit after work turns out to be "a rats' alley." It is a nest for black gangsters, pimps, and prostitutes, as well as a symbol of decay and depravity in modern life.

But a disharmony exists between Wright's description of the environment and the actions of Jake, in whom Wright's central interest presumably lies. One does not, of course, expect of Jake the type of courage and integrity that sustains Bigger's manhood in *Native Son.* But Jake has none of Bigger's virtues; he is the most despicable person imaginable. True, Jake is boxed in by circumstance, but this is true of white postal workers as well or of any workers in an industrial society. Since Jake's story takes place in the Depression years, he is lucky to have a job, and yet he habitually beats his sickly wife, gambles, and drinks. He becomes a perennial bitcher, embittered by his sexual frustration. The central meaning of Theodore Dreiser's *An American Tragedy* comes from the economic and social forces that overpower Clyde Griffiths and finally negate his aspirations; Clyde is a victim of the American dream. But such meaning does not derive from Jake's story.

There are other reasons for Jake's frustrations. At the outset of the story Jake is an extremely jealous husband, but not because Lil, his wife, is carrying on with the milkman, as Jake claims. She is in fact unable to perform sex with anyone because of the earlier abortion forced by Jake. Now she suffers from a tumor, and Jake's anxiety heightens. None of these events, however, is enumerated in a naturalistic fashion. Instead Wright concentrates on a dream Jake has so that his initial action can be reasonably accounted for. How Wright became acquainted with Freudian psychology is unknown. In discussing *Lawd Today* Keneth Kinnamon cites *The Interpretation of Dreams.*[6] Another possible source

---

6. See Kinnamon, "*Lawd Today:* Richard Wright's Apprentice Novel," 18, citing *The Basic Writings of Sigmund Freud,* trans. and ed. A. A. Brill.

is Farrell. It is generally agreed among critics that Wright, as Granville Hicks has observed, "could scarcely have failed to be influenced by James T. Farrell, who was just beginning to have a strong effect on American fiction. As Farrell had learned something about documentation from Dreiser, so Wright had learned from Farrell." Farrell had commented as early as 1943 on the relationship between naturalism and Freudianism in connection with Dreiser: "He [Dreiser] accepted as science generalizations based on the ideas of nineteenth-century materialism. In *The Financier* and *The Titan* this biologic determinism is usually explained by the word 'chemisms.' Paradoxically enough, Dreiser's appeal to 'chemisms' is made quite frequently in specific contexts concerning motivations of characters, where we can now see that the real rationale of these motivations can be most satisfactorily explained by Freudianism."[7]

Lawd Today begins with Jake's awaking from an erotic dream in which he is climbing a long winding stairway and hearing his boss's voice coming from the top of the steps. It is significant that Jake is fully awakened by the arrival of the milkman. "His loins," Wright interprets, "felt heavy and exhausted. He closed his eyes and his mind groped, thinking, *What was I dreaming?* He remembered being on the very brink of something, on the verge of a deep joy."[8] It is also significant that Jake's boss appears in this dream and harasses him. Jake battles with life on two fronts: he is socially oppressed as a worker and sexually unfulfilled as a husband. Admittedly any dream is unreal and often a medley, but adding a social theme to an already overloaded sexual image is superfluous at best. Such a strategy, so apparent from the beginning, is an example of Wright's failure to integrate the social ideas of the novel into the narrative at hand.

If social determinism cannot fully account for the life of a central character, as in *Lawd Today*, a naturalist writer often endows his hero with free will and self-assertion. The immediate model for this is Wright's own *Native Son*. Before committing his crime, Bigger, like Jake, is presented as an uneducated, uninformed individual; unlike Jake, however, Bigger is portrayed as a victim of white society who grew up in the worst black ghetto of the nation. It is thus surprising that Bigger gains identity after

7. Hicks, "Dreiser to Farrell to Wright"; Farrell, *The League of Frightened Philistines*, 13–14n.
8. Richard Wright, *Lawd Today,* 10. Subsequent references will appear parenthetically in the text as *LT.*

the murder. The crime gives him some awareness of himself and of the world, an understanding of life of which he has never been capable before. Jake, on the other hand, has as much propensity for violence as Bigger but no capacity for growth and development. If Jake can be invested with any worthy traits, they are only pretense and loquacity. The only commitment he ever makes in his life is to assert his manhood by uttering obscenities, abusing his wife, and goading her into stabbing him.

The lack of free will in Jake is best seen in his attitude toward the problem of race. Early in the story Jake bitterly complains of the fix he is in: he must pay Lil's doctor five hundred dollars. Even though he might be able to borrow the money, he will be forced to pay an exorbitant amount of interest. "Then," he thinks to himself, "there were other bills: the furniture bill and the rent bill and the gas bill and the light bill and the bill at the Boston Store and the insurance bill and the milk bill" (*LT,* 21). For all this family misfortune, he blames racism rather than capitalism. Jake has a gift of language and laconically says, *"What in the world can a man do? I'm just like a slave"* (*LT,* 20–21). The question he raises is legitimate enough, but the answer he gives in a metaphor is a non sequitur. No one doubts the relation between the question and the answer, but in the context of this scene the narrator has done away with the bridge between the economic forces and the plight of an individual. Consequently, for the reader Jake seems a bigot and ignoramus. He looks down upon Communists, Jews, Italians, Hungarians, Mexicans, Chinese, even some black people. It may well be true that in a multiracial and political society a minority has a tendency to despise another minority, but the problem with Jake is that his attitude is not derived from his thinking.

The structure of the narrative discourse results from Jake's inability to think for himself. In "Squirrel Cage," the middle section of the story, Wright interprets Jake's mind, saying "he definitely preferred the company of his own color; they understood him and he understood them" (*LT,* 103–4). Wright's observation here is accurate and also conforms to Jake's own conception of himself. But before this observation is made, Wright provides a scene in which clerks are working in the huge post office. Rather than letting Jake see the situation himself, Wright makes an interjection:

> Tables began to rattle from the thud of cards being whacked down. Hoarse shouts cut through the smoky air. Though there were no written rules of segregation, it was generally assumed

that Negroes would occupy one end of the canteen and whites the other. However, if a mixture was found nothing was said. But Jake always felt that he wanted to sit with his own race because he did not know the whites so well. (*LT*, 103)

The fact pointed out by the narrator indicates that segregation is not really a problem for Jake or any other black postal worker, or at least as serious a disadvantage as Jake thinks it is. This narrative pattern illustrates Jake's limitations in observation and judgment. Jake is too ignorant to realize that the white workers are really prejudiced, though they might not show it openly in their actions. Wright's presentation of detail is so selective that it shows how a man like Jake is incapable of observation, let alone self-determination.

Unlike Wright's self-made men, such as Bigger Thomas, Cross Damon, and Fishbelly Tucker, Jake Jackson hardly generates sympathy from the reader. Although he is not capable of reasoning, he is capable of deceiving others. He approves of graft as a way of life for anyone to get ahead; he admires people who can profit by accepting bribes. He even envies gangsters who can wield their power to intimidate the strong and the weak alike. Jealousy over women is the only emotion that influences his thought and action. He hates Germans during the war because in his eyes they are beasts and rapists of French women.

Ironically, he does not realize that his own behavior smacks of the beast. From the beginning of the story Jake is described in terms of animal temperament, a version of the atavism of which Frank Norris makes so much in *McTeague*. Jake's animalism is provoked by Lil's stubbornness, as McTeague's brutality is triggered by Trina's parsimony. Even when Jake is calm he resembles an ape in a cage running "his fingers through his hair, scratching an itchy scalp" (*LT*, 12). No wonder when he was angered by Lil moments later, "Jake gripped her arm, digging long nails into her flesh" (*LT*, 14). Only after Lil submits herself to his beating does he return to the posture of a relaxed animal. If he wins a row with her, he invariably begins to have a dream in which he is basking in the warm sun. "He stirred restlessly," says Wright, "and his shoulders twitched as though he were a child nestling deeper into a mother's bosom" (*LT*, 35). As long as Jake remains an animal in the forest he gives no one harm, but he is a menace to human society. McTeague, by contrast, is an amiable animal. One feels sorry for him because his misfortune is accidental; after all he has strived to have a good job and a good wife, the twin goals of his life. But few would feel compassion for a man like Jake. Calling *Lawd Today* "devoid of any unified relevance," a black reader notes that it is the only Wright book in which the white man or society is not made the villain.[9]

That Jake is made a villain instead of a hero not only makes this novel unique in Wright's fiction but also partly explains its failure. One of the most important requirements for a successful novel in the tradition of American literary naturalism is that it create tensions in the life of the protagonist. These tensions grow out of an environment over which he has no control and about which he understands very little and, therefore, by which he is victimized. Even though a naturalistic character is unable to control the forces outside him, he is compelled to act and wage a battle against them, thereby creating tensions. One cannot expect heroism from Jake, but in the absence of any action, let alone a challenge against the outside forces, his story must be a dull one.

Wright is, thus, least concerned with the forces in society that man must battle for survival. Most naturalist writers are clearly pessimistic determinists who observe that a person is destroyed either by competition or by submission. And his or her fate is often death. *Native Son* stands at the opposite end of this human struggle, for Bigger is victorious over the brutal facts of experience. James T. Farrell's *Studs Lonigan* is a story in which defeat comes after a long, fierce struggle. Dreiser's *An American Tragedy* stands between defeat and triumph. If naturalism deals with the tension between will and determinism, Dreiser is content to keep the tension unresolved. Compared with these novels, *Lawd Today* glaringly falls short of their power and interest, for neither does the protagonist participate in a battle of life nor does the author seek life's beauty and exaltation.

The failure in Wright's experiment in naturalism does not necessarily mean that *Lawd Today* is a failure as a novel. Within the confines of one day, one place, and one person of mediocre, if not inferior, mentality, a great deal happens and the story presents an interesting racial discourse. Of *Native Son,* James Baldwin has said that it is "the most powerful and celebrated statement we have yet had of what it means to be a Negro in America."[10] If Baldwin is right, *Lawd Today* is perhaps the most satiric and the least celebrated discourse on what it means to be black. Most

9. Ford, "The Fire Next Time?" 129–30.
10. *Notes of a Native Son,* 23.

significantly, however, Wright's satire is not only aimed at black life but, as a white critic has pointed out, "it also, insidiously, provides glimpses into what it means to be white, colorless, ubiquitous."[11] One cannot laugh at a man like Bigger who has so much dignity, nor can one belittle a man like Cross Damon who has so much intellect.

Above all, Jake is an average man, black or white, who is trying in his own way but always erring. He is a symbol, a satire on such a man. As a satire *Lawd Today* is full of cynicism and sarcasm, but Wright's remarks are rarely as bitter as are those in *Native Son*. By no means can *Lawd Today* be construed as a protest novel, but he does subtly attack society. This is why, as Russell C. Brignano has observed, "although the protest is muted in *Lawd Today* by his reportorial and journalist technique, it is implanted within the author's selection of his subject matter."[12]

Wright's is at his best with a scene in which he reigns as an impartial judge on racial issues. Neither a black nor a white point of view influences his vision; fact alone makes his judgment. Under the clamor of the crowd his voice, though quiet, carries the weight of a decree. At the end of "Part One: Commonplace," Jake and his friends walk reluctantly toward the post office for a tedious night shift. They eagerly watch a pompous parade of the Allied Imperial African War Councils in which ancient African generals are advocating the power and solidarity of black people throughout the world. Jake and his friends are impressed not only by the show but by what black people can do, just as Bigger in *Native Son* is proud of the abilities of Germans, Japanese, and Italians, who had conquered other lands. Although Jake and his comrades are convinced of the abilities of Africans, Asians, and Europeans, they are painfully reminded of the limitations imposed on them on the North American continent. This scene is immediately followed by a brief scene in which they gaze lasciviously at the carelessly exposed thighs of a white woman sitting obliquely across the aisle on a train. The taboo of interracial sex is defined in a quatrain improvised alternately by Jake and his three companions:

> Finally, Jake rolled his eyes heavenward and sang in an undertone:
> *"Oh, Lawd, can I ever, can I ever?..."*

11. Lewis Leary, "*Lawd Today:* Notes on Richard Wright's First/Last Novel," 412.
12. *Richard Wright: An Introduction to the Man and His Works*, 28.

Bob screwed up his eyes, shook his head, and answered ruefully:

"*Naw, nigger, you can never, you can never. . . .*"

Slim sat bolt upright, smiled, and countered hopefully:

"*But wherever there's life there's hope. . . .*"

Al dropped his head, frowned, and finished mournfully:

"*And wherever there's trees there's rope.*" (*LT,* 96–97)

Another important technique in Wright's satire is irony. Lewis Leary maintains that Wright's humor in *Lawd Today* is not "tainted with irony. It is genuine, as Mark Twain's at his best is genuine, with bitterness showing through but not intruding."[13] Jake's day abruptly begins as he is awakened by a loud radio broadcast announcing that it is February 12, 1936, Abraham Lincoln's birthday: "My Dear Friends, our flag is flying high today in honor of one of our greatest Americans, a man who saved his country and bestowed the blessings of liberty and freedom upon millions of his fellowmen!" (*LT,* 8). But Jake feels as though he is abandoned in "a vast Sargasso Sea—a prodigious welter of unconscious life, swept by groundswells of half-conscious emotion" (*LT,* 7). The irony sets the tone for the entire book. Jake and his black friends often dream of their good old days in the South where they used to enjoy the warmth of the sun and the quietude of the pastoral. They swam in the creek, caught catfish, and smelled magnolia trees. It is ironic that they were not accepted where they were able to live in harmony with nature. It is doubly ironic that black people in the North are physically free but mentally restless.

Jake is aware that he and other black citizens in the North are victims of racial strife, but he is not aware that they are victims of capitalism and money worship. He venerates gangsters because "it takes nerve to be a gangster! But they have a plenty of fun. Always got a flock of gals hanging on their arms. Dress swell in sporty clothes. Drive them long, sleek automobiles. And got money to throw away" (*LT,* 30). Jake emulates them by loading his closet with plenty of fancy suits. While Jake and his friends watch a sidewalk medicine show, one of them says, "a man must make a lot of money in a business like that." Since selling Universal Herb Cureal Medicine is profitable, they reason, it must be good. "I'm going to make Lil take some of that," says Jake, who believes that the quack medicine "might save her from that operation" (*LT,* 88).

13. "*Lawd Today:* Notes," 419.

He is not really concerned with whether or not it will cure Lil's tumor; he is merely concerned with saving money.

Wright's irony is least subtle when it is used in dialogue. Jake's duplicity is most revealing when he desperately tries to save his job. In order to have his job in the post office reinstated, he blatantly lies to his supervisor: "Mister Swanson, I'm a black man. You can see my skin. I loves my race. I'm proud to be black. I wouldn't do nothing on earth to drag my race down. I ain't the kind of a man what would beat his wife and stand here before you white gentlemens" (LT, 110). Jake says "I loves my race," but he does not. He says "I'm proud to be black," but in fact he is ashamed to be black; he spends hours straightening his hair. He says "I wouldn't do nothing on earth to drag my race down," but he would indeed do anything to get money and women. He says "I ain't the kind of a man what would beat his wife," but he makes a daily ritual out of beating poor Lil. Jake calls his superiors "you white gentlemens," but behind their backs he calls them "you white bastards."

While irony is a dominant form of Wright's discourse, sarcasm and cynicism are dominant elements in Lawd Today. They occur most frequently in "Squirrel Cage," where the narrator seldom intrudes into the dialogue so that the black men may speak their minds without interruption. The book characteristically becomes a satire rather than a disguised protest novel, for the narrator does not protest at all. His characters attack every ethnic, social, and economic group of Americans; in so doing they are releasing their pent-up emotions and frustrations. Black citizens think Jews mistreat them because Jews were mistreated by Europeans. Catholics accuse black men of raping their women, since "the South's sure hard" (LT, 156) on Catholics. Although Jake envies and respects anyone who has money, he hates professionals. He recalls his success in finding Lil an abortionist and reflects that such a doctor has no integrity because he takes advantage of poor workers: "It cost me five hundred iron men. . . . Boy, them quacks'll gut you if you let 'em. Quacks and mouthpieces get all a postal clerk's money. Abortions and divorces. . . . But Lawd!" (LT, 133–34). What is interesting is that the black men's views are white, middle-class views, as the reader instantly recognizes.

Other comments are directed toward white people and are distinctly the black men's own. The rich southerners, despite their wealth and power, are cowards in the eyes of black people: "The Reds sure scared them white folks down South where they put up that fight for the

Scottsboro boys" (*LT*, 152). Moreover, their hatred of the white race is so deeply ingrained in their minds that they can scarcely conceive of white blood in the Communists. Noticing that Lenin's eyes are narrow and slanted, one of Jake's friends remarks, "I'll bet you when they find out about 'im they'll find he had some Chink blood in 'im" (*LT*, 151). In particular, Jake and his friends loathe white men who exploit black women sexually. Because they cannot retaliate by exploiting white women, those black women invariably become the target of their attack. "Yeah," Jake says with exasperation, "let a nigger woman make fifty dollars a week and she begins to think she's too good for her own race. . . . It just makes my blood boil to see a nigger woman grinning at a white man like they do. And these white men around here don't give a good Gawddamn about us. We'll just be clerks as long as we stay here, but they's got a chance to rise as high as a man can go" (*LT*, 121–22).

What they call "Crackers, Rednecks, Hillbillies," their arch-rivals for livelihood, are, they are convinced, "the ones what lynch and burn us" (*LT*, 153). They think that rich white people in the South are less offensive than poor white people because the rich have no economic woes to gripe about. The poor white people thus resent black people: "They grudge you the ground you stand on" (*LT*, 153). Small wonder the description of white people that Jake and his friends give is the harshest and, from their point of view, the most accurate portrayal they ever make:

> "And don't they look awful. . . ."
> " . . . with them old bleached-out blue eyes. . . ."
> " . . . sunk way back in their heads. . . ."
> " . . . and that old dead stringy hair. . . ."
> " . . . falling down over their faces. . . ."
> " . . . like a dirty mop. . . ."
> " . . . and them old thin mouths all drawed in. . . ."
> " . . . and when they talk they whine through their noses. . . ."
> " . . . like starved cats!" (*LT*, 153)

One reason for seeing *Lawd Today* as social criticism is the width and impartiality of Wright's satiric vision. Such a derogatory depiction of white features is matched with an equally disparaging view of black features. Wright describes Jake as he wakes up in the morning:

> He stood up, fronting the mirror. The reflection showed a face round as a full moon and dark as a starless midnight. In an oily expanse of blackness were set two cunning eyes under which

hung flabby pouches. A broad nose squatted fat and soft, its two holes gaping militantly frontward like the barrels of a shotgun. Lips were full, moist, and drooped loosely, trembling when he walked. A soft roll of fat seeped out of his neck, buttressing his chin. Shaggy sideburns frizzled each temple. (*LT*,12)

Jake and the three black men also function in the novel as social critics. While they praise white people for their industriousness and system, commenting that they are "together like a army," they grieve over a chronic black attitude: "If three niggers is trying to do something, one of 'em's going to trip the others up" (*LT*, 144). In their view, white people are Machiavellian, black people are "sellouts," and yellow people do not count.

The fact that Wright was an active member of the Communist Party at the time he wrote *Lawd Today* gives a special significance to whatever views Jake and his comrades express on politics. Wright's view on American capitalism is explicitly stated throughout the book: the rich always exploit the poor; race, politics, and everything else in the United States are part of the system. Jake thus condones bribery and corruption as a capitalistic way of life. Money sometimes transcends the color lines; Jake, for example, stands in awe of Doc, a black "precinct captain. A businessman. A property owner. He's got pull with all the big politicians down in the Loop" (*LT*, 54). Even before this scene, one of Jake's comments is that "cold, hard cash runs this country, always did and always will" (*LT*, 28). Although Wright is critical of capitalism, he is also critical of Communism. Jake says of the Communists: "Now them guys, them Commoonists and Bolshehicks, is the craziest guys going! They don't know what they want. They done come 'way over here and wants to tell us how to run *our* country when their *own* country ain't run right" (*LT*, 32). Edward Margolies argues that Wright did not publish *Lawd Today* because it would be interpreted as anti-communist, but that he kept it with him in the hope that in the event he did leave the Communist Party, he would be able to publish it.[14]

However selfish and materialistic Jake may sound, his comments reflect Wright's unwavering emphasis on American life: the independent spirit of individuals. Wright chides white people who "rush about like bees. . . . Yeah, but ain't no use of a black man rushing. Naw, 'cause we

14. *Art of Richard Wright*, 91–92.

ain't going nowhere. . . . We just as well take it easy and have some fun" (*LT*, 103). Wright's critical attitude toward both Communism and capitalism is abundantly clear. Wright himself, through Jake, expresses his belief in the independence of the mind. Yet black Americans are free only within limits. Within these limits, the black American defines himself or herself. Wright defines Jake and, in so doing, transcends the mold.

To sum up, then, *Lawd Today* can be read either as a naturalistic novel or as a satire. A naturalistic interpretation will be concerned with Jake's character in the light of the society in which he lives. A reading of the novel as satire may deal with the fashion in which social and personal ills are exposed and ridiculed. Throughout the text the focus is on American society, but there is an ambiguity in Wright's treatment of the protagonist. In "Part One: Commonplace" and "Part Three: Rats' Alley," Jake appears as the protagonist as the narrative proceeds; however, in "Part Two: Squirrel Cage" in particular, Jake is used as a symbol. In this part of the story Wright constructs dialogue among Jake and the rest of the black characters without, in most cases, distinguishing the speakers. As a result, the men are cut into a single character with one voice as if in a proletarian pluralistic novel.

But the problem with this device is that *Lawd Today* is not a proletarian novel. Nor is it a novel of any political persuasion. Needless to say, there is every sign that Jake is a naturalistic character; he is examined in terms of the social and economic forces over which he has little control. A naturalistic writer, however, cannot make a story out of a character who largely disappears in the midst of a fictional experiment. It is irrelevant whether a naturalist ought to place emphasis on the forces of circumstance, as Zola does in novels like *L'Assommoir*, or on the actions of his hero, as Wright himself does in *Native Son*. In any event, the focus of this attention must necessarily be upon the interactions between will and determinism.

Wright's presentation of Jake's day, though comprehensive, is metaphorical. A literary naturalist establishes a milieu taken from life and, into it, projects characters to prove the process of a social phenomenon. What underlies the narrative in such a novel is the author's constant reminder for readers to form their own reflections. In *Lawd Today*, Wright provides as little interruption of the action as possible. Unlike Dreiser's naturalistic novel, Wright's has a severely limited time frame and only an occasional pause to indicate a transition or change of scene. By the time Jake stumbles into bed drunk and allows Lil to cut him down, readers have all but forgotten about her. Her final action, however understand-able, precipitates as if in a gothic tale. Before Roberta's murder, in *An American Tragedy*, which occurs at the end of book 2, Dreiser provides a comprehensive background of Clyde's life: his relationships with his family, including his sister Esta, who has been deserted by her lover, with all his friends and associates, and with all the girls he has attempted to allure. In Wright's novel, on the other hand, readers have no such recourse to the character's background.

There is no question that *Lawd Today* is a successful attempt at satire, particularly in "Squirrel Cage." Wright is completely impartial in treat-ing his material. If Jake is a caricature, he is a caricature of not only black men but also white men and any ordinary men and women in urban society. Wright's novel is at its best in part 2 before Jake and the black characters descend into the brothel, as *Adventures of Huckleberry Finn* is at its best in the middle chapters before Tom returns to make Huck's story a travesty. The middle section of *Lawd Today* provides the four black men with a full range of social, economic, and political commentary with no other characters intruding into their vision. These four are the funniest of all the Wright characters, for they have no inhibitions of any kind, no conflicts of interest with society. Their views are almost as candid as Huck Finn's.

The central question to be asked about *Lawd Today* is whether Wright has succeeded in combining his two experiments, one in naturalism and another in satire, to produce a racial discourse. Granted, the tragic death of a hero, whether it is in *Native Son* or *An American Tragedy*, is no laughing matter. But in both novels significant elements of satire suggest that the crimes dramatized are inevitable products of American society and that both protagonists are morally free from guilt. In *Lawd Today* the elements of humor and sarcasm are so dominant that the idea of reform, which underlies satire, is minimized. Wright has no intention of reforming Jake or society at large; indeed Jake is an average man and his foibles are those of human nature. Wright knew them deeply and succeeded in letting the reader witness them. It is true that serious satire and light humor are harmoniously wed in *Adventures of Huckleberry Finn*, but Twain's novel is basically an initiation story, not a naturalistic one. It seems difficult for any writer to mix satire and naturalism as equal bases for a novel and accomplish both ends. Such an achievement, however possible it may be, has no precedent, and *Lawd Today*, despite its merits, remains an apprentice novel.

2

Uncle Tom's Children, Earlier Fiction

T he 1938 edition of *Uncle Tom's Children,* a collection of four short stories, which appeared two years before *Native Son,* also had a generally favorable reception. James T. Farrell, appreciative of Wright's direct and realistic style, remarked in *Partisan Review* that *Uncle Tom's Children* serves as an exemplary refutation for those who wished to write "fancy nonsense about fables and allegories." In response to such readers as Granville Hicks and Alan Calmer, who wanted Wright to pace more steadily in his narrative and delve more deeply into his material, Farrell argued that Wright effectively employs simple dialogue "as a means of carrying on his narrative, as medium for poetic and lyrical effects, and as an instrument of characterization." Just as *Native Son* was extolled by white readers but condemned by a black writer, *Uncle Tom's Children* was praised by white readers but criticized by a fellow black writer. As if in return for Wright's unfavorable review of her novel *Their Eyes Were Watching God,* Zora Neale Hurston categorized *Uncle Tom's Children* as a chronicle of hatred with no act of understanding and sympathy. Like Baldwin, she too opposed Wright's politics, arguing that the stories in *Uncle Tom's Children* fail to touch the fundamental truths of black life.[1]

It is quite understandable for the three African American writers to view black life in America differently, since Baldwin grew up in New York, Hurston had the perspective of a black woman, and Wright was a product of the Deep South. To verify the authenticity of his vision Wright attached to the 1940 edition of *Uncle Tom's Children* an essay entitled

1. Farrell, "Lynch Patterns"; Hurston, "Stories of Conflict."

"The Ethics of Living Jim Crow," as perhaps Hawthorne prefaced *The Scarlet Letter* with "The Custom House." Wright's preface consists of nine episodes based on his youthful experiences in the South. The 1940 edition also included an additional story, and all five stories are closely related to the episodes described in the preface in theme and character. These stories, in turn, prefigure the theme, structure, and ideology of his later fiction. One of the most prominent ideas upon which Wright developed his fiction was his rationale for rebellion. In "How 'Bigger' Was Born," another introductory essay, attached to *Native Son*, Wright wrote:

> I felt that Bigger, an American product, a native son of this land, carried within him the potentialities of either Communism or Fascism. . . . he is a dispossessed and disinherited man; he is all of this, and he lives amid the greatest possible plenty on earth and he is looking and feeling for a way out. Whether he'll follow some gaudy, hysterical leader who'll promise rashly to fill the void in him, or whether he'll come to an understanding with the millions of his kindred fellow workers . . . depends upon the future drift of events in America. But, granting the emotional state, the tensity, the fear, the hate, the impatience, the sense of exclusion, the ache for violent action, the emotional and cultural hunger, Bigger Thomas, conditioned as his organism is, will not become an ardent, or even a lukewarm, supporter of the *status quo*.[2]

The episodes outlined in "The Ethics of Living Jim Crow" thus also serve as the basis for the rationale Wright explains in "How 'Bigger' Was Born."

Wright intended to show in *Uncle Tom's Children* that American social conditions are directly responsible for the degradations of black people. But each of the stories collected in this book shows that Wright went beyond naturalism. The pessimistic determinism often associated with naturalism taught the young Wright the meaning of racial oppression in the Deep South. A victim of oppression himself, Wright directed his energy toward rebellion. While he escaped the pessimistic outlook of naturalism, his respect for that philosophy helped him develop his own individualism and endow his characters with self-awareness. Only

---

2. *Native Son*, xx. Subsequent references will appear parenthetically in the text as *NS*.

vaguely are some of the black characters in *Uncle Tom's Children* conscious of their racially oppressive environment, but they willfully seek freedom and self-determination.

1

"Big Boy Leaves Home," the first story in the 1938 and 1940 editions of *Uncle Tom's Children*, features a young black boy's escape from his violent southern community.[3] Four innocent, happy-go-lucky black boys are discovered naked by a white woman while they are swimming in a pond and later drying their bodies on a white man's premises. When she screams, her male companion without warning begins shooting and kills two of the boys. Big Boy manages to overcome the white man and accidentally kills him. Now the two surviving boys must take flight: Bobo gets captured, but Big Boy reaches home and is told by black church leaders to hide in a kiln until dawn, when a truck will come by to take him to Chicago. While hiding, he poignantly watches Bobo be lynched and burned. Witnessing such an event gives Big Boy not only a feeling of isolation, terror, and hatred but also a sense of self-awareness and maturity. Although the events take place in less than twenty-four hours as in classical drama, the story is divided into five parts, like the acts of a play, that correspond to the crucial stages in his development from innocence, through violence, suffering, and terror, to freedom.

As the plot unfolds, it becomes apparent that the central theme of the story is the problem of miscegenation in America. The southern white community ever since the days of slavery has regarded miscegenation as prohibited if the relationship is between a white woman and a black man, but as condoned if it is between a white man and a black woman. Wright underscores these unjust sexual mores by having an angry white mob exclaim while lynching and burning Bobo: "Ah tell yuh they still here, somewhere." "But we looked all over!" "What t hell! Wouldnt do t let em git erway!" "Naw. Ef they git erway notta woman in this town

---

3. "Big Boy Leaves Home" first appeared in an anthology, *The New Caravan*, ed. Alfred Kreymborg et al. Page references to Wright's stories are to the 1940 edition of *Uncle Tom's Children*. Subsequent references to this volume will appear parenthetically in the text as *UTC*.

would be safe" (*UTC*, 46). Big Boy, the protagonist of the story, hiding in a kiln, hears this exchange and experiences the greatest fear he has ever known in his life. Not only does his friend Bobo become a scapegoat for the white people's terror, but what happens to him is also given as a lesson for the black men who dare to transgress the taboo.

Margaret Walker, a fellow black writer and friend of Wright's, considers "Big Boy Leaves Home" "a lynching story dealing with southern racism," but observes that the story has little to do with black boys' sexuality. Other critics, however, regard the story as closely related to black boys' sexual initiation. Hal Blythe and Charlie Sweet, for instance, maintain: "As a result, the Big Boys of black America are forced to retreat into the womb, never realizing their full sexual maturation. Through its sexual symbolism, then, 'Big Boy Leaves Home,' like Ralph Ellison's 'Battle Royal,' anatomizes the white racist dream of halting what it seems to fear most, the black man's sexuality."[4] By creating such a scene, Wright enables the reader to condemn the white men for the physical cruelty they perpetrate upon the innocent black boys, as well as for the psychological wound such violence inflicts upon Big Boy. Even though Big Boy can escape this ordeal and does leave home, he has not learned how to relate to the white world, let alone how to associate with white women.

The genesis of "Big Boy Leaves Home" is found in several of the episodes Wright sketches in "The Ethics of Living Jim Crow." In one episode, the young Wright felt humiliated when he saw a white man freely slap a black maid on her buttocks. Afterward she told Wright, "Don't be a fool! Yuh couldn't help it!" (*UTC*, 13). In another episode, when a black woman shoplifted at a clothing store, she was kicked in the stomach and brutalized by the white owner of the store and his son so that she was found bleeding. The black porter who witnessed the white men's brutality told Wright: "Shucks! Man, she's a lucky bitch! . . . Hell, it's a wonder they didn't lay her when they got through" (*UTC*, 9). Such an episode reveals not only that black men often acquiesce to the brutality white men perpetrate on black people, but also that white men are expected to exploit black women sexually.

It is a cultural reality that a black man's sexual relationship with a white woman was taboo in the South as late as the 1930s. At one time

---

4. Walker, *Richard Wright: Daemonic Genius,* 82; Blythe and Sweet, " 'Yo Mama Don Wear No Drawers': Suspended Sexuality in 'Big Boy Leaves Home.' "

the young Wright, a bellboy, was called up to a hotel room where a white man and a white prostitute were in bed naked. Asking Wright to buy some liquor, the woman got up and walked nude across the floor to get money from a dresser drawer. Naturally Wright watched her, but the white man was offended and said: " 'Nigger, what in hell you looking at?' . . . 'Nothing,' I answered, looking miles deep into the blank wall of the room. 'Keep your eyes where they belong, if you want to be healthy!' he said" (*UTC*, 11). In another episode, "one of the bell-boys was caught in bed with a white prostitute. He was castrated and run out of town." Immediately after this incident all the hall-boys and bellboys were warned by the hotel management that the next time it "would not be responsible for the lives of 'trouble-makin' niggers" (*UTC*, 12).

Black mothers were expected to warn their sons about the problem of miscegenation in the Deep South during the 1920s. As *Black Boy* reveals, however, Wright's mother was seldom concerned with sexual matters, let alone with miscegenation. In a way "Big Boy Leaves Home" serves as a criticism of the black mother. When Big Boy reaches home, the first person he sees is his mother, who does not console him but asks God to help him. When Big Boy tells her what happened, she exclaims: "*White* woman? . . . Lawd have mercy! Ah knowed yuh boys wus gonna keep on till yuh got into somethin like this!" (*UTC*, 32–33). An episode in "The Ethics of Living Jim Crow" is also critical of Wright's mother. Wright was involved in a fight between black and white boys in his neighborhood. While the black boys attacked the white boys with cinders that gave them only bruises, the white boys retaliated by throwing broken bottles. Wright was once injured in such a battle, sustaining a deep cut on the neck. His mother, he recalls, "came from the white folks' kitchen. I raced down the street to meet her. I could just feel in my bones that she would understand. I knew she would tell me exactly what to do next time. . . . She examined my wound, then slapped me. . . . She grabbed a barrel stave, dragged me home, stripped me naked, and beat me till I had a fever of one hundred and two. She would smack my rump with the stave, and, while the skin was still smarting, impart to me gems of Jim Crow" (*UTC*, 4).

In his later fiction as well, Wright portrays the black mother who fails to instruct her son about racism and to help him attain sexual maturity. In *Native Son*, fanatic religion is what obsesses Bigger's mother. All she can do after Bigger's capture is beg Mrs. Dalton to spare her son's life as though a slave asked his master for mercy. Even though Mrs. Thomas's willingness to plead for Bigger's safety out of her motherly love may be considered admirable, her unwillingness to fight for her daughter's safety earlier in the novel betrays her deeply ingrained prejudice against women and her inferiority complex about black women. In *The Outsider*, Cross Damon repudiates his mother not only because she taught him only subservient ethics but also because she was an epitome of sexual repression. This pious mother, Wright emphasizes, "had evoked in his pliable boy's body an aching sense of pleasure by admonishing him to shun pleasure as the tempting doorway opening blackly onto hell. . . . And this constituted his sense of dread."[5]

Not only is "Big Boy Leaves Home" based upon Wright's personal experience, but the sexual taboo that precipitates this tragedy originates from a fact both black and white people in the South knew so well. In "How 'Bigger' Was Born," Wright reminds the reader of this fact:

> In the main, this delicately balanced state of affairs has not greatly altered since the Civil War, save in those parts of the South which have been industrialized or urbanized. So volatile and tense are these relations that if a Negro rebels against rule and taboo, he is lynched and the reason for the lynching is usually called "rape," that catchword which has garnered such vile connotations that it can raise a mob anywhere in the South pretty quickly, even today. (*NS*, xii)

The white woman who suddenly appears near the swimming hole, as the story unfolds, is closely guarded and protected by the white world. "In that world," as Blyden Jackson has noted, "at least when 'Big Boy Leaves Home' was written, all Negro males, even young and with their clothes on, were potential rapists. And so this woman screams, and screams again, for someone named Jim, and Jim himself, a white man from her world, comes apace, with a rifle in his hands."[6]

Instead of being compared to the facts of racism in America, "Big Boy Leaves Home" has been compared to an ancient myth. In Ovid's *Metamorphoses*, the myth of Actaeon and Diana is told this way:

> Actaeon and his companions are out hunting at midday when Actaeon calls an end to the chase since "Our nets and spears

---

5. Richard Wright, *The Outsider*, 18. Subsequent references will appear parenthetically in the text as *O*.
6. "Richard Wright in a Moment of Truth," 172.

/ Dip with the blood of our successful hunting." Nearby, in a grotto pool nestled in a valley, the goddess Diana, herself tired from hunting, disrobed and disarmed, bathes with her maidens. Quite by accident, Actaeon, now alone, comes upon the idyllic scene. Finding no weapon nearby, Diana flings a handful of the pond's water on the hapless hunter, taunting, "Tell people you have seen me, / Diana, naked! Tell them if you can!" He flees from the scene, by stages transformed into a stag, a metamorphosis he does not comprehend (though he marvels at his own speed) until he pauses to drink. Then he "finally sees, reflected, / his features in a quiet pool 'Alas!' / He tries to say, but has no words." Stunned he hears his hounds approach. "The whole pack, with the lust of blood upon them / Come baying . . . Actaeon, once pursuer / Over this very ground, is now pursued . . . He would cry / 'I am Actaeon . . .' / But the words fail." The hounds set upon him "And all together nip and slash and fasten? Till there is no more room for wounds." Meanwhile, his companions arrive, call for him, and rue that he is missing the good show. "And so he died, and so Diana's anger / Was satisfied at last."[7]

The parallels between Wright's story and this classical myth are indeed striking. Both tales begin with idyllic scenes before the plot focuses on an initial encounter between the opposite sexes. Big Boy, the leader of the group, and three friends, who are supposed to be at school, walk through the woods, laughing, beating vines and bushes as if they are hunting anything that interests them. In the prologue, Wright refers to the legendary southern pastoral in the form of a popular song:

> *Is it true what they say about Dixie?*
> *Does the sun really shine all the time?*
> *Do sweet magnolias blossom at everybody's door,*
> *Do folks keep eating 'possum, till they can't eat no more?*
> *Is it true what they say about Swanee?*
> *Is a dream by that stream the sublime?*
> *Do they laugh, do they love, like they say in ev'ry song? . . .*
> *If it's true that's where I belong.*

As Big Boy, accompanied by his sidekicks, is pursuing his avocation in a most enjoyable environment, Actaeon, too, with his companions,

7. See Michael Atkinson, "Richard Wright's 'Big Boy Leaves Home' and a Tale from Ovid: A Metamorphosis Transformed," 251–52.

is hunting in good weather. Before the unexpected appearance of a woman, both Actaeon and Big Boy are at rest, Actaeon tired with hunting and Big Boy warming his body after swimming in the cold pond. Another point of similarity is the hero's fleeing of the scene. Before seeing Diana, Actaeon is alone after his companions have retired from hunting; upon seeing her, he flees the scene. Similarly, Big Boy flees the scene alone since two of his friends are killed and Bobo takes a separate route and eventually gets captured. Finally, both protagonists sustain serious wounds during their flight. It is, furthermore, significant that the wounding of the hero occurs in two stages. Actaeon suffers what Michael Atkinson calls "the transformative sprinkling with pondwater, which removes his humanity, and the obliterative tearing by the dogs' teeth, which destroys the last form and vestige of life."[8] In Wright's tale, Big Boy first suffers the loss of Buck and Lester, whose blood is sprinkled over him; then he suffers from watching Bobo's body be mutilated.

But the points of difference between the tales are equally striking and significant. While in the Roman myth the male protagonist alone encounters a goddess, in Wright's story a group of young boys see an adult woman. However accidental it might be, it is Actaeon who comes upon the scene where Diana is already bathing with her maidens in a secluded pond. The circumstances under which Wright's story begins are reversed: it is the lady who comes upon the scene where Big Boy is already swimming with his friends. The initial setting Wright constructs in "Big Boy Leaves Home" thus poses the serious question of whether underage boys should be judged morally wrong when they are seen naked, while swimming, by an adult woman. In the Actaeon myth, given the tradition of privacy behind it, Actaeon is clearly guilty of watching a naked goddess surrounded by her maids. If Big Boy were in the position of Actaeon, he would be arrested as a Peeping Tom in any modern society. Even if Big Boy were Peeping Tom, Big Boy's punishment would be only blindness as legend tells that Peeping Tom looked at Lady Godiva riding naked through Coventry and was struck blind. But blindness, the price Peeping Tom paid for his offense, is a far cry from the psychological wounds Big Boy and all other black boys in America indeed suffered: the shooting death of Buck and Lester caused by an army officer on leave and the lynching of Bobo perpetrated by a white mob.

8. Ibid., 257.

It is also significant that, unlike Actaeon, none of the black boys in Wright's story is alone when a member of the opposite sex appears on the scene. The woman in question, moreover, is fully protected by an adult male companion with a shotgun that could legally be used should she be molested and raped by the unarmed black boys. In the myth, however, the goddess is protected neither by anyone who can overcome a potential seducer nor by any weapon save for her flinging of a few drops of magical pondwater. In terms of crime and punishment, those who are guilty in Wright's story, the lynch mob and the woman who screams, go unpunished, whereas those who are innocent, the four black boys, are physically or psychologically destroyed. In the myth, Actaeon, the only one who is guilty, meets his death while all the innocent—Diana, her maids, and Actaeon's companions—survive the ordeal. If the Actaeon myth and the legend of Peeping Tom tell us anything significant about an ancient system of justice that meted out punishment for humankind, then the system of justice Wright condemns in "Big Boy Leaves Home" is not only unjust but fundamentally corrupt.

While "Big Boy Leaves Home" and the classical myth of Actaeon and Diana are thematically different, Wright's treatment of the sexual theme in this story has a closer resemblance to Theodore Dreiser's "Nigger Jeff." According to Donald Pizer, the germ of Dreiser's story is found in his unpublished manuscript entitled "A Victim of Justice" at the University of Virginia Library. "Nigger Jeff" as published in Dreiser's *Free and Other Stories* is slightly revised from its first published version in a magazine.[9] In *Black Boy* Wright acknowledges that he was profoundly influenced by realist and naturalist writers such as Dreiser. It is quite likely that before writing "Big Boy Leaves Home" Wright read "Nigger Jeff." Dreiser's story, in which a white mob lynches a black youth, deals with the same problems of race and miscegenation in America as does Wright's story. In "Nigger Jeff," one day a white cub reporter named Elmer Davies is sent out by the city editor to cover the lynching of an alleged black rapist, Jeff Ingalls. Jeff is first captured by a sheriff to await trial but later taken away by a mob of white men led by the brother and father of the supposed rape victim and finally hanged from a bridge

9. For a discussion of Dreiser's revision in this story, see Donald Pizer's "Theodore Dreiser's 'Nigger Jeff': The Development of an Aesthetic." References to this story are to the *Free* edition and will appear parenthetically in the text as *F*.

over a stream. After learning about the circumstances of the rape, Jeff's behavior, his family's grief, and above all the transcending beauty and serenity of nature in contrast with the brutality and criminality of the mob, Davies realizes that his sympathies have shifted.

At the outset of each story, the author stresses the peace and tranquillity of the setting where people, black and white, are meant to enjoy their lives in harmony with nature. In Wright's story, the four innocent, happy black youths, as mentioned earlier, roam about the woods and pasture, laughing, chanting, smelling sweet flowers. "A quartet of voices," Wright describes, "blending in harmony, floated high above the tree tops" (*UTC*, 17). In Dreiser's story, a young impressionable man comes upon the beautiful setting on a lovely spring day in the countryside of Pleasant Valley. Just as Big Boy and his friends are happy not only with themselves but also with the world, Davies, as Dreiser describes, "was dressed in a new spring suit, a new hat and new shoes. In the lapel of his coat was a small bunch of violets. . . . he was feeling exceedingly well and good-natured—quite fit, indeed. The world was going unusually well with him. It seemed worth singing about" (*F*, 76). Under such circumstances no one would expect violence to occur and destroy peace and harmony.

Both stories are told through the protagonist's point of view. In the beginning both Big Boy and Elmer Davies are young and naive, but the violence and injustice they witness make them grow up overnight. In the end, Big Boy, though stunned and speechless, is determined to tell the world what he has learned. As *Black Boy*, Wright's autobiography, suggests, Big Boy was modeled after the young Richard Wright himself growing up in the twenties. Dreiser's *A Book about Myself*, like *Black Boy* one of the finest autobiographies in American literature, also suggests that Elmer Davies was indeed the young Theodore Dreiser himself when the future novelist was a newspaper reporter in St. Louis in the early 1890s. As Wright fled the South for Chicago to write his early short stories, Dreiser left the Midwest for New York to write his.

In both stories, the plot, which does not hinge upon a conflict of social forces, thrives on a progression of vision. Each story opens with pastoral idylls, moves through visions of violence and injustice, and shows the hero's losing his relative state of innocence. Both writers take pains to demonstrate that the protagonist—rather than society, the antagonist—is capable of vision. The climactic scene in Wright's story, where the victim is hanged and mutilated, is presented with bright firelight. The mob is situated so close to the scene of violence that its members cannot see what is transpiring. Big Boy, hiding in the dark in a kiln, can see it far better than the mob. "Big Boy," Wright says, "shrank when he saw the first flame light the hillside. Would they see im here? Then he remembered you could not see into the dark if you were standing in the light" (*UTC*, 48). Dreiser, too, presents the climax for Elmer Davies to see rather than for the mob to see: "The silent company, an articulated, mechanical and therefore terrible thing, moved on. . . . He was breathing heavily and groaning. . . . His eyes were fixed and staring, his face and hands bleeding as if they had been scratched or trampled upon. . . . But Davies could stand it no longer now. He fell back, sick at heart, content to see no more. It seemed a ghastly, murderous thing to do" (*F*, 103–4). Seeing an asinine murder makes Davies feel as though he has become a murderer himself and seems to retard the progression of the story, but the pace of the revelation increases as Dreiser continues:

> Still the company moved on and he followed, past fields lit white by the moon, under dark, silent groups of trees, through which the moonlight fell in patches, up low hills and down into valleys. . . . In the weak moonlight it seemed as if the body were struggling. . . . Then after a time he heard the company making ready to depart, and finally it did so, leaving him quite indifferently to himself and his thoughts. Only the black mass swaying in the pale light over the glimmering water seemed human and alive, his sole companion. (*F*, 104–5)

In Wright's story, too, Big Boy remains in the kiln through the night after the mob departs and becomes the victim's sole companion. Just as morning comes for the truck to deliver Big Boy to Chicago, dawn breaks for Davies to return to his office. After the crowd departs, Davies thinks of hurrying to a nearby post office to file a partial report. But he decides against it since he is the only reporter present, just as Big Boy is, and because "he could write a fuller, sadder, more colorful story on the morrow" (*F*, 105), just as Big Boy could have when he left for Chicago in the morning. This momentary delay in Davies's action gives his revelation a heightened effect.

Moreover, Dreiser's description of dawn in "Nigger Jeff," as of the opening scene, is tinged with a transcendental vision:

> As he still sat there the light of morning broke, a tender lavender and gray in the east. Then came the roseate hues of

dawn, all the wondrous coloring of celestial halls, to which the
waters of the stream responded. The white pebbles shone pinkily
at the bottom, the grass and sedges first black now gleamed
a translucent green. Still the body hung there black and limp
against the sky, and now a light breeze sprang up and stirred it
visibly. At last he arose, mounted his horse and made his way
back to Pleasant Valley, too full of the late tragedy to be much
interested in anything else. . . . Then he left, to walk and think
again. (*F*, 105–6)

Throughout Dreiser's description of the lynching, Davies sees the signs
of evil indicated by the struggling body, the black mass, and the black
body hanging limp. The images of the dark are intermingled in his mind
with those of the light that suggest hope: "the weak moonlight," "the
pale light," "the glimmering water," "the light of morning," "a tender
lavender and gray in the east," "the roseate hues of dawn," "the white
pebbles [shining] pinkily at the bottom." As the story progresses, the
images of hope increasingly dominate those of despair.

The same pattern of imagery is also created toward the end of Wright's
story. During the night Big Boy has to protect himself from cold wind
and rain as well as a persistent dog. Even though morning arrives with
the warm sunlight and brightened air, he is still reminded of "a puddle
of rainwater" and "the stiff body" of the dog lying nearby. "His knees,"
Wright describes, "were stiff and a thousand needlelike pains shot from
the bottom of his feet to the calves of his legs. . . . Through brackish
light he saw *Will's truck* standing some twenty-five yards away, *the
engine running*. . . . On hands and knees he looked around in the *semi-
darkness*. . . . Through *two long cracks* fell *thin blades of daylight*. . . . Once
he heard *the crow of a rooster*. It made him think of *home*, of *ma* and *pa*"
(*UTC*, 51–52; emphasis added). In the final scene the nightmare that has
tormented Big Boy throughout the night is chased out of his mind and
destroyed by the blades of the sun: "The truck swerved. He blinked his
eyes. The blades of daylight had turned brightly golden. The sun had
risen. The truck sped over the asphalt miles, sped northward, jolting
him, shaking out of his bosom the crumbs of corn bread, making them
dance with the splinters and sawdust in the golden blades of sunshine.
He turned on his side and slept" (*UTC*, 53).

In the ending of "Nigger Jeff" as well, Dreiser makes the hero's
consciousness move back and forth between hope and despair as if the
images of light and dark were at war. When Davies visits the room

where the body is laid and sees the victim's sister sobbing over it, he becomes keenly aware that all "corners of the room were quite dark. Only its middle was brightened by splotches of silvery light." For Davies, another climactic experience takes place when he dares to lift the shirt covering the body. He can now see exactly where the rope tightened around the neck. The delineation of the light against the dark is, once more, focused on the dead body: "A bar of cool moonlight lay just across the face and breast" (*F*, 109–10). Such deliberate contrasts between light and dark, good and evil, suggest that human beings have failed to see "transcending beauty" and "unity of nature," which are merely illusions to them, and that they have imitated only the cruel and the indifferent that nature appears to symbolize.

At the end of the story, Davies is overwhelmed not only by the remorse he feels for the victim, as Big Boy is, but also by his compassion for the victim's bereft mother, whom he finds in the dark corner of the room:

> Davies began to understand. . . . The night, the tragedy, the grief, he saw it all. But also with the cruel instinct of the budding artist that he already was, he was beginning to meditate on the character of story it would make—the color, the pathos. The knowledge now that it was not always exact justice that was meted out to all and that it was not so much the business of the writer to indict as to interpret was borne in on him with distinctness by the cruel sorrow of the mother, whose blame, if any, was infinitesimal. (*F*, 110–11)

The importance of such fiction is not the process of the young man's becoming an artist—Big Boy or the young Richard Wright is surely not trying to become merely an artist. It is the sense of urgency in which the protagonist living in American society is compelled to act as a reformer. With his final proclamation, "I'll get it all in" (*F*, 111), Davies's revelation culminates in a feeling of triumph. Although, to Dreiser as well as to Wright, human beings appear necessarily limited by their natural environment and by their racial prejudice, both writers in their respective stories are asserting that human beings are still capable of reforming society.

In sum, protest fiction, the category to which critics have assigned "Big Boy Leaves Home," becomes successful literature only if it is endowed with a universal sense of justice, as exemplified by "Big Boy

Leaves Home" and "Nigger Jeff." Such discourse, moreover, must address an actual and pressing social issue, whether it is a lynching a white writer witnessed in a border state in the 1890s or a problem of race and miscegenation a black writer encountered in the Deep South of the 1920s. As both stories show, great social fiction can be created not so much with the artistry the author can put into it—much of which is taken for granted in these stories—as with a sense of urgency the subject matter demands. In "Big Boy Leaves Home," this urgency does not come from the quality of Big Boy's will, nor is it anything to do with the collective will of black people. Rather, it comes from the conscience of humanity, the collective will of decent individuals living anywhere. It is a revelation given to Big Boy, as it is given to Elmer Davies. And through the protagonist and the skill of a gifted writer, it is disseminated to the world at large.

2

Much of Wright's fiction has generally been regarded as existential rather than naturalistic. It is a well-established fact that Wright lived and wrote *The Outsider,* the most existential of his novels, in France, where he maintained a close contact with such influential writers as Camus, Sartre, and de Beauvoir. "Down by the Riverside" and "Long Black Song," two stories Wright had written before he came in contact with French existentialist writers, suggest an existential treatment of the protagonist. But the two stories also show that the protagonist's philosophy directly resulted from the racial oppression rampant in the South, a social phenomenon that Wright treats uniquely.

"Down by the Riverside," which was first published in the 1938 edition of *Uncle Tom's Children,* dramatizes the tragic death of a black man, Brother Mann, who uses a stolen boat during a Mississippi flood to take his pregnant wife to a hospital for the child's delivery. On the way to the hospital, Mann is discovered by the owner of the boat, a white man, who tries to shoot him; in self-defense, Mann kills the owner. When Mann reaches the hospital, he finds his wife dead. Later he is drafted by the military men in charge of rescuing flood victims. The first house to which he is sent, with a black companion, both of them in another boat, happens to be that of the owner of the stolen boat, whose family recognizes Mann. Although he considers killing them, their house suddenly tilts, the ax in his hand does not fall over their heads, and he ends up rescuing them. Once the boat safely reaches the hill, they tell the authorities that Mann is a murderer. As he flees down the riverside, he is shot to death.

Like Wright's story "The Man Who Saw the Flood,"[10] "Down by the Riverside" is a flood story based on Wright's experiences with floods in Mississippi. Both stories, written in the thirties, reflect the hard times black farmers faced in the South. "The Man Who Saw the Flood" portrays a family of three stranded by a flood and then threatened by a white store owner because of their overdue debt. Although "Down by the Riverside," like "The Man Who Saw the Flood," is concerned with an economic issue, Wright's main focus is on the racial oppression black people faced in a southern community dominated by white people. From one point of view, "Down by the Riverside," in contrast to "Big Boy Leaves Home," seems to suggest the futility of a man struggling against the chance and fate that undermine his perseverance and will to survive. From another point of view, however, this story serves as an indictment against southern racism: Brother Mann is not merely a victim of chance and fate; he is a victim of racial prejudice. On the surface, the story seems to indicate that Mann, his wife Lulu, and the unborn child all die because of the flood, a natural disaster. But the plot, as structured, ironically suggests that, were Brother Mann treated as one's brother and as a man, they would not have had to die.

White racism in the South, the culprit of their tragedy, is sketched out in "The Ethics of Living Jim Crow." In one episode, Wright relates an incident in which, while delivering packages, he had a flat tire on his bicycle. Fortunately, white men drove by and offered to take him and the bicycle along by letting him cling to the side of the car with one hand while clutching the bicycle with the other. They were drinking and offered him the flask, but he declined, saying, "Oh, no!" He was immediately hit between the eyes with an empty whiskey bottle and "fell backwards from the speeding car into the dust of the road, my feet becoming entangled in the steel spokes of my bicycle." Quite amused, the white men came out of the car and stood over him; the man who had hit him asked: "Nigger, ain' yuh learned no better sense'n tha' yet? . . .

10. Richard Wright, "The Man Who Saw the Flood," in *Eight Men*, 110–16. This short story first appeared as "Silt" in *New Masses* 24 (August 24, 1937): 19–20.

Ain' yuh learned t' say *sir* t' a white man yet?" Dazed with his elbows and legs bleeding, Wright tried to stand up, but the attacker threatened him, doubling his fists and kicking the bicycle out of the way. Another man said, "Aw, leave the bastard alone. He's got enough," and asked Wright with contempt, "Yuh wanna ride t' town now, nigger? Yuh reckon yuh know enough t' ride now?" In a rebellious mood Wright said, "I wanna walk." Once again amused, they laughed and said: "Well, walk, yuh black son-of-a-bitch!" As they left the scene, they tried to comfort him by saying: "Nigger, yuh sho better be damn glad it wuz us yuh talked t' tha' way. Yuh're a lucky bastard. 'cause if yuh'd said tha' t' somebody else, yuh might've been a dead nigger now" (*UTC*, 9–10). This episode alludes to a slave owner's condescending attitude and mentality, to which white men tried to cling in the twentieth century. A black man, still regarded as a slave, could not even decline a white man's offer; if he did, he still had to thank him and respect him for it. In the episode, Wright must have declined the offer of drink because it was dangerous to be intoxicated on the job and, if found out, he would have lost his job. Moreover, he might have felt he had no obligation to join an evildoing, however entertaining it was to the white men. They behaved as though they still owned him as a slave and expected him to entertain them. Regardless of the situation, a black man must always remain inferior to a white man. No matter how despicable the white man may be, he can still pull his rank on a black man.

In another episode included in "The Ethics of Jim Crow," Wright describes an incident in which he was riding his bicycle back to the store after making some deliveries in a white neighborhood late one Saturday night. Suddenly a police car forced him to the curb and the two policemen ordered him to get down and put up his hands. Then they got out of the car, guns drawn and faces set. Ordering him to keep still, they searched his pockets and packages. Finding nothing suspicious or incriminating, one of them told him: "Boy, tell your boss not to send you out in white neighborhoods after sundown." Wright introduces this episode by remarking, "Negroes who have lived South know the dread of being caught alone upon the streets in white neighborhoods after the sun has set. In such a simple situation as this the plight of the Negro in America is graphically symbolized." While white visitors may walk through these neighborhoods unnoticed, the color of a black man's skin makes him suspect and "convert[s] him into a defenseless target" (*UTC*, 10–11). A black man, still regarded as a servant, or an entertainer, may work for white people during the day, but in the evening, and on Saturday night in particular, when white people socialize among themselves, he does not belong to that world.

In "Down by the Riverside," the way the plot is constructed helps the narrative to make a point. The story contains some obvious coincidences, which are necessary for the issue it addresses, though some critics regard them as contrivances that undermine the story's credibility. Edward Margolies does not consider "Down by the Riverside" nearly as successful as "Big Boy Leaves Home," for "the plot becomes too contrived; coincidence is piled upon coincidence, and the inevitability of his protagonist's doom does not ring quite true." Robert Felgar also notes: "All readers of 'Down by the Riverside' have noticed a most conspicuous coincidence in Wright's arrangement of the narrative."[11] The plot at the outset presents the information that every white man in the community who owns a boat refuses to sell or loan it to Mann. The stolen boat, as Mann and the reader later learn, happens to belong to the postmaster, Heartfield. However, the white man's refusal to help Brother Mann take his pregnant wife to the hospital and the urgency for Mann's brother to steal the boat have a cause-and-effect relationship. White men are shown as greedy, like Bowman, a plantation owner who declines to exchange Mann's old mule for a boat, or another who wants as much as a hundred dollars for a boat, and also as confirmed bigots, like Heartfield, who, as Mann's brother Bob says, "hates niggers." Even though Grannie would have urged Bob not to commit a sin by "stealin them white folks boats in times like these," Wright's story argues that Brother Bob was forced to "borrow" the boat because the lives of his sister-in-law and the child yet to be born were at stake (*UTC*, 59).

By the time the boat reaches the hospital, both the mother and the child are dead. His grief and despair notwithstanding, Mann is sent down on another boat with another black man to rescue white citizens stranded in the flood rather than sent up into the hills for his own safety. Those Mann rescues happen to be Heartfield's wife and children. Although this appears coincidental, the events are inevitably connected. While the town authorities are hesitant to let, as the general says, "too many niggers [handle] these boats," they have to employ Mann to drive the boat (*UTC*, 83). Mann wishes to decline to handle it, but another

11. Margolies, "The Short Stories," 132; Feglar, *Richard Wright*, 68.

black man, young Brinkley, who has already been working with the officials, is eager to volunteer and joins the rescue mission. In front of a fellow black man with goodwill, as well as under the eye of the white authorities, Mann cannot shirk his duty.

Another coincidence, which leads to Mann's capture and execution, occurs when Mann encounters Mrs. Heartfield and her children during the rescue. When Mann is about to hack them to death with an ax, the house in which they are trapped suddenly tilts and he ends up rescuing them. But Wright has been at pains to show ever since Mann's murder of Heartfield for self-defense that Mann has willfully avoided a chance to encounter Heartfield's family. His feelings, overwhelmed by the burden of his wife's, his child's, and Heartfield's deaths, result in his inaction, his will not to see Mrs. Heartfield and her children. One critic interprets this added burden of the deaths as what covers Mann "with a cold numbness. This lack of emotion enables Mann to do as the Whites demand, even to the extent of rescuing, not killing, the remaining Heartfields."[12] In any event, his will to survive is negated by the white authorities who reject his testimony that Heartfield attempted to kill Mann before Mann killed him. The trial in this story is a parody of swift military justice, and at no point does Wright indicate that the procedures of providing a defense lawyer and witnesses for the accused were operative. Despite the social forces that deny his existence, Mann refuses to succumb till the end: "Ahll die fo they kill me! Ahll *die*" (*UTC*, 102). In defiance of death, Mann has achieved his manhood as a free man.

"Long Black Song,"[13] the third story in *Uncle Tom's Children*, has a less complicated plot than do the two previous stories. A white phonograph salesman seduces a black farmer's wife, Sarah, while her husband, Silas, is away during the day. When Silas returns home, he discovers Sarah's infidelity and fumes over it. The next day the salesman comes back, with another white man waiting in the car. Sarah leaves the house because she does not want Silas to "whip her as she had seen him whip a horse" (*UTC*, 119). Silas then exchanges gunfire with the men, killing one of them. Later white lynchers arrive and set fire to the house with Silas inside. The narrative is told from Sarah's point of view.

12. Tracy Webb, "The Role of Water Imagery in *Uncle Tom's Children*," 10.
13. "Long Black Song," like "Down by the Riverside," was also first published in *Uncle Tom's Children*.

Sarah, unconcerned with the materialistic strivings of men, is trying to recapture the memories of a past love; Silas is trying to realize his dream of owning a farm like a white man. Both dreams, however, come to naught in the face of a caste system that allows for the exploitation of others. The success of the story lies in the noble victory of Silas, who realizes at his death that his wife's disloyalty to him has been permitted by the white bourgeois code to which he so easily acquiesced. When white men sexually exploited black women other than his own wife, Silas did not think about it seriously.

The success of the narrative also stems from the way in which Wright contrasts and compares two seemingly different points of view. From Silas's point of view at his death, a black farmer falls victim to white racism, much as Brother Mann becomes the object of racial hatred and prejudice. Even though Silas has diligently worked for years in competition with white farmers, he has been unaware until his death that he has merely imitated the white farmer who believes in the system of exploiting the poor and the oppressed. P. Jay Delmar, comparing "Long Black Song" to Charles W. Chesnutt's "The Web of Circumstance," notes that both stories "share the view that a Black man's attempt to participate fully in the white economic system might very well lead to tragedy." Both Wright and Chesnutt are suggesting that "political power must precede economic power if either is to be secure against the jealousies of those already entrenched in society. Wright, for a time at least, believed that Marxist unity would provide the necessary ingredient for Black success, that 'lan' is not so important as organization."[14] In "Long Black Song," however, Wright is not concerned with what Delmar calls "Marxist unity," with which Wright does deal in the last two stories in *Uncle Tom's Children*, "Fire and Cloud" and "Bright and Morning Star." Only after Silas's wife commits adultery does Wright make him return home and proudly tell her the good news that he has succeeded in selling cotton for $250, with which he now can buy more land and hire a farmhand like a white farmer: "Ah bought ten mo acres o lan. Got em from ol man Burgess. Paid im a hundred n fifty dollahs down" (*UTC*, 115).[15]

14. "Charles W. Chesnutt's 'The Web of Circumstance' and Richard Wright's 'Long Black Song': The Tragedy of Property."

15. The landowner Silas refers to, Burgess, has the same name as the store owner in "The Man Who Saw the Flood."

Silas's rage over Sarah's infidelity, which is understandable, now arouses his pent-up feelings against the white world. After killing one of the white men as a revenge, Silas stands over the dead body and talks, as Wright says, "out of his life": "The white folks ain never gimme a chance! They ain never give no black man a chance! There ain nothin in yo whole life yuh kin keep from em! They take yo lan! They take yo freedom! They take yo women! N then they take yo life!" Silas then turns to Sarah and screams: "N then Ah gits stabbed in the back by mah own blood! When mah eyes is on the white folks to keep em from killin me, mah own blood trips me up!" (*UTC*, 125). Margaret Walker observes in *Richard Wright: Daemonic Genius:* "Not only is the story a violent and tragic piece . . . rooted in southern race hatred and sexual warfare, it foreshadows Wright's negative treatment of all women, and particularly black women."[16] I agree with Walker that Wright disparages black women elsewhere in his fiction. Sarah's infidelity, however, does not result from her weakness of character but serves in this story as a reminder that white men's sexual exploitation of black women is condoned in white society. By narrating the tragedy from Silas's point of view, Wright succeeds in making the two themes, socioeconomic oppression and sexual exploitation, intensify each other. This double vision, in turn, makes Silas as defiant at his death as it does Mann. Silas cries out in despair as though he has become a nihilist: "But, Lawd, Ah don wanna be this way! I don mean nothin! Yuh die ef yuh fight! Yuh die ef yuh don fight! Either way yuh die n it don mean nothin" (*UTC*, 125).

From Silas's point of view "Long Black Song" has a thematic resemblance to "Down by the Riverside," but from Sarah's this story is structurally quite different from the other. "Long Black Song" opens with a lullaby Sarah is singing to her baby, an action through which she induces herself to have a dream; she dreams of Tom, her lover, whom she might have married had he not gone to war. She blames the war for her plight, a sentiment that characterizes her nature as the story unfolds; "Nothing good could come from men going miles across the sea to fight. N how come they wanna kill each other? How come they wanna make blood? Killing was not what men ought to do." In the dream Tom appears with "his big black smiling face." She remembers how he used to make love to her: "Against the plush sky she saw a

16. *Richard Wright: Daemonic Genius,* 117–18.

white bright day and a green cornfield and she saw Tom walking in his overalls and she was with Tom and he had his arm about her waist. She remembered how weak she had felt feeling his fingers sinking into the flesh of her hips. Her knees had trembled and she had had a hard time trying to stand up and not just sink right there to the ground" (*UTC*, 105).

Transported with the fantasy, she finds it impossible to separate the image of Tom from the sudden appearance of a white salesman who tries to sell a phonograph at a discount and asks for a drink of water. Still remaining in her dream and now listening to the music played on the phonograph, she is willingly seduced by the salesman. During their lovemaking she continues to stay in the dream: "A liquid metal covered her and she rode on the curve of white bright days and dark black nights and the surge of the long gladness of summer and the ebb of the deep dream of sleep in winter till a high red wave of hotness drowned her in a deluge of silver and blue and boiled her blood and blistered her flesh *bangbangbang*" (*UTC*, 113). "Long Black Song" indeed has one of the most lyrical passages in American literature; Wright's portrayal of Sarah's longing for love is reminiscent of Whitman's "Song of Myself" or the undulant prose in which Gertrude Stein delineates Melanctha's highly abstract emotions in *Three Lives*.

The imagery and rhythm Wright creates for his heroine account for her vision of the world and her concept of life. From her point of view, people should spend their lives in peace and harmony as in nature. When she waits for Silas, who has gone to work in the white world, she only sees "green fields wrapped in the thickening gloam. It was as if they had left the earth, those fields, and were floating slowly skyward. . . . And far away, in front of her, earth and sky met in a soft swoon of shadow." This world is not meant for the social and economic battle in which Silas is involved. When she dreams of Tom, who has gone to war, she also sees only "a white bright day and a green cornfield" against the plush sky (*UTC*, 105). This world is not meant for men like Tom to kill, and be killed by, other men. To Silas she is an adulteress—as, to Chillingsworth, Hester was an adulteress—but Sarah has long been neglected and unloved by her husband, just as Hester had been. Observing nature, Sarah instinctively realizes that materialism and racism have no roles in love. As she sees harmony between "white bright days and the desire of dark black nights," she can only envision tenderness and love between man and woman, peace and cooperation between black and white people. She feels that "men, black men and white men, land and houses, green cornfields and grey skies, gladness and dreams, were all a part of that which made life good. Yes, somehow, they were linked, like the spokes in a spinning wheel" (*UTC*, 126).

The success of this story also comes from the tensions created between the two points of view in opposition. Silas's worldview is pessimistic and akin to a kind of nihilism that was in vogue among French existentialists such as Camus and Sartre. Sarah's, on the other hand, is optimistic and reminiscent of the transcendentalism and pantheism expressed in Whitman's "Song of Myself." However divergent the two points of view may appear as the story is told, there emerges an area of vision shared by both. The plot reveals that while Silas gains property in the fields, he loses his wife, what he considers his most important property, at home. Ironically, his wife's infidelity makes him see that what is most important in life is not money but love, a view both characters come to share. Even though Silas chooses to die in protest against racism, the stand against racism becomes a vision both share, whether it involves social or sexual relationships.

In sum, both Mann and Silas are uneducated and unread individuals, unlike Cross Damon, an existential hero in *The Outsider*. But both, unlike Big Boy, the naive and innocent protagonist in "Big Boy Leaves Home," are keenly aware that the Jim Crow conditions in the Deep South have been the culprit of their alienation. Mann and Silas, therefore, revolt against this racial oppression in their fight for survival. In each story, only his final act, a defiant suicide, enables the hero to define his own existence and achieve a personal sense of justice and freedom.

3

The last two stories in the 1940 edition of *Uncle Tom's Children* deal with Communist ideology as it affects the black communities of the South. "Fire and Cloud,"[17] the last story in the 1938 edition, takes place during the Depression and presents a black minister trusted by both black and white citizens. His dilemma is whether to dissuade his congregation from demonstrating for food they need, or to support the march at the

17. "Fire and Cloud" first appeared in *Story Magazine* 12 (March 1938): 9–41 and was awarded the *Story Magazine* Prize.

risk of violence. While many of the elders in his church cannot break with their traditional faith in passive resistance, Reverend Taylor can change and does opt for solidarity and protest. Similarly, "Bright and Morning Star,"[18] the story added to the collection in 1940, deals with the change of attitude a black woman takes toward Christianity. Aunt Sue, the mother of two revolutionary black youths, is accustomed to the attitude of forbearance preached by black church leaders, but now that she is awakened by "the bright and morning star" of Communism, she becomes a martyr instead of a victim of white power. When she is summoned by the white authorities to claim the body of her murdered son, she shoots the official dead before she is killed.

Reverend Taylor, the protagonist in "Fire and Cloud," is a mature, well-educated individual who will likely remind a contemporary reader of Rev. Martin Luther King Jr. Like King, Taylor, endowed with intellectual ability, courage, and leadership, earns respect from all people, black or white. With stoicism and endurance seldom seen in fiction or reality in America, Taylor succeeds in leading the poor and oppressed to freedom. In the previous stories, Big Boy seeks escape from a white mob, Mann tries to avoid his fate, and Silas, cornered by white vigilantes, stands his ground. None of these individuals, however courageous, is capable of reflection and planning. But when Taylor thinks of how to convince his people that in the Depression there will be no food for public relief, he reflects on his own experience in simpler times: "And they could sing as he had sung when he and May were first married; sing about picking cotton, fishing, hunting, about sun and rain. They could. . . . But whuts the usa thinkin erbout stuff like this? Its all gone now. . . . And he had to go and tell his congregation, the folks the Great God Almighty had called him to lead to the Promised Land" (*UTC*, 132). Taylor, a biblical scholar, also makes an analogy between his cause and Moses's leading the Israelites out of Egyptian slavery. Later in the story his congregation prominently sings a song based on the Moses legend.

Although the success of the freedom march hinges upon Taylor, the story is dramatized through a conflict of two forces. On the one hand, the city officials try to deny Taylor's leadership by urging Deacon Smith, a black advocate of conventional faith and subservient ethics,

18. "Bright and Morning Star" was first published in *New Masses* 27 (May 10, 1938): 97–99, 116–22, 124. The story was also published in booklet form by International Publishers in 1941.

to side with the rich. Later in the story, when Taylor is taken away in a car blindfolded and beaten, he is voted out and Deacon Smith takes over the congregation. On the other hand, the Communists in the community try to consolidate their power by appealing to white workers and black citizens. Ironically, the conflict is decided not by physical force but by moral persuasion. In the middle of the story, when the city authorities send Hadley, a white man, and Green, a black man, to Taylor to dissuade him from joining the march, Taylor tells them that he will never come to the city hall begging for food. Hadley tells Taylor, "Then the demonstrations going to be smashed. . . . *You* can stop it! You have the responsibility and the blame!" Taylor simply responds: "Gawd knows Ah ain t blame. Ahm doin what mah heart tells me t do" (*UTC*, 144).

This strong will behind Taylor's action notwithstanding, the battle would not be won without the collective will of the people. As the fire led Moses and the crowd of Israelites in the desert at night to the Promised Land, the torture with fire Taylor is inflicted with in his back leads him to his people. Through a white neighborhood he staggers to reach home with pain and blood over his body. He passes a small graveyard protected by "a high iron picket fence. A *white* graveyard, he thought and snickered bitterly. Lawd God in Heaven, even the dead cant be together!" (*UTC*, 166). Reflecting on the Communist promise that only through the unification of white workers and black people is a new world possible, Taylor now receives a revelation: on earth whites and blacks live, die, and are buried on separated lots, but in heaven they are taken in together. As he goes through the white neighborhood, he once again reflects: "Some days theys gonna burn! . . . There ain no groun yuh kin walk on that they don own! N Gawd knows tha ain right! He made the earth fer us all! He ain tol no lie when He put us in this worl n said be fruitful n multiply" (*UTC*, 167).

The first person Taylor sees upon returning home is his own son Jimmy, who informs him that Brother Smith, falsely telling the congregation that Taylor had run out, has had the Deacon Board vote Taylor out of the church. Jimmy is, at first, numb and in despair, characteristic of passive Christian resignation, but now Taylor as father tries to teach his son how black people should achieve freedom and justice: "Don be a fool, son! Don thow yo life erway! We cant do nothin erlone. . . . We gotta git wid the *people*, son. Too long we done tried t do this thing our way n when we failed we wanted t turn out n pay-off the white

folks. Then they kill us up like flies. Its the *people,* son! Wes too much
erlone this way! Wes los when wes erlone! Wes gonna be wid our folks"
(*UTC,* 171). The next day, when he meets his congregation, he preaches
them the same gospel: "All this mawning before day Ah wuz limpin thu
white folks streets. Sistahs n Brothers, Ah *know* now! Ah done seen the
sign! Wes gotta git together. Ah know whut yo life is! . . . Its sufferin! Its
hell! Ah cant bear this fire erlone! Ah know now whut t do! Wes gotta
git close t one ernother! Gawds done spoke! Gawds done sent His sign.
Now its fer us t ack" (*UTC,* 178).

Unlike Big Boy, Brother Mann, and Farmer Silas, Reverend Taylor
succeeds in his mission not because he has courage and will but because
he is blessed with vision and with capacity to convert vision to action. In
this story and elsewhere, Wright carefully distinguishes the progressive
Christian that Taylor represents from the traditional Christian, as represented by Deacon Smith, the Reverend Hammond (the black preacher
Bigger Thomas despises in *Native Son*), and Cross Damon's mother in *The
Outsider,* who is easily intimidated by white power and politics. Taylor,
always aware of such evil forces, is able to conquer them. During his
harrowing journey through the white neighborhood, he comes upon
a church where Houston, a white minister, preaches. "Even tho he
preaches the gospel Ah preaches," Taylor utters to himself, "he might
not take me in" (*UTC,* 166). Not only are traditional black Christians
unaware of the extent of segregation in churches, but they scarcely
realize that in the name of peace and harmony in race relations they
continue to abide by passive behavior as preached in their churches.

Unlike "Fire and Cloud," "Bright and Morning Star" dramatizes the
action of a black woman protagonist, Aunt Sue as she is affectionately
called by Reva, a girlfriend of her son Johnny-Boy and the daughter of a
white Communist leader. Although both Reverend Taylor and Aunt Sue
are keenly aware of racial hatred and injustice, and firmly committed
to working for deliverance, they differ in their ideas and actions. Taylor, sympathetic to Communist philosophy and inspired by Christian
legend, is convinced that only through solidarity can the oppressed
succeed in winning liberation. Although he is endowed with as much
strength of character as any other protagonist in *Uncle Tom's Children,*
he distrusts individual will and action. Through experience and work
as a preacher, he has become a pragmatist who puts his faith in a New
Jerusalem. On the other hand, Sue, born and reared in the traditional
Christian faith, is now faced with the existential dilemma of preserving

her integrity and living in an irrational world, as Cross Damon is in *The Outsider*. Moments before she is shot to death she cries out: "Yuh didnt git whut yuh wanted! N yuh ain gonna nevah git it! Yuh didnt kill me; Ah come here by mahsef" (*UTC*, 215). Uneducated and unread, she is different from Taylor, whom Marxism can inspire into collective action. Rather, Sue, like Mann and Silas, the other nonintellectuals, feels that by becoming a martyr she is able to determine her own fate. However momentarily, she is able to control her life and her world. Her defiance against the old world and the old philosophy serves as a prophecy for a new world to come.

Sue is also akin to Sarah of "Long Black Song," the only other heroine in *Uncle Tom's Children*, for both women have their thoughts and instincts grounded in nature. As Sarah awaits Silas's return, she looks at green fields and a soft afterglow spreading into the sky. As Sue waits for Johnny-Boy, she sees "the rich black earth sprawling outside in the night. There was more rain than the clay could soak up; pools stood everywhere." As Sarah wonders what is causing her baby to cry so loudly in the cradle, Sue worries about her son's "trampin in this slop all day wid no decent shoes on his feet" (*UTC*, 181). Wright says, "She yawned and mumbled: 'Rains good n bad. It kin make seeds bus up thu the ground, er it kin bog things down lika watahsoaked coffin'" (*UTC*, 181–82). She instinctively makes such a statement, an observation that there are as many good white people as there are bad white people. From the beginning of the story she instinctively perceives the bright and morning star as representing the white Communists with whom both of her sons have been associated. At the same time her common sense tells her that the reactionary white politicians attempting to purge the world of the Communists are criminals. Little wonder that she embraces Reva as if she were her daughter-in-law. A critic argues that the probability in 1938 or 1980 of a black boy and a white girl falling in love and uniting to fight "under a Marxist banner and in the deep South" was extremely small.[19] But Wright's characterization of Sue clearly demonstrates that Sue would not have regarded Reva as her daughter-in-law had she not felt the existence of genuine love between Johnny-Boy and Reva.

Not only is Sue's character portrayed in the light of her nature and instinct, but her feelings, like Sarah's, are frequently expressed through

19. See Robert Felgar, *Richard Wright*, 76.

music. In "Long Black Song," Sarah's feelings are conveyed with songs she sings or hears; in "Bright and Morning Star," when Sue is in the midst of her work, she hears a song rise up out of her childhood past and break through her half-parted lips: *"Hes the Lily of the Valley, the Bright n / Mawnin Star / Hes the Fairest of Ten Thousan t ma soul"* (*UTC*, 182). As her work at home while she is longing for her beloved son makes an allusion to the work of the Communists, the verse "the Bright n Mawnin Star" in her song becomes an expression of hope for her sons and all the people on earth.

In contrast to Sarah's portrayal, Sue's is accompanied by action. When Sue is told to bring a sheet to claim the body of her son, Wright says: "Her whole being leaped with will; the long years of her life bent toward a moment of focus, a point. . . . She stood straight and smiled grimly; she had in her heart the whole meaning of her life; her entire personality was poised on the brink of a total act" (*UTC*, 207). Later in the story, when she is determined to prevent Booker, a government informer, from giving the authorities the names of party members, she tries to reach Foleys Woods before him by crossing the creek, a dangerous obstacle; yet she acts on instinct and succeeds:

> She came to the edge of the creek and paused, wondering at what point was it low. . . . Ahll cross here, she thought. At first she did not feel the water; her feet were already wet. But the water grew cold as it came up to her knees; she gasped when it reached her waist. Lawd, this creeks high! When she had passed the middle, she knew that she was out of danger. . . . A vivid image of Booker's white face hovered a moment before her eyes and a surging will rose up in her so hard and strong that it vanished. (*UTC*, 207–8)

In her mind, the "surging will" that rises up to banish the image of Booker, a symbol of oppression, now becomes another bright star. Ever since betraying the names of the members to Booker, a hamartia on her part, she has been mired between "two abandoned worlds, living, but dying without the strength of the grace that either gave. The clearer she felt it . . . the more urgent did she feel the need to fling into her black sky another star, another hope, one more terrible vision to give her the strength to live and act" (*UTC*, 206). This star is for her to be a martyr.

Sue has thus acted even more strongly than Taylor. As Taylor's strength lies in the quality of his intellect and his support of others,

Sue's comes from within—her heart. Although Taylor and Sue reach their decisions grounded on what Edward Margolies calls "their peculiar Negro folk mysticism . . . a native Negro revolutionism,"[20] their thoughts and actions, as Wright describes them, are poles apart. Sue is more a tragic character than Taylor is a modern crusader.

Each nevertheless remains an equally great creation Wright made in this discourse, which was to influence American racial relations in generations to come. Wright succeeded in molding "Bright and Morning Star" in the well-known theoretical framework of a tragedy. He wrote in "I Tried to Be a Communist": "I remembered the stories I had written, the stories in which I had assigned a role of honor and glory to the Communist Party, and I was glad that they were down in black and white, were finished. For I knew in my heart that I should never be able to write that way again, should never be able to feel with that simple sharpness about life, should never again express such passionate hope, should never again make so total a commitment of faith."[21] Despite some disparaging remarks Wright himself made about "Fire and Cloud," history has shown that the story served as a model for the Civil Rights Movement that Dr. Martin Luther King Jr. put in action decades later.

20. "Short Stories," 137.
21. See "I Tried to Be a Communist," 56.

3

Native Son and American Culture

1

Appraising the relation of *Native Son* to American culture, Irving Howe has said: "No matter how much qualifying the book might later need, it made impossible a repetition of the old lies. In all its crudeness, melodrama and claustrophobia of vision, Richard Wright's novel brought out into the open, as no one ever had before, the hatred, fear and violence that have crippled and may yet destroy our culture."[1] Not only does Howe's statement address the problems of race, but also it reminds the reader that Wright was the first major writer to deal with sexual relationships between black and white people. Because of this racial discourse, miscegenation became no longer taboo. What happens to Bigger and Mary in *Native Son* reinforces the image central to the tragedy, an image of the forbidden sexual relationship between a black man and a white woman in particular. This sexual encounter, however spontaneous and natural, is suppressed and condemned as socially unacceptable. Since a black man and a white woman can only dream about such an experience, it has the status of myth in American culture.

In *The Long Dream*, Wright's last novel, Fishbelly Tucker gradually comes to the realization that he cannot call himself a human being until he has the freedom of sexual relationship with a woman regardless of her skin color. The problem of miscegenation thus underlies Fishbelly's battle in achieving manhood. How seriously Wright intended to deal with this problem in his work is suggested by what he says about

1. *A World More Attractive*, 98–110.

it in *Black Boy*. It is true that *Black Boy* is not focused on the hero's sexual initiation. In *Black Boy*, sex, like religion, tends to victimize rather than develop an adolescent. The only woman to whom the young Wright is sexually attracted is a black woman depicted in grotesque and physical expressions instead of pleasant and spiritual images.[2] Such a description indeed debases his attitude toward human sexuality. Even though Wright is not concerned with the hero's sexual awakening in *Black Boy*, he defines the following subjects as taboo:

> American white women; the Ku Klux Klan; France, and how Negro soldiers fared while there; Frenchwomen; Jack Johnson; the entire northern part of the United States; the Civil War; Abraham Lincoln; U. S. Grant; General Sherman; Catholics; the Pope; Jews; the Republican Party; slavery; social equality; Communism; Socialism; the 13th, 14th, and 15th Amendments to the Constitution. (*BB*, 253)

Among the nineteen topics of taboo listed, the first four are directly related to miscegenation. It is beyond dispute that miscegenation occupied the mind of the young Wright as he came of age in the Deep South. While *Black Boy* merely intimates that white men do not mind black men's talking about sex as long as it is not interracial, most of Wright's novels powerfully demonstrate this fact. Wright tries to show that miscegenation is the reason white people have a preconceived notion of black people's place in America.

But another kind of miscegenation was regarded not as myth but as history. Slavery in America allowed the plantation owner to exploit black women for sex. The scene of miscegenation as presented in *Native Son*, however, is considered a myth, for neither Bigger nor Mary takes advantage of the other for materialistic gains. The slave owner, on the other hand, took advantage of the slave woman for sex in exchange for financial compensation or because he literally owned her and could do it for nothing. This situation is similar to the white man's sexual relationship with a black woman in the story "Long Black Song," in which a man and a woman exploit each other for their own emotional or physical needs. Such a relationship, moreover, has derived from an interracial mentality widely accepted and maintained in the system of

2. Richard Wright, *Black Boy: A Record of Childhood and Youth*, 125. Subsequent references will appear parenthetically in the text as *BB*.

slavery, as Silas, the wronged black husband, accuses white men of raping black women.

By contrast, Wright portrays the interracial sexual scene in *Native Son* with genuinely human sentiments rather than with social and economic motives. Without fear of social ostracism, as Wright depicts the scene, both Bigger and Mary are involved in a purely personal relationship:

> Her lips, faintly moist in the hazy blue light, were parted and he saw the furtive glints of her white teeth. Her eyes were closed. He stared at her dim face, the forehead capped with curly black hair. He eased his hand, the fingers spread wide, up the center of her back and her face came toward him and her lips touched his, like something he had imagined. He stood her on her feet and she swayed against him.
>
> He lifted her and laid her on the bed. Something urged him to leave at once, but he leaned over her, excited, looking at her face in the dim light, not wanting to take his hands from her breasts. She tossed and mumbled sleepily. He tightened his fingers on her breasts, kissing her again, feeling her move toward him. He was aware only of her body now; his lips trembled. (*NS*, 83–84)

Wright's original description of the scene—which, as Keneth Kinnamon has pointed out, Wright deleted from the galleys in fear of censorship—bears out the reading that the sexual feelings expressed at the scene are mutual. As Arnold Rampersad has shown, the original passage included a more explicit description of Mary's sexual arousal: "He tightened his arms as his lips pressed tightly against hers and he felt her body moving strongly. The thought and conviction that Jan had had her a lot flashed through his mind. He kissed her again and felt the sharp bones of her hips move in a hard and veritable grind. Her mouth was open and her breath came slow and deep."[3]

Well before this climactic scene, Wright accounts for Bigger's sexual attraction to a white girl. Near the beginning of the novel Bigger and his friend Jack go to the movies and watch double features. *Trader Horn*, in which black men and women are dancing in a wild jungle, shows Bigger only life in a remote world. *The Gay Woman*, portraying love and intrigue in upper-class white society, quickly attracts his attention. This movie

---

3. Kinnamon, "Introduction," in *New Essays on Native Son*, 14. Wright, *Early Works*, ed. Arnold Rampersad, 524. Subsequent references to this edition of *Native Son* are given in the text as *EW*.

shows, "amid scenes of cocktail drinking, dancing, golfing, swimming, and spinning roulette wheels," a young white woman having an affair while her rich husband is too busy with his work. In contrast to the struggling young black woman Bigger is so familiar with, this young white woman appears carefree and glamorous. Jack, equally fascinated by her, tells Bigger: "Ah, man, them rich white women'll go to bed with anybody, from a poodle on up. Shucks, they even have their chauffeurs. Say, if you run into anything on that new job that's too much for you to handle, let me know" (*NS*, 33). For Bigger, then, the gay woman first seen in the movies and later realized in his own life becomes a symbol not only of success and affluence in white society but also of the fulfillment of his youthful dreams and desires. In the original manuscript, moreover, Wright included a scene in the movie theater where Bigger watches in the newsreel none other than Mary Dalton.

Bigger and Mary's sexual encounter, which the members of jury deeply resent and fail to understand, can be defended on humanistic grounds. Neither Bigger nor Mary is motivated to exploit the other: they are simply infatuated with each other. In contrast, Bigger and Bessie are interested in each other for spurious reasons, motives that do not exist in the relationship of Bigger and Mary. While Wright has great sympathy for Bigger's infatuation with Mary, he feels contempt for Bigger's treatment of Bessie. Of the latter relationship, Wright says: "It was her hankering for sensation that he liked about her. Most nights she was too tired to go out; she only wanted to get drunk. She wanted liquor and he wanted her. So he would give her the liquor and she would give him herself. . . . He knew why she liked him; he gave her money for drinks" (*NS*, 132).

It seems as though Wright in *Native Son* idolizes Mary Dalton, a liberal white girl who rebels against her racially condescending father and sympathizes with a poor black boy like Bigger. This image of a white girl, moreover, is in stark contrast to "the purity of white womanhood" the Ku Klux Klansmen try to protect in the South.[4] At the same time Wright portrays black women as if they were morally and intellectually deficient. Bigger's sister Vera is a tired and fearful girl; alcohol is what sustains Bessie. Similarly, in *The Outsider*, an existentialist novel, Wright degrades black women. Cross Damon's relationship with his mother

---

4. Richard Wright, *Pagan Spain*, 237. Subsequent references will appear parenthetically in the text as *PS*.

betrays not only their estrangement but also his hostility to her religious fanaticism (*O*, 23). The young Damon's desire to free himself from such a bondage is closely related to his inability to love any black woman, as shown by his relationship with Gladys, his estranged wife, or Dot, his pregnant mistress. The only woman he loves is the white woman Eva, the wife of his Communist friend.

Wright's idealization of white women like Mary in *Native Son* and Eva in *The Outsider,* however, does not mean that Wright was attracted to these women because they were white. "The Man Who Killed a Shadow," a short story Wright first published in French in 1949, features a white woman who tries to seduce a black man who in turn murders her.[5] The story, like *Native Son,* deals with a young black man who inadvertently kills a white woman. But the two white women are entirely different in character and circumstance. The woman in "The Man Who Killed a Shadow" is a middle-aged, sexually repressed librarian. As Saul, the black man, tries to get away, she starts screaming and he brutally strikes her to death in fear of being accused of rape. Unlike Bigger, Saul is used in the story as a symbol of sexual abandon. Ironically, Saul falls victim to a white woman's sexual exploitation of a black man.

The tragedy that befell Saul and the librarian would not have occurred if their relationship were not interracial. The scene of Mary's murder in *Native Son* also shows that Bigger is sexually aroused by Mary, and vice versa, and that he is terrified of being caught in her bedroom. In each case, racial prejudice gets in the way and prevents a man and a woman from consummating their union. Indeed, it was Richard Wright who first brought out into the open and viewed this sexual myth from a genuinely humanistic perspective.

2

When *Native Son* appeared in 1940, critics as well as readers hailed it a phenomenal success.[6] As a Book-of-the-Month Club selection it became

5. "The Man Who Killed a Shadow," in *Eight Men,* 193–209.
6. See the reviews of *Native Son* collected in John M. Reilly, ed., *Richard Wright: The Critical Reception,* 39–99. Subsequent references to these reviews are cited as Reilly; the bibliography provides information on their initial publication.

at once a best-seller, earning a popularity accorded to no previous African American novel. Sterling Brown, a distinguished black critic, was quick to recognize the revolutionary status the book achieved, asserting that if a single book could awaken the conscience of the whole nation, that book would be *Native Son*. Brown regarded as Wright's greatest achievement the creation of Bigger Thomas, not the revolutionary setting or the thrilling narrative. Brown saw Bigger's characterization as the first to exhibit "a psychological probing of the consciousness of the outcast, the disinherited, the generation lost in the slum jungles of American civilization."[7] *Native Son* has captured, as no other book has, the powerful emotions and deep-seated frustrations of black people.

Some readers, however, have not considered *Native Son* a successful novel. James Baldwin, for example, considered Bigger Thomas a monster who does not reflect the complex truths of the black experience in America. To Baldwin, Wright fails to understand the true meaning of humanity and the genuine struggle of African American life; Wright merely records "that fantasy Americans hold in their minds when they speak of the Negro." Bigger, Baldwin believed, is a misrepresentation of the black man because he "has no discernible relationship to himself, to his own life, to his own people, nor to any other people . . . and his force comes, not from his significance as a social (or anti-social) unit, but from his significance as the incarnation of a myth." The serious limitation Baldwin saw in Bigger's character is not in Wright's use of Bigger as a symbol, but in the absence of the social and human relations underlying that symbol. Baldwin would have treated Bigger's story differently: "To tell his story is to begin to liberate us from his image and it is, for the first time, to clothe this phantom with flesh and blood, to deepen, by our understanding of him and his relationship to us, our understanding of ourselves and of all men."[8] Baldwin also disagreed with Wright in his method of portraying the ordeal of black people because Baldwin saw *Native Son* as rooted in the tradition of naturalistic protest fiction. The protest novel, Baldwin argued, is written out of sympathy for the oppressed but fails to transcend their trauma or the rage such a novel expresses.

7. See Brown's review in Reilly, 95–98.
8. "Many Thousands Gone," 672, 673, 679.

Partly in response to the critical tendency to extol *Native Son*, recent critics have discussed Bigger's language in its relation to the narrator. Laura E. Tanner, for instance, makes an inquiry into what she calls the narrator's "miserable" failure in representing Bigger's voice. She attempts to account for "this textural rupture" between the narrative voice and Bigger's voice, between Wright's "sophisticated," "symbolic" language and Bigger's "unsophisticated," "awkward," "broken English." Attributing Wright's inability to fill the gap to the stylistic weakness of the novel, she concludes that "Bigger at last becomes author and narrator of his own text, driving from the novel the voices that would overwhelm his own" and that "*Native Son* is a novel about the insufficiency of novels, a story about the insufficiency of words."[9] While Tanner's reading is a conscientious effort to apply Derridian theory of discourse to Wright's discourse in *Native Son*, it explains neither the source nor the effect of the power of the narrative. Despite an effort to discard the old cloak of the New Criticism, her reading smacks of the hegemonic literary judgment that has often characterized that mode of criticism. The problem with her analysis stems from her rigid judgment of Bigger's language. "Bigger's voice," she persists, "is marked by a form of halting expression that frequently deteriorates into stuttering repetition." Bigger's language, she repeatedly argues, is characteristic of "his awkward relationship with the master language."[10] Granted, Bigger is not a literate person, but neither is Huck Finn. However awkward and clumsy Bigger's voice may sound to an educated person in the story, it does not sound so to Bigger, nor does it to the reader. Billy Budd stutters, Bartleby prefers not to talk, and Clyde Griffiths and Joe Christmas are at times utterly incoherent speakers.

On the other hand, Joyce Ann Joyce tries to show the cohesiveness between Bigger's voice and the narrative voice, "the connection between Wright's characterization of Bigger and his unique use of sentence structure and figurative language." Whereas Tanner tries to divide the narrative structure into a binary opposition, a juxtaposition of two mutually exclusive strands of language, Joyce finds "a linguistically complex network of sentences and images that reflect the opposing

9. "Uncovering the Magical Disguise of Language: The Narrative Presence in Richard Wright's *Native Son*," 134–37, 145.
    10. Ibid., 134.

or contradictory aspects of Bigger's psyche and thus synthesize the interrelationship between Wright's subject matter and his expression of it."[11] While Joyce recognizes that the power of the narrative is generated by the fierce battle Bigger wages against racist society, she cogently shows that the impact of the tragedy on the reader comes directly from Wright's complex narrative strategy. Instead of monolithically resonating the voice of Bigger as a victim of his racist environment, Wright, as Joyce argues, amply succeeds in portraying him in terms of dialectical images and ideas: sun and snow, black and white, hero and murderer, fear and blindness, humiliation and insensitivity.

Chiding Joyce for making "no distinction between 'Bigger's thoughts' and the thoughts attributed to him by the narrator," Tanner says that "Joyce fails to detect any tension generated by the placement of 'contrasting ideas inside similar grammatical structures.'"[12] The issue, however, is not whether there is any tension between the protagonist's voice and the narrator's voice, since there is always some sort of narrative tension in great novels, like *Moby-Dick, Crime and Punishment,* and *An American Tragedy.* The central question is how well the novelist uses that tension to his or her advantage to maximize the effect of the narrative. Bigger's spontaneous response and the narrator's thoughtful language do not necessarily collide because Wright creates other strands of narrative voice that mediate the two voices. But Tanner ignores the effects of such voices as the Daltons' language and the speech of Boris Max, the Marxist lawyer, let alone the effect of what is common between Bigger's voice and the narrator's. For example, the Daltons' language, larded with sociological jargon and racial condescension, sounds so far apart from both Bigger's and the narrator's voices as to create the effect of coalescing them. Tanner points out that the Daltons "utilize the master language" with ease;[13] not only do the words fall on deaf ears to Bigger, but to the reader they even sound far more awkward than Bigger's words and indeed ridiculous, thereby creating a superb parody. In Tanner's reading, just as the Daltons' language is equated with "the master language," so is Max's voice intermixed with the narrator's. Although

11. "The Figurative Web of *Native Son*," 171. Joyce's essay, originally entitled "Technique: The Figurative Web," is reprinted from her *Richard Wright's Art of Tragedy.*
12. "Uncovering the Magical Disguise of Language," 138.
13. Ibid., 136.

there is some affinity between Max's language and the narrator's and some readers might regard Max as Wright's mouthpiece, their voices at crucial points in the story are poles apart: Max's is strengthened by mind and fact as Wright's is resonated by heart and metaphor.

Although it is often true that literature and sociology, as Baldwin cautioned, are not synonymous, it is also true that a successful protest novel is a work of art that transcends the limitations of didactic writing. One of Wright's techniques to transform this sociological book into a novel is the creation of Boris Max to defend Bigger. Malcolm Cowley, generally very positive about *Native Son,* deplored Max's courtroom plea for Bigger's life as thematically weakening. He argued that Max's speech, on behalf of the whole black population, would be quite meaningful but that Bigger must die to stand as an individual, not a symbol.[14] Bigger, of course, is the major character, but he is not Wright's deepest concern until the very end of the novel. Through Max, Wright speaks for and to the nation, thereby creating a narrative voice, a point of view that is indeed sympathetic to Bigger but entirely impersonal in developing a racial discourse.

Half a century earlier Mark Twain had used a similar technique in writing *Pudd'nhead Wilson,* another important discourse on race. Like *Native Son,* Twain's book is dramatic, unsentimental, and uncompromisingly realistic.[15] While Wright and Twain both depict sensational, violent actions, they succeed in presenting objective and judicious observations about the most agonizing social issue in America.

As racial discourse, *Native Son* thrives on Max's long speech before the jury in book 3, entitled "Fate." Since this scene takes place in the final section of the novel, it makes a great impact not only on Bigger, the oppressed protagonist, but also on the nation, the oppressive antagonist. At the climactic moment in presenting his argument, Max declares:

> Multiply Bigger Thomas twelve million times, allowing for environmental and temperamental variations, and for those Negroes who are completely under the influence of the church, and you have the psychology of the Negro people. But once you

14. See Cowley's review in Reilly, 67–68.
15. The most incisive analysis with respect to the history of the composition of *Pudd'nhead Wilson* is given in Hershel Parker's "The Lowdown on *Pudd'nhead Wilson:* Jack-leg Novelist, Unreadable Text, Sense-Making Critics, and Basic Issues in Aesthetics."

see them as a whole, once your eyes leave the individual and encompass the mass, a new quality comes into the picture. Taken collectively, they are not simply twelve million people; in reality they constitute a separate nation, stunted, stripped, and held captive *within* this nation, devoid of political, social, economic, and property rights. (*NS*, 364)

Max then poses a rhetorical question to the court about whether capital punishment would deter black people from committing murder. "No!" Max says. "Such a foolish policy has never worked and never will. The more you kill, the more you deny and separate, the more will they seek another form and way of life, however blindly and unconsciously" (*NS*, 365).

How strongly Max's speech contributes to the argument of the novel is ironically shown by the weakness of Max's statement as a plea for Bigger's individual life. Not only does Max's plea fail to save Bigger, but it is doubtful that the plea convinces many readers of the justification for Bigger's brutal treatment and murder of his girlfriend Bessie. It does, however, convince the reader of the general plight of African Americans. Other scenes that have taken place long before Max's speech also contribute to its success. At the beginning of the novel Bigger complains to his friend Gus: "Goddammit, look! We live here and they live there. We black and they white. They got things and we ain't. They do things and we can't. It's just like living in jail. Half the time I feel like I'm on the outside of the world peeping in through a knot-hole in the fence" (*NS*, 23). Bigger is aware of a fence of discrimination that exists around the aviation school he dreams of attending. The poverty-stricken atmosphere in which his family is forced to live makes relationships strident and inhuman. In order to re-create for the audience in the court the condition of a family like Bigger's, Max says: "This vast stream of life, dammed and muddied, is trying to sweep toward the fulfillment which all of us seek so fondly," the pursuit of happiness guaranteed in the Constitution (*NS*, 365).

Wright presents Max's speech as a sociological analysis depicting the racial conditions in the 1930s in terms of a modern version of slavery. Similarly, Twain creates in his novel a young lawyer from upstate New York named David Wilson to provide a scientific analysis of the racial issue in the nineteenth century and of slavery in particular. The difference between the two works is obvious: the author of *Pudd'nhead Wilson* was not only a white man but also an individual, unlike Wright, who was not personally involved in the racial problems the work addresses. But Wilson's role resembles Max's, for both lawyers on behalf of the authors establish a distance from life and create an impersonal vision. For Twain as well as for Wright, the structure of the story is therefore endowed with the author's logic and objectivity.

In *Adventures of Huckleberry Finn,* a somewhat romantic novel of race, slavery is obscured in the happy ending for Jim, and other subtle and disturbing aspects of the race question are not raised. By contrast, *Pudd'nhead Wilson* ends tragically for all the major characters, white and black alike, and this connects it strongly to *Native Son.* In both works, the system of slavery, whether it is actual slavery in *Pudd'nhead Wilson* or racial discrimination and oppression in *Native Son,* is realistically portrayed. Although the story in each case is fiction, its development rests on American history. Tom Driscoll's tragedy took place in Dawson's Landing on the Missouri side of the Mississippi in 1830, and Bigger Thomas's occurred in the south side of Chicago a century later. In each novel, several generations of the American experience, a nation, a society, a local community, and an era all coalesce into a unified vision.

Another similarity is the concept of determinism Wright and Twain both use in analyzing the issues of race. From the moment *Native Son* begins, Bigger is placed in an oppressive environment; his killing of a large rat is symbolic of suppressed violence and tension. Whether he lives in a sordid, one-room apartment with his mother, brother, and sister or roams about a pool parlor with his friends, he is a frustrated young man prone to violence and transgression. Even though he is lucky enough to land a job as chauffeur for the family of a wealthy businessman, he cannot help noticing a glaring contrast between the money and power of the white ruling class and the poverty and misery of black people. This contradiction stimulates his ambition to become "somebody," but if he is denied such an opportunity, he will instinctively defend himself at all costs.

In *Pudd'nhead Wilson,* as in *Native Son,* Twain intends to demonstrate that men and women, both black and white, are victims of society at large. In such a deterministic world there are no heroes, no villains; only white society, the system of slavery in particular, becomes the culprit. No character, whether it is Roxy or Wilson, acts as an individual. The reader scarcely knows what a character thinks. Man or woman is merely a victim of circumstance and history. Just as Wright's major concern is with racism rather than with Bigger's character, Twain's aim is to assail slavery rather than the individuals involved. This is the reason some critics do not consider *Pudd'nhead Wilson* a great novel. Richard Chase, for instance, compares it unfavorably with *Huckleberry Finn*, a great novel strengthened by Twain's characterization of the hero. Chase argues that in *Pudd'nhead Wilson* "there are no characters who are capable, either by themselves or in relation to each other, of giving the book a sustained organic life."[16] Although Chase is right in maintaining that even Roxy, who is as courageous and human as anyone in Twain's stories, is not a credible character, Chase is wrong in assuming that *Pudd'nhead Wilson* is intended as a novel of character.

The most significant affinity between the two novels is that Twain and Wright both narrate in the full conviction that the crimes they dramatize are inevitable products of American society. They both convince critical readers that the protagonists are morally free of guilt. It is much easier, therefore, to understand the author's intention if the work is regarded as what Émile Zola called an "experimental novel." In such a novel, the author first establishes a milieu taken from life and observes the behaviors of the characters projected into that milieu. Zola called the experimental novelist an "experimental moralist" because the mission of such a novelist is to determine the causes of social ills so that "we wish to reach better social conditions. . . . To be master of good and evil, to regulate life, to regulate society, in the long run to resolve all the problems of [society], above all to bring a solid foundation to justice by experimentally resolving questions of criminality, is that not to do the most useful and moral human work?"[17]

Because Wright's mission in *Native Son* as racial discourse is to determine the cause of Bigger's murders, Wright places his emphasis in the third section of the book. As several critics have pointed out, book 3 is the best part of the novel. Edward Kearns, in "The 'Fate' Section of *Native Son*," argues that despite the abstractness of Bigger's speech, the third section of the novel enables Bigger to achieve his identity, a thematic strategy that serves Wright's aim. Paul N. Siegel, in "The Conclusion of Richard Wright's *Native Son*," regards Max's long speech in the courtroom as original and suggests that it does not follow a Marxist party line. Max, Siegel suggests, hands the case to a judge, thereby rejecting a trial by an all-white jury. On the strength of book 3, Wright is able to

16. *The American Novel and Its Tradition*, 156.
17. "The Experimental Novel," 178, 177.

shift the burden of Bigger's guilt to society.[18] As Wright's development of the story clearly indicates, *Native Son* is built on the inevitable results of Bigger's unpremeditated murder of a white girl. However gruesome and unbelievable his actions may appear, Bigger finds no other way to defend himself but to burn her body and make false accusations. And he cannot help killing Bessie, lest she implicate him. It is inevitable as well that Bigger is captured by white police and brought to a trial by an all-white jury. Given a racist climate, all the scenes take place one after another as if planned. The denouement of the story is convincing not only because Wright adheres to Zola's deterministic philosophy but also because the plot is partly based on the actual murder of a white woman by a black man as reported in the *Chicago Tribune* in 1938. While writing the first draft of *Native Son,* Wright read in a long series of *Tribune* articles that the case of murder "involved Robert Nixon and Earl Hicks, two young Negroes with backgrounds similar to that of Bigger." One of the articles, on May 27, 1938, reported that one Florence Johnson "was beaten to death with a brick by a colored sex criminal . . . in her apartment." The two black men, as Keneth Kinnamon notes, "were arrested soon after and charged with the crime. Though no evidence of rape was adduced, the *Tribune* from the beginning called the murder a sex crime and exploited fully this apparently quite false accusation."[19]

Book 3, and Max's speech in the court in particular, is solidly built upon what has transpired before the trial in the novel. As the lawyer Wilson discovers scientific evidence to prove Tom Driscoll's murder in *Pudd'nhead Wilson,* Max's speech seizes upon sociological evidence for the causes of Bigger's murders. Max argues with logic and eloquence that Bigger's murders have resulted from white racism rampant in Chicago. To Max, as the first two sections of the novel have proved, Bigger merely falls victim to the racist forces so familiar to the American public. As an idealist who believes in the American dream, Wright takes pains to provide a picture of what young Americans try to be— independent, economically self-reliant, and happy. Young and full of energy as Bigger is, he urges himself to pursue his dreams. If it is racism that prevents him from realizing these ideals, the result of his frustration is to save himself at the risk of killing his enemy.

18. See Phyllis R. Klotman, "Moral Distancing as a Rhetorical Technique in *Native Son:* A Note on 'Fate.'"
19. "*Native Son:* The Personal, Social, and Political Background," 68.

Just as the concept of determinism is more important than the characterization of Bigger in *Native Son*, Twain's interest in *Pudd'nhead Wilson* lies more strongly in the effects of environment on individuals than in the individuals themselves. Wilson thus conducts an experiment on behalf of the author Twain. Whether or not Wilson is a fully developed character is moot, because he is an outside observer like Max. "Isn't that pleasant—& unexpected!" Twain wrote in a letter. "For I have never thought of Pudd'nhead as a *character*, but only as a piece of machinery—a button or a crank or a lever, with a useful function to perform in a machine, but with no dignity above that."[20]

The approach Twain and Wright take to determinism, however, differs from Zola's. Zola attributes Gervaise's tragedy in *L'Assommoir*, for example, not only to her environment but to her heredity as well. Throughout *Native Son*, Bigger's behavior has nothing to do with his mother's, and there are no discernible similarities among Bigger, his sister, and his brother. In *Pudd'nhead Wilson*, Tom, the assumed white child, grows up and develops a distinctive pattern of behavior clearly traceable to his white environment but not to his black heredity. When Roxy, Tom's biological mother, reveals to her son that he was in fact born a slave, she argues that his despicable behavior derives from his black gene. "Pah! it make me sick!" she cries out. "It's de nigger in you, dat's what it is. Thirty-one parts o' you is white, en on'y one part nigger, en dat po' little one part is yo' *soul*."[21] But Roxy is wrong in her observation because she herself has been indoctrinated with the prejudice that black people are genetically inferior to white people. In the course of the story, Tom exhibits the worst traits ascribed to the corrupt white society: he is spoiled as a child, goes to Yale but comes home with offensive mannerisms, gambles away his allowance, steals, and finally murders Judge Driscoll, his benefactor.

Tom's most heinous act is the betrayal of his own mother, Roxy, since he willingly sells her down the river after she has helped him pay his debts. But his atrocities are not shown to derive from his being black; they are caused by the training the institution of slavery has forced upon black and white people alike. White and black people have both

20. *The Love Letters of Mark Twain*, 291.
21. *"Pudd'nhead Wilson" and "Those Extraordinary Twins,"* 70. Subsequent references will appear parenthetically in the text as *PW*.

been trained over the generations to treat black people as properties and commodities. Whatever is base and inferior in Tom has stemmed not from black blood but from white training. The black heredity, in fact, is shown to be superior: the white mother of the real Tom Driscoll dies shortly after she bears her son, while Roxy, when she gives birth to Chambers, Twain says, "was up and around the same day, with her hands full, for she was tending both babies" (*PW*, 5). Genetically Roxy is far more capable than her white counterpart. Moreover, Roxy "was of majestic form and stature, her attitudes were imposing and statuesque, and her gestures and movements distinguished by a noble and stately grace" (*PW*, 8).

Twain expresses his concept of determinism with poignancy in the climactic scene where Tom has no choice but to kill Judge Driscoll. Just as Bigger's killing of Mary Dalton is accidental, Tom's killing of the judge is not premeditated since his mission on that night is to steal money from his uncle's safe. He has no intention of murdering him; Twain writes: "When he was half way down he was disturbed to perceive that the landing below was touched by a faint glow of light. What could that mean? Was his uncle still up? No, that was not likely; he must have left his night-taper there when he went to bed." Since Tom feels no malice toward his uncle, he is pleased "beyond measure" when he sees his uncle soundly asleep on the sofa. But when his uncle stirs in his sleep, Tom is seized with panic and draws "the knife from its sheath, with his heart thumping and his eyes fastened upon his benefactor's face." No sooner has Tom felt "the old man's strong grip upon him, and a wild cry of 'Help! help!' [rung] in his ear," than his own fear and confusion overwhelm him and any vestiges of free will are negated at once. "Without hesitation," Twain says, "he drove the knife home— and was free" (*PW*, 94). Tom's actions, therefore, are remarkably similar to those of Bigger when Mrs. Dalton's entrance into Mary's bedroom causes him to panic: "He turned and a hysterical terror seized him, as though he were falling from a great height in a dream. A white blur was standing by the door, silent, ghostlike. It filled his eyes and gripped his body" (*NS*, 84). In each case, the protagonist falls victim to forces of social environment working against his free will and causing him to act as though he were a trapped animal. Robert Butler calls Bigger's killing of the rat, his near killing of Gus, and his killing of Mary Dalton "scenes of entrapment in which various forces inside and outside the central character restrict his consciousness and limit his free will, thereby forcing him into acts of reflexive violence that become more serious as the scenes progress."[22]

From the vantage point of slaveholders, Tom's killing of Judge Driscoll is not only criminal but immoral simply because Tom murders his benefactor. Similarly in *Native Son,* racist society refuses to recognize Bigger's killing of Mary Dalton as accidental and calls it rape and murder. In each novel, the ultimate irony is created by the narrative voice, a point of view in opposition, which informs the reader of the fact that the protagonist's killing of a white person has resulted not from his hatred of that person but from white racism, the racist conditioning of black people imposed on them by white society.

In contrast to *Native Son,* the success of *Pudd'nhead Wilson* as racial discourse largely comes from Twain's use of irony in the style and structure of the book. The opening scene is deceptive: everything seems orderly. But as the story unfolds, things are not in order as they appear. Society is corrupt: the effect of slavery on the lifestyle of Dawson's Landing is gradually revealed. The irony rests in the fact that a clear line of demarcation exists between black and white people, slaves and slave owners. As the story progresses, a deeper irony emerges: the racial distinction has become obscure through generations of miscegenation. Roxy looks white, but her blood is one-sixteenth black. The color line becomes even more obscure with Tom, who is one-thirty-second black. Moreover, he is switched with a pure white baby in the cradle. Despite his black heritage, he becomes a white man and the heir to Judge Driscoll. The dramatic irony is further intensified because nobody knows Tom's background except Roxy and the reader. The doctrine of determinism underlies Twain's theme and technique, as it does Wright's, but what enhances the effect of the story is this ironic incongruity between appearance and reality.

What is more, Twain's irony does not spare white men their lack of moral conscience. For Twain, miscegenation as condoned in the South is unquestionably immoral; he accuses slave owners of hypocrisy. His disclosure of the tradition of miscegenation is ironic, revealing that although the slave owners regard black people as animals, it is they themselves who behave like animals. They take advantage of

22. *Native Son: The Emergence of a New Black Hero,* 41.

black women for sex but fail to take paternal responsibility for their offspring. In contrast to a black woman like Roxy, these men are judged clearly immoral. What she does in switching the babies is deemed moral because her action comes from her heart, from a mother's genuine love for her child.

The most subtle irony is reserved for the ending of the novel. Immediately after Wilson's fingerprint collection proves Tom's identity, the real Tom is rescued from the throes of slavery. Twain then comments in a final scene:

> The real heir suddenly found himself rich and free, but in a most embarrassing situation. He could neither read nor write, and his speech was the basest dialect of the negro quarter. His gait, his attitudes, his gestures, his bearing, his laugh—all were vulgar and uncouth; his manners were the manners of a slave. Money and fine clothes could not mend these defects or cover them up, they only made them the more glaring and the more pathetic. The poor fellow could not endure the terrors of the white man's parlor, and felt at home and at peace nowhere but in the kitchen. (*PW*, 114)

Twain's satire is now complete: the seeming slave is free, but the free man is doomed to live like a slave for the rest of his life.

Twain's disparagement of white society is also tempered with humorous commentary on American life. Pudd'nhead Wilson's famous calendar records Twain's witty but serious charges against American society at large. Although many of the remarks have little bearing on the major themes of the novel, some of them are eloquent expressions of human folly. Chapter 21, for instance, opens with this note:

> *April 1. This is the day upon which we are reminded of what we are on the other three hundred and sixty-four.*
> —PUDD'NHEAD WILSON'S CALENDAR. (*PW*, 105)

The most satiric remark is recorded in the concluding chapter:

> *October 12, the Discovery. It was wonderful to find America, but it would have been more wonderful to miss it.*
> —PUDD'NHEAD WILSON'S CALENDAR. (*PW*, 113)

This remark on Columbus Day is followed by Twain's concluding argument. Twain asserts at the end of the story that if "Tom" had been white and free, he should rightfully have been punished. But if he had been a slave, as he should have been since he was born black, Twain suggests, he would not have committed the murder in the first place. "As soon as the Governor understood the case," Twain writes, "he pardoned Tom at once, and the creditors sold him down the river" (*PW*, 115). From a deterministic point of view, slavery was indeed the murderer and Tom was an innocent victim. Throughout the text, then, a master novelist's skill is on display, for Twain is able to present an indisputable sociological analysis with a pointed sense of humor and irony.

To present a sociological observation based on determinism, Wright uses in *Native Son* a variety of devices quite different from those in *Pudd'nhead Wilson*. There is a clear distinction, first of all, between the motives of the two novelists. Twain, a liberal thinker, wrote out of deep sympathy for the racially oppressed, and the fault he had to avoid was sentimentality. Wilson, neither the oppressor nor the oppressed, can take a neutral stand. Not only does Twain's point of view sound scientific and impersonal, but it is conveyed with humor and seldom turns into pity. Wright, on the other hand, was motivated by wrongs he had personally suffered, and his vision had no room for humor or levity. Unlike *Pudd'nhead Wilson*, *Native Son* from the first page keeps the reader vividly aware of the protagonist as the inevitable product of his environment. As the story unfolds, this portrait is gradually intensified with the events that follow his capture. The lurid trial and Bigger's defense by a radical attorney enable *Native Son* to express the whole tragedy of black people rather than one individual's pathology.

Wright's most effective technique in *Native Son* as a racial discourse is the conversion of Max's speech into a narrative voice, which in turn coordinates the findings of a sociological analysis with Bigger's personal grievances. Such a voice triumphantly counteracts the travesty that is the state's case. Unable to support his claim with factual evidence or rudimentary logic, the prosecutor piles up statements of racial prejudice and hatred reminiscent of those of Ku Klux Klansmen. Those who regard Max's speech as didactic and uninspiring are surprised at Bigger's intellectual growth at the end of the trial. The views Bigger expresses toward the end of his life become abstract; earlier he has been compelled to act by his social environment, but through Max's speech he begins to establish his own identity. As a result, he is able to conceptualize the meaning of his act and is proud of his manhood and independence.

What he achieves at the end of his life, despite the death sentence, thus contributes to Wright's thematic design.

Max's role in pleading for Bigger, then, differs from Wilson's in identifying the murderer. Max, being Jewish, has a deeper understanding of the conflict of races in America than does Wilson. Wilson, characterized as absentminded, keeps himself out of the racial strife in the local community. One can only speculate why Wright deleted in the 1940 Harper edition of *Native Son* a reference to Max's being a Jew, but because Wright's intention was to indict American society, he made Max's speech reflect a racially impersonal point of view. In the manuscript version of *Native Son*, Max states: "And, because I, a Jew, dared defend this Negro boy, for days my mail has been flooded with threats against my life. The manner in which Bigger Thomas was captured, the hundreds of innocent Negro homes invaded, the scores of Negroes assaulted upon the streets, the dozens who were thrown out of their jobs, the barrage of lies poured out from every source against a defenseless people—all of this was something unheard of in democratic lands" (*EW,* 806). This passage was deleted in the Harper edition. Max's observations on Bigger's condition in America strike the literary public, not the courtroom audience, as eminently true and brilliant. The objectivity in Max's vision therefore contrasts sharply but finely with the bigotry in the prosecutor's probing.

Despite the obvious difference in the roles Max and Wilson assume, the visions their speeches create are both ironic. As Wilson tells the court that Tom is an innocent victim instead of a murderer, Max testifies that society instead of Bigger is a murderer. Even the well-meaning Daltons—like Judge Driscoll, "respected, esteemed, and beloved by all the community," and who considers himself a "free-thinker" (*PW,* 4)—are depicted as prejudiced and condescending. Although they appear philanthropic since they donate money for black boys to buy Ping-Pong tables, they are in fact exploiters of the poor and disadvantaged. At the coroner's inquest Max questions Mr. Dalton with sarcasm: "So, the profits you take from the Thomas family in rents, you give back to them to ease the pain of their gouged lives and to salve the ache of your own conscience?" (*NS,* 304). As Benjamin Davis Jr. pointed out in his review of *Native Son*, Dalton's philanthropy as Max satirizes it resembles that of "the class of hypocritical Carnegies, Fords and Rockefellers, who are the very causes of the unemployment, poverty and misery among the Negro people, which their million-dollar gifts are falsely alleged to cure."[23] Theodore Dreiser as a young reporter in Pittsburgh in the mid-1890s witnessed such hypocrisy in Andrew Carnegie. In his magazine articles and later in his autobiography, *A Book about Myself*, Dreiser satirized Carnegie's appearance of generosity in contributing part of his huge fortunes to various libraries. In reality, Dreiser subtly noted, Carnegie was an exploiter of cheap labor in Pittsburgh, an egocentric public figure. "Selfish wealth," Dreiser remarked with a bit of sarcasm, "stands surprised, amazed, almost indignant, at the announcement that Andrew Carnegie, instead of resting in Olympian luxury on the millions he has earned, and going to the grave with his gold tightly clutched in his stiffening fingers, proposes to expend the bulk of his riches, during his lifetime, for the benefit of his fellowmen."[24]

Max's final speech in the court also abounds in irony. While Max is aware of the racist tone of the press against Bigger, he deplores "the silence of the church." "What is the cause of all this high feeling and excitement?" he asks. "Is it the crime of Bigger Thomas? Were Negroes liked yesterday and hated today because of what he has done?" Indicting the judicial system, Max says: "Gangsters have killed and have gone free to kill again. But none of that brought forth an indignation to équal this" (*NS*, 356). Personally as well, Max satirizes the landlord Dalton who refuses to rent apartments to black people anywhere but in the black belt. According to Max, then, it turns out that confining Bigger "in that forest" as a stranger had in fact made him an acquaintance of Mary, whom he murdered. And to Mrs. Dalton, Max ironically says: "Your philanthropy was as tragically blind as your sightless eyes!" (*NS*, 362). Through his killing of a white girl, Bigger is able to see himself as an individual. As James Nagel points out, this scene becomes "the pivotal point for not only the structure and theme but the imagery as well: it is a moment of 'recognition' in the classical sense."[25]

In creating literary discourse, Wright uses other stylistic and structural devices to transcend the limitations of sociological prose. The first scene, in which Bigger and his brother Buddy corner a big rat and Bigger smashes it with a skillet, suggests the plight of black people in white society. Such a violent scene implies the conditions and frustrations of

23. Review from *Sunday Worker*, in Reilly, 70.
24. "A Monarch of Metal Workers—Andrew Carnegie."
25. "Images of 'Vision,'" 113.

black people in general, but its dramatic impact is not fully appreciated until book 3, where Max delivers the eloquent speeches at the inquest and at the trial.

The scenes of confinement and estrangement are also reflected in the language of the people involved. When Mrs. Dalton is introduced to Bigger by her husband at their residence, she speaks: "Don't you think it would be a wise procedure to inject him into his new environment at once, so he could get the feel of things? . . . I think it's important emotionally that he feels free to trust his environment. . . . Using the analysis contained in the case record the relief sent us, I think we should evoke an immediate feeling of confidence." Bigger tries to listen to their conversation, Wright says, "blinking and bewildered." Her expressions such as "feels free to trust his environment," "using the analysis contained in the case record," and "evoke an immediate feeling of confidence" make "no sense to him; it was another language. . . . He felt strangely blind" (*NS*, 48). Not only does her language indicate how strange the white world appears to Bigger, it also allows Wright to satirize the condescension and estericism of social workers.

Bigger's estrangement from the white world, on the other hand, is reflected in the language of his friends and in that of his enemies. When Bigger and his friend Jack go to see the movie *The Gay Woman*, they are both puzzled by certain words used in the dialogue:

> "Say, Jack?"
> "Hunh?"
> "What's a Communist?"
> "A Communist is a red, ain't he?"
> "Yeah; but what's a red?"
> "Damn if I know. It's a race of folks who live in Russia, ain't it?"
> "They must be wild."
> "Looks like it. That guy was trying to kill somebody." (*NS*, 34–35)

This dialogue, part of which is quoted here, is a replacement for the original manuscript version, which indicates that both Bigger and Jack are well acquainted with Communism and that Bigger identifies the man kissing Mary Dalton in the newsreel as a Communist. Wright's portrayal of Bigger and Jack in the original manuscript, therefore, makes them more knowledgeable about world affairs than they are in the published version.[26] Later Bigger meets Mary and her Communist friend Jan, and their talk about Communists, demonstrations, class struggle, and black liberation bewilders him. However sympathetic their demeanor may appear, Bigger finds it difficult to understand their language. Feeling alienated from his black friends and resentful toward Mary and Jan, he even resists going into Ernie's Kitchen Shack because he dreads his black friends' asking one another: *"Who're them white folks Bigger's hanging around with?"* (*NS*, 71). Jan tells Bigger that Communists like Jan and Mary have been fighting to *"stop"* the kind of killing in a riot in which Bigger's father was also a fatality, but Bigger fails to see the connection between the Communist and Civil Rights movements. Apparently to make Bigger as uninformed and innocent a youth as possible, Wright omitted in the Harper edition a dialogue in which Peggie, the maid at the Daltons, intimates to Bigger that Mary's "wild ways" vex her conservative parents.

Another significant omission in the Harper edition is a page-long passage of Max's speech that characterizes Mary as a compassionate woman. In this passage, Max reminds the court that despite the racial segregation rampant in the country, including the very court where Bigger is standing accused of murder, she genuinely had tried to have sympathy and understanding for Bigger. "It has been said," Max emphasizes, "that the proof of the corrupt and vile heart of this boy is that he slew a woman who was trying to be kind to him. In the face of that assertion, I ask the question: Is there any greater proof that his heart is not corrupt and vile than that he slew a woman who was trying to be kind?" (*EW*, 818). By deleting such a passage, Wright made *Native Son* less didactic and avoided a cumbersome recapitulation of the earlier scene. Leaving this passage, on the other hand, would have undermined Wright's attempt to portray a black youth like Bigger as estranged from Mary, a symbol of white society. The passage would also contradict Wright's assertion that the estrangement between Bigger and Mary rather than the emotional affinity between them is what caused Mary's death. Wright attempted to prove that racism, not their infatuation with each other, resulted in the whole tragedy.

Not only do Max's speeches as they are delivered in the published version awaken in Bigger a consciousness of freedom and autonomy of

---

26. See *EW*, 472–75.

which he has not been aware before, but they also contrast sharply with the talk of Mr. and Mrs. Dalton, which is larded with sociological jargon. Moreover, Max's final speech at the trial, as Joyce Ann Joyce has noted, is comparable to the chorus in a Greek tragedy.[27] "Bigger," as Wright intimates, "was not at that moment really bothered about whether Max's speech had saved his life or not. . . . It was not the meaning of the speech that gave him pride, but the mere act of it" (*NS*, 371). That is, Max's final speech is not a description of something, but, as Aristotle said of tragedy, an action. Wright approaches Aristotelianism in the way he structures Max's dialogue with Bigger in book 3, for Bigger's response to Max is not simply a description of Bigger's sensations at the end of his life but a dynamic development in Bigger's character. This development alludes to Max's earlier observation that the actions leading to the death of Mary and Bessie were "as instinctive and inevitable as breathing or blinking one's eyes. It was an act of *creation*!" (*NS*, 366).

In contrast to *Pudd'nhead Wilson*, then, the success of *Native Son* as racial discourse also stems from a thematic design that enables Bigger to achieve a sense of freedom and independence despite his death sentence. Wright convinces the reader that Bigger has undergone an enormous development from an innocent, alienated youth to a mature, reflective person. In *Pudd'nhead Wilson*, Twain's chief interest is not in character development. Courageous and daring though Roxy is, she is not portrayed as an individualist such as Bigger becomes at the end of his ordeal. In the beginning she has some of Bigger's rebelliousness, but by the end of the story she has been reduced to the religious passivity of Bigger's mother.

These stylistic, structural, and thematic elements that buttress *Native Son* were not, of course, excised in the 1940 edition. As Twain's use of anecdote, humor, and satire in *Pudd'nhead Wilson* made the novel a unique accomplishment, Wright's devices in *Native Son* transformed what James Baldwin called "everybody's protest novel" into a successful one.[28] To Baldwin and to Wright's detractors, Bigger Thomas is not much of a character but merely a social symbol and the novel suffers from Wright's excessive reliance on symbolism and didacticism. But *Native Son* displays, as does *Pudd'nhead Wilson*, a complex interplay of social

27. *Richard Wright's Art of Tragedy*, 48.
28. Baldwin, "Everybody's Protest Novel."

and personal experiences. For both novelists, the result was a remarkably skillful fusion of the naturalistic and psychological traditions in American fiction.

3

Few critics question that *Native Son* is a superb discourse on race based upon the naturalistic tradition in American literature. Wright's work is often compared with one of the finest social novels written in that tradition, Dreiser's *An American Tragedy*. Dreiser is, among modern novelists, one of the most influential predecessors of Wright. In an episode from *Black Boy*, Wright tells of being inspired by Dreiser's fiction, which was to the fledgling writer "nothing less than a sense of life itself" (*BB*, 274). Such acknowledgment must have convinced critics that the primary source of his best-known work, *Native Son*, was *An American Tragedy*. In fact, several early reviewers of *Native Son* pointed out that the two novels share the same theme and technique. And both novels convince their readers that the crimes they dramatize are inevitable products of American society and that both protagonists are morally free from guilt. Clifton Fadiman, for instance, wrote, "*Native Son* does for the Negro what Theodore Dreiser in *An American Tragedy* did a decade and a half ago for the bewildered, inarticulate American white."[29]

Except for the obvious issues of race, Wright and Dreiser shared similar experiences before they became novelists. From their boyhoods both were economically hard-pressed; they were always ashamed that they had grown up on the wrong side of the tracks. As boys they witnessed struggling and suffering and felt excluded from society. They grew up hating the fanatic and stifling religion practiced at home. In both lives, the family suffered because of the father's inadequacies as a breadwinner; the son inevitably rebelled against such a father, and the family was somehow put together by the suffering mother. Under these circumstances, their dream of success was merely to survive; they tried to hang on to one menial job after another. As a result, both nurtured

29. "A Black 'American Tragedy' "; see also Peter Jacks, "A Tragic Novel of Negro Life in America—Richard Wright's Powerful 'Native Son' Brings to Mind Theodore Dreiser's 'American Tragedy.' "

a brooding sensibility. At twelve, Wright held "a notion as to what life meant that no education could ever alter, a conviction that the meaning of living came only when one was struggling to wring a meaning out of meaningless suffering" (*BB*, 112). This statement indeed echoes what Dreiser recorded in his autobiography:

> In considering all I have written here, I suddenly become deeply aware of the fact that educationally speaking, where any sensitive and properly interpretive mind is concerned, experience is the only true teacher—that education, which is little more than a selective presentation of certain stored or canned phases of experience, is at best an elucidative, or at its poorest, a polishing process offered to experience which is always basic.[30]

But this close kinship between the lives of Wright and Dreiser need not necessarily have resulted in the similarities between *Native Son* and *An American Tragedy*. Although both novels are obviously concerned with the crime and guilt of a deprived American youth struggling to realize his dreams of success, the characterization of the hero fundamentally differs in the two novels. Clyde Griffiths in *An American Tragedy* is seen by Dreiser as a representative type, and the novel's psychological focus serves to delineate the frustrations of not only an individual but also a class. Bigger Thomas in *Native Son* is presented as a particular individual in Wright's imagination. Wright's essay "How 'Bigger' Was Born" suggests an extension of Bigger to include all those rebels the author had known in the South, and even white victims of the system who actively fought against it. Nevertheless, within the confines of the novel itself, we find no other character remotely like Bigger, once the murder triggers the creation of his personality, and no similar identification between character and author. It is significant in this regard that, as *Black Boy* demonstrates, Wright always considered himself unique, an outsider, not only from white persons but also from most of the black persons with whom he grew up.

It would seem that both authors, being literary naturalists, used authentic court records. Dreiser drew on the Gillette murder case in upstate New York; Wright on the Leopold and Loeb kidnapping-murder as well as the Robert Nixon murder trial and conviction in Chicago. The titles of both books strongly imply that Clyde and Bigger are

---

30. Theodore Dreiser, *Dawn*, 586.

the products of American society and that society, not the individuals involved in the crimes, is to blame. But doesn't a naturalistic novel *always* create tensions in the life of the hero, growing out of an environment over which he has no control and about which he understands very little and, therefore, by which he is *always* victimized? If so, *Native Son* does not appear to fit into this genre. Bigger's transcendence of the type of defeated, determined protagonist of which Clyde in *An American Tragedy* is a good example provides the clearest distinction between the two works. Despite the obvious parallels between *Native Son* and *An American Tragedy*, the comparison is of limited value, and this reading is to show significant differences between the two books.

It is true that both novels employ crime as a thematic device. In *Native Son*, the murder of Bessie is the inevitable consequence of Mary Dalton's accidental death; in *An American Tragedy*, Clyde's fleeing of the scene of the accident that kills a child is what leads to his plotting of murder later in the story. Without the presence of crime in the plot neither author would have been able to make significant points about his protagonist. But the authors' focus is different in the two books. Wright's center of interest, unlike Dreiser's, is not crime but its consequences—its psychological effect on his hero. Before committing his crime Bigger is presented as an uneducated, uninformed youth; indeed he is portrayed as a victim of white society who grew up in the worst black ghetto of the nation. We are thus surprised to see him gain identity after the murder. The crime gives him some awareness of himself and of the world of which he has never been capable before. We are surprised to learn that after the murder Bigger is well versed in world affairs. "He liked to hear," Wright tells us, "of how Japan was conquering China; of how Hitler was running the Jews to the ground; of how Mussolini was invading Spain" (*NS*, 110). By this time he has learned to think for himself. He is even proud of Japanese, Germans, and Italians, because they "could rule others, for in actions such as these he felt that there was a way to escape from this tight morass of fear and shame that sapped at the base of his life" (*NS*, 109–10).

Book 1 of *Native Son* is entitled "Fear," and ironically Wright's characterization of Bigger makes his stature deliberately smaller and less courageous than we might expect of a fighter against racial oppression. No wonder Mary Dalton's death is caused by Bigger's fear of white people and their world. His killing of Mary is an accidental homicide. In *An American Tragedy*, Clyde is placed in a situation so oppressive that only violence can provide the hope of dignity. But the oppression for Clyde has a corollary of hope, not fear, on his part. Clyde is an optimistic character, always seeking opportunities for success in life. While Bigger can only kill accidentally, Clyde in the same position can consciously plot murder. Even though the boat into which Clyde lures Roberta overturns when he has not planned it, and her actual death may legally prove to have been accidental, Clyde is not entirely innocent. On this ground alone the interpretation of the death of a girl as a central episode vastly differs between *Native Son* and *An American Tragedy.*

Throughout his story Dreiser implies that Clyde's aspirations to rise in the world are not matched by his abilities. Near the beginning Dreiser makes known that Clyde, overly impressed by every sign of success in his future, "lacked decidedly that mental clarity and inner directing application that in so many permits them to sort out from the facts and avenues of life the particular thing or things that make for their direct advancement."[31] This is why whatever he does is so inept that he is easily caught after the crime. At the trial, Clyde after such a harrowing experience is called by the prosecutor "a loose, wayward and errant character" (*AT,* 525). Before execution Clyde remains "a mental and moral coward," as his defense attorneys have presented him. Not only has he become a puppet of his own lawyers for their political purposes but he ends his life as an immature youth without a sense of remorse, let alone self-confidence.

By contrast, Bigger after committing two crimes has for the first time redeemed his manhood. Bigger tells Max: "But really I never wanted to hurt nobody. That's the truth, Mr. Max. I hurt folks 'cause I felt I had to; that's all. They was crowding me too close; they wouldn't give me no room. Lots of times I tried to forget 'em, but I couldn't. They wouldn't let me" (*NS,* 388). Bigger's earlier evasion of life has been converted to participation. The fact that he had killed a white girl, a symbol of beauty for white society, makes him "feel the equal of them, like a man who had been somehow cheated, but had now evened the score" (*NS,* 155). Bessie's murder also marks a new development in Bigger's manhood. For the first time he desires to be at peace with himself. Bigger is no longer a slave but a free man who claims his right to "create." Bessie's

31. Theodore Dreiser, *An American Tragedy,* 169. Subsequent references will appear parenthetically in the text as *AT.*

murder results from a willful act, a clear departure from the accidental killing of Mary Dalton.

Despite a death sentence handed down by his white rulers, Bigger now proclaims his own existence. Even Max, who has taken a sympathetic attitude toward the racially oppressed, is bewildered by Bigger's deep urges for freedom and independence. "I didn't want to kill," Bigger tells Max. "But what I killed for, I *am!*" (*NS*, 391–92). Having overcome white oppression, Bigger now stands as a heroic exemplar for the members of his race. His brother Buddy, he realized, "was blind. . . . went round and round in a groove and did not see things." Bigger sees in Buddy "a certain stillness, an isolation, meaninglessness" (*NS*, 103). And he finds his sister and mother to be equally weak. "Bigger," says Wright, "was paralyzed with shame; he felt violated" (*NS*, 280).

Finally, in both *Native Son* and *An American Tragedy* a preacher appears before the trial to console the accused. But in *Native Son* the black preacher is described in derogatory terms. Bigger immediately senses that the Reverend Hammond possesses only a whitewashed soul and functions merely as an advocate of white supremacy. Wright offers this explanation: "The preacher's face was black and sad and earnest. . . . He had killed within himself the preacher's haunting picture of life even before he had killed Mary; that had been his first murder. And now the preacher made it walk before his eyes like a ghost in the night, creating within him a sense of exclusion that was as cold as a block of ice" (*NS*, 264).

During his act of liberation, too, Bigger is consciously aware of his own undoing and creation. To survive, Bigger is forced to rebel, unlike Clyde, who remains a victim of the tensions between individual will and social determinism. In rebelling, Bigger moves from determinism to freedom. Bigger knows how to escape the confines of his environment and to gain an identity. Even before he acts, he knows exactly how Mary, and Bessie later, has forced him into a vulnerable position. No wonder he convinces himself not only that he has killed to protect himself but also that he has attacked the entire civilization. In *An American Tragedy*, Dreiser molds the tragedy of Clyde Griffiths by generating pity and sympathy for the underprivileged in American society. In *Native Son*, however, Wright departs from the principles of pity and sympathy that white people have for black citizens. In "How 'Bigger' Was Born," Wright admits that his earlier *Uncle Tom's Children* was "a book which even bankers' daughters could read and weep over and feel good about." In *Native Son*, however, Wright did not allow for such complacency. He warns readers that the book "would be so hard and deep that they would have to face it without the consolation of tears" (*NS*, xxvii).

The meaning of *Native Son* therefore derives not from crime but from its result. Dreiser's interest in *An American Tragedy*, on the other hand, lies not in the result of crime but in its cause. While Bigger at the end of his violent and bloody life can claim his victory, Clyde at the end of his life remains a failure. *Native Son* thus ends on an optimistic note; *An American Tragedy* as a whole stems from and ends on the dark side of American capitalism. F. O. Matthiessen is right in maintaining that the reason for Dreiser's use of the word *American* in his title "was the overwhelming lure of money-values in our society, more nakedly apparent than in older and more complex social structures."[32] Furthermore, Helen Dreiser seems to confirm Dreiser's central thought in interpreting materialism as the cause of Clyde's tragedy. On Dreiser's choice of the Chester Gillette murder case for fictionalization, she comments:

> This problem had been forced on his mind not only by the extreme American enthusiasm for wealth as contrasted with American poverty, but the determination of so many young Americans, boys and girls alike, to obtain wealth quickly by marriage. When he realized the nature of the American literature of that period and what was being offered and consumed by publishers and public, he also became aware of the fact that the most interesting American story of the day concerned not only the boy getting the girl, but more emphatically, the poor boy getting the rich girl. Also, he came to know that it was a natural outgrowth of the crude pioneering conditions of American life up to that time, based on the glorification of wealth which started with the early days of slavery and persisted throughout our history.[33]

Dreiser's fascination with this subject resulted in his treatment of Clyde as a victim of the American dream. Bigger, too, a product of the same society, cherishes a dream of his own. Like anyone else, he reads the newspapers and magazines, goes to the movies, strolls the crowded streets. Bigger is intensely aware of his dreams: "to merge

32. *Dreiser*, 203.
33. *My Life with Dreiser*, 71–72.

himself with others and be a part of this world, to lose himself in it so he could find himself, to be allowed a chance to live like others, even though he was black" (*NS*, 226). Unlike Dreiser, Wright must have clearly recognized his hero's sense of alienation from the rest of the world. It is an alienation that Wright himself, not Dreiser, often experienced as a boy and as a man. But it never occurs to Bigger that he can pursue such a dream. Indeed, throughout the text Wright amply documents the prevailing social mores, economic facts, and public sentiments to prove that Bigger's actions, attitudes, and feelings have already been determined by his place in American life. It is understandable for James Baldwin to say of *Native Son* that every black person has "his private Bigger Thomas living in the skull."[34] Given such a determined state of mind, Bigger would not be tempted to pursue his dreams. Ironically, the racial oppression and injustice in fact enhance his manhood. To Clyde Griffiths, however, the flame of temptation is brighter and more compelling. He is easily caught, and he thrashes about in a hopeless effort to escape the trap. Under these circumstances, "with his enormous urges and his pathetic equipment,"[35] as Dreiser once characterized the plight of such an individual in America, there is no way out for Clyde but to plot murder.

The central meaning of *An American Tragedy* thus comes from the economic and social forces that overpower Clyde and finally negate his aspirations. Where a Bigger Thomas before liberation must always remain an uninformed, immature youth, a Clyde Griffiths is one whose mind is already ingrained with that glorious pattern of success measured by money; one must climb the social ladder from lower to middle to upper class. At the beginning of the story Dreiser directly shows how the family's mission work in which Clyde is compelled to take part looks contrary to his dreams. Dreiser at once comments that "his parents looked foolish and less than normal—'cheap' was the word. . . . His life should not be like this. Other boys did not have to do as he did" (*AT*, 12). A basically sensitive and romantic boy, he cannot help noticing the "handsome automobiles that sped by, the loitering pedestrians moving off to what interests and comforts he could only surmise; the gay pairs of young people, laughing and jesting and the 'kids' staring, all troubled him with a sense of something different, better, more beautiful than his,

34. "Many Thousands Gone," in *Notes of a Native Son*, 33.
35. Quoted by Matthiessen in *Dreiser*, 189.

or rather their life" (*AT*, 10). The function of this scene is in great contrast to that of a similar scene in *Native Son*. Near the beginning Bigger goes to the movies to see the double feature. The portrayal of upper-class white society in *The Gay Woman*, after quickly attracting his attention, quickly loses it, and *Trader Horn*, in which black men and women are dancing in a wild jungle, shows him only life in a remote world. Bigger is thus placed in no-man's-land; he is only vaguely aware that he is excluded from both worlds. Unlike Wright, Dreiser places his hero in *An American Tragedy* at the threshold of success and achievement.

Clyde is also a victim of sexual forces. Early in the story his family is confronted by his older sister Esta's elopement, pregnancy, and desertion. Although Clyde is aware that sex leads to exploitation and misery on the part of the girl, he does not blame the whole problem on the seducer. This ambivalence in his attitude toward sex foreshadows his own affair with Roberta. For Bigger, sex is merely a biological force that plays a minor role in his life. For Clyde, however, sex is not only viewed materialistically but weighed in the gradations of the economic and social scale. Clyde is first attracted to the incipient whore, Hortense Briggs, because her eyes remind him of an alcove in the hotel hung with black velvet. To her suggestion that "fellows with money would like to spend it" on her, Clyde boasts: "I could spend a lot more on you than they could" (*AT*, 79). To win her love he must buy her an expensive fur coat beyond his means. Sondra Finchley, his ultimate love, for whom he is forced to sacrifice his second girlfriend, Roberta, is called "the most adorable feminine *thing* he had seen in all his days" (*AT*, 219; emphasis added). Dreiser can make us feel what Clyde feels: "Indeed her effect on him was electric—thrilling—arousing in him a curiously stinging sense of what it was to want and not to have—to wish to win and yet to feel, almost agonizingly that he was destined not even to win a glance from her" (*AT*, 219–20). In short, sex becomes not a romantic force of love but the symbol and substance of material success in the American dream.

Thus Clyde is presented as a helpless victim of society. Characterized by the defense attorneys as a man of weak character, he is not strong enough to oppose the system, nor is he well equipped to transcend his spurious dreams. On the contrary, Bigger in *Native Son* is represented to his disadvantage by the defense attorney. A more convincing argument in that courtroom would have been, as discussed earlier, for the defense to plead insanity rather than to demonstrate that Bigger was a victim of society. In Clyde's defense in *An American Tragedy*, neither pleading insanity nor demonstrating societal victimization occurs. Jephson most faithfully equates Clyde's infatuation with Sondra with a "case of the Arabian Nights, of the ensorcelled and the ensorcellor. . . . A case of being bewitched, my poor boy—by beauty, love, wealth, by things that we sometimes think we want very, very much, and cannot ever have" (*AT*, 681). Dreiser's theme therefore becomes the baffling problem of justice. Jephson, Dreiser's mouthpiece during the trial, tells Clyde and the court: "Clyde—not that I am condemning you for anything that you cannot help. (After all, you didn't make yourself, did you?)" (*AT*, 675). This pronouncement is later echoed by Clyde's own reflections in the prison:

> Was it not also true (the teaching of the Rev. McMillan— influencing him to that extent at least) that if he had led a better life—had paid more attention to what his mother had said and taught—not gone into that house of prostitution in Kansas City—or pursued Hortense Briggs in the evil way that he had— or after her, Roberta—had been content to work and save, as no doubt most men were—would he not be better off than he now was? But then again, there was the fact or truth of those very strong impulses and desires within himself that were so very, very hard to overcome. (*AT*, 784)

Other naturalists who often show their characters being destroyed by overwhelming forces always remind us how small and helpless human efforts are. "Men were nothings," says Frank Norris toward the end of *The Octopus*, "mere animalcules, mere ephemerides that fluttered and fell and were forgotten between dawn and dusk."[36] Dreiser never does this because he is always seeking the possibility of magnitude and self-determination in human existence. No matter how small and weak a man like Clyde may prove to be, Dreiser never gives up searching for his humanity and individual worth. In an interview in 1921 Dreiser flatly stated his predilection for little men that was to explain his treatment of Clyde Griffiths: "I never can and never want to bring myself to the place where I can ignore the sensitive and seeking individual in his pitiful struggle with nature."[37]

Both Wright and Dreiser are intensely concerned with the forces in society that one must battle for survival. Some naturalist writers see

36. *The Octopus*, 343.
37. Matthiessen, *Dreiser*, 189.

human beings easily destroyed by social forces, while others make their novels thrive upon such a battle. Wright's racial discourse shows that his hero stands at the opposite end of this human struggle, for Bigger, unlike Clyde, is victorious in his battle against the social forces. True, Bigger is condemned to die as a murderer, but this defeat is really a triumph for Bigger, who has rejected society's rules and values and established his own. Dreiser, on the other hand, stands between defeat and triumph. If naturalism faces the tension between will and determinism, Dreiser is content to keep the tension unresolved. Despite Clyde's destruction in the end, Dreiser refuses to indict life. Instead he tenaciously seeks its beauty and exaltation until the end.

The two novelists' divergent attitudes toward the problem of guilt are reflected in the style and structure of their books. *Native Son* is swift in pace and dramatic in tone and displays considerable subjectivity, involving the reader in experiences of emotional intensity. The thirties were hard times for both white and black people, and it was not possible to take a calm and objective view of the situation. Wright himself was a victim of the hard times, and he could speak from his heart. Moreover, Bigger Thomas is a conscious composite portrait of numerous black individuals Wright had known. As indicated in "How 'Bigger' Was Born," all of them defied the Jim Crow order, and all of them suffered for their insurgency (*NS*, xii). As in the novel, Wright lived in a cramped and dirty flat, and he visited many such dwellings as an insurance agent. In Chicago, while working at the South Side Boys' Club, he saw other prototypes of Bigger Thomas—fearful, frustrated, and violent youths who struggled for survival in the worst slum conditions.[38]

The twenties, the background of Dreiser's novel, had not of course erupted into the kind of social strife witnessed a decade later. Unlike the hostile racial conflicts dramatized in *Native Son*, what is portrayed in *An American Tragedy* is Clyde Griffiths's mind, which is deeply affected by the hopes and failures of the American dream. A later reviewer of *An American Tragedy* accused Dreiser of scanting, "as all the naturalists do, the element of moral conflict without which no great fiction can be written, for he fobbed the whole wretched business off on that scapegoat of our time, society."[39] But the depiction of such a conflict was not

38. See Richard Wright, "The Man Who Went to Chicago," in *Eight Men,* 210–50; and Keneth Kinnamon, *The Emergence of Richard Wright,* 120.
39. J. Donald Adams, "Speaking of Books."

Dreiser's intention for the novel in the first place. Rather, the poignancy of Clyde's tragedy comes from his helpless attraction and attachment to the dream society had created. Dreiser defines this essential American psyche in an essay:

> Our most outstanding phases, of course, are youth, optimism and illusion. These run through everything we do, affect our judgments and passions, our theories of life. As children we should all have had our fill of these, and yet even at this late date and after the late war, which should have taught us much, it is difficult for any of us to overcome them. Still, no one can refuse to admire the youth and optimism of America, however much they may resent its illusion. There is always something so naïve about its method of procedure, so human and tolerant at times; so loutish, stubborn and ignorantly insistent at others, as when carpetbag government was forced on the South after the Civil War and Jefferson Davis detained in prison for years after the war was over.[40]

In contrast to Bigger's violent life, Clyde's mind can be conveyed only by a leisurely pace and undramatic tone. Dreiser's approach is basically psychological, and this allows us to sympathize with the character whose principal weakness is ignorance and naïveté. Consequently we become deeply involved with Clyde's fate. Above all, the relative calmness and objectivity with which Clyde's experience is traced stem from a mature vision of the tribulations shared by any of us who have ever dreamed.

The lack of dramatic tone in *An American Tragedy* is also due to the novel's changes of setting. Dreiser's restless protagonist begins his journey in Kansas City, flees to Chicago, and finally reaches his destination in upstate New York. In contrast, Wright achieves greater dramatic intensity by observing a strict unity of setting. All of the action in *Native Son* takes place in Chicago, a frightening symbol of disparity and oppression in American life. Wright heightens the conflict and sharpens the division between the two worlds early in the novel. In the beginning, the Thomases' apartment is described as the most abject place imaginable, while the Dalton mansion suggests the white power structure that ravages black people and destroys their heritage. The conflict is obvious throughout, and the descriptions of the two households

40. "Some Aspects of Our National Character," 24.

present ironic contrasts. Whereas everything at the Thomases' is loud and turbulent, at the Daltons' it is quiet and subdued. But the true nature of the racial oppressor is later revealed: Mr. Dalton, real estate broker and philanthropist, tries to keep black residents locked in the ghetto and refuses to lower the rents. During the trial, the prosecutor, the press, and the public equally betray the most vocal racial prejudice and hatred, as mentioned earlier. Thus the central action of book 3 is for the defense to confront and demolish this wall of injustice if Bigger is to be spared his life.

The narrative pattern in *An American Tragedy* is entirely different. Although the novel is divided into three parts, as is *Native Son*, Dreiser's division is based upon changes of time and characters. Each part has its own complete narrative, and one part follows another with the same character dominating the central scene. Each unit is joined to the other not only by the principal character but by the turn of events that underlies the theme of the novel. Book 1 begins with Clyde's dreams of success but ends in an accident that forebodes a disaster. This narrative pattern is repeated in book 2, beginning with a portrayal of the luxurious home of Samuel Griffiths in Lycurgus and ending with the murder. Book 3 opens with a depiction of Cataraqui County, where Clyde is to be tried and executed. Clyde's defense, resting upon the most sympathetic interpretation of his character as a moral and mental coward, clearly indicates the possibility of hope but nonetheless ends on a note of despair. The death of a child caused by an automobile accident at the end of book 1 does not make Clyde legally guilty, but his fleeing the scene of the accident makes him morally culpable. This pattern is also repeated at the end of book 2, where he willfully ignores Roberta's screams for help, an act of transgression for which he is tried and punished. Such a narrative pattern is not given to the death of Mary and Bessie in *Native Son*, since one murder is necessarily caused by the other. Despite the fact that Bessie's death is caused by a premeditated murder, Bigger's crime does not raise the same moral issue as does Clyde's

There are also many other parallels that thread the three parts together in *An American Tragedy*. Esta's seduction and abandonment by a traveling actor early in the story foreshadow what happens to Roberta. Clyde's attraction to Hortense Briggs has a great deal in common with his helpless enticement to Sondra Finchley with her beauty and wealth. Roberta and Clyde, in fact, come from similar backgrounds, both trying to extricate themselves from the past in order to realize their dreams of social and economic success. Furthermore, the entire book is enclosed, in the beginning and in the end, by almost identical vignettes. The novel opens with Clyde and his family preaching on a street of Kansas City at dusk of a summer night and closes with an almost identical scene in San Francisco, with Russell, Clyde's nephew, now taking his place. Dreiser's implication is unmistakable: given the same temperament and circumstance, Russell will grow up to be another Clyde Griffiths and encounter another American tragedy.

Such parallels and ironies not only dominate Dreiser's narrative structure but also constitute the naturalistic detail that characterizes a Zolaesque experimentation. A literary naturalist, as does a scientist experimenting in a laboratory, minutely observes how a given character acts in accordance with his or her milieu. In *An American Tragedy*, unlike his earlier novels such as *Sister Carrie*, Dreiser conducts his experiment with the characters not once but twice to prove the process of a natural phenomenon. What underlies the plot development in this novel is Dreiser's constant reminder for readers to refer to their own flashbacks and reflections.

In *Native Son*, Wright allows readers as little interruption of the action as possible. Unlike *An American Tragedy*, Wright's discourse has no chapter divisions and only an occasional pause to indicate a transition or change of scene. Before Mary's murder, for example, Wright gives readers only three brief glimpses of Bigger's life: his relations with his family, his gang, and his girlfriend. Before Roberta's murder, on the other hand, which occurs at the end of book 2, Dreiser provides a comprehensive background of Clyde's life: his relationships with his family including Esta, with all his friends and associates, and with all the girls with whom he has attempted to make friends. Whereas Dreiser's presentation is complete and direct, Wright's is selective and metaphorical.

Wright thus differs from the traditional naturalist who piles detail upon detail to gain verisimilitude. He is more akin to his contemporaries like Faulkner and Steinbeck in using the devices of the symbolic novel. He writes with great economy, compressing detail in small space and time; readers must supply the rest. But his ideas are scarcely misinterpreted, because *Native Son*, as James Baldwin aptly pointed out, is a protest novel with the author's voice dominating the discourse. Baldwin argues that although this authorial voice records black anger as no African American before him had done, that is also, unhappily, the overwhelming limitation of *Native Son.* What is sacrificed, according to Baldwin, is a necessary dimension to the novel: "the relationship that Negroes bear to one another, that depth of involvement and unspoken recognition of shared experience which creates a way of life. . . . it is this climate, common to most Negro protest novels, which has led us all to believe that in Negro life there exists no tradition, no field of manners, no possibility of ritual or intercourse, such as may, for example, sustain the Jew even after he has left his father's house."[41] Bigger is therefore meant to be not so much a character as a symbol, though some critics consider this a confusion in the book. Edward Margolies, for instance, observes an inconsistency of tone in book 3, "where the reader feels that Wright, although intellectually committed to Max's views, is more emotionally akin to Bigger's." What Margolies regards as inconsistent might more profitably be interpreted as a thematic juxtaposition of points of view, the personal (Bigger's) and the ideological (Max's), with both of which Wright is sympathetic.[42]

In *An American Tragedy,* the author's voice is relatively absent. In *Sister Carrie,* for example, Dreiser is noted for a lengthy philosophical commentary inserted at every significant turn of event, as well as for a strong tendency to identify with his characters, especially his heroine. But in *An American Tragedy* Dreiser's comments are not only few but short. Despite Clyde's resolution to work hard and steadily once he has reached the luxurious world of the Green-Davidson, Dreiser's comment is devastatingly swift: "The truth was that in this crisis he was as interesting an illustration of the enormous handicaps imposed by ignorance, youth, poverty and fear as one could have found" (*AT,* 384).

In contrast to *Native Son,* Dreiser in *An American Tragedy* also reduces the author's omniscience by relying upon indirect discourse. When Clyde is helplessly trapped between his loyalty to Roberta and his desire for Sondra, the insoluble dilemma is rendered through his dreams involving a savage black dog, snakes, and reptiles. About the possibility of Roberta's accidental murder, Dreiser depicts Clyde trying to dismiss the evil thought but at the same time being enticed to it. Clyde's actual plot to murder, suggested by the newspaper article, now thrusts itself forward, as the narrator says, "psychogenetically, born of his own turbulent, eager and disappointed seeking" (*AT,* 463).

41. *Notes of a Native Son,* 27–28.
42. *Art of Richard Wright,* 113.

This crucial point in Clyde's life is explained in terms of a well-known myth:

> there had now suddenly appeared, as the genie at the accidental rubbing of Aladdin's lamp—as the efrit emerging as smoke from the mystic jar in the net of the fisherman—the very substance of some leering and diabolic wish or wisdom concealed in his own nature, and that now abhorrent and yet compelling, leering and yet intriguing, friendly and yet cruel, offered him a choice between an evil which threatened to destroy him (and against his deepest opposition) and a second evil which, however it might disgust or sear or terrify, still provided for freedom and success and love. (*AT*, 463–64)

The immediate effect of such a passage for the reader is to create compassion for the character whose mind is torn between the two forces with which he is incapable of coping. Given Clyde's weaknesses, then, the reader is more likely to sympathize with than despise such a soul.

On the contrary, Bigger's manhood—which is as crucial a point in his life as Clyde's dilemma is in his—is rendered through direct discourse. It is not the narrator's voice but the character's that expresses his inner life—the newly won freedom. His murder of a white girl makes him bold, ridding him of the fear that has hitherto imprisoned him. In the midst of describing Bigger's intoxication over his personal power and pleasure, Wright shifts the tone of the narrative to let Bigger provide a lofty voice of his own. While preparing a ransom note, Bigger utters: "Now, about the money. How much? Yes; make it ten thousand. *Get ten thousand in 5 and 10 bills and put it in a shoe box.* . . . That's good. . . . He wrote: *Blink your headlights some. When you see a light in a window blink three times throw the box in the snow and drive off. Do what this letter say*" (*NS*, 167). Even more remarkable is Bigger's final statement to Max:

> "What I killed for must've been good!" Bigger's voice was full of frenzied anguish. "It must have been good! When a man kills, it's for something. . . . I didn't know I was really alive in this world until I felt things hard enough to kill for 'em. . . . It's the truth, Mr. Max. I can say it now, 'cause I'm going to die. I know what I'm saying real good and I know how it sounds. But I'm all right. I feel all right when I look at it that way." (*NS*, 392)

Bigger's utterance, in fact, startles the condescending lawyer. At this climactic moment Max, awestruck, "groped for his hat like a blind man"

(*NS*, 392). Interestingly enough, Dreiser's presentation of Clyde in the same predicament is given through indirect discourse:

> He walked along the silent street—only to be compelled to pause and lean against a tree—leafless in the winter—so bare and bleak. Clyde's eyes! That look as he sank limply into that terrible chair, his eyes fixed nervously and, as he thought, appealingly and dazedly upon him and the group surrounding him.
>
> Had he done right? Had his decision before Governor Waltham been truly sound, fair or merciful? Should he have said to him—that perhaps—perhaps—there had been those other influences playing upon him? . . . Was he never to have mental peace again, perhaps? (*AT*, 811)

In contrast to this portrait of Clyde, who is largely unaware of his guilt and his manhood, the final scene of *Native Son* gives the ending its dramatic impact. Despite his crimes and their judgment by white society, Bigger's final utterance elicits from readers nothing but understanding and respect for the emerging hero.

The sense of ambiguity created by Dreiser's use of portraits, dreams, and ironies in *An American Tragedy* is thus suited to the muddled mind of Clyde Griffiths. Bigger Thomas, however, can hardly be explained in ambivalent terms, for he has opted for the identity of a murderer. Clyde is presented as a victim of the forces over which he has no control, and Dreiser carefully shows that Roberta's murder—the climax of the book— has inevitably resulted from these forces. The principal interest of the novel, centering upon this crime, lies in Clyde's life before the murder and its effect on him. In book 3, Clyde is depicted not merely as a victim of society but more importantly as a victim of his own illusions about life. In the end, then, he remains an unregenerate character as Dreiser has predicted earlier in the story.

Like Clyde, Bigger in *Native Son* is presented in the beginning as a naive character, and his life is largely controlled by fear and hatred. He kills Mary Dalton because he fears his own kindness will be misunderstood. He hates in turn what he fears, and his violence is an expression of this hatred. But unlike Clyde, he has learned through his murders how to exercise his will and determination. Each of the three sections of *Native Son* is built on its own climax, and book 3, "Fate," is structured to draw together all the noble achievements of Bigger's life. Significantly, each of the changes in Bigger's development is also measured by his own language. The difference in characterization between the two Americans is therefore reflected in the style and structure of the novels. Granted, both novelists deal with similar material, but their treatments of a young man's crime and guilt in American society vastly differ in ideology and in discourse.

4

The City

Quest for Freedom

O ne of the central themes in nineteenth-century American fiction was the white man who left his community in quest of pastoral peace of mind. Not only was he able to live in harmony with nature, but he would find a bosom friend in a stranger, a dark-skinned man from whom he learned the values of life he had never known. Natty Bumppo in James Fenimore Cooper's Leatherstocking novels makes such a friendship with Chingachgook and Hard-Heart, noble savages of the American wilderness. Ishmael in *Moby-Dick* is ritualistically wedded to Queequeg, a pagan from the South Seas. Huck Finn discovers a father figure in Jim, a runaway slave. In modern African American fiction, on the contrary, a black man is deeply suspicious of the pastoral scene. He finds the rural South a living hell and dreams of the northern city as offering deliverance from racial prejudice and exclusion. Richard Wright, while being careful not to romanticize American urban life, shows that a black man can find the city a better place to live than the rural community that has defined his past and can succeed in creating a self in the city.

Wright's desire to create the self in his own life is well documented in his autobiography *Black Boy*. His success in fictionalizing such an impulse is also evident in his work, particularly in *Native Son* and *The Outsider*. "Reduced to its simplest and most general terms," he asserts in "Blueprint for Negro Writing," "theme for Negro writers will rise from understanding the meaning of their being transplanted from a 'savage' to a 'civilized' culture in all of its social, political, economic, and emotional implications."[1] By "savage culture," Wright means the origin of black people in Africa as well as the history of slavery in the South. By "civilized culture" he implies the promised land of the American city in the North after emancipation.

Although the motive for a white man's quest for pastoral idylls has little to do with race, his urgent need, nonetheless, is to escape from some sort of social and emotional tension he suffers in living with other individuals. In *Moby-Dick* Ishmael confesses his motive for becoming a whale hunter: "especially whenever my hypos get such an upper hand of me, that it requires a strong moral principle to prevent me from deliberately stepping into the street, and methodically knocking people's hats off—then, I account it high time to get to sea as soon as I can."[2] The root of Ishmael's anxiety is the crush of individuals that occurs in a crowded community; Ishmael's action betrays the basic elements of national character—individualism and freedom.

Just as white men want to exercise the rights of liberty and individuality, it is nothing unusual in modern America for black men to desire to acquire such privileges. One of the reasons black men in Wright's work move from a rural to an urban environment is precisely the absence of individuality and independence within the black community in the South. More than any other book, *Black Boy* is a satire on the black community, where people are united by race and religion but are not encouraged to generate the spirit of individualism. Clearly the young Wright rebelled against such tradition. For those who did not seek independence and freedom, such a community would be a haven. Ralph Ellison has observed: "In some communities every one is 'related' regardless of blood-ties. The regard shown by the group for its members, its general communal character and its cohesion are often mentioned. For by comparison with the cold impersonal relationships of the urban industrial community, its relationships are personal and warm."[3] To Wright, however, such an environment in the South does not produce meaningful relationships among people and is even detrimental to the creation of manhood.

The lack of individuality among black people in the South has taken a heavy toll on black character. The oppressive system, Wright observes in *12 Million Black Voices*, "created new types of behavior and new patterns

1. "Blueprint for Negro Writing," 47.
2. Herman Melville, *Moby-Dick*, 23.
3. "Richard Wright's Blues," 208.

of psychological reaction, welding us together into a separate unity with common characteristics of our own."[4] He provides an illustration of this behavior so familiar to plantation owners:

> If a white man stopped a black on a southern road and asked: "Say, there, boy! It's one o'clock, isn't it?" the black man would answer: "Yessuh."
> If the white man asked: "Say, it's not one o'clock, is it, boy?" the black man would answer: "Nawsuh."
> And if the white man asked: "It's ten miles to Memphis, isn't it, boy?" the black man would answer: "Yessuh."
> And if the white man asked: "It isn't ten miles to Memphis, is it, boy?" the black man would answer: "Nawsuh."
> Always we said what we thought the whites wanted us to say. (12, 41)

What Wright calls "the steady impact of the plantation system" also had its effect on the education of black children. In many southern states the white authorities edited the textbooks that black children were allowed to use, automatically deleting any references to government, constitution, voting, citizenship, and civil rights. The school authorities uniformly stated that such foreign languages as French, Spanish, and Latin were not suitable for black children to learn. This provincial policy is reminiscent of the famous scene in *Adventures of Huckleberry Finn* in which Jim cannot understand why a Frenchman cannot speak English. In an attempt to teach Jim that English is not the only language spoken on earth, Huck says:

> "S'pose a man was to come to you and say Polly-voo-franzy— what would you think?"
> "I wouldn't think nuffn; I'd take en bust him over de head— dat is, if he warn't white. I wouldn't 'low no nigger to call me dat."
> "Shucks, it ain't calling you anything. It's only saying, do you know how to talk French?"
> "Well, den, why couldn't he say it?"
> "Why, he *is* a-saying it. That's a Frenchman's *way* of saying it."

Failing to convince Jim that there are languages other than English and cultures other than English and American, Huck utters in frustration

---

4. Richard Wright, *12 Million Black Voices*, 41. Subsequent references will appear parenthetically in the text as *12*.

and with irony: "I see it warn't no use wasting words—you can't learn a nigger to argue."[5] In *12 Million Black Voices* Wright reports that white men "become angry when they think that we desire to learn more than they want us to" (*12*, 64).

To Wright, the effect of white subjugation in the South was most visible in the black communities of the Mississippi Delta. By the time he was fourteen he was able to read and write well enough to obtain a job, in which he assisted an illiterate black insurance salesman. On his daily rounds to the shacks and plantations in the area, he was appalled by the pervasiveness of segregated life: "I saw a bare, bleak pool of black life and I hated it; the people were alike, their homes were alike, and their farms were alike" (*BB*, 151). Such observations later infuriated not only white segregationists but also many black citizens who wrote letters to the FBI and denounced *Black Boy*. Some letters called Wright "a black Nazi" and "one of the biggest spreaders of race hatred." Another black protester complained: "I am an American Negro and proud of it because we colored people in America have come a long way in the last seventy years. . . . We colored people don[']t mind the truth but we do hate lies or anything that disturb[s] our peace of mind." According to Addison Gayle, Senator Bilbo of Mississippi condemned *Black Boy* on the floor of the U.S. Senate on June 7, 1954, calling it "the dirtiest, filthiest, lousiest, most obscene piece of writing that I have ever seen in print . . . it is so filthy and dirty . . . it comes from a Negro, and you cannot expect any better from a person of his type."[6]

This absence of individuality and self-awareness among black people in the South often leads to the compromise of their character. Individually, Fishbelly and his father in *The Long Dream* are powerless to assert themselves. Although they are not forced to cooperate with the white police, greed often sacrifices their moral integrity. They are fully aware that their illicit political connections will make them as wealthy as the white people. What is worse, not only politics but also sex is dealt with in its sordid context: the hero's ritual of initiation into manhood is performed in a house of prostitution.[7]

5. Mark Twain, *Adventures of Huckleberry Finn*, 79.
6. *Richard Wright: Ordeal of a Native Son*, 173.
7. "Fire and Cloud," Wright's earlier short story, also deals with the corruption of the black leadership in southern cities.

Although some black men are able to escape the southern environment and move to the industrial North, they find it difficult to rid themselves of the corrupting system they have learned in the South. Jake Jackson of *Lawd Today,* as noted earlier, is tempted to do anything if he can make money. He is so corrupted that he admires politicians who accept bribes and gangsters who intimidate people. "I always said," Jake boasts, "that we colored folks ought to stick with the rich white folks" (*LT,* 58). What unites people like Fishbelly Tucker and Jake Jackson is the fact that though they can escape and, like the protagonist of *Black Boy* and Big Boy in "Big Boy Leaves Home," can for the most part free themselves from the racial strictures in their lives, they ultimately fail to find themselves. Even though they are physically free of the subjugating system, mentally they have failed to become individuals with autonomy and integrity.

Wright told Irving Howe that "only through struggle could men with black skins, and for that matter, all the oppressed of the world, achieve their humanity."[8] To Wright, freedom for black people can become a reality only when all black people acquire independent vision as outsiders. No matter how courageous Silas, the black farmer in "Long Black Song," may appear, his fight against the racial oppressors makes little impact on black liberation as a whole because his rebellion is motivated by a private matter. I agree with Edward Margolies, who says: "Yet Silas's redemption is at best a private affair—and the Negro's plight is no better as a result of his own determination to fight his oppressors with their own weapons. He is hopelessly outnumbered."[9] The black emancipation from the rural South, Wright warns, must be accompanied by the vision of the outsider. Ely Houston, the New York District Attorney in *The Outsider,* speaks as Wright's mouthpiece: "Negroes, as they enter our culture, are going to inherit the problems we have, but with a difference. They are outsiders and they are going to *know* that they have these problems. They are going to be self-conscious; they are going to be gifted with a double vision, for, being Negroes, they are going to be both *inside* and *outside* of our culture at the same time" (*O,* 129).

Houston's admonition can be easily heeded by a black intellectual like Cross Damon, but to most of Wright's uneducated black men the

8. Irving Howe, "Black Boys and Native Sons," 109.
9. *Art of Richard Wright,* 67.

fear of persecution is what threatens their freedom and existence. In *Black Boy,* Wright is continually at pains to show that white people have a preconceived notion of a black man's place in the South: the black man serves the white people, he is likely to steal, and he cannot read or write. A black man is not likely to be executed for petty theft; there are relatively few restrictions on the subjects he is allowed to discuss with white men. Even sex and religion are the most accepted subjects of conversation, for they are the topics that do not require positive knowledge or self-assertion on the part of the black man. As pointed out earlier, however, interracial sex is taboo (*NS*, xii), and black men had to risk their lives if they were caught in the act. Horace R. Cayton, a sociologist and Wright's close friend and associate, observes that for a black man "punishment in the actual environment is ever present; violent, psychological and physical, leaps out at him from every side."[10]

It is well documented that the principal motive behind black people's exodus from the rural South to the industrial North is their quest for freedom and equality. Wright himself, a victim of racial prejudice and hatred, fled to Chicago in search of the kind of freedom he had never experienced in the feudal South. "For the first time in our lives," he wrote, "we feel human bodies, strangers whose lives and thoughts are unknown to us, pressing always close about us" (*12*, 100). In stark contrast to the situation in the South, where black people were not allowed to communicate freely with white citizens, the crowded and noisy apartments in the northern cities became hubs of interracial mingling and communication, places where the migrant black people came in close contact with "the brisk, clipped men of the North, the Bosses of Buildings." Unlike the southern landlords, the city businessmen, Wright discovered, were not "at all *indifferent.* They are deeply concerned about us, but in a new way" (*12*, 100).

In the industrial city a black man functions as part of a "machine." Unlike his life in the rural South, which depends upon "the soil, the sun, the rain, or the wind," his life in the North is controlled by what Wright calls "the grace of jobs and the brutal logic of jobs" (*12*, 100). By living and working ever so closely with the white bourgeoisie, the minority workers in the city strive to learn their techniques. Consequently, Wright notes, black workers "display a greater freedom and

10. "Discrimination—America: Frightened Children of Frightened Parents," 264.

initiative in pushing their claims upon civilization than even do the petty bourgeoisie."[11] The harsh conditions under which black workers must produce and compete with white workers become an incentive to achieve a higher social and economic status. In short, the black man of the industrial North is given a chance to shape his own life. Economically man is a machine and his production is measured not by his race, but by his merit.

Clearly, the businessmen of the city are not concerned about the welfare of the black workers recently fled from the rural South. Like the self-proclaimed philanthropist Dalton in *Native Son,* they take an interest in the black people because their business would prosper if the black men's economic status improved. Focusing on such economic facts in the city, Wright carefully constructs a racial discourse in which a character like Dalton functions as a symbol for the ambivalent and contradictory ways of the city. Mr. Dalton thus has given millions for social welfare, especially for the NAACP, and ostensibly donated money to buy Ping-Pong tables for black children. Bigger Thomas does not know this, nor is he aware that Mr. Dalton's contribution comes from the exorbitant rents charged to the black tenants living in his overcrowded and rat-infested apartments. However ironic this may be, the fact remains that Bigger feels grateful for getting a job and that, for him at least, his employer does not appear a racist. Despite the severe living conditions in which black people are placed, the fierce competition they face, and the traumas they suffer, the city nevertheless provides them with possibilities of freedom and equality. The competition the black man faces in the city creates a tension quite different in nature from the tension in the segregated South. One of Jake's friends in *Lawd Today* says: "The only difference between the North and the South is, them guys down there'll kill you, and these up here'll let you starve to death" (*LT,* 156).

What impressed Wright when he arrived in Chicago from the Deep South was the relative absence of discrimination. "It was strange," he wrote in *American Hunger,* "to pause before a crowded newsstand and buy a newspaper without having to wait until a white man was served."[12] Although he was allowed to sit beside white men and women on a streetcar, as are Jake Jackson and his black companions in *Lawd*

11. "Blueprint for Negro Writing," 38.
12. Richard Wright, *American Hunger,* 1–2. Subsequent references will appear parenthetically in the text as *AH.*

Today, he began to feel "a different sort of tension than I had known before. I knew that this machine-city was governed by strange laws" (*AH,* 2). *American Hunger* also intimates an episode that suggests some white citizens were not as much obsessed with the problems of race as were southerners, and that a black man was often treated by the white citizens as an equal. Besides liberals such as the Hoffmans, the family of the Jewish delicatessen owner, underground gangsters also treated black people with equality and compassion, as Wright notes in *12 Million Black Voices:* "through the years our loyalty to these gangster-politicians remains staunch because they are almost the only ones who hold out their hand to help us, whatever their motives. . . . The most paradoxical gift ever tendered to us black folk in the city is aid from the underworld, from the gangster, from the political thief" (*12,* 121–22). One time, Wright obtained employment as a porter in a Jewish delicatessen and felt he had to lie about his absence from that job to take his civil service examination for a better paying job in the post office. But it turned out that his employer would have gladly consented for him to take the examination and that he would not have had to lie about something so important and beneficial to himself. In *The Outsider* the realistic details woven in the life of Cross Damon are those of the problems caused by living in the city. Cross is not in any way handicapped in his life or work because he is a black man. He is physically and mentally a tired man; he is bored with routine work just as are his fellow workers, black or white. Because of an early and unfortunate marriage, he has to support a wife he does not love and their children; he has a pregnant mistress who is trying to force him to marry her. To forget his miseries he takes to drinking. But such problems have little to do with Cross's being a black man.

Earning a livelihood in industrialized society as does Cross Damon, however, takes a heavy toll. Like Sartre's Mathieu, Cross finds himself in a state of incomprehensible disorder and meaninglessness. To black men such as Cross Damon and Fred Daniels of "The Man Who Lived Underground," the city takes on the appearance of a labyrinthine metropolis, where the pervading mood is aimlessness, loneliness, and lack of communication. Man is treated as a machine and not expected to communicate or intermingle with his fellow human beings. The controlling image of Wright's city is that of a crowded place inhabited by the people, black and white, who are alienated by displacement and industrialization.

The dehumanizing influences of urban life on nonintellectuals like Bigger Thomas make their personalities warp and harden. In the heart of Chicago, Wright witnessed numerous examples of the Bigger Thomas type—nervous, fearful, frustrated. "The urban environment of Chicago," Wright recalls, "affording a more stimulating life, made the Negro Bigger Thomases react more violently than even in the South. More than ever I began to see and understand the environmental factors which made for this extreme conduct" (*NS*, xv). These black youths, moreover, are alienated not only from the white civilization but also from their own race. Based on this reality, Bigger is depicted as "resentful toward whites, sullen, angry, ignorant, emotionally unstable, depressed and unaccountably elated at times, and unable even, because of his own lack of inner organization which American oppression has fostered in him, to unite with the members of his own race" (*NS*, xxi).

While Bigger Thomas of *Native Son*, buttressed by Wright's own experience in Chicago, is depicted as a hero able to transcend these obstacles of city life and gain self-confidence, another black man, Jake Jackson of *Lawd Today*, is presented as a degenerate character largely unaware that industrialization and capitalism have hopelessly corrupted his soul. Wright makes it clear that while Jake is not legally a criminal, as is Bigger, Jake is a latter-day slave. If Jake is a victim of the economic system, he is also a worshiper of the shoddy values of the system that exploits him. Jake and Bigger are products of the same civilization, but Jake, unlike Bigger, is incapable of transcending the dreadful effects of the social environment. Jake Jackson among Wright's characters is often the object of disparaging remarks by critics, but there are some notable exceptions. Granville Hicks, finding some interest in Jake's personality, calls this character uneducated, frustrated, and "erring but alive." Lewis Leary, regarding Jake as a caricature of the white world, calls him "incongruously, enduringly alive."[13]

Even though the dominant influences of the urban environment on the black men lead to dehumanization and isolation, the same environment can provide them with avenues for transcendence. In fact, Chicago, New York, and later Paris, unlike the southern cities, offered Wright education, free access to libraries, political affiliation, and introduction to realist writers such as Theodore Dreiser, Sinclair Lewis, and John Dos

13. Hicks, "Dreiser to Farrell to Wright"; Leary, "*Lawd Today*: Notes," 420.

Passos and French existentialist novelists such as Sartre and Camus. It is a well-known fact that Wright learned how to write fiction by associating with the John Reed Club of Chicago, a leftist writers' organization. Not only did he find intellectual stimulation in Communist philosophy, but also, as Blyden Jackson points out, he found among the members of the Communist Party the warm and sustained relationships whose lack was the cause of his loneliness in the South.[14]

On the one hand, Wright's ideological fascination with Communism is overtly expressed in such early short stories as "Fire and Cloud" and "Bright and Morning Star," which take place in the southern environment. The chief reason Wright joined the Communist Party was not his belief in the economics of Communism, nor his attraction to trade unionism, nor his curiosity about its underground politics. His vision was the possibility of uniting isolated and oppressed people all over the world. His own experience in the cities had convinced him that industrialization and commercialization have a tendency to lead people to isolation and loneliness. On the other hand, his personal attraction to Communism is alluded to in *The Outsider*. After accidentally gaining a new identity, Cross Damon leaves Chicago for New York, a cosmopolitan city, where he befriends a Communist couple, the Blounts, not because of sympathy for their ideology, but simply because he finds in them urbanity, liberalism, and lack of racial bigotry, the qualities he had not earlier found in white people. To a total stranger in a huge metropolis, the sudden appearance of the Blounts, who offer him food, shelter, and companionship, is indeed an oasis.

As an artist, however, Wright in his own life became disillusioned with the Communist Party. To his dismay he learned that the party insisted on discipline over truth, and that factionalism within the party preempted dialogue and criticism. The party was interested in a fledgling writer as long as his imaginative ability would result in the writing of pamphlets acceptable to party principles. "It was inconceivable to me," Wright wrote, "though bred in the lap of southern hate, that a man could not have his say. I had spent a third of my life traveling from the place of my birth to the North just to talk freely, to escape the pressure of fear" (*AH*, 92). Not only did he find the party practice repressive, but he realized that blind adherence to Communist ideology would leave an

14. "Richard Wright: Black Boy from America's Black Belt and Urban Ghettos," 301.

artist little room for concentration and reflection. "The conditions under which I had to work," Wright felt, "were what baffled them. Writing had to be done in loneliness and Communism had declared war upon human loneliness" (*AH*, 123).

In *The Outsider*, Cross Damon murders not only the Fascist landlord but also the Communist associate, a symbolic act of terror in asserting himself. If his New York landlord is a painful reminder of the Ku Klux Klansmen of the South, his Communist companion equally stands in the way to his freedom and independence. Now with Eva, the wife of the murdered Communist, in his arms, Cross reflects on this climactic action:

> They'll think I did it because of Eva! No; Communists were not unintelligent; they could not seriously think that. There was one thing of which he was certain: they would never credit him with as much freedom to act as they had. A certain psychological blindness seemed to be the hallmark of all men who had to create their own worlds. . . . All other men were mere material for them; they could admit no rivals, no equals, other men were either above them or below them. (*O*, 369)

Unlike Clyde Griffiths in Dreiser's *An American Tragedy*, a victim of the materialistic civilization, Cross Damon has learned through his murders how to exercise his will. And before death he is finally able to declare his independence.

Similarly, the last word in *Native Son* is not expressed by the white authorities who hold Bigger in jail, nor the white liberals who are sympathetic to black people. The final statement is given not by the Communist lawyer Max, but by Bigger, a black man who has at last achieved his goal in life: "I didn't know I was really alive in this world until I felt things hard enough to kill for 'em. . . . It's the truth, Mr. Max. I can say it now, 'cause I'm going to die" (*NS*, 392).

Bigger's dismissal of the Reverend Hammond's attempt to console the accused before the trial is also a symbolic act that suggests the black man's rejection of religion. In the same way, Cross rejects his mother, the product of southern black piety. While Wright dismisses Christianity as useless for black people's freedom and independence, he values the black church in the city because it enhances their community life. In *12 Million Black Voices*, he observes: "Despite our new worldliness, despite our rhythms, our colorful speech, and our songs, we keep our churches alive. . . . Our churches are centers of social and community life, for we have virtually no other mode of communion and we are usually forbidden to worship God in the temples of the Bosses of the Buildings. The church is the door through which we first walked into Western civilization" (12, 130–31). Both Bigger and Cross reject religion because in a complex modern society it functions only as a ritual; it offers only irrational escape, blind flight from reality. Both men, having conquered the forces of the urban environment, have now severed themselves from the last remnants of religious and political influence. They both have become rugged individualists, the willed creators of their past, present, and future in a chaotic and hostile world. Margaret Walker notes, "Wright's philosophy was that fundamentally all men are potentially evil. . . . Human nature and human society are determinants and, being what he is, man is merely a pawn caught between the worlds of necessity and freedom. . . . All that he has to use in his defense and direction of his existence are (1) his reason and (2) his will."[15]

But Cross's search for meaning in his life is a departure from Bigger's achievement of manhood. In Chicago, the problem of race, the avowed conflict between black and white people, becomes the catalyst for Bigger's manhood. In New York, the issue that torments Cross is not the conflict of race; the larger issue he faces is man's existence or annihilation. In creating Cross, Wright departed from the social issues confronting a black man and asked the universal question of what man is. In terms of plot, the accidental killing of a white woman in *Native Son* whets Bigger's creative impulses. To Cross, Eva becomes an essence he tries to find in the meaningless existence. He has fallen in love with her because they both suffer from the same wound; she was forced to marry a man she did not love just as Cross was once married to a woman he did not love. It is the city environment that enables Cross to love a white woman. For Cross the consummation of his love for Eva is the ultimate purpose of his new life.

Although both men seek freedom and independence in their lives, the visions they gain before death are poles apart. Bigger's last words—"I didn't know I was really alive in this world until I felt things hard enough to kill for 'em" (*NS*, 392)—signal the affirmation of life. Cross, tasting his agonizing defeat and dying, utters: "I wish I had some way to

15. "Richard Wright."

give the meaning of my life to others. . . . We're strangers to ourselves" (*O*, 439). Whereas Bigger's vision is full of joy and hope, Cross's is tinged with sadness and estrangement.

Noting Cross's action to kill without passion and his indifference to the emotions of others, a critic has called the philosophy of this metaphysical rebel most consistently nihilistic. To another critic, moreover, Cross represents "the moral and emotional failure of the age."[16] The reason for calling Cross nihilistic lies in his uncharacteristic remark, "Maybe man is nothing in particular" (*O*, 135). Cross's statement, however, seems to be based upon Wright's worldview, the philosophy of the absurd, which was in vogue after World War II. Nihilists are convinced of the essential absurdity of human existence, but Cross is not. Cross is passionately in search of order, eternity, and meaning. In the light of his actions in the novel, not in view of Wright's occasional philosophy, Cross ends his life as a failed humanist rather than a nihilist.

As Wright endowed Bigger Thomas with the capacity to assert his freedom and independence, Wright also endowed Cross Damon with the power to create an essence. Bigger, despite his lack of education, challenged and transcended the unjust forces of the urban environment. Cross, placed in the cosmopolitan climate where he is able to shed the last vestiges of the obsolete Christian ethics as well as the stifling Marxist ideology, stumbles onto the philosophy of existentialism. Rejecting such a philosophy, however, he instead defines his own way of life. His revolt is not so much against the nothingness and meaninglessness of existence as it is against man's inability to make illogical phenomena logical. Despite his own failure, the revelation he gains at the end of his life suggests the possibilities of harmony and love among all men. Bigger and Cross have walked different avenues in the city, but in the end they have both been able to "uphold the concept of what it means to be human" in America.[17]

16. See Charles I. Glicksberg, "Existentialism in *The Outsider*" and "The God of Fiction," and Margolies, *Art of Richard Wright*, 135.

17. Quoted from Wright's unpublished journal, September 7, 1947, in which he wrote: "Sartre is quite of my opinion regarding the possibility of human action today, that it is up to the individual to do what he can to uphold the concept of what it means to be human." See Michel Fabre, "Richard Wright, French Existentialism, and *The Outsider*," 186.

5

Black Boy
A Record of Childhood and Youth

*B*lack Boy is generally acclaimed not only as the finest autobiography written by a black author but as one of the greatest autobiographies ever written in America. Critics, however, are not in agreement on what kind of autobiography it is. W. E. B. Du Bois, for instance, wondered about the authenticity of the book, saying, "The [sub]title, 'A Record of Childhood and Youth,' makes one at first think that the story is autobiographical. It probably is, at least in part. But mainly it is probably intended to be fiction or fictionalized biography. At any rate the reader must regard it as creative writing rather than simply a record of life." Yet even if one regards the book as a creative discourse rather than an actual record of life, and despite its felicities of language, *Black Boy*, Du Bois felt, falls short of its possible effectiveness because it is "so patently and terribly overdrawn."[1] Those who are not impressed by the book criticize its excessive emphasis on violence, meanness, and despair. Moreover, they are not convinced of the authenticity of *Black Boy* as an autobiography because they feel that the world, as bad as it is, cannot be so bad as Wright says it is.

Even those who are convinced of *Black Boy*'s authenticity do not necessarily consider it a higher accomplishment than *Native Son*. When the book appeared, many distinguished writers became its advocates: Sinclair Lewis, William Faulkner, Gertrude Stein, Henry Miller, Ralph Ellison, Lionel Trilling. Among them Faulkner, who perhaps knew black

1. "Richard Wright Looks Back."

life in the South as well as anyone, wrote to Wright that he was deeply moved by *Black Boy,* but commented that what is said in it is better said in *Native Son.* "The good lasting stuff," Faulkner wrote, "comes out of one individual's imagination and sensitivity to and comprehension of the sufferings of Everyman, Anyman, not out of the memory of his own grief." This response by a fellow novelist suggests that *Black Boy* suffers as a work of art because Wright's method in it is less impersonal than it is in a novel like *Native Son.* To Faulkner, art cannot be created when too much is made of one's own life; dealing with impersonal forces of nature and society in such a novel as *Native Son* requires a sense of detachment. For this reason Faulkner said, "I hope you will keep on saying it, but I hope you will say it as an artist, as in *Native Son.*"[2]

Faulkner's assessment of *Black Boy* is based on the assumption that the book is an autobiography. But the narrator of the book takes such an impersonal approach that *Black Boy* as a whole may not sound like a usual autobiography. As Du Bois has noted, there is a genuine paucity of personal love or affection expressed toward Wright's mother in *Black Boy.* But the young Wright amply expresses his awe and wonder at her suffering: he is unable to understand why she was deserted by her husband, broken by paralysis, and overwhelmed by every unimaginable circumstance she had to face. His reaction, as a narrator, is intellectual rather than personal. By contrast, in Theodore Dreiser's autobiography of youth, *Dawn,* the narrator's wonder at his equally suffering mother is tinged with personal sorrow and sympathy. In short, Wright's intention in *Black Boy* seems to have been to portray his experience with naturalistic objectivity, rather than from a personal point of view.

A literary naturalist, such as Wright had become by the time he wrote *Black Boy,* is a sociologist who takes a milieu from life and projects characters that act in accordance with the milieu. The naturalist must record, without comment or interpretation, what actually happens. If Wright regarded himself as a fictional persona in *Black Boy,* he would be less concerned either with his own life or with his own point of view. The focus of his interest in the book would be on the events that occurred outside his life. It is understandable, then, that Wright's account of his own life would not be entirely authentic. One might even suspect that Wright's self-portrait would abound with fictional accounts, and indeed

2. "Letter to Richard Wright."

many differences between *Black Boy* and his life have been pointed out. One reviewer's objection to the book as autobiography is based on discrepancies found between Wright's accounts in the book and in "The Ethics of Living Jim Crow."[3] For example, Wright describes a fight between himself and a group of white boys in which he was injured behind the ear; according to *Black Boy*, his mother later ushered him to a doctor, whereas in his "Ethics of Living Jim Crow," Wright relates that "a kind neighbor saw me and ushered me to a doctor, who took three stitches in my neck" (*UTC*, 4). Also in *Black Boy* Wright often refers to his mother as a cook "in the kitchens of the white folks" and describes her as less intellectual than she really was (*BB*, 27). In fact, Ella Wilson, his mother, before her marriage to his father, was considerably well educated and taught school. Edwin R. Embree, who was familiar with Wright's youth and early literary career, testifies that Ella Wilson was light brown and good looking and that her book learning enabled her to obtain teaching positions at twenty-five dollars a month.[4]

These discrepancies, however, are not a major reason for calling *Black Boy* a fictionalized autobiography. Even though parts of the book are fictional, it is nevertheless autobiographical and should not be equated with a novel. No one for a moment can overlook the fact that it portrays Wright himself; if it concerns others, their lives are necessarily intertwined with his. But the most important distinction *Black Boy* bears as autobiography is Wright's intention to use the young self as a mask. The attitudes and sentiments expressed by the young Wright are not totally his own but represent the responses of those he called "the voiceless Negro boys" of the South.[5] Such a device makes *Black Boy* a unique autobiography just as a similar technique makes *Native Son* a unique novel. Wright tells us that Bigger Thomas is a conscious composite portrait of numerous black individuals he knew in his life (*NS*, xii).

1

What makes *Black Boy* not only a unique autobiography but also one of the most influential discourses on race in America is its artistry.

3. Beatrice M. Murphy, review of *Black Boy*.
4. "Richard Wright: Native Son."
5. Wright, "The Handiest Truth to Me to Plow Up Was in My Own Hand."

What impresses many readers about the book is that it tells bitter truth about life. Wright cannot be criticized for his subject matter, for he is not responsible for the world he did not make. Above all, *Black Boy* impresses the reader because Wright remains an artist throughout the text. As in his best fiction his language, unlike the language of a typical naturalist, is terse, lucid, and vivid; his presentation is moving and dramatic. Horace R. Cayton, a sociologist who intimately knew Wright's method, quotes him as saying:

> I have always taken the writing of literature very seriously, and I've looked upon fiction and writing in general as a means of revealing the truth of life and experience rather than purely as a means of entertaining people. In other words, I feel that literature ought to be a sharp instrument to reveal something important about mankind, about living, about life whether among whites or blacks. That is why my work hews so close to facts, and yet why I try to float these facts on a sea of emotion, to drive them home with some degree of artistic power, as much as humanly possible, to the level of seriousness which characterizes science. I want people to enjoy my books but I want them to be moved and conditioned by them.[6]

A bitter man, in short, can be a great artist as well.

The most obvious device Wright uses in *Black Boy* is blending a narrative with lyrical passages that extol the glory of the southern landscape:

> There was the wonder I felt when I first saw a brace of mountainlike, spotted, black-and-white horses clopping down a dusty road through clouds of powdered clay.
>
> There was the delight I caught in seeing long straight rows of red and green vegetables stretching away in the sun to the bright horizon.
>
> There was the faint, cool kiss of sensuality when dew came on to my cheeks and shins as I ran down the wet green garden paths in the early morning.
>
> There was the vague sense of the infinite as I looked down upon the yellow, dreaming waters of the Mississippi River from the verdant bluffs of Natchez.
>
> There were the echoes of nostalgia I heard in the crying strings of wild geese winging south against a bleak, autumn sky. (*BB*, 14)

6. "Discrimination—America," 263.

On the one hand, the factual details of the landscape are floated "on a sea of emotion"; on the other, they create powerful irony. While Wright's lyricism exhibits the deep love of black people in the South for their soil, it also recalls that they were rejected by the very soil they loved. Such incongruity sets the tone of the entire discourse, as it does in other texts. In *Lawd Today*, for example, Jake Jackson and his black friends often dream of their good old days in the South where they used to enjoy the warmth of the sun and the quietude of the pastoral: swimming in the creek, catching catfish, smelling the magnolia trees. In "Big Boy Leaves Home" a sudden tragedy strikes four black boys enjoying an idyllic country life in the Deep South. It is ironic that black persons were not accepted where they could live in harmony with nature.

Poetic passages in *Black Boy* also vividly convey the various emotional responses the hero has to living in the South. Such language often blends disparate images that are unified only by their intensity of feeling. Some images—"spotted, black-and-white horses," "long straight rows of red and green vegetables," "the yellow, dreaming waters of the Mississippi River"—all suggest a harmony of nature and society. Others—"the crying strings of wild geese" and "a solitary ant carrying a burden upon a mysterious journey" (*BB*, 14)—allude to racial anxiety and tension. Still others—"a [tortured] delicate, blue-pink crawfish that huddled fearfully in the mudsill of a rusty tin can" (*BB*, 14) and "a chicken [leaping] about blindly after its neck had been snapped by a quick twist of my father's wrist" (*BB*, 15)—depict cruelty and sadism.

In these images Wright interpolates such a statement as "Each event spoke with a cryptic tongue. And the moments of living slowly revealed their coded meanings" (*BB*, 14). This, however, does not signal that each of the images evoked has a point-for-point correspondence with a specific event in reality. It would be inept to argue that "a brace of mountainlike, spotted, black-and-white horses clopping down a dusty road" alludes to miscegenation. It would also be perverse to compare the chicken leaping with its neck cut off to a victim of racial violence. Wright's imagery often appears unrelated to actuality because facts of life are elevated to a higher level of consciousness and sensibility. "The relationship between reality and the artistic image," he says in "Blueprint for Negro Writing," "is not always direct and simple. The imaginative conception of a historical period will not be a carbon copy of reality. Image and emotion possess a logic of their own."[7] Gerian Steve

7. "Blueprint for Negro Writing," 48.

Moore is correct in observing that *Black Boy* "presents the black man in retreat from his society. . . . Wright was an artist engaged in the process of trying to discover his place in a society that denied him." But I do not agree with his contention that Wright as autobiographer is inferior to Malcolm X in understanding his relationship to society and giving "his art a definite focus."[8]

In establishing his own world Wright is able to shape the images at will. At the end of *Black Boy* he is a nineteen-year-old who has been initiated to be a burgeoning writer by American realists such as H. L. Mencken, Theodore Dreiser, Sinclair Lewis, and Sherwood Anderson. These writers made him realize, more than anything else, that he had long been shut out of the intellectual life in America. He knew what hunger and hatred meant in his youth and he had learned to live with them, but he now had a new hunger for the freedom of the mind. "I seemed forever condemned," he says, "ringed by walls" (*BB*, 274). This image of imprisonment recurs throughout the book. He remembers that at four he tried to burn down his grandmother's house by setting fire to the white curtains. "I crossed restlessly to the window," he recalls, "and pushed back the long fluffy white curtains—which I had been forbidden to touch—and looked yearningly out into the empty street" (*BB*, 9). As he grew older and was allowed to play in the street, he one day saw a host of chained convicts, all black, dressed in their black-and-white-striped clothing, a spectacle that at once reminded him of zebras confined in the zoo.

In Wright's imagery, reality can also be altered at will. In his portrayal of the black community, he makes disparaging remarks about its character and action: black people are often shortsighted, selfish, superstitious. The most satiric description is accomplished through images of their religious life. From the beginning Wright's personality was stamped into realism, and his sense of living, he tells us, was as profound as what the church was trying to teach. No wonder the images of burning lakes, ugly beasts, and disfigured monsters that he associated with Granny's Seventh Day Adventist doctrine lost their emotional appeal once the young Wright stepped out of the church into the bright sunshine and the world of people (*BB*, 113). Depicting a religious institution in such terms suggests not only his sincere disbelief in original sin, but also a sense of bleakness, shallowness, and pettiness he found in his community.

8. "Richard Wright's *American Hunger*," 85.

As some critics have noted, *Black Boy* is relatively free from the hero's references to his own sexual awakening. Edward Margolies considers sex in *Black Boy* in terms of "violence (the dangers inherent in relationships with white prostitutes); bravado (adolescent boys speaking of their prowess); obscenities (which Wright learned at the age of six); or condescension and rejection (Wright's fending off the daughter of his landlady in Memphis because she was incapable of understanding the depths of his sensibilities)." Katherine Fishburn maintains that *The Long Dream* has more detail and a much more thorough treatment of a young black man's sexual maturation than does *Black Boy*.[9]

Sex in this book is treated much like religion, for Wright knew during his adolescent years that one could be easily victimized by sexual forces. The only time sexual attraction is mentioned is in connection with a church service where Wright at twelve was infatuated with the elder's wife. His "desires," however, are "converted into a concrete religious symbol," depicted in grotesque and physical expressions instead of pleasant and spiritual images: "a black imp with two horns; a long, curving, forked tail; cloven hoofs, a scaly, naked body; wet, sticky fingers; moist, sensual lips; and lascivious eyes feasting upon the face of the elder's wife" (*BB*, 125). Such an impulse indeed debases his attitude toward human sexuality. His ease in fending off such biological forces can be contrasted to the young Fishbelly Tucker's unsuccessful struggle with his sexual awakening in *The Long Dream*. In that novel, sex is dealt with in its sordid context, a house of prostitution.

If Wright can debase the character of black people, he can also recast in new images of freedom any facts in his own life that seemed unworthy of human dignity. Whenever the young Wright felt his conduct restricted at home, he immediately let his mind take a flight outside as if transcending the oppressive family life. Under the spell of "the pervading smell of sweet magnolias," he saw "the rolling sweep of tall grass swaying and glinting in the wind and sun." The predominant image at this scene is symbolic of his long-suppressed desire for a peaceful intermingling of black and white people: "There was the suspense I felt when I heard the taut, sharp song of a yellow-black bee hovering nervously but patiently above a white rose." Such an atmosphere, however, is never allowed to grow unreal as it does in the church elder's sermons

9. See Margolies, *Art of Richard Wright*, 17–18, and Fishburn, *Richard Wright's Hero: The Faces of a Rebel-Victim*, 14.

that indulge in grotesque creatures and supernatural events. For the image of a bee and rose is followed by a stark reality: "the baffled stares of white folks who saw an old white woman leading two undeniably Negro boys in and out of stores on Capitol Street." Later this scene is juxtaposed with another scene in which two lines of people form at the ticket window in a train station (*BB*, 54–55). The most dramatic action takes place toward the end of the book; in his fifteenth year, he feels educationally behind the average American youth but is conscious of self-determination and the danger involved in his action. "Somewhere in the dead of the southern night," he declares, "my life had switched onto the wrong track and . . . the locomotive of my heart was rushing down a dangerously steep slope, heading for a collision, heedless of the warning red lights that blinked all about me, the sirens and the bells and the screams that filled the air" (*BB*, 187).

Another dramatic device he uses to express his racial views in *Black Boy* is dialogue. Wright's racial discourse is at its best when much of the episode is interlaced with revealing dialogue. The narrator deliberately creates a scene in which two individuals, usually the young Wright and an opponent, confront each other with an exchange of laconic statements. These remarks not only reveal the gullibility of an antagonist but also compel the reader to identify with the hero. Once Wright encountered in an elevator a black youth who exposed his buttocks for a white man to kick so that he might earn a quarter. Wright tells us he felt "no anger or hatred, only disgust and loathing," and that he confronted this youth:

> "How in God's name can you do that?"
> "I needed a quarter and I got it," he said soberly, proudly.
> "But a quarter can't pay you for what he did to you," I said.
> "Listen, nigger," he said to me, "my ass is tough and quarters is scarce." (*BB*, 250)

At thirteen years of age Wright was forced to seek a job as a houseboy. A white woman looking for an "honest" black boy gave Wright an interview:

> "Now, boy, I want to ask you one question and I want you to tell me the truth," she said.
> "Yes, ma'am," I said, all attention.
> "Do you steal?" she asked me seriously.
> I burst into a laugh, then checked myself.

"What's so damn funny about that?" she asked.
"Lady, if I was a thief, I'd never tell anybody." (*BB*, 160)

Another stylistic device congenial to his purposes, whether in his use of imagery or in dialogue, is irony. Often a statement by an antagonist inadvertently betrays more than he wants to say, or there is a marked contrast between what he wants to say and what his words mean to the reader. For example, Wright's boss at an optical company in Jackson, Mississippi, originally from Illinois, professes himself unprejudiced and boasts that he wants to "break a colored boy into the optical trade." But he cautions the young Wright: "You're going to have a chance to learn a trade. But remember to keep your head. Remember you're black" (*BB*, 205). Ironically, the warning suggests that rebelling against the Jim Crow law, as Wright was resolved to do, would be considered insane.

What, then, underlies the white man's conception of a black male? Most significantly, black men are categorized as animals, a mentality inherited from the days of slavery. Not only are black people considered to be white people's servants, but they are expected to entertain white people as though they were animals in the zoo. Wright cites an incident in which his foreman at a company he worked for instigated antagonism between him and a black boy employed at another company so that the two black boys would try to stab each other. Wright, avoiding the trap, agreed instead to fight a boxing match to satisfy the whim of the white employer. "I suppose," Wright reasons, "it's fun for white men to see niggers fight. . . . To white men we're like dogs or cocks" (*BB*, 260). Even killing among black men would not prick a white man's conscience. Such an inhuman attitude echoes that of the white public at the trial of Bigger Thomas for the murder of Bessie in *Native Son*. White people are less disturbed by a black person's killing another black person than by a black person's killing a white person.

Another degrading assumption white men hold about black men is that, since they are treated as animals, they are not supposed to possess intellectual capabilities. The reasons the young Wright loses employment are often related to his intelligence, which poses a threat to the white man's sense of superiority. Wright points out, for instance, that some black men tried to organize themselves and petitioned their white employers for higher wages and better working conditions. But such a movement was swiftly met with further restriction and brutality. Throughout the book Wright continues to demonstrate that white citizens in the South would rather have black people who stole goods and properties than black individuals who were conscious, however vaguely, of the worth of their own intelligence and humanity. For Wright, racism induces black deceit and encourages black irresponsibility. It is superb irony that black people are rewarded in the degree that they can make white citizens feel safe and let them maintain their moral superiority.

Such rhetorical skills enable Wright to develop his racial discourse with poignancy. His aim is to bring home his hard-won conviction that racial problems stem not so much from the individuals involved as from a system inherited from the past. The white race, therefore, is as much a victim as the black race. Many episodes in *Black Boy* show that the kind of sympathy white southerners felt for black people was nothing more than racial condescension. Although white people in the South considered themselves decent, compassionate human beings, their behavior revealed a deep-seated, unconscious attitude reminiscent of Aunt Sally's response to Huck Finn. When Huck reports that a steamboat has just blown out a cylinder-head downriver and killed a black man, she replies nonchalantly: "Well, it's lucky; because sometimes people do get hurt."[10] What Twain and Wright share is the genuine feeling that an intense individualist possesses; both artists feel their own great powers and yet recognize the hopelessness of trying to change the world.

The artist that Wright has become can ask himself at the conclusion of *Black Boy:* "From where in this southern darkness had I caught a sense of freedom? Why was it that I was able to act upon vaguely felt notions? What was it that made me feel things deeply enough for me to try to order my life by my feelings? The external world of whites and blacks, which was the only world that I had ever known, surely had not evoked in me any belief in myself. The people I had met had advised and demanded submission. What, then, was I after? How dare I consider my feelings superior to the gross environment that sought to claim me?" (*BB*, 282).

But Wright's presentation of that environment in *Black Boy* proves his triumph. Although he suffered, he refused to remain passive and saved himself from the pathetic ambivalences of the oppressed. Rather than indulging in self-pity, he devoted his energy to reading and writing.

10. Twain, *Adventures of Huckleberry Finn*, 218.

In so doing he discovered that the magic of words, as he remembered from his early childhood, was not a mere reflection of the environment but could become "the gateway to a forbidden and enchanting land" (*BB*, 49). For, as he has asserted elsewhere,[11] art has its own autonomy, like the self Wright created in *Black Boy*. Art can transcend the realms of social, political, religious power and judgment.

2

The uniqueness of Wright's discourse in *Black Boy* can be explained in another way. Since the narrator is a spokesman for the voiceless black youths of the South he had known, he must be objective and scientific in his observations. Thus *Black Boy*, though not intended as such, is a convincing sociological study. Like sociology, it not only analyzes a social problem but offers a solution. Wright attempts to study the ways in which black life in the South was determined by the environment, and, to borrow Émile Zola's words, he wants to "disengage the determinism of human and social phenomena so that we may one day control and direct these phenomena."[12] Like Zola, he constantly tries to make his investigation systematic and unbiased. Such writing therefore deals with the specific social forces in the environment of a black boy: white racism, black society, and black family.

James Baldwin has accused Wright of believing that "in Negro life there exists no tradition, no field of manners, no possibility of ritual or intercourse."[13] Unlike Baldwin, who grew up in a highly religious black community in Harlem, Wright in the Deep South witnessed the essential bleakness of black life in America. The central issue, however, is whether such human traits as tenderness, love, honor, and loyalty are innate in the African American tradition, as Baldwin believed, or are fostered, won, struggled, and suffered for, as Wright believed. Elsewhere Wright tells us that he wrote *Black Boy* "to tell a series of incidents strung through my childhood, but the main desire was to render a judgment on my environment. . . . That judgment was this: the environment the South

11. See Wright, *White Man, Listen!* 185.
12. "The Experimental Novel," 181.
13. Baldwin, *Notes of a Native Son*, 28.

creates is too small to nourish human beings, especially Negro human beings."[14] Wright, therefore, squarely places the burden of proof upon white society, contending with enough evidence and justification given in *Black Boy* that the absence of such human qualities in black people as tenderness and love stemmed from years of white oppression.

What disturbed Wright at first was not the failure of many black and white citizens alike to see the facts of racism, but their inability to recognize malice in the minds of white racists. *Black Boy* recounts an incident in which Wright was wrongfully accused of addressing a white employee at an optical company without using the title "Mr." Another white employee later corroborated the accusation by telling Wright: "Didn't you call him *Pease*? If you say you didn't, I'll rip your gut string loose with this f-k-g bar, you black granny dodger! You can't call a white man a liar and get away with it!" (*BB,* 209). Consequently Wright was forced to leave his job. Resenting a black man's obtaining what they considered a white man's occupation, these white men deliberately created a falsehood to deny Wright a livelihood.

Not only did white racism succeed in separating black and white people, but it had devastating effects on black life. Critics, both black and white, have complained that Wright in *Black Boy* lacks racial pride. It is true that he is critical of the black community in the South, but it is not true that he places the blame on the black community itself. His intention is to show that a racist system produced a way of life that was forced on black people. In terms of social determinism, *Black Boy* provides a literary experiment to demonstrate uniformity in black behavior under the influence of social forces. "Wright," Edward Margolies observes, "traps the reader in a stereotyped response—the same stereotyped response that Wright is fighting throughout the book: that is, that all Negroes are alike and react alike."[15]

Most black people, he admits, do adjust to their environment for survival. But in so doing they lose individuality, self-respect, and dignity. This is perhaps why Benjamin Davis Jr. attacked Wright's portrayal of the Southern black community. "*Black Boy,*" Davis complained, "says some wholly unacceptable things about the Negro's capacity for genuine emotion."[16] For Wright, however, it is the circumstances in which black

14. Wright, "The Handiest Truth," 3.
15. *Art of Richard Wright,* 19.
16. "Some Impressions of *Black Boy.*"

people find themselves that cause the personalities to warp, and this in turn results in various forms of hypocritical, erratic, and despicable behavior.

About white men's sexual exploitation of black women, Wright is as critical of black women as of white men, because black women expect and readily condone white men's behavior. Once a black maid who had been slapped playfully on her buttocks by a white nightwatchman passing by told the indignant Wright who had witnessed the incident: "They never get any further with us than that, if we don't want 'em to" (*BB*, 218). Understandably such portraits of black men and women made some readers feel that Wright unduly deprived black people of their personal honor and dignity. For Ralph Ellison, Wright's novel lacks "high humanity," especially among its black characters. As Dan McCall correctly argues, however, "Wright is trying to show us how this gross state came about. He refuses to dress up his Negroes in an imported Sunday best because he has a far larger task before him."[17] Wright explains:

> I began to marvel at how smoothly the black boys acted out the roles that the white race had mapped out for them. Most of them were not conscious of living a special, separate, stunted way of life. Yet I knew that in some period of their growing up—a period that they had no doubt forgotten—there had been developed in them a delicate, sensitive controlling mechanism that shut off their minds and emotions from all that the white race had said was taboo. (*BB*, 216)

This absence of individuality and self-awareness among black people in the South often leads to the compromise of their character. Individually, Fishbelly and his father in *The Long Dream* are powerless in asserting themselves. Although they are not forced or coerced to cooperate with white police, greed often leads them to sacrifice their moral integrity. They are fully aware that their illicit political connections will make them as wealthy as the white people.

One of the remarkable insights *Black Boy* offers is that social determinism takes its heaviest toll in black family life. One would assume that if black boys are mistreated in society at large, they would at least be protected in their family. But in Wright's early childhood his father

17. McCall, *The Example of Richard Wright*, 118–19.

deserted his wife and children; not only did Wright become a casualty of the broken family, but his father himself was a victim of the racial system in the Deep South. "From the white landowners above him," Wright observes, "there had not been handed to him a chance to learn the meaning of loyalty, of sentiment, of tradition" (*BB*, 43).

As a result, the young Wright was subjected to the crushing blow of family antagonisms. His grandmother's Seventh Day Adventist doctrine as practiced at home epitomizes this hostility and strife. Wright saw "more violent quarrels in our deeply religious home than in the home of a gangster, a burglar, or a prostitute. . . . The naked will to power seemed always to walk in the wake of a hymn" (*BB*, 150). While Granny held on to the helm of the family, several of Wright's uncles also attempted to administer their authority. One of them, enraged by Wright's impolite mannerisms, scolded his nephew for not acting as "the backward black boys act on the plantations"; Wright was ordered "to grin, hang my head, and mumble apologetically when I was spoken to" (*BB*, 174).

Based upon Wright's vision, it seems as though black adults, subjected to racism in white society, in turn felt compelled to rule their children at home. The adults had grown up in a white-dominated society in which they were permitted no missteps. That Wright's worst punishments, such as those he was given by his mother for setting fire to his grandmother's house, were inflicted by his closest relatives suggests how deeply black life was dominated by white racism.

In this respect, *Black Boy* can be closely compared to Angelo Herndon's *Let Me Live* (1937). Both writers depict the forces of segregation that had devastating effects on their educations and job opportunities. Both describe poverty and hunger in the plights of their families. But, while Wright grew up without his father and with his bedridden mother and hostile relatives, Herndon was able to rely on the traditional family loyalty—a father with trust and confidence in his son and a warm-hearted, loving mother. It is quite understandable that Wright, compared to his black contemporaries, acquired a much more sinister vision of the black family.

3

Despite the naturalistic philosophy that underlies Wright's racial discourse, the miracle of *Black Boy* is that its hero, by the time he leaves for Chicago, has not become the patient, humorous, subservient black man of the white myth. Nor does he end up as the degraded, grinning, and perpetually frustrated black man or as a murderer like Bigger Thomas. Throughout the book Wright's interest lies in creating a manhood as a direct challenge to the overwhelming forces of racist society. *Black Boy* reveals how self-creation can be thwarted and mauled, but unlike James Farrell's *Studs Lonigan* or Dreiser's *An American Tragedy*, in Wright's work the hero's spirit remains unbroken. Most important, however, what distinguishes *Black Boy* from any other naturalistic work is that it is the story of a man estranged from his own race by sensitivity and intellect, yet alienated from the white race by the color of his skin.

Finding himself in no-man's-land, the young Wright attempted to create his own world. Although *Black Boy* is predominantly a portrayal of southern society, it reads also as a self-portrait. Despite the devastating effects of the society upon his own life, he came to the conclusion that anything was "possible, likely, feasible, because I wanted everything to be possible." Early in the book he rationalizes this passion for ego: "Because I had no power to make things happen outside of me in the objective world, I made things happen within. Because my environment was bare and bleak, I endowed it with unlimited potentialities, redeemed it for the sake of my own hungry and cloudy yearning" (*BB*, 82–83).

About this process of self-creation, critics have charged that he deliberately degrades black life to dramatize the emergence of the self as a hero. W. E. B. Du Bois says: "After this sordid, shadowy picture we gradually come upon the solution. The hero is interested in himself, is self-centered to the exclusion of everybody and everything else." John M. Reilly also argues that Wright "will not risk telling experiences inconsistent in any way with his image of himself as an alienated peasant youth in rebellion against the hostile Southern caste system. . . . Wright suppresses his connections with the bourgeoisie. Had he mentioned these connections, Wright might have modified the picture of a bleak and hostile environment, but there is no question of falsification." But given his life as we know it today, one can scarcely deny the authenticity of the events recounted in the book, nor are the episodes about racism unbelievable or unconvincing. Although Du Bois argues that "the suffering of others is put down simply as a measure of his own suffering and resentment," it is understandable that Wright did so in order to make his own life representative of the voiceless black boys, as well as to intimate that they too are capable of self-creation.[18]

Whether or not the hero is too selfish and proud an achiever to be credible can be judged by how convincingly his maturation is portrayed. In his early childhood Wright acquired a hatred for white people, not based on his own experience but derived from other black children. Like any child, black or white, Wright had his vision circumscribed by blinders and colored glasses. As he grew older, however, he realized that the roots of racial hatred did not exist in any individuals but stemmed from an inherited system. The white race was as much its victim as the black race. From this vantage point, he took social determinism to be a threat to his autonomy and began to wage a battle. By the time he was nineteen, he had become aware that his life experiences "had shaped me to live by my own feelings and thoughts" (*BB*, 276).

It was the crushing effects of environment and temperament that Wright learned so well from his immediate relatives. When he was a young boy, one of his uncles was murdered by his white business competitors, and his grandmother was a religious fanatic. The greatest blow to his childhood came from his own father, who succumbed to the temptation of sex and alcohol. When he saw his father again a quarter of a century later, he realized that, "though ties of blood made us kin, though I could see a shadow of my face in his face, though there was an echo of my voice in his voice, we were forever strangers, speaking a different language, living on vastly distant planes of reality" (*BB*, 42). Not only is Wright denying the influence of heredity on his own character, but he is distinguishing between two men subjected to the same environment. His father, Wright concludes, "was a black peasant who had gone to the city seeking life, but . . . whose life had been hopelessly snarled in the city, and who had at last fled the city— that same city which had lifted me in its burning arms and borne me toward alien and undreamed-of shores of knowing" (*BB*, 43).

What, then, were the forces in his life that the young Wright learned to ward off in his struggle for independence? During his youth he witnessed how deeply superstitious religion had trapped the minds and hearts of black people. As a child he was impressed with the elders at church for the inspiring language of their sermons: "a gospel clogged

18. Du Bois, "Richard Wright Looks Back"; Reilly, "Self-Portraits by Richard Wright," 34.

with images of vast lakes of eternal fire, of seas vanishing, of valleys of dry bones, of the sun burning to ashes, of the moon turning to blood, of stars falling to the earth, of a wooden staff being transformed into a serpent, of voices speaking out of clouds, of men walking upon water, of God riding whirlwinds, of water changing into wine, of the dead rising, of the blind seeing, of the lame walking; a salvation that teemed with fantastic beasts having multiple heads and horns and eyes and feet" (BB, 113). But such sensations departed quickly once he left the church and saw the bright sunshine with the crowd of people pouring into the streets. To him none of these religious ideas and images seemed to have anything to do with his life. He knew not only that religion had a capacity to mesmerize people in the black community, but also that it was used by "one individual or group to rule another in the name of God" (BB, 150).

Although Black Boy is strung with a series of episodes that illustrate forms of racial oppression, the center of attention lies in the hero's transcendence of that oppression. Racial oppression is caused not only by the external forces of society but also by the internal problems of the oppressed. "Some," Wright admits, "may escape the general plight and grow up, but it is a matter of luck."[19] To the hero of Black Boy, most of the oppressed were victims of racial prejudice, failures in the battle for survival. No wonder an anonymous reviewer, calling Black Boy "the most ferocious exercise in misanthropy since Jonathan Swift," was appalled by the hatred Wright expresses toward both white and black people.[20] Obviously, the reader misunderstood Wright's intention, for the book is not meant to be a satire like Gulliver's Travels, in which the narrator assails and loathes every conceivable human vice and depravity. Rather, Black Boy is Wright's honest attempt to refute a naturalistic philosophy of life. Its hero is a catalyst in accomplishing this task.

In "Blueprint for Negro Writing," Wright asserts that "theme for Negro writers will rise from understanding the meaning of their being transplanted from a 'savage' to a 'civilized' culture in all its social, political, economic, and emotional implications."[21] In Black Boy, his chief aim is to show how this youth, whom the South called a "nigger," surmounted his obstacles in the civilized culture. The most painful

19. Wright, "The Handiest Truth."
20. Newark Evening News, March 17, 1945.
21. "Blueprint for Negro Writing," 47.

stance he took in this struggle was to be an intense individualist; he created selfhood and exerted his will at the risk of annihilation. In scene after scene both the black community and the white one kept piling crushing circumstances upon him, but no matter how unbearably they were pressed down on him, he refused to give in. Only under such pressure can one discover one's self. For others, this process of creation might have been aided by chance, but for him "it should be a matter of plan." With himself an exemplar, Wright defined the mission as "a matter of saving the citizens of our country for our country."[22]

The reader could be puzzled by this youth's individuality and fortitude if the seed of manhood had not been sown in the child. Despite a critic's disclaimer to the contrary, *Black Boy* contains ample evidence for the child's precocity and independence. Reviewer F. K. Richter observed that *Black Boy* is an unconscious demonstration of Aristotle's entelechy that manhood resides in childhood. But he maintains that because Wright fails to provide indispensable factors that made the child grow, "the book loses some of its value as autobiography and non-fiction and takes on, however slightly, a quality of fiction."[23] Wright's earlier self is presented even to the point of betraying his vanity. When he moved to his grandmother's house after his family was deserted by his father, he took pride in telling the timid children of the new neighborhood about his train ride, his cruise on the *Kate Adams* on the Mississippi River, and his escape from the orphanage (*BB*, 46). Moreover, the young child is presented as a rebel who refused to compromise with the dictates of society and family. Once he was dismayed to find out that the man who had beaten a black boy was not the boy's father. Although Wright was told by his mother that he was "too young to understand," he responded with a resolution: "I'm not going to let anybody beat me" (*BB*, 31). This bellicose attitude gave rise to an even more awesome resolution, of which he later became capable when he heard the story of a black woman who had avenged her husband's murder by a racist. Rumor had it that when she was granted permission to claim her husband's body for burial, she took with her a shotgun wrapped in a white sheet and, while kneeling down before the white executioners, shot four of them—an incident that served as the exact prototype of "Bright and Morning Star." *Black Boy* records the young Wright's belligerency:

22. Wright, "The Handiest Truth," 3.
23. Richter, review of *Black Boy*, in Reilly, 171.

> I resolved that I would emulate the black woman if I were ever
> faced with a white mob; I would conceal a weapon, pretend
> that I had been crushed by the wrong done to one of my loved
> ones; then, just when they thought I had accepted their cruelty
> as the law of my life, I would let go with my gun and kill as
> many of them as possible before they killed me. The story of
> the woman's deception gave form and meaning to confused
> defensive feelings that had long been sleeping in me. (BB, 84)

Becoming an aspiring rebel inevitably led to being a misfit. In Wright's
life, however, it was his innate character that allowed this to happen.
How self-assertive the young Wright was can be best shown in a comparison between him and his playmates. Although he identified himself
with a mistreated group, there was a crucial difference between him
and other black children. They constantly complained about the petty
wrongs they suffered, but they had no desire to question the larger
issues of racial oppression. Their stance resembles that of the young
Fishbelly in *The Long Dream*; just like his father before him, Fishbelly
servilely worships the powerful white citizens. He falls in love with the
values of the white world because such demeanor can offer him material
rewards and make his manhood less painful to achieve. The young
Wright, on the other hand, found among the black boys no sympathy
for his inquiring mind. As a result he was forced to contemplate such
questions for himself.

As early as twelve years old, Wright held "a sense of the world
that was mine and mine alone, a notion as to what life meant that no
education could ever alter, a conviction that the meaning of living came
only when one was struggling to wring a meaning out of meaningless
suffering" (BB, 112). His decision to leave the South seven years later, his
final action in the book, was based upon such conviction, as if the seed of
manhood had already been in the child. Without mental companionship
to rely on, however, he withdrew and turned inward like the antihero
of an existentialist novel. In his recoil he once again discovered that the
revelation of all truths must come through the action and anguish of
the self.

It was at this point in his ordeal that he came in contact with the
writings of American realists such as Mencken, Dreiser, and Anderson.
It was their ideas, he tells us, that literally delivered his brooding sensibility to a brighter horizon, a vision that "America could be shaped
nearer to the hearts of those who lived in it" (BB, 283). It was also at

this point that he decided to head North to discover for himself that one could live with dignity and determine one's own destiny. Because he knew he could not make the world, he sought to make things happen within him and caught a sense of freedom, and in so doing he discovered the new world.

6

The Outsider, Racial Discourse, and French Existentialism

1

Critics have for the most part regarded the Harper edition of *The Outsider* published in 1953 as existential. They have also noted parallels between Wright and European existentialist novelists in the treatment of the metaphysical rebel, calling Cross Damon's philosophy most consistently nihilistic.[1] It is well known that Wright lived and wrote *The Outsider* in France, where he maintained a close contact with such influential writers as Camus, Sartre, and de Beauvoir. Moreover, these French existentialists can conveniently be placed side by side with Wright's protagonist, who contemplates human existence through his exhaustive reading of Nietzsche, Hegel, Kierkegaard, and Dostoyevsky.

But Arnold Rampersad's edition of *The Outsider,* published by the Library of America in 1991, further suggests that Wright's original intention for *The Outsider* was not as existential as critics have thought. For the Harper edition, as Rampersad has shown, the original length of 741 typescript pages was shortened to 620 pages, a 16.3 percent reduction. The difference between the two versions is partly stylistic but also has to do with Wright's intention for the book as racial discourse.

1. See Glicksberg, "Existentialism in *The Outsider*" and "The God of Fiction." Michel Fabre specifically indicates that Wright's composition of *The Outsider* was influenced by Camus's *The Stranger.* See Fabre, "Richard Wright, French Existentialism, and *The Outsider,*" 191.

Most of the block cuts suggest that the novel as originally conceived was not as avowedly existentialist as critics have characterized the Harper edition as being. The original version suggests that Cross Damon is not a black man in name only. Not only is his plight real, but all the incidents and characters he is involved with, which at times appear to be clumsily constructed symbols, nonetheless express well-digested ideas. He is not "pathetically insane," as a reviewer described him.[2] The novel bewildered black reviewers as well, not because of Wright's novel philosophy, but because Wright seemed to have lost contact with his native soil.[3] But a detailed comparison of the two versions will show not only that Cross Damon as originally portrayed is not simply an embodiment of a half-baked philosophy, but also that he is a genuine product of American society.

Wright's intention in the Harper edition of *The Outsider* is to express a version of existentialism in which human action is taken as the result of an individual's choice and will. Early in the novel Damon's wife, Gladys, complains to her husband that white people intimidate her. He in turn admonishes her that one must exert one's will to exist. "It's up to us to make ourselves something," he argues. "A man creates himself" (*O*, 51). Initially Damon is attracted to his Communist mentor Gil Blount for his ideology and action. After Blount's death Damon realizes that he epitomized "a modern man." "Life, to him," Damon reflects, "was a game devoid of all significance except that which he put into it" (*O*, 370). Damon, however, killed Blount because Blount had attempted to wield the Communists' power over Damon's will.

Corollary to Damon's idea of self-creation is his abhorrence of human dependence on others. Damon loses his interest in Gladys because, as Wright observes, "it was the helplessness of dependence that made her fret so. Men made themselves and women were made only through men" (*O*, 51). In order to characterize modern man as self-reliant and autonomous, Wright deleted a number of passages in which people are portrayed as passive and dependent on others. Both editions of the novel begin with a scene in which Damon, tired with his long work at the post office, tries to rest his body on one of his companions. But his friend, a short man, chides him, saying, "Hell, naw! Stand on your

2. James N. Rhea, review of *The Outsider*.
3. See Saunders Redding, review of *The Outsider*; Lloyd Brown, "Outside and Low."

own two big flat feet, Cross!" (*O*, 1).[4] The opening scene is, indeed, identical between the two versions except for three sentences allusive to a racial feature of the black men: "Tiny crystals trembled whitely between their dark faces. The shoulders of their overcoats were laced with icy filigrees; dapples of moisture glowed diamondlike on their eyebrows where the heat of their blood was melting the snow" (*LW*, 371). This passage was deleted, since Damon and his black friends, conscious of their racial background, give the impression that having been born black is responsible for their plight. Such an implication contradicts Wright's portrait of a self-made man.

Among the sequences and incidents cut out of the original manuscript, the extended Hattie episode, which runs fourteen pages in two scenes, is the longest. Hattie is a young black widow who is lost in her life and is trying to cling to others for help. Damon finds himself easily tempted by this lonely woman, but he staves off the temptation. Even before this episode, Wright also deleted a sentence from Damon's conversation with Ely Houston, a district attorney he happens to meet on the train: Damon says to Houston, "The American Negro, because of his social and economic situation, is a congenital coward" (*LW*, 505). Even though Damon characterizes the African American as a helpless victim of society rather than a courageous, self-sufficient individual, he is not aware that he himself remains a coward. The irony in Wright's portrayal of Cross Damon rests in the fact that while Damon disparages black women like Gladys and Hattie as weak and dependent, he himself does not always act like a strong man. The original manuscript thus includes an episode in which Damon, pursued by Communist agents, desperately tries to save his life by begging Hattie to hide him in her apartment and promising to give her $250 for her help. An existentialist like Meursault in *The Stranger* and Raskolnikov in *Crime and Punishment* would not stoop to such an action as does Wright's protagonist.

Cross Damon as originally conceived strikes one as an egoist, a selfish individual, rather than an indifferent, audacious human being compelled to do nothing in the face of the void and meaningless universe. This seems to be why Wright excised the two opening paragraphs of book 4, entitled "Despair." In this passage Damon confesses his selfish motive for murdering Blount and Herndon. Damon accomplished his

---

4. Also *Later Works*, ed. Arnold Rampersad, 369. Subsequent references to this version will appear parenthetically in the text as *LW*.

goal, Wright observes, "as much for a dawning reverence for her as for the protection of his own self-love" (*LW*, 618).

In the original version of the novel, the character of Eva Blount, Damon's love, is strikingly similar to that of Damon. He falls in love with Eva because both have suffered from a loveless marriage. In stark contrast to an existentialist, Eva is as passionately in search of meaning in existence as is Damon. "Her sense of guilt," Wright says, "was throwing her on his side; she had long been wanting to be free of Gil and now that she was free she wants to unburden her guilt on to someone else, on to Herndon" (*LW*, 642). Significantly, Wright eliminated this passage to make Eva as selfless and passive a person as Damon. As a result, she is portrayed as "as calm as marble. Balling a handkerchief in her right fist, she sat looking bleakly in front of her. His eyes caught hers and he saw in them a glint of recognition. Yes, she's with me. She thinks I'm a victim too" (*O*, 253–54).

Despite the fact that Eva has fallen prey to the Communists, as has Damon, Wright's aim in the Harper version is to endow her character with courage and autonomy. To strengthen her individualism, Wright omitted two sentences from Eva's diary in which she expresses an outrage against the Communists: "The Party lifted me up in its hands and showed me to the world, and if I disown them, they'll disown me . . . What a trap!" (*LW*, 594). Such a passage intimates that she has been deprived of freedom and independence and become a helpless victim of the Communists. Omitting this passage makes Eva akin to Damon and hence more attractive to him. His affinity for her, in turn, whets his craving for freedom and independence from a totalitarian philosophy. While his intimate relationship with Eva constitutes a credible event in *The Outsider* as a naturalistic protest novel, it also plays a crucial role in Wright's dialectics between oppression and freedom.

Wright's chief interest in *The Outsider* thus lies in an exposition of what freedom means to certain individuals. As Damon disparages Gladys and Hattie, he repudiates his own mother not only because she is the product of the traditional Christianity of the South but also because she failed to challenge the lack of freedom and individualism that prevailed in African American life. To make Mrs. Damon freer of a religious dogma, Wright cut out a long speech by her in which she admonishes her son to abide by God's law. "If you feel you can't master yourself," she warns him, "then take your problem to God. . . . Life is a promise, son; God promised it to us and we must promise it to others. Without that promise, life's nothing . . . Oh, God, to think that at twenty-six you're lost" (*LW*, 391). It is only natural that Damon should find his peace of mind in a liberal woman like Eva. Wright also tries to show how religion gets in the way of achieving freedom. In his flight to New York Damon meets a priest he regards as "a kind of dressed-up savage intimidated by totems and taboos that differed in kind but not in degree from those of the most primitive of peoples." The priest's demeanor shows Damon that good and evil are not discovered by "the edicts of any God" but by human actions, for it is only the individual who is responsible for the consequences of his or her actions (*LW*, 494).

To Damon, law, like religion, is created to inhibit human actions. A truly liberated individual does not control his or her actions under the law. Instead an existentialist creates his or her own law and abides by it. For this reason, Wright deleted a long passage in which Damon discusses how law has the capacity to inhibit individuality and creativity in human life but at the same time provide the freedom of choice. "Implied in law," Damon asserts, "is a free choice to each man living under the law; indeed, one could almost say a free challenge is embedded in the law" (*LW*, 700). Since this ambivalence in Damon's interpretation of law is embodied in Houston, Wright also deleted several sentences that specifically refer to Houston: "Cross shrewdly suspected that Houston, a self-confessed outlaw, knew this, felt it; and it was what had made him become an active defender of the law; he *had* to represent the law in order to protect himself against his own weakness and fear" (*LW*, 700). Wright made such an omission to strengthen his argument that one's moral obligation is to the individual and not to society, as well as to justify Damon's murder of the men who had deprived him of individual freedom.

Wright's emphasis on the autonomy of human action is also reflected in the style of the novel. While Wright partly intended the book to be a social protest, his chief aim was to mold a black man's life upon existential tenets. Just as Damon's statement in the original manuscript that the black person in America is a victim of the social and economic environment was excised from the Harper edition, other descriptions of naturalistic determinism were also deleted. The subway accident in which he is involved makes him feel as if he were imprisoned in himself. He is "so swamped . . . by himself with himself that he could not break forth from behind the bars of that self to claim himself" (*LW*, 488). A stranger who witnessed the accident tells Damon: "Brother, your blood is the tomato sauce. Your white guts is the spaghetti. And your flesh is the meat, see? You'd be surprised how like a plate of meatballs and spaghetti you look when you get minced up in one of those subway wrecks" (*LW*, 470). Such a description was omitted, for it is a cynical remark about the gruesome condition of a human being.

To make *The Outsider* akin to existential novels by Sartre and Camus, Wright also eliminated much of the profane and sexually allusive language. The Harper edition, for instance, does not include an expression Eva writes in her diary as she accuses the Communists of having deceived her into marrying her husband: "Goddam this deception!" (*LW*, 595). In describing the ground where Joe, a friend of Damon's, lies after Damon has killed him, Wright originally wrote: "some of the grounds spilled over a bloodstained Kotex which still retained the curving shape of having fitted tightly and recently against the lips of some vagina; there was a flattened grapefruit hull whose inner pulpy fibres held a gob of viscous phlegm" (*LW*, 485). The passage was changed to "some of the grounds spilled over a flattened grapefruit hull" (*O*, 115). Similarly, passages including such sentences as "Sarah's breasts heaved" and "her lips hung open and she breathed orgiastically" were deleted (*LW*, 556).

At a crucial point in the development of the story Wright went to great pains to revise the original manuscript to express an existential philosophy. On the one hand, Wright came to recognize a close relationship between Damon's actions and his social and psychological background; on the other hand, he tried to demonstrate in Damon's life a nihilistic view of the world as stated earlier in the book: "man is nothing in particular" (*O*, 135). As the story progresses, however, the feeling of isolation and loneliness increasingly dictates Damon's action. Reading Eva's diary makes him realize that Eva's love for him came out of her sympathy for his oppressed life just as his love for her was intensified by his compassion for her personal predicament. This revelation leads to his statement on his deathbed—"To make a bridge from man to man" (*O*, 439)—a clear contradiction to his earlier view of man.

Although Damon's final vision makes the Harper version of *The Outsider* less existential than originally intended, it suggests that Wright was ambivalent in expressing his view of human existence. In both versions, he intended to portray an outsider as an individual with courage and audacity, but as the story unfolds, Damon finds himself increasingly alienated and realizes that, however imperfect society may be, he cannot live without relating to others. It is ironic that Wright's hero is determined to be an outsider but in his heart wants to be an insider. A character like Cross Damon is sometimes larger than the author's occasional philosophy and is able to speak for himself. Wright the philosopher only gets in his way; Wright the artist remains true to his character. In the end, the interest of the story lies not in Wright's mind but in his heart, the genuine feelings Wright himself had experienced in American society.

2

A comparison of *The Outsider* with Camus's *The Stranger*, a typical French existentialist novel, further suggests that *The Outsider* is not as existential as it appears. Although the likeness in theme, character, and event between *The Outsider* and *The Stranger* has been pointed out, it has not been studied in any detail. In general, critics have regarded Wright's philosophy in *The Outsider* as nihilistic, as mentioned earlier. Charles I. Glicksberg, in "Existentialism in *The Outsider*" and "The God of Fiction," saw parallels between Wright and Camus in their treatment of the metaphysical rebel, calling Cross Damon's philosophy most consistently nihilistic. More recently, critics have demonstrated Camus's influences on Wright in his conception of Cross Damon. According to Michel Fabre, Wright read *The Stranger* in the American edition at a very slow pace, "weighing each sentence, 'admiring' its damn good narrative prose," and then remarked:

> It is a neat job but devoid of passion. He makes his point with dispatch and his prose is solid and good. In America a book like this would not attract much attention for it would be said that he lacks feeling. He does however draw his character very well. What is of course really interesting in this book is the use of fiction to express a philosophical point of view. That he does with ease. I now want to read his other stuff.[5]

Edward Margolies in his comparison of Damon and Meursault pointed out that "both men kill without passion, both men appear unmoved

5. Fabre, "Richard Wright, French Existentialism, and *The Outsider*," 191.

by the death of their mothers; both men apparently are intended to represent the moral and emotional failure of the age."[6]

It would be quite tempting to compare the two works if they were the products of the same age and the particular philosophy they dealt with was in vogue. Moreover Camus's indifferent philosopher can conveniently be placed side by side with Wright's protagonist, a self-styled existentialist. One suspects, however, that the comparison of the two novels would never have been made if the two novelists had not both been caught up in the philosophical context of existentialism. This meant that the literary likeness was taken for granted. Meursault kills a man; he is charged with a murder, tried, and convicted in a world of court, jury, and judge. But Damon kills more than one man, not only an enemy but also a friend, a mentor, and an ally, and is responsible for the suicide of a woman he loves. But he is never charged with a crime, brought to trial, or convicted. Unlike Meursault, who encounters his death in the world of daylight in Algiers, Damon is himself murdered by two men, the agents of the Communist Party, on a dimly lit street in New York. *The Outsider,* therefore, is fiction of a different order, brought together with *The Stranger* in an assumed definition of human existence in the modern world. Although the two novels are regarded largely as existentialist, the crucial details that differentiate the narratives make Meursault and Damon radically different in their ideology and action.

It is time to reexamine *The Outsider* as a discourse on race; that is, it is important to redefine the black tradition and experience that underlie this work. Comparing this novel with an avowedly existentialist novel like Camus's *The Stranger* will reveal that Wright's novel is not what critics have characterized it to be. A detailed comparison of this novel with *The Stranger,* a novel of another culture and another tradition, will show not only that Wright's hero is not simply an embodiment of a half-baked philosophy but also that he is a genuine product of the African American experience. Such a reevaluation of the book will also clarify misconceptions about Wright's other books.

The disparity of the two books becomes even more apparent when seen in the light of the less fashionable literary philosophy, naturalism. To some American writers, such as Stephen Crane and Theodore Dreiser, naturalism is a doctrine that asserts the indifference of the universe to

6. *Art of Richard Wright,* 135.

the will of man. The indifference of the universe is most poignantly described by Stephen Crane in "The Open Boat": "When it occurs to a man that nature does not regard him as important, and that she feels she would not maim the universe by disposing of him, he at first wishes to throw bricks at the temple, and he hates deeply the fact that there are no bricks and no temples. Any visible expression of nature would surely be pelleted with his jeers."[7] Dreiser describes the forces of nature in *Sister Carrie*:

> Among the forces which sweep and play throughout the universe, untutored man is but a wisp in the wind. Our civilisation is still in a middle stage, scarcely beast, in that it is no longer wholly guided by instinct; scarcely human, in that it is not yet wholly guided by reason. . . . As a beast, the forces of life aligned him with them; as a man, he has not yet wholly learned to align himself with the forces. In this intermediate stage he wavers— neither drawn in harmony with nature by his instincts nor yet wisely putting himself into harmony by his own free-will.[8]

Camus, though his naturalistic vision is not conveyed with Dreiser's massive detail or analyzed by Zola's experimental method, nevertheless constructs his novel to dramatize a climactic assertion of universal indifference. Wright's novel, on the other hand, is filled with events and actions that exhibit the world's concerns with the affairs of people. The outside world is indeed hostile to Damon, a man of great will and passion. Refusing to be dominated by it, he challenges its forces. But Meursault, remaining mostly a pawn, is not willing to exert himself against the forces that to him have no relation to existence.

Heredity and environment, the twin elements in naturalistic fiction, are more influential to human action in *The Stranger* than they are in *The Outsider*. Although heredity has little effect on Meursault's behavior, environment does play a crucial role. Meursault is consistently shown as indifferent to any of society's interests and desires: love of God, marriage, friendship, social status. He is averse to financial success or political power; he receives only what is given or acts when acted upon. He is, like Dreiser's Sister Carrie, "a wisp in the wind"; he is more drawn than he draws.[9] This explains his passivity. Camus painstakingly

7. *Great Short Works of Stephen Crane*, 294.
8. *Sister Carrie*, 83.
9. Cf. *Sister Carrie*, 83–84.

accounts for human action just as Zola or Dreiser demonstrates the circumstances under which it occurs.

Camus shows that Meursault, who had no desire to kill the Arab, merely responded to pressures applied by natural forces. The blinding sun and the glittering knife held by the Arab caused Meursault to fear and forced him to pull the trigger. If the man with the knife had been a Frenchman, Meursault would not have acted with such rashness. Given the history of Arab-French colonial relations, Meursault's antagonism toward the Arabs might have subconsciously triggered his action. Camus's emphasis in this narrative, however, is on the elements of chance, that is, the blinding sun and the glittering knife, rather than on social elements such as the disharmony between the French and the Arabs.

This idea of chance and determinism is absent in Wright's concept of human action as it is exhibited in *The Outsider*. Each of the four murders committed by Damon is premeditated, the suicide of a woman is directly related to his actions, and his own murder is a reprisal for the actions he could have avoided. In each case it is made clear that Damon has control over his action; in each murder he is capable of exerting his will or satisfying his desire. In marked contrast to Meursault, Damon exerts himself to attain the essences of his own existence. They are the very embodiments of the abstract words of society—*friendship, love, marriage, success, equality,* and *freedom*—to which he cannot remain indifferent. Wright takes pains to show that they are not empty dreams. The fact that Damon has been deprived of them at one time or another proves that they constitute his existence.

The Outsider represents a version of existentialism in which human action is viewed as the result of an individual's choice and will. To Wright, the individual's action must be assertive and, if need be, aggressive. This is perhaps why he was more attracted to Sartre and de Beauvoir than to Camus. In an unpublished journal Wright wrote: "Sartre is quite of my opinion regarding the possibility of human action today, that it is up to the individual to do what he can to uphold the concept of what it means to be human. The great danger, I told him, in the world today is the very feeling and conception of what is a human might well be lost. He agreed. I feel very close to Sartre and Simone de Beauvoir."[10]

If Wright's protagonist is considered an existentialist actively in search of an essence in the meaningless existence, Meursault seems a

10. See Fabre, "Richard Wright, French Existentialism, and *The Outsider*," 186.

passive existentialist compelled to do nothing in the face of the void and meaningless universe. Focused on the definition of existence, their views are alike: Damon at one time says, perhaps uncharacteristically, "Maybe man is nothing in particular" (O, 135). The point of disparity in their worldview, however, is the philosophy of the absurd. While Meursault is convinced of the essential absurdity of existence, Damon is not. If one considers human life inherently meaningful, as does Damon, then it follows that his actions to seek love, power, and freedom on earth are also meaningful. Conversely, however, if one judges life absurd, as does Meursault, then it follows that his actions are also absurd.

What is absurd is this dilemma of Meursault between his recognition of chaos and his search for order. It is the conflict between his awareness of death and his dream of eternity. It is the disparity between the essential mystery of all existence and one's demand for explanation. The fundamental difference in attitude between Meursault and Damon is that Meursault seeks neither order, nor a dream of eternity, nor explanation, while Damon is passionately in search of such an essence. Meursault's passivity, moreover, stems from Camus's attitude toward his art. Camus tries to solve the existentialist dilemma by arguing that an artist is not concerned to find order, to have a dream of eternity, or to demand explanation, but to experience all things given. The artist describes; he does not solve the mystery of the universe that is both infinite and inexplicable.

Whereas Camus's hero resists action, Wright's is compelled to act. Wright endows his hero with the freedom to create an essence. Damon's revolt is not so much against the nothingness and meaninglessness of existence as it is against one's inability to make illogical phenomena logical. In the eyes of the public, Damon is as guilty of his murder of the fascist as Raskolnikov is guilty of his murder of the pawnbroker in *Crime and Punishment*. Likewise, Damon's killing of his friend Joe is similar to Raskolnikov's killing of the pawnbroker's sister Lizaveta. In the case of Joe or Lizaveta the murderer has no malice toward the victim but intentionally kills to protect himself from prosecution. Both crimes result from premeditated actions; Meursault's killing of the Arab is accidental.

Some critics find a contradiction in Damon's view of the world. Early in the story Damon considers man "nothing in particular" (O, 135), but at the end of his life he asserts, "We must find some way of being good to ourselves. . . . Man is all we've got. . . . I wish I could ask men to meet themselves" (*O*, 439). Likewise his inaction initially makes him see nothingness and meaninglessness in human existence, but in the end his action results in his realization of loneliness and "horror" on earth (*O*, 440). In short, what appears to be a contradiction in Damon's view of existence is rather a reflection of activeness and aggressiveness in his character.

The chief difference in philosophy between the two books derives from the differing philosophies of the two novelists, Wright and Camus. Although both men are regarded as rebels against society, the motive behind the rebellion differs. Damon rebels against society because it oppresses him by depriving him of the values he and society share, such as freedom of association and opportunity for success. Meursault is aloof to society because he does not believe in such values. Moreover he does not believe in marriage or family loyalty. His obdurate attitude toward society is clearly stated in Camus's preface to the American edition of *The Stranger:*

> I summarized *The Stranger*—a long time ago, with a remark that I admit was highly paradoxical: "In our society any man who does not weep at his mother's funeral runs the risk of being sentenced to death." I only meant that the hero of my book is condemned because he does not play the game. In this respect, he is foreign to the society in which he lives; he wanders, on the fringe, in the suburbs of private, solitary, sensual life. And this is why some readers have been tempted to look upon him as a piece of social wreckage. A much more accurate idea of the character, at least one much closer to the author's intentions, will emerge if one asks just how Meursault doesn't play the game. The reply is a simple one: he refuses to lie. To lie is not only to say *more* than is true, and, as far as the human heart is concerned, to express more than one feels. This is what we all do, every day, to simplify life. He says what he is, he refuses to hide his feelings, and immediately society feels threatened.[11]

If Meursault is characterized by his refusal to play society's game, Damon is a type of person who cannot resist playing such a game. While society is threatened by Meursault's indifference to it, in *The Outsider* it is Damon rather than society that feels threatened.

This estranged personality of Meursault is reflected in his relationship with his mother. Some critics have used his calm acceptance of the

---

11. Camus, *Lyrical and Critical Essays*, 335–37.

bereavement as evidence for his callousness.[12] But the fact that he does not cry at his mother's funeral would not necessarily suggest that he is devoid of emotions. Had Meursault thought her death would have spared her the misery of her life or that death would be a happier state for man, he should not have been aggrieved by the passing away of his mother. What makes him a peculiar character, however, is the fact that an experience that would be a traumatic one for others is for him devoid of any meaning. *The Stranger* thus opens with the protagonist's unconcerned reaction to his mother's death: "Mother died today. Or, maybe, yesterday; I can't be sure."[13] But as the story progresses he becomes a more sensitive individual. He is indeed disturbed during the vigil by the weeping of his mother's friend. And every detail, whether it is the driving home of the screws in the coffin lid or the starting of the prayers by the priest, is minutely described. Throughout the story there is no mention of Meursault's disliking his mother. He fondly reflects on her habits and personality; he affectionately calls her *Maman*.

By contrast Damon's relationship with his mother betrays not only the estrangement between them but also his hostility to the racist society that had reared her. It is only natural that Damon should rebel against such a mother, who moans, "To think I named you Cross after the Cross of Jesus" (*O*, 23). He rejects his mother not only because she reminds him of southern black piety but also because she is an epitome of racial and sexual repression:

> He was conscious of himself as a frail object which had to protect itself against a pending threat of annihilation. This frigid world was suggestively like the one which his mother, without knowing it, had created for him to live in when he had been a child. . . . This God's NO-face had evoked in his pliable boy's body an aching sense of pleasure by admonishing him to shun pleasure as the tempting doorway opening blackly onto hell; had too early awakened in him a sharp sense of sex by thunderingly denouncing sex as the sin leading to eternal damnation. . . . Mother love had cleaved him: a wayward sensibility that distrusted itself, a consciousness that was conscious of itself. Despite this, his sensibilities had not been repressed by God's fearful negations as represented by his mother; indeed,

12. See, for instance, Robert de Luppe, *Albert Camus*, 46–47.
13. *The Stranger*, trans. Stuart Gilbert, 1. Subsequent references will appear parenthetically in the text as *S*.

his sense of life had been so heightened that desire boiled in him
to a degree that made him afraid. (*O*, 17–18)

The young Damon's desire to free himself from such a bondage is
closely related to his inability to love any black woman, as shown by
his relationship with Gladys, his estranged wife, or Dot, his pregnant
mistress. The only woman he loves is the white woman Eva. He feels
an affinity with her, for he discovers that she, too, is a fearful individual
and that she had been deceived into marrying her husband because
of a political intrigue. He is, moreover, tormented by the envenomed
abstraction of racial and political myths. Unlike the white phonograph
salesman who seduces the wife of a black man in "Long Black Song,"
Damon is permanently frustrated. Because *The Outsider* portrays a rich
variety of racial and political animosities, his love life is defined in terms
of forces beyond his control. To him the consummation of his love for
Eva is the ultimate purpose of his new existence. It is understandable
that when that goal appears within reach and yet is taken away from
him, he finds only "the horror" that he has dreaded all his life (*O*, 440).

Meursault's relationship with women, on the contrary, is totally un-
inhibited socially and psychologically. His relationship with Marie is
free from the kinds of racial and political entanglements that smother
Damon's relationship with Eva. Meursault, the perfectly adjusted man,
does not suffer from any kind of repression. His action for love is
motivated from within according to logic rather than convention or
sentiment. In his life, love of woman is as natural an instinct as is eating
or resting; love is more akin to friendship than to marriage. He helps
Raymond, for he says, "I wanted to satisfy Raymond, as I'd no reason
not to satisfy him" (*S*, 41). Meursault is kind and benevolent, as Damon
is not; he is relaxed and content, while Damon is tense and frustrated.

Meursault's indifference to existence is epitomized by his love life.
His attitude toward Marie bears a sort of impersonal, superhuman mode
of thought. To the public such an attitude is inhuman, unconventional,
and unethical. His view of love is no different from that of death;
interestingly enough, his sexual relations with Marie begin immediately
after his mother's death. If death occurs beyond human control, so does
love. His meeting with her takes place by mere coincidence, and the
relationship that develops is casual and appears quite innocent:

While I was helping her to climb on to a raft, I let my hand
stray over her breasts. Then she lay flat on the raft, while I trod

water. After a moment she turned and looked at me. Her hair was over her eyes and she was laughing. I clambered up on to the raft, beside her. The air was pleasantly warm, and, half jokingly, I let my head sink back upon her lap. She didn't seem to mind, so I let it stay there. I had the sky full in my eyes, all blue and gold, and I could feel Marie's stomach rising and falling gently under my head. We must have stayed a good half-hour on the raft, both of us half asleep. When the sun got too hot she dived off and I followed. I caught up with her, put my arm round her waist, and we swam side by side. She was still laughing. (S, 23–24)

Even when a marriage proposal is made by Marie, his indifference remains intact: "Marie came that evening and asked me if I'd marry her. I said I didn't mind; if she was keen on it, we'd get married" (S, 52).

Meursault's indifference is also reflected in his reaction to the crime of which he is accused. Partly as a corollary to the nature of the crime, he is passive rather than active. Unlike Damon, he commits a crime without malice or intention. He kills the Arab not because he hates the victim but partly because he sympathizes with his friend Raymond, whose life has been threatened. Given this situation, it would be more natural for him to defend his friend than the hostile stranger. Meursault's crime is a crime of logic; it is not a murder. Camus's purpose for using crime in *The Stranger* is to prove that society, rather than the criminal, is in the wrong. Camus's intention is to prove that his hero is innocent, as well as to show that Meursault's logic is far superior to society's. When crime appears innocent, it is innocence that is called upon to justify itself. In *The Stranger*, then, it is society, not the criminal, that is on trial.

Because Meursault is convinced of his innocence, he attains at the end of his life his peace of mind, a kind of nirvana:

With death so near, Mother must have felt like someone on the brink of freedom, ready to start life all over again. No one, no one in the world had any right to weep for her. And I, too, felt ready to start life all over again. It was as if that great rush of anger had washed me clean, emptied me of hope, and, gazing up at the dark sky spangled with its signs and stars, for the first time, the first, I laid my heart open to the benign indifference of the universe. (S, 154)

Damon is also convinced of his innocence at the end of his life. What the two novels share is not only that the hero is prosecuted by society, but that society—the prosecutor, jurors, and judge—seems to him to be always in the wrong. Camus's hero refuses to play society's game; as a result he is sentenced to death by society. Society expects him to grieve over his mother's death and refrain from having a casual affair with a woman during the mourning. But Wright's hero, induced to play society's game, loses in the end. He is tempted to participate in the normal activities of society such as a love affair and a political association. Tasting his agonizing defeat and dying, he utters:

> I wish I had some way to give the meaning of my life to others. . . . To make a bridge from man to man . . . Starting from scratch every time is . . . is no good. Tell them not to come down this road. . . . We must find some way of being good to ourselves. . . . We're different from what we seem. . . . Maybe worse, maybe better . . . But certainly different . . . We're strangers to ourselves. (*O*, 439)

The confession at the end of his life suggests that he, unlike Meursault, has always felt obliged to justify his actions. He has finally realized that they always collided with society's interests and values. As an outsider, he trusted no one, not even himself, nor did society trust him. While maintaining in his last breath that "in my heart . . . I'm. . . . *innocent*" (*O*, 440), he is judging society guilty. While Meursault is a victim of his own crime, Damon is a victim not only of his own crime but also of society's. Meursault, who refuses to justify his actions, always feels innocent: "I wasn't conscious of any 'sin'; all I knew was that I'd been guilty of a criminal offense" (*S*, 148).

Although both novels employ crime as a thematic device, the authors' focus differs. Camus's center of interest is not crime but its consequences—its psychological effect on his hero. Before committing his crime Meursault is presented as a stranger who finds no meaning in life. After he is sentenced to death he realizes for the first time that his life has been enveloped in the elusive beauty of the world. "To feel it so like myself, indeed, so brotherly," he says, "made me realize that I'd been happy, and that I was happy still" (*S*, 154). In *The Outsider* crime is used, like accidental death or suicide, to create a new life for the hero. He murders the fascist Herndon as a reprisal; he intentionally kills the Communist Blount out of his desire for a white woman. In stark contrast to Camus's hero, to whom death has brought life and happiness, Wright's hero in the end is once more reminded of his own estrangement and horror. The kind of fear Damon suffers at the end of his struggle is clearly absent in Meursault's life. A critic, in comparing Meursault to Clyde Griffiths, the hero of Theodore Dreiser's *An American Tragedy*, comments: "Passivity in *L'Etranger* is strength, and only the strong can be indifferent. When Meursault receives this almost Buddhist illumination, he loses the two great distractions from life: hope and fear. He becomes happy, rather than terrified, in the face of his expected execution; he no longer hopes for some wild chance to deliver him from it. This prisoner is alone and freed, from within."[14]

The two novelists' divergent attitudes toward the problems of crime and guilt are also reflected in the style and structure of their works. *The Stranger* is swift in pace and dramatic in tone and displays considerable subjectivity, involving the reader in the consciousness of the hero. The reader's involvement in the hero's dialectics is intensified because the book consists of two parts dealing with the same issue. The first part involves the reader in a few days of Meursault's life, ending with his crime; the second re-involves the reader in the same experiences through the trial in court. Since the hero's experiences are viewed from different angles, they never strike one as monotonous or repetitious. The chief reason for the juxtaposition is for the hero, and for Camus, to convince the reader that what appears to society to be a crime is not at all a crime in the eyes of an existentialist.

This juxtaposition also elucidates the discontinuity and unrelatedness of Meursault's experiences in the first half of the story despite the reordering and reconstruing of those experiences in the second half. As the incidents and actions in the first half are discontinuous, so is time. No days are referred to in Meursault's life except for Saturday and Sunday, his days off. Of the months only August is mentioned since Meursault, Mason, and Raymond plan to have their vacation together; of the seasons only summer. By the same token, there is no mention of the day of the month. And Meursault's age is unknown; he is merely "young."[15] As there is nothing unique about his concept of time, there is nothing unique about his experience. As points in time are discontinuous, so are experiences. At his trial the prosecutor accuses him of moral turpitude, for Meursault shed no tears at his mother's funeral and casually started an affair with Marie immediately after. To

14. Stropher B. Purdy, "*An American Tragedy* and *L'Étranger*," 261.
15. The most precise analysis of Camus's concept of time is presented by Ignace Feuerlicht in "Camus's *L'Étranger* Reconsidered."

Meursault, his mother's death, his behavior at the funeral, and his love affair are not only devoid of meaning in themselves, but discontinuous, unrelated incidents.

Similarly, the threatening gesture of the Arab, the sweating in Meursault's eyebrows, the flashing of the sun against his eyes, and the firing of his revolver occur independently of one another. If his eyes were blinded by the sun and the sweating of his eyebrows, his pulling of the trigger would not have been a logical reaction. When he is later asked by the prosecutor why he took a revolver with him and went back to the place where the Arab reappeared, he replies that "it was a matter of pure chance" (*S*, 110). If he does not believe that he is "morally guilty of his mother's death" (*S*, 128), as charged by the prosecutor, it would be impossible for him to admit that he is morally guilty of the Arab's death. This is precisely why he tells the priest that he is guilty of a criminal offense but that he is not a sinner (*S*, 148).

Swift and intensive though Camus's probing of Meursault's character is, the reader is deliberately kept from coming to an easy conclusion about Meursault's guilt. By contrast, the reader is instantly made aware of Damon's guilt in unambiguous terms. In *The Outsider* truly heinous crimes are constructed in advance with all the plausible justifications. Before the reader is made aware of Damon's guilt, the author has defined in unequivocal terms the particular traits in Damon's character and the particular forces in society that led to his crimes. In so doing Wright creates a clear pattern by which Damon's motives for crime are shown. Whereas there is no such relatedness in Meursault's motives for action, there emerges in *The Outsider* a chain of events that can scarcely be misinterpreted. The murder of the fascist is committed side by side with that of the Communist. Another example of this relatedness in Damon's actions is, as Margolies observes, the pattern in which Damon rejects the black women as he destroys the Communists and fascist: "When Cross murders two Communists and a fascist, his motives seem to derive more from what he regards as his victims' desire to enslave him psychologically, rather than from any detached, intellectualized, conscienceless 'compulsion' on his part. What the Communists and fascist would do to Cross if they had him in their power is precisely what his mother, wife, and mistress had already done to him. In a sense, Cross murders his women when he crushes his enemies."[16] Damon kills

16. *Art of Richard Wright*, 133.

both men with malice: he murders Herndon because of his hatred for the fascist and racist and Blount because of his passion for the white woman. Unlike Meursault, Damon is conscious of his guilt in the instant of committing his crime.

Because Damon's actions are predetermined and interrelated, Damon is constantly made conscious of the passage of time. The problems in his manhood and marriage, for example, are related to those of his childhood. His desertion of his wife is analogous to his rejection of his mother, just as the Communists' rule over workers in modern times is akin to slavery in the past. *The Outsider* opens with a scene at dawn in which Damon and his friends "moved slowly forward shoulder to shoulder and the sound of their feet tramping and sloshing in the melting snow echoed loudly" (*O*, 1). Like Jake Jackson in *Lawd Today*, Damon, bored with routine work, finds the passage of time unendurable. In *The Stranger*, Meursault is least concerned with time; he never complains about the monotony of his work. In fact, he dislikes Sundays because he is not doing his routine job. Damon, on the contrary, wishes every day were Sunday, or reminisces about Christmastime in a certain year. Damon's friend Joe Thomas reminds Damon of their happy days in the past: "Remember that wild gag he pulled at Christmastime in 19 . . . ? . . . When the hell was that now? Oh, yes! It was in 1945. I'll never forget it. Cross bought a batch of magazines, *Harper's, Atlantic Monthly, Collier's, Ladies' Home Journal,* and clipped out those ads that say you can send your friends a year's subscription as a Christmas gift" (*O*, 5).

Meursault says whether he dies at thirty or at seventy it doesn't matter. For him life has no more significance than death. For Damon life is all that matters. If his earlier life is not worth living, a new one must be created. Therefore, a freak subway accident, in which he is assumed dead, offers him another life and another identity. All his life he plans his actions with hope for the future and with denial of the past. Such an attitude is emblematic of the African American tradition, the deep-seated black experience, as expressed in the spirituals. While Edgar Allan Poe's writings sometimes smack of morbid romanticism, that erotic longing for death, the spirituals reverberate with energy and vitality and convey the sense of rejuvenation. However violent and destructive Damon may appear, he inherently emerges from this tradition. Meursault, on the other hand, is the very product of the nihilistic spirit that hovered over Europe, particularly France, after World War II.

Despite Wright's effort to relate Damon's actions to his social and psychological background, *The Outsider* remains imperfect as a novel; but as a racial discourse it closely reflects American social reality. Some of its faults are therefore structural rather than philosophical. Given the kind of life Damon has lived, it is not difficult to understand his nihilistic view of the world when he states that "man is nothing in particular" (*O*, 135), or his conciliatory vision that man "is all we've got. . . . I wish I could ask men to meet themselves" (*O*, 439). But, as some critics have pointed out, it is difficult to believe that a young man with such mundane problems, renewing his life through a subway accident, suddenly emerges as a philosopher discussing Nietzsche, Heidegger, and Kierkegaard. J. Saunders Redding considers *The Outsider* "often labored, frequently naive, and generally incredible." Another reviewer finds it impossible to relate Wright's "passionless slayer" to the Cross Damon of book 1 and says, "We can identify with the first Cross Damon, but not the later one. Wright goes out of his way to make this identification impossible."[17] While in *The Stranger* the two parts of the story are so structured that each enlightens the other, in *The Outsider* the hero's life before and after the accident are constructed as though they were two tales.

This weakness notwithstanding, *The Outsider* is unquestionably a powerful statement made by an outsider who refuses to surrender his will to live. One can scarcely find among black heroes in American fiction such a courageous and tenacious, albeit violent, man. As compared to Bigger Thomas, Wright's celebrated hero, Damon stands taller and poles apart simply because Damon is endowed with an intellectual capacity seldom seen in African American fiction. It is no wonder that when the novel came out, critics in general, both white and black, who were unfamiliar with such a character, failed to appreciate Wright's intention and execution in the book. Orville Prescott's *New York Times* review was a typical white critic's reaction to *The Outsider*. With due respect for Wright's previous successes, Prescott politely insisted that Wright must have deplored Damon's moral weakness and irrational behavior at the end of the book, and further remarked, "That men as brilliant as Richard Wright feel this way is one of the symptoms of the intellectual and moral crisis of our times." Saunders Redding, in his review in the

17. See Redding's review in *Baltimore Afro-American,* in Reilly, 225–27; and Melvin Altschuler, "An Important, but Exasperating Book," in Reilly, 203–4.

Baltimore Afro-American, quoted earlier, noted that Wright's brand of existentialism, instead of being a device for the representation of truth, "leads away from rather than toward reality." Arna Bontemps was even sarcastic in *Saturday Review:* "The black boy from Mississippi is still exploring. He has had a roll in the hay with the existentialism of Sartre, and apparently he liked it."

. The strengths of *The Outsider* become clearer as this novel is compared with *The Stranger.* Although Damon professes to be a nihilist, as does Meursault, he is never indifferent to human existence, as is Meursault. Camus's hero is called a stranger to society as well as to himself; he is indifferent to friendship, marriage, love, success, freedom. Ironically, Damon, who seeks these things in life, fails to obtain them. It is ironic, too, that Meursault, to whom they are at his disposal, is indifferent to them. Wright's hero, an outsider racially as well as intellectually, struggles to get inside. Damon wants to be treated as an individual, not as a second-class citizen or a person whose intellectual ability is not recognized. By contrast, Camus's hero, an insider but a stranger, strives to get outside.

It is hardly coincidental, then, that both novels are eloquent social criticisms in our times. *The Outsider* is an indictment against American society, for not only does Wright maintain Damon's innocence but he shows most convincingly that men in America "hate themselves and it makes them hate others" (*O,* 439). *The Stranger,* on the other hand, is an indictment against French society, for Camus proves that while the criminal is innocent, his judges are guilty. More significantly, however, comparison of the two novels with their differing characters and traditions reveals that both Wright and Camus were writing ultimately about a universal human condition.

7

Black Power
Race, Politics, and African Culture

1

Racial conflict in America has stirred the imagination of distinguished novelists like Mark Twain and William Faulkner, not to mention such African American writers as Zora Neale Hurston, Ralph Ellison, James Baldwin, and Toni Morrison, but none has dealt with the problem as deeply and as widely as has Richard Wright. In his earlier fiction, *Uncle Tom's Children* and *Native Son*, as well as in his earlier nonfiction, *12 Million Black Voices* and *Black Boy*, Wright addresses racial issues that affect American society in general and the lives of African Americans in particular. As he theorizes in "Blueprint for Negro Writing," his earlier work serves as a model for the African American writer who "is being called upon to do no less than create values by which his race is to struggle, live and die." Such writing, Wright says, is endowed with "a consciousness which draws for its strength upon the fluid lore of a great people, and moulds this lore with the concepts that move and direct the forces of history today."[1] By contrast, *Black Power* (1954), *The Color Curtain* (1956), and *Pagan Spain* (1957), the three books in his main period of nonfiction, were not only written while he was in exile in another country but are also concerned with race, culture, and politics on another continent.

1. "Blueprint for Negro Writing," 43.

In his earlier work, Wright took great pains to express the long-suppressed voices of black people in America—personally as in *Black Boy*, individually as in *Uncle Tom's Children* and *Native Son*, and collectively as in *12 Million Black Voices*. "Blueprint for Negro Writing" emphasizes that the voices must convey "the nationalist implications of their lives," the spirit of freedom and independence in black people that is also ingrained in the national character. Although freedom and independence for all Americans are guaranteed in the Constitution, Wright charges, these rights are not upheld and are often denied black people. To him black nationalism "means a nationalism . . . that knows its ultimate aims are unrealizable within the framework of capitalist America."[2] To support his assertion, he uses Marxism in analyzing the relationship between the economic disparity of black and white people and racial oppression.

The Outsider, which preceded *Black Power*, was written partly under the influences of French existentialist novelists, especially Sartre and Camus. Wright's own existential thinking in *The Outsider* had an immediate impact on his writing of *Black Power*. In *The Outsider*, however, Cross Damon is not consistently an existentialist: he wavers in his judgment, particularly when concerned with political thoughts. In a highly theoretical discussion with the Communist Party dialectician Blimin, Damon posits various approaches to the accomplishment of modern industrialism, pragmatic ideas that counteract capitalistic exploitation. Judging Russian Communism merely as one of the Marxist theories and practices, Damon accuses the Russian leaders of a dictatorship, a smoke screen under which they rule, deprive the people of individualism, and, ironically, exploit them. In short, Russian Marxism is antithetical to Damon's version of existentialism.

Another influence *The Outsider* had on the writing of *Black Power* was Wright's idea of "a double vision," explained by Ely Houston, New York District Attorney. "Negroes, as they enter our culture," Houston as Wright's mouthpiece says, "are going to inherit the problems we have, but with a difference" (*O*, 129). Even though Damon tries to alienate himself from the world, while dying he seizes upon a vision that enables him to see himself as belonging to American culture. The acquisition of independent vision, something Wright considers imperative for African

2. Ibid., 42.

Americans, would also apply to the leaders of the Third World. In *Black Power*, Kwame Nkrumah's success is attributed not to his pragmatic application of Russian Marxist tactics, but to his principles of autonomy and self-reliance, a vision that he had achieved by living in the West as an outsider as well as in Africa as an insider. *Black Power*, as a nonfiction narrative, also draws its impetus from a double vision Wright himself establishes throughout the text. In 1953, when he traveled to Africa to write *Black Power*, not only was he an American exile in Paris, an outsider, but his African experience convinced him that he was an outsider in Africa as well, but an insider of American culture.

The motive for writing *Black Power* is clearly given at the beginning of the book. Nkrumah as prime minister of the colonial Gold Coast had written a letter of recommendation for Wright's travel, stating that the purpose for his visit was to "do some research into the social and historical aspects of the country."[3] The brief preface, "Apropos Prepossessions," indicates that the audience for the book is the West and that Wright intended both to comment on politics in this emerging nation and to analyze the mysterious tribal culture. Even though his discussion of politics is based on a layman's understanding of economics and history and his cultural criticism is largely intuitive rather than anthropological, his conclusions yield startling revelations about African culture and an African American's visceral reactions to it.

Wright's intention to relate discourse on politics to that on culture is revealed in the very first pages of the book, in the passages "To the Unknown African" and in three quotations, from Countee Cullen, Walt Whitman, and Robert Briffault. "To the Unknown African" conveys an observation derived from Wright's African experience that the African was victimized by slave traders "because of his primal and poetic humanity." African culture, Wright remarks, "created a vision of life so simple as to be terrifying, yet a vision that was irreducibly human." The quotations from both Cullen and Whitman suggest that Africans, the inheritors and products of nature, have been exploited by a materialistic civilization. To Cullen, Africa three centuries ago was inhabited by "Strong bronzed men, or regal black / Women from whose loins I sprang / When the birds of Eden sang?" Before Europeans appeared with their machines, the continent had thrived on its pastoral idylls replete with

---

3. Richard Wright, *Black Power: A Record of Reactions in a Land of Pathos,* before preface. Subsequent references will appear parenthetically in the text as *BP.*

"*Spicy grove,* cinnamon tree." Now it exists at the services of Western traders who exploit African products. In a similar vein, Whitman's line *"Not till the sun excludes you do I exclude you"* expresses not merely his compassion for African Americans but strongly their natural and divine heritage. And Briffault's passage alludes to Westerners' underestimation of and prejudice against the African heritage: "The entire course of development of the human race, from whatever point of view it may be regarded, whether intellectual, economic, industrial, social, or ethical, is as a whole and in detail coincident with the course of transmitted social heredity." Whitman's line and Briffault's statement, though, provide two different interpretations of the human race. Whitman considers the sun a sign of Africa as well as of nature: black people must be free as nature is free, for the sun does not exclude them. While Whitman sees humans as natural beings, Briffault considers them social beings.

In *Culture and Imperialism,* Edward Said has recently proposed two separate definitions of the word *culture.* In one definition culture means "all those practices, like the arts of descriptions, communication, and representation, that have relative autonomy from the economic, social, and political realms and that often exist in aesthetic forms." Another definition equates culture with "a concept that includes a refining and elevating element, each society's reservoir of the best that has been known and thought, as Matthew Arnold put it in the 1860s."[4] Partly because the second definition, evoking a Victorian critic and aesthetician, is outdated and is mindful of Euro-centrism, and primarily because such a categorization of culture smacks of "cultural war," this definition scarcely fits Wright's analysis of African culture. His study was intended as a search for the intrinsic elements of African culture, what he calls the "primal and poetic humanity" that has made the African people African as well as human. In the course of his investigation not as an anthropologist or social historian but as a creative writer, he discovers the innate human values shared by all cultures with, to borrow Chomskian terms, the "deep structure" of African culture. As a result, Wright's portrayal often takes issue with characteristics reported by anthropologists and historians, descriptions that often reflect the "surface structure" of the culture.

Because Wright attempted to seek out the deeply rooted human values, insulated as they were from economic and political circumstances, Said's first definition applies to *Black Power.* Wright, in fact,

4. *Culture and Imperialism,* xii–xiii.

found such a human value as tribal and familial kinship to be a crucial element for the survival of African culture. The sense of loyalty is so profoundly ingrained in African character that Nkrumah used it to solidify his otherwise fragile socialist government. Wright's observation of human values differs from those of anthropologists and historians simply because such investigators have a tendency to analyze the values in terms of Western culture and from the perspective of Western aesthetic standards. Whereas anthropological and sociological interpretations are inclined to be monolithic, Wright's views are cross-cultural and often multicultural.

His comparative stance thus makes *Black Power* a subjective but informed study that confirms his a priori concept of African history and culture. *Black Power,* indeed, has an affinity with an ideological novel like *The Outsider* rather than with a satiric one like *Lawd Today. Lawd Today* is narrated by the author, who makes a series of commentaries on various individuals appearing on the scenes. Instead of many voices engaged in complex dialogues, *Lawd Today* privileges a single, authoritative voice that expresses Wright's moral and social views, just as Swift presents his moral and political ideas in *Gulliver's Travels.* By contrast *Black Power* is narrated in the form of multiple discourse. Throughout the text, the narrator's consciousness remains a battleground where other voices—those of Africans and colonialists, of politicians and workers, of journalists and social scientists—are engaged in various discussions.

As multiple voices are presented, the narrator assumes a variety of poses—traveler, journalist, political scientist, historian, and philosopher. In fact, before writing *Black Power,* Wright had been not only a Marxist sympathizer in politics but a novelist in the tradition of American realism represented by Dreiser, Lewis, and Anderson. In *Black Power,* the multiple views and opinions develop at two seemingly different levels of the narrative. At one level, the book, like a picaresque novel, tells a number of unrelated episodes found on the road; at another level the narrator contrasts Marxist politicians with British colonialists, imperialistic British officials with liberal-minded British subjects, Nkrumah's associates with his rivals, Anglicized Africans with indigenous Africans. As a travelogue, the book portrays fascinating rituals and customs in tribal life: hiding the corpse and representing the dead by their nails and hair at the funeral service; fearing, revering, and abstaining from sexual relations with menstruating women. At the same time the book provides degrading portraits of African and Western men: on a ship

Wright encountered a Nigerian Supreme Court justice who, during a stopover on a coastal island, visited a brothel with European prostitutes; at a cocktail party given in Wright's honor, a British guest told hilarious jokes about some natives, as if they were slaves, calling them savages and damned fools. Instead of discussing the negative characteristics of such men, Wright lets them unwittingly reveal themselves. While *Black Power* thrives upon such episodes, they in turn reveal the ways in which European colonialism and imperialism had eroded the social mores of Africans and Westerners alike.

Because each of the many descriptions of personal conduct and opinion is linked to a particular culture and a particular way of seeing and understanding experience at a particular point in history, there arises an intense dialogue—sometimes assumed, sometimes vocalized—among these different points of view. For example, Wright, though an outsider, clearly saw that Nkrumah, an insider, tried to relate tribal culture with leftist politics. On the other side of the historical development, Wright observed a tacit conflict between the Christian missionary and African nationalism, as well as overt strife between colonial exploitation and Marxist politics. Unlike a typical novel of ideas, *Black Power* constantly presents a dialogue as it is manifested in its concrete, living totality— that is, a discussion as it takes place in a context to represent the point of view of an actual, specific individual or group of people. The discourse in *Black Power* thus resembles that in *Black Boy*, in which the central vision is personal, or echoes that in *12 Million Black Voices*, which presents a collective, historical outlook. The uniqueness of *Black Power*, though, lies in a coalescence of personal, collective, and historical perspectives. This narrative strategy in *Black Power* is similar to the creation of a nonfictional persona John M. Reilly sees in *American Hunger*. "Without protecting his ego," Reilly explains, "he extends sympathy toward those from whom he differs, acknowledging the significance of the understanding of collective life he shares with them, while retaining confidence in the integrity of his own analysis of reality."[5]

The conclusions drawn from the dialogues and episodes are not only representative and objective but ultimately personal. "This volume," the preface states, "is a first-person, subjective narrative on the life and conditions of the Colony and Ashanti areas of the Gold Coast, an

5. "The Self-Creation of the Intellectual: *American Hunger* and *Black Power*," 221.

area comprising perhaps the most highly socially evolved native life of present-day Africa" (*BP*, xiv). In contrast with a conventional travelogue or autobiography, Wright's nonfiction, *Black Power* in particular, begins its discourse with very personal, subjective assumptions about the subject matter, goes through a series of external visions, and yet returns to its original premise and rationalization. In Socratic dialectics, opposing values and beliefs genuinely counteract one another, but in Wright's discourse, a priori, humanistic points of view prevail over materialistic, racially oppressive attitudes in a form of self-creation as seen in *Black Boy*. In *Black Power*, given an African American writer's experience in America and abroad, the narrator compellingly subverts, in the name of universal humanism, the representations of colonialism and imperialism, convention and hegemony. Wright thus attained such privileged dominance over the dialogues that occurred in his African journey that he had the audacity to advise as prominent a world statesman as Nkrumah.

2

Although *Black Power* turned out to be Wright's personal and subjective analysis of African culture, his immediate motive in writing the book was to observe the birth of an independent African nation, Ghana, and to account for the political activities involved in that event. The twofold motive of the book is suggested by the fact that Wright had some difficulty in deciding on its title. As Michel Fabre indicates, Wright considered such titles as "This Heritage," "Black Brothers," "Dark Heritage," "Africa Turns Black," "Ancestral Land," and "Ancestral Home," all of which represent the major perspectives he acquired in his travel. But, as he wrote to Margrit de Sablonière, "The title: *Black Power* means political and state power. I did not have in mind any racial meaning."[6]

Upon Wright's arrival in the Gold Coast in 1953, the country was still a colonial state under British rule; Kwame Nkrumah (1909–1970), head of the Convention People's Party, was leading the state to the threshold of independence. Nkrumah was the prime minister from 1957 to 1960 of

6. Quoted in Nina Kressner Cobb, "Richard Wright and the Third World," 238.

the British Commonwealth nation and served as the first president of the independent Ghana between 1960 and 1966. Before independence, the country, then comprising the Gold Coast colony, the Ashanti kingdom, the Northern territories, and the Togoland trust territory, was the direct descendant of a West African empire that had flourished in the fourth through thirteenth centuries. Nkrumah was a tribal member-turned-intellectual who had been educated in England and lived in America as well as in the Soviet Union. He was enormously popular among his people because of his ability to use a leftist political strategy and because of the respect and support given him by the British government.

Although Wright's visit was made possible by Nkrumah's official invitation and both cherished a warm, friendly relationship, one can hardly overlook remarkable differences between their backgrounds. Wright found Nkrumah a pragmatic Marxist: Nkrumah was trying to reconcile tribal life with a classless social structure, on the one hand, and empower the workers with the support of the colonialists, on the other. By contrast, Wright was not a pragmatist, nor was he entirely sympathetic to Marxist theories, to which he had paid serious attention while in Chicago and New York in the 1930s and 1940s before becoming a permanent exile in Paris in 1947. While living in the northern cities of the United States, he "held consciously in [his] hands Marxist Communism as an instrumentality to effect such political and social changes" (*BP*, xi). The reason for his disenchantment with Communism is given in *American Hunger:* even though Communist doctrine can be put into practice for workers, it deprives intellectuals like him of freedom of thought. "It was inconceivable to me," he writes, "though bred in the lap of southern hate, that a man could not have his say. I had spent a third of my life traveling from the place of my birth to the North just to talk freely, to escape the pressure of fear. And now I was facing fear again." He broke with the Communist Party because it demanded that he subordinate his writing to its needs. "Writing," he responded, "had to be done in loneliness and Communism had declared war upon human loneliness."[7]

In *Black Power* he reiterates the reason for his relinquishing of membership in the Communist Party. His leaving the party "was caused

---

7. *American Hunger*, 92, 123. The manuscript for the book was originally included in the manuscript for *Black Boy* but omitted from the Harper edition of *Black Boy* in 1944.

by my conviction that Marxist Communism, though it was changing the world, was changing that world in a manner that granted me even less freedom than I had possessed before" (*BP,* xi). Although the circumstances under which he disagreed with Communist doctrine in America differ from those Nkrumah faced in West Africa, Wright further makes this observation: "Perhaps, in time, I could have brought myself to accept this Communist suppression of freedom on a temporary basis, but when historic events disclosed that international Communism was mainly an instrument of Russian foreign policy, I publicly and responsibly dropped its instrumentality and disassociated myself from it" (*BP,* xi–xii). He wants the reader to know that Communism in America stifled the artistic integrity of a writer and warns Nkrumah that Communists are intent on undermining the political integrity of a liberator like Nkrumah.

As long as Communism succeeded in devising a system by which oppressed and disadvantaged people could be liberated, Wright would have continued his association with its movement. From today's vantage point, his warning to Africans about Communism was indeed prophetic, but it was also aimed at the dangers inherent in capitalism, as he stressed in the preface:

> Yet, as an American Negro whose life is governed by racial codes written into law, I state clearly that my abandonment of Communism does not automatically place me in a position of endorsing and supporting all the policies, political and economic, of the non-Communist world. Indeed, it was the inhuman nature of many of those policies, racial and otherwise, that led me to take up the instrumentality of Communism in the first place. (*BP,* xii)

By "the inhuman nature" of non-Communist policies, he clearly indicts capitalism for its exploitation of the poor and the less privileged. To account for this inhuman system of economics and politics, he uses the Marxist analysis of African colonial history.

His Marxist interpretation of economic history focuses on the most painful and inhuman event in human history, the slave trade. He places as an epigraph to part 1, "Approaching Africa," a passage from Eric Williams's *Capitalism and Slavery:* "Only in one particular did the freedom accorded in the slave trade differ from the freedom accorded in other trades—the commodity involved was man" (*BP,* 1). The epigraph is a poignant reminder for Wright, who was taken by a friend of

Nkrumah's to a large, modern store that exported timber, where he was asked by the sales clerks about his ancestors. One of them nonchalantly asked, "What part of Africa did you come from, sar?" After a pause another persisted, "Haven't you tried to find out where in Africa you came from, sar?" Embarrassed and offended, Wright responded with a note of irony: "Well . . . you know, you fellows who sold us and the white men who bought us didn't keep any records" (BP, 35). Recording such a conversation reveals his belief that the culprit of the slave trade was not only colonialism but also capitalism and its corollary, greed. Greed, therefore, corrupted Western buyers and African sellers alike. Constantly reminded of the detrimental aspects of capitalism, he became critical of the West's imposition of industrialism on African life. At one point he visited a tribal community that looked poor but offered spiritual warmth and family kinship. "And suddenly," he comments, "I was self-conscious; I began to question myself, my assumptions. I was assuming that these people had to be pulled out of this life . . . had to become literate and eventually industrialized. But why? Was not the desire for that mostly on my part rather than theirs? I was literate, Western, disinherited, and industrialized and I felt each day the pain and anxiety of it. Why then must I advocate the dragging of these people into my trap?" (BP, 147).

Despite this skepticism about the inevitable industrialization and modernization of Africa, Wright could not find at hand any alternative economic or political solutions, nor could he help merely observing the ways in which Nkrumah's Convention People's Party was operating. In a lengthy discussion with one Dr. Ampofo, a distinguished African physician trained in Edinburgh, he confirmed his view that Nkrumah's party was not a Communist movement, for the Communists had called his movement "corrupt, bourgeois nationalism." Wright remarks: "Some aspects of this movement seem to partake of Leftism; other aspects are almost religious in their emotional expression. Sometimes one must use Marxist ideas to aid one in trying to grasp what one is looking at, but Marxism cannot satisfactorily account for this." For one thing, this colonial state in the early 1950s did not have much industry and hence had no need for many workers to be recruited from the tribal communities. Since there were no masses of people in the country, there arose no class consciousness. The race consciousness in the Gold Coast, as Wright realized, was not as acute as that of African Americans, and yet there arose a passionate political movement. "There's a creative energy in these people," the physician told him. "The Akan is a stubborn and proud man. There is in him a consciousness of national humiliation and there is a deep race consciousness, deeper than you think." When the men reached the point of discussing a mysterious ritual called *juju,* a tribal oath binding the Akan men, the dialogue verged on disbelief and absurdity on both sides, and they changed the topic (*BP,* 198–201).

The tribal people and the Westernized intellectuals and businessmen Wright met all betrayed hesitancy, apathy, and at times lack of self-confidence in their country. The stagnation, he recognized, interfered with Nkrumah's efforts to modernize the political machinery. The ultimate problem in this situation derived from European colonialism and imperialism, which had oppressed African culture for the past five or more centuries. As Wright observed the struggle of this country, he saw that the religious customs of the people were upheld by Nkrumah and his followers undisturbed partly because the British had adopted only indirect rule over the masses and their daily living. As often in non-Western countries, tribal rituals and customs in Ghana were kept intact in the hinterland while Westernization took place in the coastal area. To operate their mines and timber industry, however, the British imposed their social and economic system on tribal life; consequently, with the exhortation of the missionaries, the African people's faith in their own religion had gradually been destroyed. This impact of colonialism upon African life, in turn, created massive detribalized Africans who led frustrating lives in two cultures and believed in neither of them.

Similarly, Wright points out that in America the native American Indians, rather than African Americans, were the first to be enslaved by Europeans in the new world. And the European colonialists, finding the native Americans temperamentally unsuitable for hard labor in a warm climate, exploited poor white servants and convicts. In every experiment to harness human beings to the workforce under the banner of progress, as Wright emphasizes, the colonialists were intent on destroying the traditional and spiritual values in the lives of the victims. In a speech to the people of Ghana, he stated: "I'm one of the lost sons of Africa who has come back to look upon the land of his forefathers. In a superficial sense it may be said that I'm a stranger to most of you, but, in terms of a common heritage of suffering and hunger for freedom, your heart and my heart beat as one" (*BP,* 77). The sincerity and warmth in this speech are poignantly contrasted with the disgrace and coldness betrayed by one Judge Thomas, a high-ranking puppet of the British imperialists, who visited a "shabby whorehouse" on the Canary Islands, as mentioned earlier. "Mr. Justice," Wright says, "represented the victory of enlightenment: he could read, he could vote, he was free; but he was adamant against the hungers of the new generation." With pathos and bitterness, Wright finishes his portrait of this African intellectual: "Mr. Justice's grandfather had been a hero to him, but I doubted if Mr. Justice's children would regard him in a heroic light. He wanted his children to be black Englishmen" (*BP*, 27).

By various juxtapositions of personalities and ideas Wright advances his argument not through a book of protest but through a book of analysis. He shows how deeply and widely colonialism and imperialism had left their marks on the oppressed. "Colonialism and imperialism," as Frantz Fanon notes, "have not paid their scores when they withdraw their flags and their police forces from our territories. For centuries the Capitalists have behaved in the undeveloped world like nothing more than criminals."[8] Fanon's characterization of these Europeans reflects Wright's image of a thief muffled in the cloak of a teacher or preacher: "So this was the White Man's burden that England had been so long complaining about? How cleverly the whole thing had been explained to the outside world! How wrapped up and disguised in morality had this lust for gold become!" (*BP*, 151). By way of a casual conversation with a young African electrician, Wright illustrates an overwhelming irony in modern African history. "And after they had taught you to read," he told the African, "you read, didn't you? And when you read you found out that the British had taken your country? Is that it?" The man responded slowly and evasively: "I know the history of my country, sar. We were conquered" (*BP*, 148).

What is remarkable about Wright's discourse on history is its demonstration that the damages inflicted on African culture had not always been at the hands of the colonialists and imperialists, but had also come from a lack of courage and integrity on the part of Africans, a trait derived from the invaders, in tacit collaboration with the materialistic Europeans and Africans. Wright had a sustained discussion about crime with Mr. X, a Scotland Yard–trained law-enforcement officer Wright called the most liberal-minded Englishman. Wright assumed that Africans' criminal behavior was different from that of colonialists,

8. *The Wretched of the Earth*, 101.

but Mr. X told him: "The same thing that makes an Englishman steal makes an African steal. There's but one slight difference: the African is more prone to be prouder of his theft than the Englishman." Not only did this discussion allude to the idea of a thief noticing another thief, but both discussants agreed that the African thief's crime could be exonerated more justifiably than the Englishman's because the African would have been acting in order to get even with colonial injustice. The motive for killing, as Wright realized, was also the same as that for stealing, for, as Mr. X explained, "The African feels that he has done right, most of the time" (*BP,* 209).

The culprits of colonialism in the Gold Coast, however, had not always been just the merchants of England; they had also included the Christian missionaries, who should have objected to the inhuman, immoral trade of goods for people. If the missionaries had read history, as Wright did, "the industrial and mercantile interests could come to terms with a rising nationalism" (*BP,* 55). To him they were jealous by their religious nature and panicked at the prospect of a popular nationalism that was to create new institutions, attitudes, and values for Africans. Ironically, Nkrumah's nationalism became a new form of religion, "politics *plus!*" (*BP,* 56). The missionaries over the centuries, moreover, had been bent upon infusing in the minds of Africans the superiority of their religion, race, and culture. Their attitudes had in turn bred the inferiority of the African people; consequently, African life psychologically came to reflect the European assumptions of African inferiority. A typical African intellectual, for instance, loved the white person simply because that person looked powerful, secure, and occasionally generous, and at the same time the African hated him or her because the white person's power was used to strip the black person of dignity, tradition, and humanity. With a bit of sarcasm, Wright mentions Africans' buying canned food imported from Europe, their relying on kerosene in lieu of local fats, their abandoning of weaving and buying of wools from Lancashire, their going to the Christian churches for social activities and going to "the Stool House" for rituals to propitiate the spirits of their ancestors. What was, in the beginning, merely the Western assumption of the inferiority of the African became a reality, because the degrading conditions in which the African was forced to live created the inferiority complex, a self-deception.

In sum, racial and political discourse in *Black Power* gains its intensity by juxtaposing binary points of view, a clear-cut rather than dialectical structuring of signals and reverse signals. Throughout the text Wright gives the signal that the colonialists, imperialists, and missionaries indoctrinated Africans with an inferiority complex, while at the same time giving the reverse signal that the Europeans cherished and clung to their superiority complex. The Europeans residing in West Africa, as Wright saw, were materialistic and often greedy; they failed to understand, and find an affinity for, the African way of life. In reverse, the Africans' outlook on life was largely spiritual and genuinely religious, however superstitious they appeared to an African American like Wright. The narrator presents the signals in presenting the colonial businessmen: they wanted to get rich; that is, they wanted Africans to remain poor. Similarly, the British soldiers in Africa had no compunction in killing the natives because they regarded them as their enemies. Wright's narrative leads to an ironic, perhaps sarcastic, pair of signals about the Christian crusaders in Africa, whose mission was to "save" (*BP,* 158). But, isolated, lonely, and away from home, they were bent upon saving themselves.

3

In contrast with the social and political conditions of the colonial state, the indigenous culture in the region Wright visited was shrouded in deep religious mysteries. He met the King of Ashanti, Otumfuo Sir Osei Agyeman Prempeh II, whose lineage dates back to an ancient kingdom that flourished at the time of the Roman empire. Not only was Wright given an audience by the king, but he was presented by the king's grandson to the chief of Mampong, Nana Asofo Kamtantea II. He then was met, with varying levels of ceremony, by various personages, all men, who occupied royal and tribal ministerial positions in the hierarchies of the kingdom and tribes. His observations and impressions about Ashanti's tribal culture thus led to his analyses and theories about African culture, a body of fact and knowledge that had little relevance to the political operation of the state.

Wright came away with the notion that whereas the profound myths, traditions, and customs constituting African culture were in the way of its modernization, they were still the essence and power that buttressed what he calls the African survival. He disagreed with the anthropologists and social historians who characterized African culture as primitive and irrational. But "the African will always seem a 'savage,' " he says, just as the new developments in the non-African world are "fantastic" to the African (*BP,* 117). The Western definition of the inferiority of the African race, he explains in *Black Power,* had derived from the hegemonic assumptions of academicians, assumptions that were only remotely related to the underlying assumptions of the African beliefs. In short, African culture looks irrational to Westerners just as Western culture does to Africans.

Despite an attempt to separate the African and non-African perspectives of African culture, Wright could not help searching for the commonalities of the two cultures. Partly guided by his Marxist predilections, he found an affinity between African tribalism and Communism. During his visit to a tribal community in Akan, he came upon a young American-educated informant who provided him with a description of the dependence of tribal life on family kinship:

> "The uncle's sister's blood flows in the nephew's veins. . . .
> Look, if an African makes £100,000, do you think he can keep it?
> No. His family moves in and stays with him until that money is
> gone. You see, the family here is more of an economic unit than
> in the West. . . . Let's say that an African family has gotten hold
> of a few thousand pounds. They'll hold a family meeting and
> decide to send Kojo, say, to London to study medicine. Now,
> they are not giving that money to Kojo; they are *investing* it in
> him and when he masters his medical subjects, returns home,
> and starts practicing, the family stops working and goes and
> lives with Kojo for the rest of their lives. That's their way of
> collecting their dividends, a kind of intimate coupon clipping,
> you might say." (*BP,* 100)

Emphasizing the tight organization of modern tribal society, the informant told Wright that tribal members seldom became wealthy but that they "never starve. . . . It's Communism, but without any of the ideas of Marx or Lenin. It has a sacred origin" (*BP,* 100).

The genesis of African survival, then, is what Wright understood to be the African concept of divinity, based on *The Akan Doctrine of God* by Dr. J. B. Danquah, "lawyer, philosopher, politician, dramatist, and long-time nationalist leader" (*BP,* 171–72), the book recommended by the informant. Wright also consulted Eva L. R. Meyerowitz's *The Sacred State of the Akan,* which Wright says "some Ashanti intellectuals sneer at" (*BP,* 335). Danquah and Meyerowitz both indicate that the Ashanti traditionally consider the sun the origin of their society, a concept and practice remindful of the ancient religion of Shintoism, the Japanese state religion, in which the sun goddess called Ama-Terasu Ohmi Kami (Heaven-Shining Great God) rules the universe. From another perspective, the division of the sexes as practiced in the Akan religion is akin to the Confucius analects that male and female children over seven years of age must not sit together. Although Wright's interpretation of African religion was largely derived from his reading, much of his understanding came intuitively from his own observations of tribal life. As the sun, which to Africans, and indeed to all humanity, seems the most powerful sign of nature, and thus controlled their lives, so did the king rule over his tribes, the chief over his families, the father over his children. The salient distinction Wright saw between the native African communism and the family system in the West, whether it was capitalistic, socialistic, or communistic, was the Africans' belief in the power of nature and their traditional denial of individualism. The African communism, another informant told Wright, saves an individual from want, "for all he has to do is go to another relative and sponge on him. Individual initiative is not very popular in Africa. Why amass a lot of money? You'll have to give it away anyhow" (*BP*, 245). Given his own hostility to the suppression of individualism in any form, Wright was not convinced of the values the informant tried to explain. But the African's testimony once more reminded him of materialism and pecuniary greed, the twin culprits in Western life that had spared African life.

The primacy of kinship over individualism, though it originated from the African tradition, was a defense mechanism to fend off the onslaught of industrialism and imperialism, a form of African nationalism that opposed the cross-cultural political conditions in Africa. Wright's description of his visit to the Ashanti tribes, therefore, focused on his attempt to decipher their concepts of life and existence. What he at first saw struck him as indeed primitive and superstitious, but he was nevertheless transported with joy and excitement. And eventually he came away with awe and respect, gaining a great sense of pride in African culture he had not had before.

What he saw in the religious practices suggests that he considered some of it extremely superstitious: "All of this seems bizarre to me; I can't conceive of myself ever believing any of it" (*BP*, 336–37). For example, he was told that accidents often occurred to African log transporters because of their carelessness in handling their vehicles and because of their belief in "*juju*" (*BP*, 327), a superstition even the natives laughed about. Such an anecdote made him realize that African workers, lacking self-confidence, blamed others for their own failure. From another perspective, however, much of the African religious belief seemed quite abstract and hence highly philosophical and psychological. He was impressed by the African concept of time, which "oscillated between the present and the past." Believing in a circular movement of time, the African "exerted his will to make what had happened happen again" (*BP,* 174–75). Africa, he thought, could use Western technology and industrialization, but such a concept of time would be detrimental to modernization. On arrival in Africa, before going to Kumasi, the Ashanti capital, Wright stayed in Accra, the coastal city. At once he noticed that houses in the city had no street numbers, a lack that not only indicated a chaotic urban development but also suggested a circular concept of time and place. Having no numbers assigned to individual houses suggested that they had come to their existence regardless of order and location and that the city functioned like a maze. Jack B. Moore has recently written about Wright's impressions of Accra, which looked sordid and decaying, and remarks: "True, the Old Slave Market in Christiansborg is crumbling, its walls rotting and columns broken into rubble . . . but that is made to seem not a symbol of the old life's death, but of the constant decay of matter in the city where Ghana's new life will soon be constructed and centered."[9]

Although Wright appreciated the ancestral worship not only characteristic of the African religion but typical of other religions such as Buddhism and Hinduism, he was unable to penetrate the detail and symbolism of its mystery. He had no difficulty understanding, for example, the dedication of an African woman's life to preparing and serving food to "the bones of the dead king" (*BP,* 272), a ritual analogous to a Buddhist woman's service in offering food to statues of the Buddha. Just as a menstruating woman is feared in Ashanti life, a Shintoist woman in the same condition abstains from consecrating the food to be presented at the household shrine. On the other hand, he found it difficult to appreciate the symbolism of the Golden Stool, "upon which no man sits but which itself lies upon its side upon a special throne of its own." Wright simply interpreted the stool as "the magic that makes more than a million people one. Ashanti is vaguely Oriental;

9. "'No Street Numbers in Accra': Richard Wright's African Cities," 71.

there is something hidden here, a soul that shrinks from revealing itself" (*BP*, 273). In effect, Western language is incapable of representing the depth of the tribal culture. Africans, conscious of the unwritten history, have created "methods of verbal jockeying to cast doubt into the minds" of the Westerners who would attempt to understand them. To Wright, language could not account for such culture, for "the Ashanti had secrets *behind* secrets; and if I pried out *those* so-called secrets, he could at once allude to still other and more dreadful secrets behind *those* secrets, and so on" (*BP*, 290).

Judging such rituals and customs as the vestiges of a primitive culture, the British were bent upon shattering what had once given meaning to the Ashanti. It is sheer irony that the colonialists and imperialists, with their condescension and with the support of the missionaries, contributed to the rise of the nationalism of the Ashanti, "a hunger to regain control over their lives and create a new sense of their destinies" (*BP*, 91). It is also ironic, for instance, that bribery, a colonial vice learned from greedy British businessmen, was an illegal and criminal conduct in Western society but had an unwitting resemblance to the tradition of favoritism regarded as correct and viable, and on occasion honorable, in tribal customs.

The destructive forces of Western culture notwithstanding, African culture resisted its influences and kept intact its own basic, primal view of existence. In *Black Power*, Wright is adamantly opposed to the Western concept of "African survivals," the perspective of those who measure the cultural development in terms of science and technology and whose goal in life is to amass a fortune. "The African attitude toward life," he maintains, "springs from a natural and poetic grasp of existence and all the emotional implications that such an attitude carries." How much African culture an African retained under European oppression or when the person was transplanted to another culture such as America "is not a racial, but a cultural problem, cutting across such tricks as measuring of skulls and intelligence tests." For an illustration, Wright contrasts the cultural traits of a person of African heritage with those of a European immigrant:

> There is no reason why an African or a person of African descent—in America, England, or France—should abandon his primal outlook upon life if he finds that no other way of life is available, or if he is intimidated in his attempt to grasp the

new way. (It must be said, however, that the African, in his effort to assimilate the Western attitude, starts from a point of reference that is not completely shared by the Irish, the Italians, the Poles, or other immigrants. The tribal African's culture *is* primally human; that which *all* men once had as their warm, indigenous way of living, is his. . . .) There is nothing mystical or biological about it. When one realizes that one is dealing with two distinct and separate worlds of psychological being, two conceptions of time even, the problem becomes clear; it is a clash between two systems of culture. (*BP,* 266)

Although the African would easily adjust to a new environment, the rational, urban, and industrial way of living in the West, that person would as easily retain much of his or her primal and often uniquely African philosophy of life.

The attacks of the British forces on the Ashanti around the turn of the nineteenth century, for instance, had resulted in the stronger retention of their way of life. Nkrumah consequently was to gain from what the British had tried to eliminate. From the vantage point of tribal life, the African people had come to realize that the defense of their culture meant renewal of their faith in themselves. John M. Reilly maintains that the despairing characteristic of *The Outsider* is absent in *Black Power* because what African culture has come to mean to an African in *Black Power* is "positive renewal of his faith in the possibility of human reconstruction."[10] Gaining self-confidence in their own culture, Africans realized that it was also characteristic of universal human values. Such values as awe of nature, family kinship and love, faith in religion, and honor all had made what Wright calls "African survivals" possible. This primal outlook that he witnessed in African life, buttressed as it was by universal humanism, was in singular contrast with the predominantly materialistic view of life held by the British colonialists.

On the basis of Danquah's *The Akan Doctrine of God,* Wright was persuaded of the African belief that spirits reside in inanimate objects like trees, stones, and rivers. He also witnessed Africans' belief in ghosts and in the spirits of the dead. For Africans, moreover, life and death are not diametrically opposed. "Life in the ghost world," he remarks, "is an exact duplicate of life in this world. A farmer in this world is a farmer there; a chief here is a chief there. It is, therefore, of decisive

10. "The Self-Creation of the Intellectual," 225.

importance when one enters that world of ghostly shades to enter it in the right manner. For you can be snubbed there just as effectively and humiliatingly as you were snubbed here" (*BP*, 214). The African religion furthermore does not recognize, as Whitman does not, the existence of hell and sin, nor does it distinguish between good and evil, as he does not in "Song of Myself." "When the family is the chief idea," Wright quotes Danquah as saying, "things that are dishonorable and undignified, actions that in disgracing you disgrace the family, are held to be vices, and the highest virtue is found in honor and dignity. Tradition is the determinant of what is right and just, what is good and done" (*BP*, 215–16). Africans thus reject the original sin in Christian doctrine: "The notion that, because two remote ancestors had sexual relations and bore a child, there was imposed upon all mankind a threat of suffering, is, to the African mind, simply ridiculous" (*BP*, 216–17). Whereas the Akan religion and Christianity share the concept of life after death, the Akan religion resembles other religions such as Buddhism and Hinduism in its belief in incarnation and in the existence of soul in the nonhuman living. "Death," Wright observes, "does not round off life; it is not the end; it complements life." To him the African religion looks "terrifying" but not "primitive" (*BP*, 217), as any Eastern religion would strike Westerners as terrifying rather than primitive.

Before commenting on Ashanti life, he quotes a passage from Edmund Husserl's *Ideas:*

> Not only might human development have never overstepped the pre-scientific stage and been doomed never to overstep it so that the physical world might indeed retain its truth whilst we should know nothing about it; the physical world might have been other than it is with systems of law other than those actually prevailing. It is also conceivable that our intuitable world should be the last, and "beyond" it no physical world at all. (*BP*, 239)

Husserl's passage suggests the preeminence of the physical world over the scientific vision of that world and a reliance on intuition rather than on history in the search for truth. Wright thus applies Husserl's idea of human beings and their environment to an analysis of the African existence. This relationship of human beings to their world is, in some respects, reminiscent of Emerson, who emphasizes the preeminence of the spiritual and transcendental over the material and empirical. As Emerson urges his readers to think, not for the sake of accomplishing material things, but for the sake of realizing their own spiritual world, Wright interprets the primal outlook in African culture to mean the primacy of spirit over matter.

As the African concept of life is based on awe of nature, the concept of society is derived from the kinship and love in the family. "The state," Wright explains, "is owned by a female king, just as a child is regarded as being owned by its mother; the state is ruled by a male king, just as a family is headed and its affairs managed by a father. Hence, female kings are founders of states, the 'mother' of everybody in the state" (*BP,* 334– 35). As the state is buttressed by women, the family is matrilineal in its inheritance. "When a man takes a wife," an African physician informed Wright, "he cannot leave the family and live with her; he has to bring her into his family. She becomes a daughter in his family in addition to being a wife" (*BP,* 201). Africans indeed fear and revere woman, Wright stresses, because of her innate biological power, signified by the moon and the tides of the seas, and because of her longevity. "Food, and children to help to grow more food," Wright realizes, "were the crux of existence. Pray the ancestors to let us have more children so that there will be more hands to grow more food" (*BP,* 262–63). The supremacy of woman in the African state and family, therefore, reflects the universal idea of mother nature, and womanhood in *Black Power* constitutes a quintessential representation of African character.

Wright's discussion on the preeminence of woman in African culture is in striking contrast to his analysis of African American history in *12 Million Black Voices.* The latter work describes the ways in which African American men in the northern cities with their physical power and skill, competing with white workers, eclipsed the roles of African American women. Houston A. Baker Jr. has recently written an essay, "On Knowing Our Place," which, based on a historical study of *12 Million Black Voices,* shows a distinction between African American male and female places. Baker sees Wright's African American men as collaborators of northern machine culture and his African American women as domestics.

4

Before arriving in Africa, Wright had intended *Black Power* to be an objective report on the social and political conditions of a colonial state on the verge of its independence. But his journey into its hinterland shifted his focus: he became more interested in exploring the psychological and philosophical attitudes of the people. As a result, he succeeded beyond all expectations in grasping their basic way of life. While he felt awe and had a deep respect for their instinctively natural, poetic attitudes toward existence, he came away with the impression that some of the rituals and customs, as well as most of the superstitions, were in the way of building a modern nation.

Observing African life as a historian rather than as a novelist, Wright tried to exclude race from his consideration, but he could not at times help reminding himself of his own racial heritage. Interviewed by *L'Express* in 1960, Wright stated: "I am opposed to any racial definition of man. I write about racial problems precisely to bring an end to racial definitions. And I do not wish anybody in the world in which we live to look at it from a racial perspective, whether he is white, black, or yellow."[11] Although he dismissed as stereotyping the remarks made by his "defensive-minded Negro friends" that Africans are innately gifted with music and dancing, "a genius of our own" (*BP*, 5), he vividly remembered how beautifully and rhythmically African Americans had danced in storefront churches and on the plantations of the Deep South. As late as 1960, half a decade after his travels in Africa, when interviewed on radio in Paris, he was still self-conscious. Asked about the religious nature of the African people, he replied:

> When I tried to work with African Negroes, I found in their minds something mystical, a metaphysical element. And I wonder what it can be. Because it is absent in me. I think there may be a great strength in the religious spirit of American Negroes, but I wonder whether one can build a strong society upon such consciousness. I really don't know. For me, it is an open question. I wonder.[12]

Not only was he ambivalent about the spiritual and metaphysical heritage of African Americans, but his experience in Africa also created in him a sense of diffidence that this heritage, however deeply it was ingrained in them, might be detrimental to their advancement in the

11. "Interview with Richard Wright," in *Conversations with Richard Wright*, 201.
12. Georges Charbonnier, "A Negro Novel about White People," in *Conversations with Richard Wright*, 237.

twentieth-century world of cross- and multiculturalism. I agree with Edward Said, who has recently discussed the interdependence of cultures: "Western imperialism and Third World nationalism feed off each other, but even at their worst they are neither monolithic nor deterministic. Besides, culture is not monolithic either, and is not the exclusive property of East or West, nor of small groups of men or women."[13]

As for Africans, Wright was not entirely impressed by their familial and tribal life. While he admired close relationships that buttressed the Ashanti family and tribe, he was troubled by the denial of individualism. All his life he believed in the twin values of American life: individualism and freedom. He was thus torn between his admiration for strong family kinship and tribal unity and cooperation on the one hand and his very American, almost Emersonian, drive toward individualism on the other hand. Not only did Wright remain ambivalent on this subject, but to him this characteristic of unity and lack of individualism in African life was a sign of the paradox of Africa.

The open letter he wrote Nkrumah on his way home, included at the end of *Black Power,* also reflects his ambivalent feelings about African culture in general and Nkrumah's political strategy in particular. On the one hand, Wright was emotionally attracted to the tribal life, but on the other, he was critical of its mysterious elements. Politically as well, he was sympathetic toward Marxism for its idealistic theories but antagonistic to its dictatorial power. Although he was convinced of the inevitable industrialization capitalism would bring about in Africa, he was extremely apprehensive of the exploitation of human power, a new form of slavery, that industrialism would introduce into Africa. Whether his argument is concerned with people or politics, his emphasis is placed on self-creation, the generation of confidence in Africans themselves individually or as a culture. One may easily draw an analogy between the young Wright's self-creation and his transcendence of racial oppression through the power of language as shown in *Black Boy* and the African's life under colonial and imperialistic oppression as studied in *Black Power.* One may also see a parallel between the transformation of tribal life to industrialized society in West Africa as reported in *Black Power* and the exodus of African Americans to the northern cities as portrayed in *12 Million Black Voices.*

13. *Culture and Imperialism,* xxiv.

In the letter to Nkrumah, Wright is understandably polite in discussing the negative aspects of African life. "To think about Africa" he begins the penultimate chapter of the book, "is to think about man's naïve attempt to understand and manipulate the universe of life in terms of magical religion" (*BP*, 334). Yet he cautions Nkrumah that the modernization of African society, even with the support of Western liberalism and democracy, would be arrested by "a gummy tribalism" (*BP*, 344). "AFRICAN LIFE MUST BE MILITARIZED!" he warns, "not for war, but for peace; not for destruction, but for service; not for aggression, but for production; not for despotism, but *to free minds from mumbo-jumbo*" (*BP*, 347; emphasis added).

To Wright, then, the Africans' enchantment with such superstitions in tribal life was a sign of their lack of self-confidence, the signal for their transformation. For Africans to gain self-confidence, he urges as though he were Emerson: "Be merciful by being stern! If I lived under your regime, I'd ask for this hardness, this coldness" (*BP*, 346). Emerson wrote at the end of his poem "Give All to Love": "Heartily know / When half-gods go, / The gods arrive." Emerson's poem is an admonition that stoical self-reliance must be kept alive underneath one's passion. As long as we rely on others, "half-gods," we cannot reach our enlightenment. African culture, Wright thought, had not developed its character to the extent that the people could become "stout, hard, sharply defined; there is too much cloudiness in the African's mentality, a kind of sodden vagueness that makes for lack of confidence, an absence of focus that renders that mentality incapable of grasping the workaday world." What is worse, the colonialist or imperialist deliberately had kept the African's mentality "static" for the sake of "his own perverse personal salvation." Given this background, Wright urges Nkrumah: "*You must be hard!*" (*BP*, 343).

Echoing his own experience with Communism, Wright recommends that although Marxism is an idealistic and yet practical doctrine for liberation of the oppressed the world over, its method must be devised by Africans. "Russia will not help you," he stresses, "unless you accept becoming an appendage of Moscow; and why should you change one set of white masters for another . . . ?" (*BP*, 346). Robert Felgar draws an analogy between *Black Power* and *Native Son:* "Wright sees, in short, a continental recapitulation of the American treatment of its blacks: the 350-year history of the black man in America is the history of black Africa for the last 2,000 years. Bigger Thomas has reappeared as the whole of Africa; the European-American West represents the Daltons and the Buckleys; the opportunistic Communists play themselves; and the essential relationship among those protagonists in both scenarios is identical."[14] Felgar's comparison is an intriguing one. If this reading implies that Max in *Native Son* is analogous to the Communists in *Black Power*, it seems a far-fetched analogy, for Max plays the role of an entirely trusted, altruistic, and extremely compassionate defender of Bigger, unlike the defense lawyers of Clyde Griffiths in Dreiser's *An American Tragedy*. In *Black Power*, on the contrary, Communism, and Russian Marxism in particular, is untrustworthy, dictatorial, and unreliable for Nkrumah and his state, and hence rejected. Nor does Wright recommend the Western form of capitalism, which would lift African workers from tribal bondage to "industrial slavery." The only solution he envisions is for a popular political leader like Nkrumah to find his "*own* paths," his "*own* values." Wright urges him to "feel free to *improvise!* The political cat can be skinned in many fashions; the building of that bridge between tribal man and the twentieth century can be done in a score of ways" (*BP*, 346). His advice on Communism in 1954 was, indeed, prophetic, as what has happened to Angola and Cuba well attests. Significantly, his advice to Nkrumah was for the Gold Coast to use Marxism, a theory that made the relation of class to production meaningful in the modern nation, but "drop it" if it proved useless.

Wright's argument was for Africans to preserve their primal attitudes in their hearts rather than manifest them in their rituals and customs. Above all, he urged African politicians and intellectuals to create pragmatic policies with firm discipline and self-determination. "The burden of suffering that must be borne," he asserts, "impose it upon *one* generation! Do not, with the false kindness of the missionaries and businessmen, drag out this agony for another five hundred years while your villages rot and your people's minds sink into the morass of a subjective darkness" (*BP*, 346). Although modern Africa is making her progress "at a snail's pace" (*BP*, 345), Wright predicts that her values, which are spiritual and genuinely humanistic, will eventually prevail over Western values, which, created by technology and industrialism, are materialistic and predominantly mechanistic.

To halt stagnation and make the African progress deliberate and unfaltering, he implies, requires a double vision on the part of African

14. *Richard Wright,* 141.

leaders. As Ely Houston in *The Outsider* lectures Cross Damon that African Americans, gifted with a double vision, are at once living both inside and outside American culture, so does Wright admonish Africans to see themselves endowed with a critical vision and to gauge for the sake of their own lives both spiritualism and materialism, tradition and modernism, Communism and capitalism. From today's perspective, indeed, Africans are living both inside and outside Western culture, a culture that has become increasingly international and multiple.

8

The Color Curtain, Multiculturalism, and American Racial Issues

1

As its subtitle indicates, *The Color Curtain* constitutes a report on an international and multicultural conference held outside the West. The narrative structure of the book, however, suggests that Richard Wright's nonfiction work was intended as a travelogue. Unlike a typical travelogue, which describes a journey from home to elsewhere, Wright's travel begins not in America but in Europe and ends in Asia. Living in Paris as an exile, Wright traveled to Madrid by train and then from Madrid to Jakarta by plane with brief stops at Cairo, Karachi, Calcutta, and Bangkok. Much of the initial narrative consists of planned interviews he conducted on the train and plane with a variety of fellow travelers, intellectuals of diverse cultural backgrounds, including a young anti-racist Dutch woman; a young Indonesian-born Dutch female journalist; a dark-skinned twenty-six-year-old woman with an Irish Catholic mother and an Indian Moslem father; a male, middle-aged, married, Westernized, Indonesian educator, whom Wright dubs "the H. L. Mencken of Indonesia";[1] a male, single, restless Indonesian student of political science; and a young male Pakistani journalist educated by Christian missionaries.

1. Richard Wright, *The Color Curtain: A Report on the Bandung Conference*, 53. Subsequent references will appear parenthetically in the text as *CC*.

What distinguishes *The Color Curtain* from Wright's other books like *Black Boy* and *Uncle Tom's Children* is the multiculturalism that underlies his discourse in it. While Wright's observations and analyses deal with diversity in culture and religion, his overall vision is unified in terms of race. The participants of the Bandung Conference, as a reviewer of the book points out, "found in the very fact of being nonwhite a basis of unity and, in relation to that fact, the events of history and the problems of the present and of the future were discussed."[2] Because Wright in *The Color Curtain* is concerned with cultural diversity as well as with racial unity, his observations at the conference have a direct corollary with his comments on American racial issues in his other books. The Bandung Conference thus taught Wright that the progress of nonwhite people in Asia and Africa would come about through the peaceful coexistence of diverse cultures and through the scientific and technological assistance the West was to give the East. Such a lesson makes a strong allusion to Wright's observations on American racial issues. The advancement of racially oppressed people in the United States, Wright seems to imply, should be achieved through mutual respect for diverse cultural heritages and through the assistance society is obligated to give the educationally and economically disadvantaged.

How closely the problems discussed in *The Color Curtain* are related to racial and cultural problems in America is suggested by an anecdote Wright includes in the book. During the conference Wright met a white American woman reporter who intimated to him that her black roommate made a ritual of secretly straightening her hair at night. Puzzled by her roommate's habit, the reporter asked Wright why this black woman felt it necessary to straighten her hair despite the fact that her hair "seems all right." Wright replied: "Because you were born with straight hair, and she wants to look as much like you as possible" (CC, 185). He hastened to add that the Hindus, who had lived under British rule for centuries, had been conditioned to regard white skins as superior. Likewise, some young Japanese women are eager to have cosmetic surgery performed on their eyelids so that their eyes look just like those of Western women. Referring to the black roommate, Wright responded to the journalist: "Can you blame her? It's a tribute that she pays to the white race. It's her way of saying: 'Forgive me. I'm sorry that I'm black; I'm ashamed that my hair is not like yours. But you see that I'm doing all that I can to be like you'" (CC, 187).

2. Ellen Logue, "Review of *The Color Curtain*."

Such an episode clearly suggests that the center of Wright's interest in *The Color Curtain* lies in generating self-esteem on the part of the nonwhite population of the world. To Wright, a black woman's straightening of her hair or a Japanese woman's cosmetic surgery means a psychological suicide. "That is why," he declares, "twenty-nine nations are meeting here in Bandung to discuss racialism and colonialism. The feeling of inferiority that the white man has instilled in these people corrodes their very souls. . . . And though they won't admit it openly, they hate it" (*CC*, 187). The Bandung Conference, in short, was for the descendants of the old cultures to regain their pride and confidence.

Just as the close relationship and friendship Wright established with Kwame Nkrumah provided him with enormous insight into Africa, the dialogues among the Asian leaders and intellectuals he heard at the Bandung Conference enabled him to understand various Asian cultures. Above all, in *The Color Curtain*, he is impressed by the Westernized elite of Asia, who are able to look at their cultures from both Eastern and Western points of view. In the introductory section of *Black Power* Wright describes himself as a member of the Westernized elite he describes in *The Color Curtain*, a nonwhite individual who is educated in the West. Such an intellectual has the vantage of being able to see both worlds from another, and third, point of view. In his African journey Wright came to realize that the African American like him is the product of neither Africa nor America but of both cultures. Just as he urges African Americans not to return to Africa, he urges Westernized Asians not to go back to their religions and cultures. In his eyes, the new Asian leaders play the role of a bridge between the East and the West.

There are some differences in ideology between *The Color Curtain* and *Black Power*. Interestingly, reviews of *The Color Curtain* were more favorable than those of *Black Power*, since in *The Color Curtain* Wright takes a less anti-colonial and more pro-West stance. Furthermore, he is decidedly anti-Communist, admonishing the elite of the Third World against sympathizing with world Communism. In the *New York Times Book Review* Tillman Durdin, himself an elite of Indonesia, concurred with Wright's conclusion: the crucial question facing Asians is whether Asia will be dominated by Communism or by democracy. As Wright recognizes in *The Color Curtain* that the emerging nations in Asia were anti-Communist, he observes in *Black Power* that Africa was decidedly anti-colonialist. Realizing that building a new African culture must be accomplished by building self-confidence, he urges Nkrumah to militarize his nation. If such a militant tactic is construed as Communist or Fascist, Wright has faith that an African leader like Nkrumah will not become a dictator. Arming Africa, as discussed in the previous chapter, must be "not for despotism, but to free minds from mumbo-jumbo" (*BP*, 342–49).

Wright in *Black Power* argues that the Western influences on Africa in the form of imperialism and Christian missionaries have all but destroyed once-flourishing civilizations. It is, therefore, understandable that the new Africa is anti-colonialist in principle and militaristic in tactic. In *The Color Curtain*, on the other hand, Wright observes that Asian democracy and Communist China are politically at war and that the only way in which new Asian cultures can surpass their adversary is through the help of Western science and industry. That he took an anti-Communist stance in *The Color Curtain* was prophetic, for not only has Communism failed to influence the Third World but the Soviet Union has collapsed in recent years. It is also prophetic that he regarded the problems of Asia and Africa as "beyond left and right" (*CC*, 9). The Third World, in his view, was confronted with more profound issues like colonialism, racialism, and war or peace—on which both left and right could and did agree.

Between *Black Power* and *The Color Curtain*, both of which are part of Wright's discourse on multiculturalism, there emerges a distinct pattern of development in his point of view. The ideas Wright generates in *Black Power*, as his dialogue with Nkrumah suggests, are largely personal. While *Black Power* reads as a psychological, introspective inquiry into the race question, *The Color Curtain* becomes a social, economic, and political projection into the future. Throughout *The Color Curtain* his observations on multiculturalism in Asian nations lead to his analysis of the race issue at home. Although his view of race and culture in America is not stated in the book, he clearly draws various analogies between the racial and cultural problems in the Third World and those in America.

2

These indirect references to American racial issues become apparent as the discourse develops, but such an intention is hinted before it begins. At the outset of the book Wright's wife questions him about his qualifications for writing such a book. He replies:

> I don't know. But I feel that my life has given me some keys to what they would say or do. I'm an American Negro; as such, I've had a burden of race consciousness. So have these people. I worked in my youth as a common laborer, and I've a class consciousness. So have these people. I grew up in the Methodist and Seventh Day Adventist churches and I saw and observed religion in my childhood; and these people are religious. I was a member of the Communist Party for twelve years and I know something of the politics and psychology of rebellion. These people have had as their daily existence such politics. These emotions are my instruments. They are emotions, but I'm conscious of them as emotions. I want to use these emotions to try to find out what these people think and feel and why. (CC, 15)

Wright's emphasis on the emotions that underlie the burden of his race consciousness echoes what Wright told Horace R. Cayton, a sociologist who intimately knew Wright's method of writing. According to Cayton, Wright's theory of writing called for a type of writing in which the author must "float" facts of life "on a sea of emotion" and "drive them home with some degree of artistic power . . . to the level of seriousness which characterizes science."[3] Unlike a typical literary naturalist such as Zola, Wright does not hesitate to express emotions side by side with his portrayal of social facts.

In *Black Power*, his emotions are expressed on several different levels. When he viewed the Gold Coast, he did so as a Western intellectual, an African American, an exile in Paris, a man of New York and Chicago, and a southerner. "As a Negro," as Russell C. Brignano has noted, "he approached Africa, as it unfolded before him, with attitudes and emotions different from those of a white Westerner."[4] In *The Color Curtain*, as in *Black Power*, Wright approached Asia with the same point of view and feeling. As *Black Boy* tells more about the young Wright than about the South, *The Color Curtain* reveals more about the mature Richard Wright than about the Bandung Conference.

Among the characteristics of the Third World, multiculturalism is what unites Wright's vision of that world with his feelings about his

3. "Discrimination—America," 263.
4. *Richard Wright: An Introduction*, 91.

own country. While attending the conference, he was keenly aware that Indonesians were anxious to annihilate the Dutch colonial culture but were uncertain as to what kind of culture was best for their nation. The informant who provided Wright with this sentiment reminded him that Indonesia consists of "several" cultures—Muslim, Christian missionary, overseas Chinese, and Polynesian. To this informant and other Westernized Asian attendees of the conference, Indonesian culture emerged as a challenge to the traditional concept of race and culture. The Asian masses, as this informant pointed out, used to think that "some vague, metaphysical principle in nature had decreed that Africa was for the blacks, China for the yellows, Europe for the whites, etc." "It was amazing," Wright remarks parenthetically, "how widespread this feeling was in Asia and Europe, but less in Asia than in Europe." He learned that the uneducated Asians took their racial and cultural environment for granted and believed that "nature had ordained the present arrangement." At the same time he realized that those Westernized Asians "who had been shaken up, as it were, by war, racial prejudice, or religious persecution, had become awakened and felt that the world belonged to all of those who lived in it" (CC, 43).

Wright also learned that this perspective on multiculturalism could be put into action by a politician like President Sukarno of Indonesia. Asians, as Wright saw, did not fall victim to their cultural environment; they were instead taking advantage of their diversity in religion and race. "Sukarno," Wright argues, "was not evoking these twin demons; he was not trying to create them; he was trying to organize them" (CC, 140). On the one hand, Asian leaders were deeply religious men, products of the mystical cultures; on the other, the Third World populations had been subjugated on the assumption that they were racially inferior. To defend their cultures from colonialism, Asian leaders tried to generate a racial consciousness, which was "slowly blended with a defensive religious feeling." The Bandung Conference showed Wright that the double consciousness of race and religion "had combined into one: *a racial and religious system of identification manifesting itself in an emotional nationalism which was now leaping state boundaries and melting and merging, one into the other*" (CC, 140).

Wright's account of the Asian consciousness of race and religion is closely related to his vision of African American life. In other books, as detailed earlier, Wright tends to show uneducated black people victimized by religion. In *Native Son* Bigger's mother is obsessed with religion, and Cross Damon's in *The Outsider* is the product of the traditional Christianity in the South that taught black children subservient ethics. Consequently, he rejects her not only because she reminds him of southern black piety but also because she is the epitome of racial and sexual repression. Similarly, Bigger makes a disparaging remark about the Reverend Hammond: "And now the preacher made it walk before his eyes like a ghost in the night, creating within him a sense of exclusion that was as cold as a block of ice" (*NS*, 264).

Whereas these black characters fall victim to their racial and religious consciousness, Wright also created a man and a woman in *Uncle Tom's Children* who take advantage of their racial and religious heritages. Thus, the Reverend Taylor, the civil rights leader in "Fire and Cloud," is faced with deciding whether to dissuade his congregation from demonstrating for the food they need or to support the march at the risk of violence. While many of the elders in his church cannot break with their traditional faith in passive resistance, the Reverend Taylor can change and does opt for solidarity and protest. Aunt Sue, the mother of two revolutionary black youths in "Bright and Morning Star," is accustomed to the attitude of forbearance preached by black church leaders, but when she is awakened by "the bright and morning star" of Communism, she becomes a martyr instead of a victim of white power.

Like Rev. Martin Luther King Jr., the Reverend Taylor, endowed with intellectual ability, courage, and leadership, earns respect from all people, black and white. What Wright calls the "melting and merging" of the racial and religious consciousness, as seen in Reverend Taylor and Aunt Sue, alludes to what Wright witnessed in many of the leaders of the emerging nations. He quotes one Winburn T. Thomas, a longtime missionary in Asia, as saying:

> Strange as it may seem to Western observers, many Asians are both Christians and Communists. At one time, six of the seven leaders of the Travancore, India, Communist Party representatives were baptized Christians. There are two Communist Party representatives in the Indonesian parliament who also hold membership in the Batak Church.
>
> The sharp ideological lines and distinctions frequently drawn by Westerners are blurred in Asia. It is not uncommon for a Japanese to say that he is at once a Buddhist, a Confucianist, and a Christian. (*CC*, 168–69)

Wright realized at the conference that although "the two doctrines of life, Christianity and Communism, are opposed," they are "at bottom . . . not as opposed as one would think. There are deep underground, emotional connections. Seen through Asian eyes, the two philosophies share much of the same assumptions of hope" (CC, 168). To Wright, then, the peaceful coexistence of religion and politics accounts for the tenacity and pragmatism of the Asian mind (CC, 170).

The key to the prosperity of the new nations in Asia is the leaders' insight in creating harmony out of diversity in their cultural legacy. Above all, as Wright was convinced, the Asian leaders were flexible and pragmatic in adopting democracy and capitalism. They readily admitted that Asia as a whole was handicapped with antiquated technology and work ethics. Paula Snelling, a reviewer of *The Color Curtain* who had lived in Indonesia, found Wright's account of "the myth of white superiority upon Asia" illuminating, even though she admitted that his knowledge of the philosophical and cultural history of these people was inadequate. What the Asian elite, Wright, and Snelling shared is a vision of harmony and prosperity that prevailed in Asia after World War II.

White Man, Listen!—a nonfiction work that appeared a year after *The Color Curtain*—expresses much the same view as *The Color Curtain.* The new leaders of the Third World, as Wright portrays them, "stand poised, nervous, straining at the leash, ready to go, with no weight of the dead past clouding their minds, no fears of foolish customs benumbing their consciousness, eager to build industrial civilizations."[5] Wright considers Jawaharlal Nehru of India, for instance, exemplary of the Asian African elite. For Nehru, India is "a halfway house between East and West" (CC, 166). Wright admires Nehru because Nehru's thinking is autonomous: his greatness "consists of his being what his country is: part East, part West. If one day Nehru says that the perplexities facing Asia are moral, then he is acting in a Western manner; if the next day he says that the world is gripped by a power struggle, he is looking upon life as an Asian" (CC, 165).

Nehru's role as a bridge between East and West can also be attributed to other leaders of the Third World. Dr. Mohammed Natsir, a former prime minister of Indonesia and a staunch Muslim, believed that Islam had made his country neutral in the battle between Communism and

5. *White Man, Listen!* 63.

capitalism. "There will be no need for Communism in Moslem countries," he told Wright. "Pan-Islam will represent a world force, socialistic in nature, keeping a middle ground between Communism and Capitalism." Social and economic progress for a country like Indonesia was possible not only because its leaders were knowledgeable about diverse cultures and ideologies but also because they had unwavering faith and confidence in their legacy. In short, Wright calls Natsir "more pro-Islam than anti-Communist or pro-Capitalist" (CC, 123).

Among the Asian and African elite, Wright found Carlos P. Romulo, a member of the Philippine cabinet and the chairman of the Philippine delegation to the Bandung Conference, the most pro-Western. In keeping with Romulo's ideas, Wright asserted that the West had the moral obligation to assist the East in its technological and economic development. Wright was remarkably impressed by Romulo's speech to the Asian African delegates at the conference. Romulo, while criticizing the West for having fostered racism, acknowledged its positive influences on the East. He reminded the Third World representatives that it was Western political thought that had given Asia and Africa their "basic ideas of political freedom, justice and equity." He maintained that it was Western science that after World War II had "exploded the mythology of race." Romulo's idea of cooperation between the East and the West, based upon secular and rational thought and feeling on the part of the Asian and African elite, warranted "the West's assuming the moral right to interfere." To Wright, the elite of the Third World were "more Western than the West in most cases. . . . And those two bases of Eastern and Western rationalism must become one!" If the spirit of coexistence and coprosperity should fail at this point of human history, "the tenuous Asian-African secular, rational attitudes will become flooded, drowned in irrational tides of racial and religious passions." The final message Wright received at the conference was that the development of Asian and African cultures would be accompanied by peace rather than war, which characterized Marxism, and that the development would be toward "a rapid industrialization" rather than "a static past" (CC, 219–20).

The sentiment of peace and prosperity that prevailed at the conference is expressed earlier in Wright's discourse by a young Eurasian woman. Single, born in Singapore of an Irish Catholic mother and Indian father of Moslem faith, she had lived in the East as well as in the West. She felt that no state in the East or the West should promote religion; Christianity had had no deep effect either on herself or in Malaya, her country. Because of her mixed racial, religious, and national heritage, she was always interested in world affairs. Having a sense of loyalty to both East and West, she did not want to see the Third World isolated as a racial and political bloc. "I feel for both sides," she told Wright. "I love Asia and I love Europe and I don't want to see a clash." Conscious of her Asian roots, she was strongly attracted to a prosperous Asian country like Japan: she called the Japanese "a powerful, civilized, 'yellow' people." Having witnessed both the British and the Japanese occupations of Malaya, she felt ambivalent about Japan. As Wright says, "she respected the Japanese and feared them." She respected the Japanese "because of their 'pride' and 'strength' and 'development,' and she would certainly have liked to belong to a 'colored' nation if that nation resembled, say, the British or the American" (*CC*, 34–44). The Eurasian journalist's attitude toward Japan has an affinity with that of Bigger, who is proud of the Japanese. To Bigger, the Japanese could rule others rather than be ruled as other nonwhite people often were (*NS*, 109).

3

The effects of multiculturalism on the Third World thus bear a strong resemblance to those on African American life. "All intelligent Asians," as an Indonesian educator declared, "now know that the Western white man is praying for us to fight among ourselves, and that we'll never do." In his view, Western people, admitting that colonialism had failed, were attempting to reconquer that world by dividing the people of the Third World. "Fighting among ourselves," he says, "is the white man's only chance of getting back. We're closing ranks. The white man will be disappointed" (*CC*, 67). Solidarity among the oppressed, particularly among black people, is the most powerful weapon against racism, as Wright shows in "Fire and Cloud" when the Reverend Taylor succeeds in uniting his congregation. With stoicism and endurance buttressed by his racial and religious consciousness, Taylor succeeds in leading the poor and the oppressed to freedom.

Wright makes the colonial policy of divide and rule akin to white people's encouragement for black people to fight among themselves. Such a racist mentality, as discussed earlier, pervades Wright's fiction. The trial in *Native Son* shows that the white public is not enraged as much by Bigger's murder of his black girlfriend as by his accidental killing of a white girl. In *Black Boy*, Wright describes how the foreman at a company he worked for instigated antagonism between the young Wright and a black boy employed at another company. The culprit in this incident is the racist mentality that regards black men as animals, an attitude inherited from the old days of slavery. Not only are black people considered to be white men's servants, but they are expected to entertain white rulers as though they were animals in the zoo. Even killing among black men would not prick the white man's conscience.

Another affinity between colonialism in the Third World and racism in America can be seen in the appeal Marxism had to nonwhite people. "I agree with Nehru," a Pakistani journalist maintained. "Colonialism and not Communism is the main danger. Get rid of colonies and you'll not have a trend toward Communism." Reminding Wright that Russia was a colonial state before she became the Soviet Union, a Marxist state, he argued that the American fear of world Communism was "shortsighted and unhistorical." He considered Marxists' friendly posture toward Asia understandable and realistic, because a Marxist, a leftist, was ideologically opposed to a colonialist, a rightist. "But," he concluded, "we would have risen without the Communists" (*CC*, 67–68). Much of Wright's early fiction demonstrates that black intellectuals in America in the Depression years were strongly attracted to Marxist philosophy. *Black Boy*, for example, includes an episode in which the young Wright wondered why he could not eat when he was hungry and "why some people had enough food and others did not" (*BB*, 26). The purpose of Chou En-lai of Communist China in attending the Bandung Conference was to promote the understanding that Marxism was a revolutionary call addressed to socially and economically oppressed people everywhere. Chou En-lai's appeal, as Wright saw, won sympathy from the leaders of the Third World partly because the Chinese were racially akin to the people of that world. In America, on the other hand, it was the Depression of the 1930s, an economic environment, that made a black intellectual like Wright fascinated by Marxism. The Reverend Taylor's freedom march, as "Fire and Cloud" indicates, is triumphant primarily because the black people form an alliance with the workers, the economically oppressed.

What the victims of colonialism and racism have in common was a sense of insecurity. In the Third World, as in America, the psychic growth of the people has been stunted by the dictatorial policies of the rulers. Sukarno's keynote speech makes it clear that the people of the Third World are "living in a world of fear." Sukarno emphasizes: "The life of man today is corroded and made bitter by fear. Fear of the future, fear of the hydrogen bomb, fear of ideologies. Perhaps this fear is a greater danger than the danger itself, because it is fear which drives men to act foolishly, to act thoughtlessly, to act dangerously" (CC, 138). This psychological state of Asians and Africans strongly resembles that of black people in America. The anxiety a black man feels in a white-dominated society is vividly described in book 1 of *Native Son*, entitled "Fear." Wright takes pains to show that Bigger hangs psychologically suspended in a no-man's-land, neither in the white world of rich people he sees in the movie *The Gay Woman* nor in the world of African natives depicted in *Trader Horn*.

The colonial policy is to deprive the natives of autonomy and self-determination, and this oppressive policy has created anxiety and fear in their minds. "For many generations," Sukarno underscores, "our peoples have been the voiceless ones in the world. We have been the unregarded, the peoples for whom decisions were made by others whose interests were paramount, the peoples who lived in poverty and humiliation" (CC, 139). What Sukarno says about the people of the Third World indeed echoes what Wright reports in *12 Million Black Voices*. The lack of individuality among black people in the South, as Wright shows, has taken a heavy toll on the black character. The oppressive system, in his analysis, "created new types of behavior and new patterns of psychological reaction, welding us together into a separate unity with common characteristics of our own" (*12*, 41).

What Wright calls "the steady impact of the plantation system" also affected the education of black children. In many southern states, as mentioned earlier, the white authorities edited the textbooks that black children were allowed to use, automatically deleting any references to government, constitution, voting, citizenship, and civil rights. In *12 Million Black Voices* Wright reports that white men "become angry when they think that we desire to learn more than they want us to" (*12*, 64).

Just as the racist tradition was upheld in depriving black citizens of education, colonialism persisted in indoctrinating natives with Eurocentrism. Before the people of the Third World can move from a colonial state to an independent state, they must establish a sense of confidence not only in their tradition and culture but also in their ability to industrialize. The first part of the Bandung communiqué, therefore, stresses the economic development of Asians and Africans. The swiftest way for them to rid themselves of their feeling of inferiority was through development of their industries. "When the day comes," as Wright notes, "that Asian and African raw materials are processed in Asia and Africa" by themselves for their benefit, "the supremacy of the Western world, economic, cultural, and political, will have been broken once and for all on this earth" (*CC*, 203). The Pakistani journalist, quoted earlier, told Wright that the Asian elite "knew in his heart that the West had been irrevocably triumphant in its destruction of his culture, but he insisted that when he embraced a new way of life he was going to do so on his own terms, with no monitoring or overlordship from Westerners" (*CC*, 71).

What this Asian intellectual advocates is a new awareness among Asians and Africans that a reorganization of economic and industrial power was not sufficient in itself and that a sense of autonomy and confidence must come from the Third World, not from the West. Like *The Color Curtain, 12 Million Black Voices* is intended not only as a report on the progress of black people in America from a subjugating environment in the South to an industrial society in the North, but also as a history of how the northward movement of African Americans led to an increase in their self-esteem and, above all, an independent vision. Wright told Irving Howe, one of the most distinguished liberal critics of our time, that "only through struggle could men with black skins, and for that matter, all the oppressed of the world, achieve their humanity."[6]

To Wright, freedom for black people can become a reality only when all black people acquire independent vision as outsiders. No matter how courageous Silas, the prosperous black farmer in "Long Black Song," may appear, his fight against the racial oppressors makes little impact on black liberation as a whole because his rebellion is motivated by a private matter. Black emancipation from the rural South, Wright warns, must be accompanied by the vision of the outsider. "Negroes, as they enter our culture," Ely Houston, the New York District Attorney in *The Outsider* says, speaking as Wright's mouthpiece, "are going to inherit the problems we have, but with a difference. . . . they are going to be both *inside* and *outside* of our culture at the same time" (*O*, 129).

The achievement of independent vision, which Wright considers imperative for African Americans, is also what characterizes the new

6. *A World More Attractive*, 109.

Asians and Africans. Wright thus found at the Bandung Conference that the harbingers of the Third World were not only well educated in Western culture and philosophy but also proud of their history and tradition. He indeed envisioned "the Westernized and tragic elite of Asia, Africa, and West Indies" as "men who carry on their frail but indefatigable shoulders the best of two worlds."[7] Their double vision is what enables them to acquire the basic ideas of democracy and freedom from the West but reject the inhuman aspects of capitalism: greed and materialism. Buttressed by the spirit of their tradition, they are able to sustain some of the fundamental values of humanism: peace, loyalty, love, and kinship. Such an extolment of their qualities also speaks of the liberated black people Wright envisioned in America.

7. *White Man, Listen!* v.

9

Pagan Spain

Cultural and Racial Discourse

U pon its publication in 1957, *Pagan Spain* appeared to signal a departure from Wright's earlier nonfiction and from *Black Power* (1954) and *The Color Curtain* (1956) in particular. While the two previous travelogues are focused on the non-Western world—African and Asian cultures, respectively—*Pagan Spain* is primarily concerned with a Western culture. But what is common among the three works is that the narrator is distinctly an American. Although Wright claims an African heritage, in *Black Power* and *The Color Curtain* he does not speak like an African. Even though he speaks in *Pagan Spain* as a European resident, he still remains an American. If these works are read as travelogues, commentaries on foreign cultures, his perspectives strike one as realistic, impartial, and critical.

That *Pagan Spain* contains many disparaging remarks about Spanish culture is partly responsible for the fact that the book has been published in such European countries as Germany, Holland, Sweden, and Italy, but not in Spain. Wright's aim at achieving objectivity is indicated by his interview with a magazine reporter in 1959: "*Pagan Spain* is about a journey—or rather it's a descriptive account of three automobile trips I made in Spain, the Spanish people I met, the fiestas, flamencos, bullfights, the feeling of the country, the warmth of the people and the incredible poverty."[1] As this statement suggests, his intention for the book—unlike *The Color Curtain*, in which the informants

1. Barry Learned, "U.S. Lets Negro Explain Race Ills, Wright Declares," 185.

are predominantly intellectuals, what he calls the Asian elite—was to deal with all classes of the Spanish people, including aristocrats and gypsies, businessmen and workers, dancers and prostitutes, matadors and pimps, priests and shop clerks. As a result, *Pagan Spain* turns out to be not only a vivid portrayal of Spain after World War II but an acute cultural criticism.

As Hemingway in the 1920s took advice from Gertrude Stein that in part led to his writing such books on Spain as *The Sun Also Rises* (1926) and *For Whom the Bell Tolls* (1940), Wright eagerly listened to the legendary authoress when he arrived in Paris in 1946. "You'll see the past there," she told him. "You'll see what the Western world is made of. Spain is primitive, but lovely. And the people! There are no people such as the Spanish anywhere. I've spent days in Spain that I'll never forget. See those bullfights, see that wonderful landscape" (*PS*, 1–2). Despite Stein's urging, however, he postponed his journey for nearly a decade. In the summer of 1954 at the urging of his friends Alva and Gunnar Myrdal, the well-respected Swedish sociologists, he finally drove past the Pyrenees to Barcelona. In contrast to Gertrude Stein's romanticized, traditional, and ritualistic view of Spanish culture, *Pagan Spain* is dedicated to the Myrdals, *"who suggested this book and whose compassionate hearts have long brooded upon the degradation of human life in Spain"* (*PS*, dedication).

This dedication intimates that his immediate motive for the book was to explore the fate of Spanish exiles and victims under Franco's totalitarian regime. Reflecting on his own experience in America, he says: "I had never been able to stifle a hunger to understand what had happened there and why. . . . An uneasy question kept floating in my mind: How did one live after the death of the hope for freedom?" (*PS*, 2). What the Myrdals called "the degradation of human life in Spain" reminded him of his birth under a racist government in Mississippi, of his formative twelve years under the dictatorship of the American Communist Party, and of a year of his intellectual life under the terror of Argentine dictator Juan Perón. "The author," as a reviewer noted, "gives his reader bitter, stark facts at the same time that he unwittingly reveals his own bitter, hurt self."[2] His avowed opposition to Franco's totalitarianism, evident throughout the text, thus contributed to the fact that *Pagan Spain* received better reviews in the United States than did *Black Power* or *The Color Curtain*.

2. Mary Ellen Stephenson, "Spain Gets Bitter Barbs from Visitor."

But some American readers "were shocked to see" a black writer discuss a white culture. Before Wright, a usual pattern had been for a Western anthropologist or a Western writer like Joseph Conrad to comment on Asian or African life. If Wright considered himself an African, his situation would have been the opposite of that of a Western writer. He thus declared: "I was reversing roles."[3] If, on the other hand, he regarded himself as an American writer, his comments on Europe, indeed, signaled a reversal of the comments of Alexis de Tocqueville and D. H. Lawrence, whose views of American culture remain classic. Similarly, from today's vantage point, Wright's view of Spain remains a unique cultural criticism.

Three years after the publication of *Pagan Spain, L'Express,* in its interview with him, posed this question: "Is there in the United States an important output of Negro literature, and do you number many friends among these writers?" In response he stated:

> Yes, many. Negro literature in the United States is actually so important that it even preoccupies our government. American blacks are testifying against the most modern of Western countries. . . . In the United States, the tendency is to tell black writers: "Don't be preoccupied with your experience as Negroes. Don't be polarized by it. You are people. Write exactly as any other people would do on any other subject." I would be inclined to tell them, "On the contrary, take your ghetto experience as a theme, for this precisely is a *universal* topic."[4]

In effect, Wright is suggesting that one's racial experience is a representation of universal experience. By analogy, then, a Spaniard's experience represents not only Spanish culture but also universal experience. Not surprisingly Wright's observations in *Pagan Spain* are closely related to those on African American experience.

1

What underlies Wright's cultural discourse in *Pagan Spain* is a notion that Spain, despite its history, was not nearly as Christian as it looked. His chief interest, therefore, lies not in examining the Catholic church as

---

3. "Interview with Richard Wright," in *Conversations with Richard Wright,* 203.
4. Ibid., 204–5; emphasis added.

it became entangled with Franco's totalitarian regime, but in exploring the intriguing boundaries of Spanish religiosity. Initially he was puzzled by the Falangists, made up of *"half monks, half soldiers"* (*PS*, 60). He saw all of them worship a statue of the Virgin Mary that had been carved by Saint Luke. "It is further claimed," Wright recounts, "that it was brought to Spain by St. Peter himself in A. D. 30." He was also told: "Hermán Cortés came here to ask blessings from the Black Virgin. Even Columbus made a pilgrimage here" (*PS*, 60). As his exploration of Spain's religious character delves into the past in contrast to the present political situation, and into the interior in contrast to the Catholic church as a modern institution, his expressions become increasingly flexible, fluid, and dynamic. An anonymous reviewer interpreted *Pagan Spain* primarily as Wright's indictment against the machinations of the church and the state: "It is the Spain of the ready thumb of the church and the state, the thumb which twists and turns the lives of the poor mortals beneath it, shaping and moving the poor mortals in a way repugnant to much of the world."[5] While he relies on conventional metaphor, symbolism, and imagery in describing religious practices, he is bent on creating representations that strike the reader as unconventional, metonymical, and psychoanalytical.

Anyone commenting on the political situation of Spain in the 1950s could not help seeing the exploitation of the Catholic church by the politicians. Their strategy was to equate Spanish Catholicism with Spain's glorious past; Catholicism was pitted against Protestantism, which the majority of Spaniards perceived as a decadent, materialistic religion. "The average Spaniard," Wright says, "knows nothing of Protestantism." Even Spanish intellectuals feel "uneasy when the subject of Protestantism is mentioned" (*PS*, 137). Juan Perrone, S.J., in his catechism in 1950, asserted that Protestantism came into existence in Spain to propagate Socialism and Communism. But from Wright's point of view, Spanish Protestantism was far more concerned with the lives of the poor and socially oppressed than was Catholicism. Reflecting on his own Protestant background, he sympathized with the Spanish Protestants for "the needless, unnatural, and utterly barbarous nature of the psychological suffering" they had undergone at the hands of the religious and political officials. What interested him was a psychological,

5. See "No Castles in Spain," in Reilly, 290.

uncanny affinity that existed between the Protestants in Spain and African Americans, Jews, and other oppressed minorities in America. "It is another proof, if any is needed today," he argues, "that the main and decisive aspects of human reactions are conditioned and are not inborn" (*PS*, 138).

Economically Catholicism in Spain fared worse than Protestantism. The Protestants were known for their ability to cope with reality, while the Catholics were slow in adapting themselves to life changes in general and industrialization in particular. To Wright, Protestantism, however suitable for industrialism and modernism, was rejected in Spain, just as was "the murderous rationalism of sacrificial Communism . . . in favor of an archaic collective consciousness based on family symbols: One Father, One Mother, One Spirit" (*PS*, 240).

This definition of Spanish Catholicism as archaic, unrealistic, and impractical, however, is only superficially characteristic of Spanish religiosity. Although Ferdinand and Isabel had driven the Moors out of Spain in 1492 under the banner of Catholicism, Spanish culture kept intact, as Wright notes, "all the muddy residue of an irrational paganism that lurked at the bottom of the Spanish heart" (*PS*, 240). He thus maintains that the Spanish people would turn back the clock of history and cling to paganism. The social, religious, and familial customs and rituals of this predominantly Catholic nation, as he shows throughout the book, reflect a religious philosophy that is not Catholic but primitive and primeval.

As for the sources of paganism in Spain, he relies on the commonly held view: "the pagan streams of influence flowing from the Goths, the Greeks, the Jews, the Romans, the Iberians, and the Moors lingered strongly and vitally on, flourishing under the draperies of the twentieth century" (*PS*, 193). From time to time, he also implies that paganism in Spain came from Asia through Buddhism and possibly Confucianism, both of which antedate Christianity by five hundred years or more. Spanish paganism, he speculates, was related to the Egyptian divinity, and the Akan God, which fascinated him when he traveled in West Africa, as discussed in *Black Power.*

But the most convincing argument for Spanish paganism is derived from his examination of the Black Virgin at Montserrat, one of the famous tourist attractions in Spain. "The ascent to Montserrat," he says, "was breath-taking. We climbed, spinning and circling slowly round the naked mountain peaks on tiny roads that skirted the sheer edges of cloud-filled chasms whose depths made the head swim" (*PS*, 60–61). The representations such a passage creates are avowedly Freudian, though Wright deemphasizes them, and his approach to Spanish national character is unmistakably psychoanalytical:

> More and more nations of seriated granite phalluses, tumefied and turgid, heaved into sight, each rocky republic of erections rising higher than its predecessor, the whole stone empire of them frozen into stances of eternal distensions, until at last they became a kind of universe haunted by phallic images—images that were massive, scornful, shameless, confoundingly bristling, precariously floating in air, obscenely bare and devoid of all vegetation, filling the vision with vistas of a non- or superhuman order of reality. (*PS*, 61)

The phallic images that dominate the geological environment of the Black Virgin do not allude to what Saunders Redding called "a paganism as gross and a venality as vulgar as the temples of Baal."[6] To Wright, such images represent, not *prurience,* a physical, as opposed to psychological, emotion, but *procreation,* a "non- or superhuman order of reality."

Wright indeed defines the genesis of the Virgin as non-Western. The Virgin in Spain is "a perhaps never-to-be-unraveled amalgamation of Eastern and African religions with their endless gods who were sacrificed and their virgins who gave birth perennially" (*PS*, 240). In singular contrast to the male principle of life for which Christianity stands, Spanish religiosity emphasizes the female principle in life the Virgin symbolizes. In portraying the statue of the virgin, Wright seizes upon the Virgin's black face exhibiting "a kind of quiet, expectant tension" (*PS*, 62). Her facial feature recalls a mixture of the Roman and the Oriental. Moreover, the infant Christ seated on her lap, possessing "that same attitude of quiet, tense expectancy," resembles her (*PS*, 63). Wright continues to speculate: "Maya, the mother of Buddha, was supposed to have been a virgin. Chinese temples have long had their images of the Holy Mother sitting with the Child on her lap. The Egyptians worshiped Isis, mother of Horus, as a virgin, and she was called Our Lady, the Queen of Heaven, Mother of God" (*PS*, 65).[7]

---

6. Redding, from the *Baltimore Afro-American,* in Reilly, 299.
7. As noted in the chapter on *Black Power,* the supreme, pantheistic divinity in Shintoism, the Japanese state religion, is the Goddess Ama-Terasu Ohmi Kami, literally translated as "Heaven-Shining Great God."

In all these religions, then, the image of the mother symbolizes how human beings feel about their birth. Divinity or superhumanity, as he maintains, "is inescapably bound up with sex." As human beings throughout history have worshiped the mother, "the female principle in life," Spaniards have worshiped the Black Virgin (*PS*, 65). A reviewer of *Pagan Spain*, an American Catholic priest, called Wright's interpretation of paganism in Spain heretic: "Montserrat, for him, can be accounted for according to the categories of Freud's pan-sexual theories. This attempt to explain religious phenomena in the crude terms of sexual sublimation has well been described as a type of Machiavellian denigration. There is no space here to expose the fallacy."[8]

Viewing religion in Spain, as Wright does, from the vantage point of superhumanism reveals that Spaniards were scarcely conscious of class and racial differences. Rather than staying at a hotel, he chose to spend the first night with a Spanish family in a village. To his surprise the family took him into their Christian fellowship even before they knew his name. "To these boys," he remarks, "it was unthinkable that there was no God and that we were not all His sons" (*PS*, 9). Even the Falangists' book of political catechism includes this dialogue:

ARE THERE THEN PEOPLE WHO WITHOUT BEING BORN IN SPAIN ARE SPANIARDS?
Yes; all who feel themselves to be incorporated in the destiny of Spain.
AND CAN THERE BE PEOPLE BORN IN SPAIN WHO ARE NOT SPANIARDS?
Yes; children of foreigners and those who disassociate themselves from the destiny of the Motherland.
THEN, DO YOU SEE CLEARLY THAT FOR US THE MOTHERLAND IS NOT THE LAND IN WHICH WE ARE BORN BUT THE FEELING OF FORMING PART OF THE DESTINY OR AIMS WHICH THE MOTHERLAND MUST FULFILL IN THE WORLD?
Yes.
WHAT IS THIS DESTINY?
To include all men in a common movement for salvation.
WHAT DOES THIS MEAN?
Ensure that all men place spiritual values before material. (PS, 23)

To the Western industrialized world, the primacy of the spiritual over the materialistic looks irrational and primitive. Wright calls Spanish

8. Francis E. McMahon, S.J., "Spain through Secularist Spectacles," in Reilly, 300.

paganism "an infantile insistence upon one's own feelings as the only guide and rule of living . . . to sustain their lives by being overlords to the 'morally' less pure, to the 'spiritually' inferior" (*PS*, 151). It was not class and race but faith in universal superhumanism that determined one's superiority or inferiority in Spain.

2

Pagan Spain ends with the lasting impression made on Wright by the Virgin during his third and final visit to Seville. The hooded penitents in the procession were upholding the Virgin as if the Ku Klux Klan in the South were trying to protect white womanhood. But he says, "Some underlying reality more powerful than the glittering Virgin or southern white women had gripped these undeniably primitive minds. They were following some ancient pattern of behavior and were justifying their actions in terms that had nothing whatever to do with that pattern" (*PS*, 237). By "some ancient pattern of behavior" he means Spanish paganism, which has its psychological origin in the female principle of life. Though the Virgin in Spain was an established symbol of Catholicism, she was in reality a representation of paganism, the principle of eternal procreation: "A God died that man might live again, and the Virgin stood eternally ready to give birth to the God that was to die, that is, the Man-God" (*PS*, 238). Just as Wright was awed by the procreating image of the Virgin at Montserrat, he was struck again by what he witnessed in Seville: "The cross was held high and on it was the bloody, bruised figure of a Dying Man. . . . But behind the Dying Man was the Virgin ready to replenish the earth again so that Life could go on" (*PS*, 239), a spectacle remindful of the matriarchalism of the Ashanti, or the sun goddess in Japanese Shintoism.

Spanish religiosity, based as it was on sexuality, betrays another paradox. Toward the end of his travels Wright met a naturalized Spanish woman who told him, "The Church here will tell you that the people here love God so much that sex has been conquered. But all that you hear about here is sex. When I first came here, I thought that the Spanish had just discovered sex—they talked so much about it, and they still do. Sometimes they act as if they invented sex." To her, life was "upside down here" (*PS*, 212–13). Spaniards were obsessed with sex as much as with the Virgin; they were overly concerned with innocence as much as with sex. Such a contradiction revealed itself in all aspects of Spanish life. "Even the prostitution, the corruption, the economics, the politics," Wright observed, "had about them a sacred aura. *All was religion in Spain*" (*PS,* 192).

Although the preeminence of religion over sexuality suggests sexual repression on the part of Spanish men, it took a heavier toll of Spanish women. Antifeminism was rampant in all segments of Spanish society. At home men dominated women: "The women ate silently with one eye cocked in the direction of their men, ready at a moment's notice to drop their knives and forks and refill the half-empty masculine plates" (*PS,* 90). In public, men tended to move away from women and vice versa, a common occurrence indicating separation of the sexes. Young women, Wright saw, were always protected from contact with men so that virginity was guarded until marriage. At a hotel he found an American woman intimidated by the manager who claimed that she had refused to pay for baths she did not take. The Spaniard "smiled and explained . . . that men were not, perhaps, superior to women, but they were certainly more intelligent. His air was one of cynicism and his manner asked me to join him in his masculine game of domination" (*PS,* 74). As a fellow traveler, Wright admonished the woman not to be hysterical: "You are acting like a Negro. . . . Negroes do that when they are persecuted because of their accident of color. The accident of sex is just as bad. And crying is senseless" (*PS,* 76).

Not surprisingly, Franco's Falangists were bent on brainwashing young women. The government officials imposed a "moral" position on Spanish women. While women were protected, men were allowed to exploit prostitutes, a blatant antifeminist contradiction. Under the Falangist doctrine, feminine heroism was defined as subservience to men: *"though for [women] heroism consists more in doing well what they have to do every day than in dying heroically."* Women's temperament, the catechism continued, *"tends more to constant abnegation than to heroic deeds"* (*PS,* 77). Women under the Franco regime were called heroic if they sacrificed the pleasures of life for the sake of the dictatorship.

For Wright, the Falangist concept of the state, which denied the liberal doctrines of Jean-Jacques Rousseau and the right of universal suffrage, was in direct opposition to superhumanism. This political repression, in turn, resulted in a sexual repression evident in the Flamenco dance. During his visit to the legendary Granada, Wright met an accomplished

Flamenco dancer. He was deeply impressed by her performance as well as by the audience. "I pantomimed," he says, "what I wanted to say and they were willing to take time to imagine, to guess, and, in the end, to understand; and they were patiently determined to make others know and feel what they thought and felt." The dancer "began a sensual dance that made a kind of animal heat invade the room" (*PS*, 171). Even before the performance he was keenly aware of the frustration of the people. He assured the dancer, whose husband had died fighting for the republic against Franco: "I shall tell [Americans] that the people of Spain are suffering" (*PS*, 170). Wright was also a witness to the orgiastic ecstasy of the gypsy dance, the emotion that Western culture in general and modern Spanish culture in particular had long suppressed. Though a tourist himself, he watched the audience: "The Germans, Swiss, Americans, Englishmen gazed open-mouthed at an exhibition of sexual animality their world had taught them to repress" (*PS*, 167), a spectacle that suggests Carl Jung's collective, unconscious repression. Instead of emphasizing sexuality for the cause of repression, Jung theorized that the primal, universal, collective unconsciousness has a sexual as well as nonsexual component. According to Jungian psychology, personality consists of the persona, which is consciously presented to the world, and the anima, which is unconsciously repressed. When Wright explored the Black Virgin at Montserrat, he seemed to be more impressed by the collective, racial unconsciousness akin to Jungianism than by the sexual repression in Freudianism. To his Spanish companion Wright said, "Pardo, don't you see that conglomeration of erect stone penises? Open your eyes, man. You can't miss. I'm not preaching the doctrines of Freud. Let the facts you see speak to you" (*PS*, 66).

Whether sexual repression in Spain was viewed collectively or individually, its chief cause was the church. The church, which condemned sex, made Spaniards more conscious of it. Compared to other countries, Spain had the highest rates of prostitution in the city as well as in the village. "To be a prostitute was bad," Wright quips at the church, "but to be a prostitute who was not Catholic was worse" (*PS*, 21). This collective, almost unconscious, sexual repression that permeated Spanish society manifested itself in a vicious circle of prostitution and the church. Spanish Catholicism was "a religion whose outlook upon the universe almost legitimizes prostitution" (*PS*, 151). The Spanish people largely acquiesced in a circular argument the church had maintained over the centuries: "Sin exists, so declares this concept. Prostitution is sin, and proof of sin. So prostitution exists." This universal prostitution, then, was not regarded as something that must be eradicated, a cynical sign that "the work of salvation is not yet complete" and that the church must make "a more strenuous effort" to save men as well as women in the name of God (*PS*, 152).

From a sociological perspective, the church and prostitution helped each other. The church took great pride in its generosity by accepting fallen women under any circumstances with open arms: "a prostitute can at any time enter a church and gain absolution" (*PS*, 152). Such generosity, however, was not always considered by Spanish men as a genuinely religious endeavor. Rumor ran rampant throughout the country that some priests openly took advantage of "lonely" women as well as prostitutes who sought salvation in the church. Since sexual freedom was condoned by the church, Spanish laymen were jealous of the sexual lives of the priests. A Spanish man felt that "if they can do it and get away with it, so can I." Wright reflects, "I, for one, feel it naïve in our Freudian, twentieth-century world even to allude to the bruited sexual lives of priests and nuns. I do not know nor am I interested in whether they have sexual lives or not. I hope that they do, for their own sake; and I'm sure that God does not mind" (*PS*, 154). Given the paganism and superhumanism that characterized Spanish religion and culture, Wright's reflection emphasizes a conviction that human sexuality, as exhibited at Montserrat as well as in the Spanish Catholic church, was the best and absolute proof of the existence of God.

From an economic point of view, prostitution and poverty were intertwined in Spain. In the middle of the twentieth century, Spain was the poorest nation in western Europe. As an American, Wright paid homage to Seville, where Christopher Columbus's body was interred in the cathedral. Despite the surrounding lands rich with orange groves, olive gardens, and wheat and rice farms, "the impression of poverty was so all-pervading, touching so many levels of life that, after an hour, poverty seemed to be the normal lot of man." Recollecting the fertile southern landscape and the teeming city life in the America he had left behind, and Paris and the peaceful southern provinces of France, Wright comments, "I had to make an effort to remember that people lived better lives elsewhere" (*PS*, 178). Seville, a capital of "white slave" trade, was not only a glaring metonym for sexuality, but the whole nation "seemed one vast brothel" (*PS*, 187). In Spain, poverty and sexuality indeed went hand in hand.

Spanish sexuality begins in childhood. "No people on earth," Wright stresses, "so pet and spoil their young as do the Spanish" (*PS*, 152). A Spanish woman at an early age is trained to be a "seductress." Once married to a poor man, she can justify selling her body if it is to feed her children. On a national level, sex is regarded as a medium of exchange for goods and services. Significantly as well, "white slavery between Spain and the bristling brothels of North Africa is a wide-scale, well-organized, and genially conducted business—prostitution being perhaps the biggest business in the Mediterranean world" (*PS*, 150). Just as a poor young mother in the village is tempted to become a prostitute for the sake of feeding her hungry children, a young domestic earning low wages in a coastal city is enticed to travel to North Africa as a prostitute rather than "to be an ill-clad, half-starved slave to some spoiled, bourgeois Spanish wench" (*PS*, 151). Prostitution flourished in Spain, for there was behind this indigenous poverty a persistent pagan outlook upon life, a love of ritual, dance, sex, and nightlife.

3

Among the rituals, customs, and social activities Wright saw in Spain, bullfighting profoundly influenced his understanding of Spanish culture and religion. On the surface, a bullfight was a representation of the Spaniard's love for ritual and ceremony, "a delight in color and movement and sound and harmony" (*PS*, 151). But, underneath, this cruel ritual smacked of the central paradox of Spanish religion. On the one hand, bullfighting as a religious ritual found its sanction and justification in the canons and practices of Spanish Catholicism. On the other, however, it was antithetical to Spanish paganism, what Wright calls superhumanism as represented by the Black Virgin at Montserrat. Whereas Spanish Catholics believed in the sanctity of saving the human soul over protecting the nonhuman life, pagans, such as Buddhists and Hindus, made no distinction between human beings and the rest of the animate world because they believed that the soul resides in animals as well. The paradox of bullfighting is also apparent in the yelling of "*Olé!*" when the matador incites the bull. The expression means "For God's sake!"—a pagan religious phrase of the Moors—but the audience, as Wright points out, was not aware of its pagan origin. Thus the matador and the audience were invoking the name of God in keeping with the Christian as well as the pagan tradition. Wright makes a reference in a footnote to Américo Castro's *The Structure of Spanish History* (*PS*, 90).[9]

As the opening section of *Pagan Spain*, "Life after Death," reaches its apogee with the concept of eternal procreation, the female principle in life, as represented by the Black Virgin of Montserrat, the following section, "Death and Exaltation," culminates with the portrayal of a bull-fight Wright attended in Barcelona. At the beginning of the journey into Spain he befriended a Catalan family with whom he stayed for a short period. They told him that Spaniards, and Catalans in particular, "don't shrink from dark skins" and that they were traditionally miscegenational (*PS*, 80). But once he went into a village he was constantly stared at as if he were a total stranger, one who did not belong to Europe. "Amidst these naïve yokels," he felt, "I became something that I had never been before, an object that was neither *human* nor *animal*, my dark skin and city clothes attracting more attention than even the bullfighters" (*PS*, 131–32; emphasis added). Interestingly enough, while Spaniards would consider him neither human nor animal, it seemed as though bullfighting was a religious ritual that reflected both Catholicism, a religion eminently concerned with the human soul, and paganism, a superhuman and pantheistic philosophy of life encompassing all forms of life on earth.

From this ambivalent point of view, Wright's description of the bull-fight is a unique achievement. Above all, he was able to describe not only how the bullfighter faced death, but also how the bull himself felt:

> Chamaco's left hand now grasped the muleta firmly; he turned away from the bull, looking at him sideways, letting the red cloth drop below his left knee. He now lifted his gleaming sword chin high and sighted along the length of it, pointing its sharp, steel tip at the tormented and bloody mound of wounds on the bull's back. . . . The bull's horns rushed past his stomach as Chamaco tiptoed, leaning in and over the driving horns, and sent the sword to its hilt into the correct spot in the bull's body.
>
> The bull halted, swayed. Chamaco stood watching him, gazing gently, sadly it seemed, into the bull's glazed and shocked eyes. . . .
>
> I watched the bull. He sagged, his eyes on his tormentor. He took an uncertain, hesitant step forward, and then was still.

9. Américo Castro, *The Structure of Spanish History*, 113.

Chamaco lifted his right hand high above the bull's dying head;
it was a gesture that had in it a mixture of triumph and compassion. The bull now advanced a few feet more on tottering legs,
then his back legs folded and his hind part sank to the sand, his
forelegs bent at the knees. And you saw the split second when
death gripped him, for his head nodded violently and dropped
forward, still. A heave shook his body as he gave up his breath
and his eyes went blank. He slid slowly forward, resting on his
stomach in the sand, his legs stretching straight out. He rolled
over on his back, his four legs already stiffening in death, shot
up into the air. (PS, 111–12)

Although Wright vividly depicts man's battle against beast—the triumph of man's will over nature's power, as sanctioned by Catholicism—
his implication is unmistakable: the bullfight is a crime against life,
nature, and God. Viewed from any religious vantage point, it is a blatant
representation of the depravity of the human soul. At the conclusion of
the bullfight, he says: "The man-made agony to assuage the emotional
needs of men was over" (PS, 112).

What agonized Wright the most about this ritual—as it would perhaps any humanist—was the behavior of the audience in the bullring
in the aftermath of the slaughter. He was appalled to see the spectators
wildly rush to the dead bull, kick its testicles, stomp them, spit at them,
and grind them under their feet, "while their eyes held a glazed and
excited look of sadism" (PS, 134). Even though the bull was dead, they
looked as though they were venting long-repressed feelings toward
themselves. Such a behavior reflected one that occurred during the
performance as well: "The peak of muscle back of his neck gushed blood.
That was the way it had been planned. The means were cruel; the ends
were cruel; the beast was cruel; and the men who authored the bloody
drama were cruel. The whirlpool of discordant instincts out of which
this sodden but dazzling drama had been projected hinted at terrible
torments of the heart" (PS, 102). As noted earlier, the cruelty of a bullfight
is a reflection of man-centered Catholicism, in which the beast, part of
nature, is regarded as man's adversary. In a pagan religion the followers
are taught to respect man as well as beast. Significantly enough, Wright
was quick to point out that, though the predominant sentiment of the
crowd was sadistic, there were some who had compassion for the bull:
"the crowd began to howl, protesting, disapproving, fearing that the
bull was being punished too much, would be too weak to fight well"

(*PS*, 104–5). This sentiment of the spectators was a sign not only of paganism but also of universal humanism.

The sadism displayed on the part of the spectators also involved the bullfighter. One Whitney, an American who lived in Spain to become a bullfighter, informed Wright that the bullfight "has the intensity of religious emotion" and that the bullfighter is expected to offer his life to the bull. "Without that, there is no bullfight," Whitney explained (*PS*, 130). "More and more, when you're in the ring, you're not fighting the bull; you're trying to live up to the legend the public has built up about you. They ask for risks and they boo you when you refuse to take them. When the bullfighter believes in his legend and tries to obey the crowd, he's on his way to the graveyard" (*PS*, 131). Such a testimony suggests that Spaniards were fascinated by the cruelty perpetrated not only on the bull but also on the bullfighter, a perverted psychology akin to one often seen among the spectators who enjoy watching race car accidents.

In Wright's description of the bullfight, the cruel treatment of the dead bull by the spectators is suggestive of the lynch victims he had witnessed in the South. In the poignant portrayal of a lynching in "Big Boy Leaves Home," the victim is hanged from a tree and burned alive as the white mob chants in an ecstasy of joy. Big Boy, hiding in a kiln, watches Bobo lynched and burned: " 'LES GIT SOURVINEERS!' . . . 'Everybody git back!' 'Look! Hes gotta finger!' . . . 'He's got one of his ears, see?' . . . 'HURRY UP N BURN THE NIGGER FO IT RAINS!' . . . Bobo was struggling, twisting; they were binding his arms and legs. . . . The flames leaped tall as the trees. The scream came again. Big Boy trembled and looked. The mob was running down the slopes, leaving the fire clear. Then he saw a writhing white mass cradled in yellow flame, and heard screams, one on top of the other, each shriller and shorter than the last. The mob was quiet now, standing still, looking up the slopes at the writhing white mass gradually growing black, growing black in a cradle of yellow flame" (*UTC*, 49).

In *The Long Dream*, Chris, the protagonist's friend, is lynched for having had sexual relations with a white girl; consequently he is castrated and white women are fascinated by his genitals. Wright describes the scene in which a black physician examined Chris's body: "He rolled the corpse upon its back and carefully parted the thighs. 'The *genitalia* are gone,' the doctor intoned. Fishbelly saw a dark, coagulated blot in a gaping hole between the thighs and, with defensive reflex, he lowered his hands nervously to his groin. 'I'd say that the genitals were pulled out by a pair of pliers or some like instrument,' the doctor inferred. 'Killing him wasn't enough. They had to *mutilate* 'im. You'd think that disgust would've made them leave *that* part of the boy alone. . . . No! To get a chance to *mutilate* 'im was part of why they killed 'im. And you can bet a lot of white women were watching eagerly when they did it. Perhaps they knew that that was the only opportunity they'd ever get to see a Negro's genitals—.' "[10] Watching the bullfight, Wright was filled with horror at the sadism the ritual created: "It had been beautiful and awful and horrible and glorious," he thought, "and ought to have been forbidden." When he confessed, "I was revolted, but hungry for more . . . indignant, but bewitched, utterly" (*PS*, 109), he was also expressing the paradox of Spanish character.

This sadism, a sign of human selfishness, to which he thought Spaniards were prone, was in contrast to the African primal outlook upon life he saw among the Ashanti. As he reported in *Black Power*, he was enormously impressed by the African reverence for nonhuman life, an innate faith in nature that was absent in Christianity in general and Catholicism in particular. In his journey into Africa, Wright also found a strong resemblance between the Akan religion and a pagan religion such as Buddhism. An African, he wrote in *Black Power*, "dared not cut down a tree without first propitiating its spirit so that it would not haunt him; he loved his fragile life and he was convinced that the tree loved its life also" (*BP*, 262). The Akan religion and Buddhism share the common faith that mankind is not at the center of the universe. Small wonder that Wright, as he watched the bull being slaughtered, poured out his deepest sympathy toward it; he was genuinely concerned about how it felt as most of the Spaniards were ecstatic about its tragic death.

If the bullfight was viewed as a uniquely Christian ritual, it was nothing more than a religious practice in which followers were taught not only how to accept the inevitability of death but also how to create death, a means of sacrificing animal life for the benefit of human life. This human selfishness, this egoism, manifested itself in the drama enacted in the bullring: "*There was no doubt but that this beast had to be killed!* He could be allowed to linger along; he could be played with, teased even, but he had to go, for there was no possibility of coming to terms with

10. See Richard Wright, *The Long Dream*, 78. Subsequent references will appear parenthetically in the text as *LD*.

him. . . . This beast had not only to be slain, but *ceremoniously* slain—slain in a manner that would be unforgettable" (*PS*, 97). For Wright, the drama signified the mystery and miracle of human life. The mystery rested upon "why the human heart hungered for this strange need"; the miracle involved "the heart's finding that a rampaging bull so amply satisfied that need" (*PS*, 98).

As the Catholic priest offered faithful prostitutes absolution, the matador as a lay priest offered a mass in front of a huge audience in the bullring, the guilty penitents. What the priest and the matador shared was a common practice in which they themselves gained salvation in their work. But Wright realized that the matador's work was far more disciplined than the priest's. Whitney, the American bullfighter, told him that bullfighters in Spain "are not supposed to touch women or liquor. This is not to help you in fighting the bull; it is to keep you in condition to recuperate when you are gored. And make no mistake, you will be gored" (*PS*, 130). When the lives of the priest and the matador are compared, Whitney's observation that the bullfight, buttressed as it is by intensely religious emotion, always requires risk of one's life seems an ironic understatement.

Relying on Whitney's experience and understanding, Wright was fascinated by the emotional aspect of the bullfight. Whitney told him: "The essence of the bullfight is not in moving around, but in standing still. And that's a hard thing to do. When you're holding that muleta and facing a bull, your instinct prompts you to run. And if you do, you're dead, for the bull can outrun you. You must plant your feet in the sand and face death" (*PS*, 129). Whitney's understanding was derived from Juan Belmonte, the most celebrated matador in Spain. Wright was interested in Belmonte's characterization of bullfighting as "a spiritual exercise and not merely a sport. Physical strength is not enough." Wright interpreted this exercise as "the conquering of fear, the making of a religion of the conquering of fear. Any man with enough courage to stand perfectly still in front of a bull will not be attacked or killed by that bull" (*PS*, 113). Wright was told the local legend of a matador who stood sill reading a newspaper and of a bull that ignored him. But Wright thought it humanly impossible and inconceivable for a man to remain still against a surging beast that weighs ten times as much as he does.

While Juan Belmonte's concept of bullfighting was concerned with the emotional aspect of the sport, the test of courage in the face of death,

Hemingway was interested in portraying the technical and artistic aspects of the rite. Hemingway describes Romero's bullfight in *The Sun Also Rises* as though he were creating a painting:

> The bull did not insist under the iron. He did not really want to get at the horse. He turned and the group broke apart and Romero was taking him out with his cape. He took him out softly and smoothly, and then stopped and, standing squarely in front of the bull, offered him the cape. The bull's tail went up and he charged, and Romero moved his arms ahead of the bull, wheeling, his feet firmed. The dampened, mud-weighted cape swung open and full as a sail fills, and Romero pivoted with it just ahead of the bull. At the end of the pass they were facing each other again. Romero smiled. The bull wanted it again, and Romero's cape filled again, this time on the other side. Each time he let the bull pass so close that the man and the bull and the cape that filled and pivoted ahead of the bull were all one sharply etched mass. It was all so slow and so controlled. It was as though he were rocking the bull to sleep. He made four veronicas like that, and finished with a half-veronica that turned his back on the bull and came away toward the applause, his hand on his hip, his cape on his arm, and the bull watching his back going away.[11]

As Wright in *Pagan Spain* discusses the concept of Belmonte, who, fighting the bull closely, displayed his courage in facing death, Hemingway in *The Sun Also Rises* also refers to Belmonte's principle of always working close to the bull. "This way," Jake Barnes, Hemingway's mouthpiece, says, "gave the sensation of coming tragedy. People went to the corrida to see Belmonte, to be given tragic sensations, and perhaps to see the death of Belmonte."[12] Because Belmonte in the novel is neither a major character nor a representation of bullfighting as a religious rite, Hemingway underplays Belmonte's role and underscores Romero's bullfight as a central image of lovemaking:

> The bull was squared on all four feet to be killed, and Romero killed directly below us. He killed not as he had been forced to by the last bull, but as he wanted to. He profited directly in front of the bull, drew the sword out of the folds of the muleta and sighted along the blade. The bull watched him. Romero spoke to

11. *The Sun Also Rises*, 216–17.
12. Ibid., 214.

the bull and tapped one of his feet. The bull charged and Romero waited for the charge, the muleta held low, sighting along the blade, his feet firm. Then without taking a step forward, he became one with the bull, the sword was in high between the shoulders, the bull had followed the low-swung flannel, that disappeared as Romero lurched clear to the left, and it was over. The bull tried to go forward, his legs commenced to settle, he swung from side to side, hesitated, then went down on his knees, and Romero's older brother leaned forward behind him and drove a short knife into the bull's neck at the base of the horns. The first time he missed. He drove the knife in again, and the bull went over, twitching and rigid.[13]

Wright, on the other hand, depicts the bullfight as a test of one's courage in the face of death. He thus watched this drama of life for man, or death for beast, as it unfolded in the bullring. "Man and beast," he wrote, "had now become fused into one plastic, slow-moving, terrible, delicate waltz of death, the outcome of which hung upon the breath of a split second" (*PS*, 109).

In contrast to Hemingway's treatment of the matador, Wright was interested in bullfighting as a profession. Compassionate as he was, Wright was troubled to see a bullfighter too young to be risking his life, but Wright was told by a Spanish informant that the boy, coming from a poor family, had become rich: "Pain caused by a bull's horn is far less awful than pain caused by hunger" (*PS*, 107). Such a fact of poverty recalls a social and economic environment that bred prostitutes for the sake of feeding hungry children. Observing the young matador's performance, Wright also felt that the young man "did not quite believe in the value of what he had done . . . and harbored some rejection or doubt about the Niagara of applause that deafened his ears" (*PS*, 113). The boy thus regarded the bullfight as nothing more than his livelihood: neither emotionally nor philosophically was he concerned with his profession.

4

Despite the deeply religious tradition, whether Catholic or pagan, that buttressed its culture, Spain in modern times revealed degradation at

13. Ibid., 220.

all levels of society. Before Wright begins his discourse, he quotes these lines from Carl Sandberg:

> *I tell you the past is a bucket of ashes.*
> *I tell you yesterday is a wind gone down,*
> *a sun dropped in the west.*

Wright is alluding to his own observation that the vestiges of the glorious past were scarcely visible in modern Spain. Not only did Spain lose its political influence in the modern world, but its spiritual tradition fell victim to materialism and a decadent commercialism. Even though Spain remained a vital part of the capitalist world, its development was hampered by its outdated social and economic policies and practices. *Pagan Spain* thus begins with a quotation from Nietzsche, *"How poor indeed is man,"* and ends with Wright's own statement, "How poor indeed he is." By "he," Wright means the twentieth-century Spaniard who has lost touch with "the *rich* infinities of possibilities looming before the eyes of men," the "hearts responding to the call of a high courage," and "the will's desire for a new wisdom" (*PS*, 241; emphasis added). For Wright, the Spanish people were indeed economically poor; but more important, they seemed *poor* at adapting themselves to a modern progressive culture.

Throughout the text Wright tries to demonstrate the conservatism that gripped Spanish life individually as well as collectively. He saw, for instance, a Spanish Communist leader carry a statue of the Virgin on his back in an Easter procession because the statue was from his own neighborhood. To Wright's informant, this was a glaring contradiction. "I cannot support that kind of nonsense," the man uttered. "That man had sworn that he did not believe in God. Yet there he was carrying the Virgin. How can you fight with men who twist and turn like that?" (*PS*, 215).

Conservatism and traditionalism in Spain, on the other hand, had little effect on race relations. Surprisingly, Wright found Spaniards for the most part free of racial prejudice. Only a few of them showed a trace of the racism to which he was so accustomed in America and by which he was on occasion disturbed in France. Not only was he welcomed by Spaniards personally and affectionately wherever he visited, but he found them, the young intellectuals in particular, invariably antiracist, anti-anti-Semitic, anti-Franco, anti-imperialist, anti-Russian, and anti-American.

For Wright, Spaniards as a whole possessed an innate virtue that enabled them to relate to their fellow human beings on a personal and spiritual level rather than in terms of a social and political relationship, a man-made practice that plagued race relations in America. Such a virtue notwithstanding, Wright found Spaniards to be as pecuniarily greedy as Americans, with a materialistic outlook upon life that also degraded their culture. Historically Spanish colonialists had been regarded as less resistant to miscegenation than other Europeans, and yet, as a Spanish informant told Wright, "We gave them our culture in a way that no other European nation ever did, and we meant it. But we were greedy; we were after gold. And that ruined us" (*PS*, 213).

One of the culprits responsible for Spain's cultural stagnation was the church. Spanish intellectuals were all in agreement that reforming the archaic tradition must begin "at the cradle" and with "a new generation" (*PS*, 204). But the church, in collaboration with Franco, the Falange, and the army, was always in the way of change. Earlier in his discussion of Spanish character Wright posed this question:

> But why was Spain a dictatorship? I had long believed that where you found tyranny, such as exists in Russia, you would also find a confounding freedom secreted somewhere; that where you had a stifling bureaucracy, such as in France, there was a redeeming element of personal liberty; that where you had a police state, such as was in Argentina, you had under it, disguised, a warm comradeship; and that where you had a restrained and reserved attitude, such as is in England, you had, somewhere nearby, equalizing it, a licentious impulse to expression. *Did that principle hold true in Spain?* (*PS*, 12)

Wright's subsequent observations confirmed that a sense of freedom and open-mindedness existed in Spain only on the surface of daily life.

Otherwise, as Wright recognized, the Spanish mind was stifled by its own uniquely religious and irrational consciousness. Indeed, Spanish culture was irrational as Akan culture was irrational. And the sacredness and irrationality of Spain were in contrast to the secular mind-set that had liberated the rest of Europe from its past. Even compared with some parts of Africa, and most of Asia, Spain lagged behind in its progress toward modernism. "The African," Wright notes, "though thrashing about in a void, was free to create a future, but the pagan traditions of Spain had sustained no such mortal wound" (*PS*, 193). Africa and Asia, as he saw, were endowed with seeds of modernism while Spain sadly was locked in tradition and religion.

Such a critical view of Spain notwithstanding, Wright was nevertheless sympathetic toward the energetic maternal instinct of the Spanish woman, without which Spanish culture would not have survived after World War II. He discovered, for example, a strong affinity between the indigenous matriarchalism in the Ashanti, as discussed in *Black Power*, and the stalwart womanhood in Spain. Spain, beleaguered as it seemed by modernism and multiculturalism, withdrew into the past to regain its usable elements however irrational and primeval they might have appeared in the eyes of the world. Over the centuries Spanish men had built a state but never a society, a fact of history that betrayed another paradox of Spanish culture. Wright was convinced above all that Spanish women, not Spanish men, had borne the burdens of an economically poor nation. As women worked and reared children, men idled away their time talking abstract nonsense in the countless establishments of entertainment that flooded an otherwise chaotic landscape. If there was a semblance of society, it was based only on the hearts and minds of the women whose devotion to life stabilized Spain. This apotheosis of Spanish womanhood is thus derived from the female principle in life, a salient characteristic of pagan Spain.

10

Eight Men, Later Fiction

*E*ight Men (1961), a posthumous collection of seven short stories and a novella, "The Man Who Lived Underground," was published two years after Wright's death. "The Man Who Was Almost a Man," the first short story in the collection, was originally published in *Harper's Bazaar* in 1940 under the title "Almos' a Man." The story as published in *Eight Men* is slightly revised from the *Harper's* version. As Michel Fabre indicates, it is also a revised version of the last two chapters of Wright's unpublished novel "Tarbaby's Dawn," portraying a black boy as he grows up on a white man's farm. Wright wrote the part of the novel from which "Almos' a Man" derives, as Fabre suggests, as early as 1934. This part of the novel describes the boyhood and early life of a black boxer; what is common between the episode and "Almos' a Man" is the black adolescent's rebellion against a white-dominated society.[1]

While "The Man Who Lived Underground" overtly expresses Wright's existential philosophy, "The Man Who Was Almost a Man" presents a superbly controlled but eminently realistic narrative of a black youth growing up in the South during the Depression years. All of the stories in *Eight Men* deal with a variety of black characters in different circumstances, but the collection as a whole is primarily concerned with black oppression in white society. Two selections, "The Man Who Was Almost a Man" and "The Man Who Saw the Flood," focus on the racial problems black farmworkers and their families faced in the South in the 1930s. The stories in *Eight Men*, however, all differ in technique and style and produce a variety of effects.

1. See Fabre, *Unfinished Quest,* 626, 135.

1

In "The Man Who Was Almost a Man" a seventeen-year-old black boy, Dave Saunders, works along with his father for a farmer, Jim Hawkins. Dave dreams of owning a gun, which to him symbolizes manhood. Other workers, black and white, taunt him, his father often beats him, and his mother collects his wages from Hawkins. The black workers, in particular, treat Dave "as though he were a little boy," and he cannot stand it.[2] Having a gun with him, he thinks, would force them to respect him and treat him as an equal. He also believes that his possession of a gun might deter his father from beating him.

Even though his mother is more sympathetic to his needs than his father is, she cannot approve of his buying a gun. When he tells her, "Ma, Ah kin buy one fer two dollahs," she says, "Not ef Ah knows it, yuh ain!" As he pleads with her, saying, "But yuh promised me one," she flatly responds, "Ah don care whut Ah promised! Yuh ain nothing but a boy yit!" (EM, 16). Hawkins pays his wages to her instead of him because, as she tells him, "Ah knows yuh ain got no sense" (EM, 16). But the real reason for her initial denial of his request is her fear that if his father finds out about the gun, he is certain to blame her for allowing their son to have the money in the first place. From Dave's point of view, however, it is quite natural to think that possessing a gun would protect him from harassment and ridicule by other men. From an adult point of view, it is naive to think that owning a gun constitutes achieving manhood.

As if to resolve the ambivalence between the two points of view, his mother eventually gives Dave two dollars for him to buy a used handgun from a local storekeeper. He promises her that he will give the gun to his father. Rather than surrendering what he has bought with his own money, Dave sleeps that night with it under his pillow. The next morning, getting up earlier than anyone else, he goes out in the fields to learn how to fire the gun and accidentally kills Jenny, Hawkins's mule. He commiserates with Jenny, who has endured the drudgery as much as he has, but none of the people on the farm, including his father, believes that the shooting was an accident. Hawkins demands that Dave work two years to pay for the mule. To Hawkins, whether the shooting of

---

2. Richard Wright, "The Man Who Was Almost a Man," in *Eight Men*, 11–26. Subsequent references to the stories in this collection will appear parenthetically in the text as *EM*.

Jenny is accidental or not, Dave is responsible for the loss of property and must pay for it. Hawkins sarcastically tells him, "Well, looks like you have bought you a mule, Dave" (*EM*, 23).

Under the thumb of his father, who is under the thumb of Hawkins, Dave finds no way out of the predicament but to rebel. "He remembered other beatings," the narrator says, "and his back quivered." Dave, through the same narrative voice, reflects: "Naw, naw, Ah sho don wan im t beat me tha way no mo. Dam em all! Nobody ever gave him anything. All he did was work. They treat me like a mule n then they beat me. He gritted his teeth. N Ma had t tell on me" (*EM*, 25). Dave's reflection, as the quoted passage indicates, is conveyed simultaneously from his and the narrator's points of view; that is, the passage shifts back and forth between Dave's voice and the narrative voice. Such a narrative technique not only helps Dave express his deeply felt emotions, but it also objectifies his grievances.

Because his mother, who is the closest to Dave, is under his father's thumb as well, she is unable to defend her son. Not only is Dave forced to rebel against his father and Mr. Hawkins, but he finds utterly unfair the drudgery he has endured as poor Jenny has. He has now reached the point where he feels compelled to act by attacking Hawkins, a symbol of slaveholder mentality. Dave feels as though he would shoot at Hawkins's house had he one more bullet left. "Ah'd like t scare ol man Hawkins jusa little," he says, "Jusa enough t let im know Dave Saunders is a man" (*EM*, 26).

Hearing a freight train approaching from afar, Dave resolves to leave Hawkins's farm. "He jerked his head, listening," Wright says. "From far off came a faint *hoooof-hoooof; hoooof-hoooof; hoooof-hoooof*. . . . He stood rigid. Two dollahs a mont. Les see now. . . . Tha means it'll take bout two years. Shucks! Ah'll be dam!" (*EM*, 26). Just as the Mississippi was to Huck and Jim a symbol of escape, independence, and freedom, modes of transportation such as trains, trucks, and planes appear frequently in Wright's work. Bigger Thomas in *Native Son* dreams of flying an airplane; Big Boy in "Big Boy Leaves Home" escapes in a covered truck; and in *The Long Dream* Fishbelly Tucker dreams of riding a locomotive and, after his father's death, leaves Clintonville, Mississippi, for a flight to Paris. In this story, Dave's final action is to jump onto the passing freight train heading north.

Like Bigger, Dave has not been allowed to find his own identity as a man. Early in *Native Son*, one might recall, Bigger complains to his friend

Gus: "Goddammit, look! We live here and they live there. We black and they white. They got things and we ain't. They do things and we can't. It's just like living in jail. Half the time I feel like I'm on the outside of the world peeping in through a knot-hole in the fence" (*NS*, 23). Although Bigger and Dave are both physically competent workers, neither has much choice in his employment. Bigger chauffeurs the daughter of a wealthy businessman in Chicago as Dave works for a prosperous farmer in the South. Like Bigger, who accidentally kills his employer's daughter, Dave fatally shoots his employer's mule by accident. By a fatal accident, however, each protagonist is awakened to his manhood and to a sense of freedom and independence he has not known before.

Although Dave's desire to achieve manhood has been prompted by a climate of racial prejudice, Dave's story has more to do with his adolescent state of mind than with the racial problems he has faced. Since Bigger's family, unlike Dave's, is poverty-stricken, *Native Son* is less concerned with Bigger's personal state of mind than with the social and economic problems affecting that state of mind. Dave and Bigger have grown up in entirely different environments: Dave works along with his family on a farm, while Bigger, separated from his family, drives around the urban ghetto. Compared to Bigger, who is treated as nobody in such a world, Dave is regarded as a good worker under his parents' guidance, however stifling and misguided it may be. All Dave wants is to be treated as an equal to other men. Bigger, on the other hand, is forced to commit a crime in order to declare his existence as a man. Bigger is judged guilty for murdering his black girlfriend, but Dave escapes the unjust world as an innocent youth because he has accidentally destroyed only his employer's property.

What makes Dave's story poignant is the young protagonist's naïveté. He is neither a violent black youth like Bigger Thomas nor an erudite existentialist like Cross Damon. Nor is Dave a frightened victim of racial harassment like Big Boy. Although much of Wright's fiction at times smacks of protest, "The Man Who Was Almost a Man" expresses from various vantage points Wright's ideas of adolescent rebellion. Wright's argument is not confrontational as in his Communist stories such as "Fire and Cloud" and "Bright and Morning Star." Above all, Dave's story has a universal appeal, for the story evokes memories of adolescence anywhere and anytime.[3] Dave could be any adolescent who is conscious

---

3. See James Baldwin, "The Survival of Richard Wright."

of the brewing of talent and confidence within himself and is compelled to rebel against authority.

Dave's immediate goal in the battle of life is self-realization. He is painfully aware that no one on Mr. Hawkins's farm, even his own father, is concerned about his manhood. Each man, Dave feels, must discover a set of values for himself and test them against his own experience without guidance and authority. His parents, especially his father, try to keep their son a mere boy and ignore his adolescent wishes and dreams. In search of self-realization Dave is akin to Bigger in *Native Son* and Cross in *The Outsider*, for none of these characters receives guidance and support from his family or friends. Dave closely resembles Fishbelly in *The Long Dream* because both characters reject their fathers, as does Huck Finn, to achieve their manhood. Dave's search for self-realization is reminiscent of that of an existential character whose aspiration is to create his or her own world for freedom and independence.

What makes Dave different from such characters as Huck Finn and Meursault in Camus's *The Stranger* is the racist society in which Dave has grown up. Instead of going home that evening with a gun, as his mother has told him to do, Dave stays out in the fields, "aiming it now and then at some imaginary foe. But he had not fired it; he had been afraid that his father might hear. Also he was not sure he knew how to fire it" (*EM*, 18). His real use for a weapon is to tell the world not only that he should be treated as a man, but also that he should be treated as an equal to a white man. By owning such a weapon, Dave is convinced, his family can defend themselves should they be harassed or attacked by white people. He tells his mother that when he obtains a gun, he will give it to his father. Her approval of Dave's purchase of a gun hinges upon his promise to hand it to his father. She, like Dave, feels that a black man is entitled to own a gun to protect his family. "Here," she says. "Lawd knows yuh don need no gun. But yer pa does. Yuh bring it right back t me, yuh hear? Ahma put it up. Now ef yuh don, Ahma have yuh pa lick yuh so hard yuh won fergit it" (*EM*, 17). That Dave fails to keep his promise creates a sense of ambiguity because his action cannot indicate whether he is fighting for his manhood or against racism, or both.

This ambivalence is also related to the development of the story. Even before the shooting of the mule, Dave is aware of Hawkins's exploitation of black workers. When Hawkins finds Dave getting up early and going out in the fields, he suspiciously asks, "What're yuh doing here so early?" Dave merely replies, "Ah wuz fixin t hitch up ol Jenny n take her t the fiels." Hawkins at once demands extra work from him: "Good. Since you're so early, how about plowing that stretch down the woods?" (*EM*, 19). Since Hawkins employs both black and white farmhands, his racist attitude suggests that black workers have to put in more hours and effort than white workers for the same wages. Despite such an injustice, this story is less violent and confrontational than Wright's other Depression stories simply because Dave's parents, particularly his father, feel grateful to Hawkins for their employment and do not complain about their work. In this story, then, Wright depicts racial oppression and exploitation not only in terms of a black adolescent's rebellion against his father, but also in the context of a racial rift between black and white workers.

That "The Man Who Was Almost a Man" deals with the issues of race and manhood is also related to the irony of the story. While Dave's punishment is a form of racial oppression and exploitation, his accidental killing of a mule and his subsequent escape from a racist society constitute a form of freedom and self-creation. His final action, in turn, thrives on an ambiguity, for the story closes with an emerging hero who sits on top of a boxcar with his gun intact but with no money and no prospect of future action. "Ahead the long rails," Wright describes, "were glinting in the moonlight, stretching away, away to somewhere, somewhere where he could be a man" (*EM*, 26). "The Man Who Was Almost a Man," in sum, is one of the finest stories of initiation in American fiction that deals with the problems of race and adolescence at the same time.

2

"The Man Who Lived Underground"[4] has largely been regarded as an existentialist work. "The ultimate impression one carries away," Edward Margolies commented, "is not merely that of social protest, but

4. The novella originally appeared as "The Man Who Lived Underground" in *Cross-Section: A Collection of New American Writing*, ed. Edwin Seaver, 58–102. Parts of the novella had earlier been published as "The Man Who Lived Underground: Two Excerpts from a Novel" in *Accent*, 2 (spring 1942): 170–76. Subsequent page references to the novella are to "The Man Who Lived Underground," in *Eight Men*, 27–92.

rather protest against the nature of man, the human condition—what Camus called the metaphysical protest." Russell C. Brignano considered Fred Daniels, "the anonymous main character . . . created by Wright before his associations with the French existentialists," as "almost a purely existential hero." "Wright," David Bakish observed, "had read Dostoyevsky, Camus, Sartre, and other existential writers, but such a philosophy was instinctive to a sensitive outsider like Richard Wright, and like freddaniels." Pointing out the differences between Wright's work and Dostoyevsky's *Notes from Underground,* Michel Fabre read the story as an "existential parable" presenting the humanist message that while an individual can impose masks upon himself, he "acquires his identity from other men."[5] Few critics, however, have spoken of the ambivalence in Wright's expression of existentialist philosophy in this story.

Critical estimates of "The Man Who Lived Underground" have also varied over the years. When it appeared in *Eight Men,* after Wright's death, Saunders Redding characteristically dismissed it as "a first-class Gothic tale." Despite the extraordinary vividness and stylistic innovations, Redding observed, "It is as if Gabriel, brandishing his trumpet and filling his lungs with air to blow the blast of doom, managed only a penny whistle's pipe." Irving Howe, Wright's consistent champion, found in the story not a congenial expression of existentialism but an effective narrative rhythm, "a gift for shaping the links between sentences so as to create a chain of expectation." Howe felt that Wright thrived on naturalism, for when he moved from his naturalistic style to "a more supple and terse instrument," he went astray, and his naturalistic detail was as "essential to his ultimate effect of shock and bruise" as understatement to Hemingway's effect of irony and loss. James Baldwin, who had earlier detested Wright's portrayal of Bigger Thomas in *Native Son,* considered *Eight Men* a reflection of Wright's authentic rage. Although Baldwin did not provide a detailed discussion of "The Man Who Lived Underground" in his essay "The Survival of Richard Wright," he seemed to have the story in mind when he wrote, "Wright's unrelentingly bleak landscape was not merely that of the Deep South, or of Chicago, but that of the world, of the human heart." "Implicit in the story," Margaret

5. Margolies, *Art of Richard Wright,* 77; Brignano, *Richard Wright: An Introduction,* 143–44; Bakish, *Richard Wright,* 45; Fabre, "Richard Wright: The Man Who Lived Underground" and *Unfinished Quest,* 241.

Walker recently said, "is the existential dilemma of the marginal man who seeks in a stream of consciousness manner, to affirm himself as a human being." To Walker, "The Man Who Lived Underground," which links *Native Son* to *Black Boy*, was a crucial work in establishing Wright as a novelist of ideas.[6]

The ambivalence in Wright's expression of existentialist thought and the variance in the readings of the novella derive from the multiplicity of Wright's intentions. Contrary to disclaimers, the racial issue is a major theme in "The Man Who Lived Underground." "*All* literature is protest," Wright told Baldwin. "You can't name a single novel that isn't protest." To this manifesto, Baldwin "could only weakly counter that all literature might be protest but all protest was not literature."[7] Throughout the story, then, Fred Daniels is not a black man in name only. Not only is his plight real, but all the major incidents and characters he is involved with, which at times appear to be clumsily constructed symbols, nevertheless reflect the racial struggle and oppression from which a black man like him suffers. Once confined in the sewers Daniels is completely isolated from the white world, and the only group of people he encounters is a black congregation in a basement church. "After a long time," the narrator says, "he grew numb and dropped to the dirt. Pain throbbed in his legs and a deeper pain, induced by the sight of those black people groveling and begging for something they could never get, churned in him" (*EM*, 33). Such a scene is not inserted as a symbol but serves as a graphic detail of the futility and oppression of black people. Once he is mistaken for a black attendant working for a white grocer, who is away for supper. When a white woman asks for a pound of grapes, Daniels lifts up a bunch, which weighs much more than a pound, puts them in a bag, and hands them to her. "Thanks," she says, "placing a dime in his dark palm." "He flung the dime to the pavement," the narrator says, "with a gesture of contempt and stepped into the warm night air" (*EM*, 49). Not only do such episodes make for depth and solidity, but they are subtle expressions of ideology and protest.

Placing two crucial episodes at the beginning and end of the story, respectively, shows how seriously Wright deals with issues of race.

6. Redding, review of *Eight Men*, in Reilly, 346; Howe, "Richard Wright: A Word of Farewell," in Reilly, 350; Baldwin, *Nobody Knows My Name*, 149; Walker, *Richard Wright: Daemonic Genius*, 174.
7. Baldwin, "Alas, Poor Richard," in *Nobody Knows My Name*, 157.

Unlike a typical antihero of the modern novel, such as Ralph Ellison's *Invisible Man*, Daniels has no choice but to flee to the underground world. He has no choice as well but to confess to a crime he did not commit. The narrator at once intimates that Daniels "was tired of running and dodging" (*EM*, 27), a case history of oppression and persecution. The reader learns later that Daniels has falsely been accused of the murder of one Mrs. Peabody. Her identity as a white woman is not suggested until the midpoint of the story. Immediately after the episode in the grocery, as Daniels steps into the world above, the narrator says, "A few shy stars trembled above him. The look of things was beautiful, yet he felt a lurking threat." Walking toward a deserted newsstand, Daniels sees "a headline: HUNT NEGRO FOR MURDER" (*EM*, 49). In contrast to Orpheus, whose motive for descending to the underworld was to free Eurydice, Daniels scarcely remembers his wife, who is mentioned only once along with a woman he used to work for. Unlike Orpheus, Daniels utters to himself, "I'VE GOT TO HIDE" (*EM*, 27), the very first statement of the story, because he is black.

At the end of the story the racial theme is once again intensified. Unable to comprehend Daniels's vision of the underworld, Lawson, one of the policemen, shoots him down, insisting, "You've got to shoot his kind. They'd wreck things" (*EM*, 92). To Daniels, what Lawson calls "things" means the system of oppression black people have been suffering in America. Lawson's other statements are not as explicit and direct as this one. While another policeman observes that Daniels is suffering from "Delusions of grandeur," Lawson says, "Maybe it's because he lives in a white man's world" (*EM*, 89). Lawson's view is ambivalent, for it may mean, as Stephen Soitos notes, "a black man will never be accepted in a white world,"[8] or it may suggest that white society has caused what the policemen regard as Daniels's malady. The irony of Lawson's statement, of course, rests in the fact that white society, and the policemen in particular, rather than black people, and Daniels in particular, are sick and corrupt.

The racial theme in "The Man Who Lived Underground" is not only intensified with this kind of irony and satire, but it also thrives on Wright's style of understatement throughout the story. For one thing, Wright solved in this work the naturalist writer's stylistic problem by

8. "Black Orpheus Refused: A Study of Richard Wright's *The Man Who Lived Underground*," 24.

eliminating the excessive accumulation of detail. The details of oppression and violence with which scenes in *Uncle Tom's Children* and *Native Son* are saturated have disappeared in this story; instead such details are replaced by equally realistic but selective incidents, images, and dreams. To the imaginative reader, a black man trapped in the sewer is more disturbing than a black man forced to kill a white woman accidentally in her bedroom. Whereas Wright's earlier books contain blatant racists galore, the problem of racism in "The Man Who Lived Underground" is focused sharply but subtly on the white policemen. Lawson is the cruelest individual, determined to treat Daniels as a second-class citizen. Earlier in the story, when Murphy, another policeman, learns that Daniels has lived in the underground cave on "pears, oranges, bananas, pork chops," Lawson asks Daniels with a smile, "You didn't eat any watermelon?" (*EM*, 89). By contrast, the two other policemen appear merely curious about his underground life, if not slightly sympathetic to him. Limiting the portrayal of cruelty to one individual as Wright does in this story heightens the sense of a black man as a victim of a white man's inhumanity. Such stylistic and structural devices as understatement and scene reduction also make the thematic development ambivalent, for it is not clear whether Wright's intention is to protest against white racism or the human condition in general, or both.

Wright's idea of the universal human condition finds its congenial expression in the middle of the story as Daniels, now settled in the underground cave, tries to develop a dialectic. "Maybe *any*thing's right, he mumbled. Yes, if the world as men had made it was right, then anything else was right, any act a man took to satisfy himself, murder, theft, torture" (*EM*, 64). What Daniels calls "the world as men had made it" is precisely the fact of human history, not a utopia, philosophy, or religion. For him, of course, it constitutes a world of racism and oppression. If such a world were deemed right, then, it would follow that any one person's offense—"murder, theft, torture"—would be right. What Daniels is saying rings true because one person's offense, however serious it may be, can scarcely compare with even a fraction of the past, not to mention the future, injustice in American society.

Even though the world of racism and oppression is judged wrong, except perhaps by Ku Klux Klanners, it does not necessarily follow that "any act a man took to satisfy himself, murder, theft, torture" was right. To determine whether such an act is right or wrong, Daniels as an experiment steals precious jewels and hundred-dollar bills from the businesses he visits at night. Although he steals the money—and readily admits it is a criminal offense—he considers his act quite different from that of an embezzler he witnesses, since Daniels has no intention of spending the money. The embezzler is obviously guilty, but Daniels feels as though he himself is innocent. He nevertheless considers himself guilty because the money and jewels are lost to those who owned them. On the contrary, he does not feel guilty when a white woman buys a bunch of grapes at a bargain price while the store owner is not present and Daniels pretends to be an attendant, for instead of handing her dime to the store owner, he throws it away.

This personal feeling of guilt and innocence is further pitted against the societal judgment of Daniels's act. The other tools and merchandise such as a cleaver, a radio, and a typewriter that he steals in the underworld, the narrator reasons, "were all on the same level of value, all meant the same thing to him. They were the serious toys of the men who lived in the dead world of sunshine and rain he had left, the world that had condemned him, branded him guilty" (*EM*, 55). Whereas an individual's judgment of self-conduct as right or wrong is ambivalent, the societal assessment of individual conduct is one-sided. Experience has taught Daniels that society always imposes its own rules on a person, and such ideals as democracy, equality, and individuality all sound hollow.

The ambivalence in Daniels's judgment of human behavior and the conflict between the personal and societal judgments, therefore, lead to a nihilistic spirit Wright attempted to express in this story. For Daniels, at least, a human action, whether it is well intended or not, has no meaning. For a person to find value in his or her act or in a society that has victimized the person is sheer futility. If such value should exist, Daniels argues, it should be annihilated.

Although Daniels's argument resembles that of Cross Damon in *The Outsider*, who declares early in his struggle for existence, "Maybe man is nothing in particular" (*O*, 135), Wright's manner of expounding nihilism in "The Man Who Lived Underground" vastly differs from that in *The Outsider*. In contrast to Daniels's life, any act in which Damon is involved, whether it is the estrangement of his family, the suicide of his white mistress, or his betrayal of his friend and mentor, is minutely described. Reflecting on Daniels's life in the underworld, the reader finds it difficult to understand, much less judge. Only once does he mention his nameless wife and only briefly does he speak about having worked for a woman named Mrs. Wooten. Only once does he identify himself by spelling his name on the typewriter he has stolen: freddaniels. Typing his entire name in lowercase suggests that he is not a special person since what is spelled out is not a compound word or a proper noun. Above all, the reader learns that Daniels was arrested for the murder of a woman, not because he was an important person in the community or was in some way involved in the murder, but because he happened to be at the scene for no particular reason.

In *The Outsider,* on the other hand, Wright seems to have taken the risk of contradicting himself not only because of the naturalistic accumulation of detail but because of his insistence that Damon judges life inherently meaningful. The difference between "The Man Who Lived Underground" and *The Outsider,* then, derives from a difference of character. While Daniels resists action, Damon compels himself to act. Unlike Daniels, Damon is endowed with the freedom to create an essence; his action results in something, whether it is love or hatred, happiness or tragedy, life or death. Damon is guilty of his murder of the fascist as Raskolnikov is guilty of his murder of the pawnbroker in *Crime and Punishment.* As Damon's murder of the fascist Herndon is analogous to Raskolnikov's murder of the pawnbroker, Damon's killing of his friend Joe is similar to Raskolnikov's killing of Lizaveta, the pawnbroker's sister. Damon's murder of Herndon is also similar to Bigger's murder of Bessie in *Native Son.* In each case, the murderer has no malice toward his victim but kills to protect himself from prosecution. Both crimes result from premeditated actions, but none of Daniels's actions in the underworld lead to crimes as such. The experience Damon gains earlier in the novel makes him see nothingness and meaninglessness in human existence, but in the end his actions result in a realization of loneliness and "horror" on earth (*O*, 440). What appears to be a contradiction in Damon's view of existence is rather a reflection of his aggressive character. Making Damon more active a character than Daniels enables Wright to put less emphasis on the concept of nihilism in *The Outsider* than in "The Man Who Lived Underground."

As an expression of nihilism, "The Man Who Lived Underground" has a closer kinship with Camus's *The Stranger* than it does with *The Outsider.*[9] The similarity between the two novellas becomes even more

9. See Fabre, "Richard Wright, French Existentialism, and *The Outsider,*" 191.

apparent if seen in the light of the less fashionable literary philosophy, naturalism. To some American novelists, such as Stephen Crane and Theodore Dreiser, naturalism is a doctrine that asserts the indifference of the universe to the will of man. The indifference of the universe is most poignantly described by Stephen Crane in "The Open Boat"; the forces of nature are expressed by Theodore Dreiser in *Sister Carrie:* "Among the forces which sweep and play throughout the universe, untutored man is but a wisp in the wind."[10] Although Camus's naturalistic vision is not conveyed with the naturalist's typical massive detail or analyzed by Zola's experimental method, Camus nevertheless constructed *The Stranger* to dramatize a climactic assertion of universal indifference. Like Daniels, Meursault remains an inactive, passive character and seldom exerts himself against the forces that to him have no relation to existence. Like Daniels, Meursault is consistently shown as indifferent to society's interests and desires: love of God, family, marriage, friendship, social status. Just as Daniels is indifferent to the jewels and hundred-dollar bills scattered all over the cave, Meursault is averse to financial success and political power. Like Daniels, Meursault receives only what is given or acts only when acted upon. Both men resemble Sister Carrie, "a wisp in the wind"; they are more drawn than they draw.

If *The Outsider* represents a version of existentialism in which human action is viewed as the result of an individual's choice and will, Daniels, like Meursault, seems a passive existentialist compelled to do nothing in the face of the void and meaningless universe. Another point of similarity in their worldviews is the philosophy of the absurd: Daniels and Meursault are both convinced of the essential absurdity and futility of human existence. What, moreover, is absurd and futile to Daniels is a dilemma between his realization of chaos in the world above and his search for order in the world below. It is a conflict between his awareness of isolation and his dream of association. It is the disparity between the essential mystery of all existence and his demand for explanation. The ultimate irony in Daniels's story, then, lies in the fact that once he resolves his dilemma and begins to show his new vision to the world above he is shot to death.

In stark contrast to the ending of *The Stranger*, in which Meursault remains content with "the benign indifference of the universe" (*S*, 154),

10. See Dreiser, *Sister Carrie*, 83.

the conclusion of "The Man Who Lived Underground" suggests that Daniels has reached at the end of his life a frame of mind far different from Meursault's. The narrator in Daniels's story says: "He knitted his brows in an effort to remember, but he was blank inside. The policeman stood before him demanding logical answers and he could no longer think with his mind; he thought with his feelings and no words came" (*EM*, 79). His underground life has shown that he is liberated from desire, greed, and hatred and more significantly that he is free even of thoughts. Daniels's state of mind at the end of his life is reminiscent of that of Wright, who composed this haiku shortly before his death:

> It is September
> The month in which I was born
> And I have no thoughts.[11]

It is difficult to conjecture whether Wright had Zen philosophy in mind when he wrote "The Man Who Lived Underground." But there is much evidence to indicate that at least toward the end of his life Wright was interested in Zen aesthetics, especially in haiku.[12] That Japanese haiku is not the expression of a poet's subjective, emotional, or intellectual life can easily be seen in R. H. Blyth's four-volume selection of classical haiku, which Wright consulted with great enthusiasm.

As Blyth amply shows in these volumes, haiku masters such as Basho and Buson and their followers endeavored to achieve satori, the enlightenment of self, through poetry. Satori, as in Zen, is a state of *mu*, nothingness. The state of nothingness is absolutely free of any thought or emotion; it is so completely free that such a consciousness corresponds to that of nature. This state of nothingness, however, is not synonymous with a state of void, but functional. And its function is perceived by the senses. If, for example, the enlightened person sees a tree, that person sees the tree through his or her enlightened eye. The tree is no longer an ordinary tree; it now exists with different meaning. The tree exhibits satori only when the viewer is enlightened. As Daniels hides himself in the underworld, he encounters a large rat with beady eyes and tiny

---

11. See Fabre, *Unfinished Quest*, 513.
12. For an extensive study of Wright's haiku, see Robert Tener, "The Where, the When, the What: A Study of Richard Wright's Haiku." For a recent discussion of Zen philosophy and aesthetics, see Yoshinobu Hakutani, "Emerson, Whitman, and Zen Buddhism."

fangs; a dead baby floating in the sewer; and a corpse, its blood drained out into a bottle—objects by which one would be frightened. Unlike the young Bigger Thomas in *Native Son*, who kills a large rat with a skillet, Daniels lets the rat go "spinning in the scuttling stream" (*EM*, 30). Upon seeing the baby, he thinks it may be alive and instinctively tries to save it, but he realizes moments later that it is "dead, cold, nothing, the same nothingness he had felt while watching the men and women singing in the church" (*EM*, 34). In contrast to Tyree Tucker in *The Long Dream*, for whom obtaining corpses brings prosperity, Daniels regards embalming as a process of turning man into nature. What Daniels has witnessed in the underground world enables him to acquire a new vision of life, for the narrator says: "He saw these items hovering before his eyes and felt that some dim meaning linked them together, that some magical relationship made them kin. He stared with vacant eyes, convinced that all of these images, with their tongueless reality, were striving to tell him something" (*EM*, 59).

What Daniels envisions among such disparate images is a mysterious linkage that unites them. The ultimate goal of Zen teaching is for a person to discover his or her place in the totality of the universe. The totality of the universe in Zen philosophy has an affinity with that in American transcendentalism. Emerson, in a moment of exaltation, envisioned a transparent eyeball merging into a divine light, an image of infinity and oneness. Similarly, "Passage to India" is Whitman's demonstration of monism: the world is one, spirit and matter are one, man and nature are one. In "Crossing Brooklyn Ferry," the people separated by time and space are united in an image of seagulls. This concept of unity and infinity is also the basis for Zen's emphasis on transcending the dualism of life and death. Dogen (1200–1254), whose work *Shobogenzo* is known in Japan for his practical application rather than his theory of Zen philosophy, observed that since life and death are beyond man's control, there is no need to avoid them.[13] Dogen's teaching is a refutation of the assumption that life and death are entirely separate entities as are seasons or day and night. Among Wright's characters, Daniels is the closest to an individual unconcerned about the matter of life and death. While leading the policemen to his cave, he is clearly threatened with a possibility of death. Lawson, irritated with Daniels's strange behavior,

13. For Dogen's teaching on death, see Kodo Kurebayashi, *Introduction to Dogen Zen*, 44–50.

stares at his face for a long time without uttering a word, reaches his hand to his holster, and draws his gun. Laughing and staring at Lawson's face, Daniels says, "Mister, I got a gun just like that down there. . . . I fired it once then hung it on the wall. I'll show you." Despite the death threat, Daniels has achieved some kind of enlightenment, for he "looked brightly at the policeman; he was bursting with happiness" (*EM*, 90). It is no wonder that Lawson had earlier branded Daniels as insane when he said that he truly loved people as he watched through the underground holes how they lived.

A significant aspect of Daniels's kinship with Zen is his self-reliance. While living underground, Daniels seizes an opportunity to observe black people in prayer in their basement church. Hearing them singing, *"Jesus, take me to your home above / And fold me in the bosom of Thy love,"* Daniels "was crushed with a sense of guilt" (*EM*, 32), not because society, including himself, was in any way responsible for the conditions of their lives, but because they were "groveling and begging for something they could never get" (*EM*, 33). Like Emerson, Wright in this parable is emphasizing man's independence from God's power and influence. For Wright, an individual must achieve enlightenment by himself or herself even at the risk of losing sight of God, and this is somewhat akin to the doctrine of Zen. Unlike the other sects of Buddhism, Zen is not a religion as such, which teaches the follower to have faith in a monolithic deity. Like American transcendentalism, Zen teaches one a way of life completely different from what one has been conditioned to lead. In Zen, anyone possesses Buddhahood and all one must do is realize it. One must purge one's mind and heart of any materialistic thoughts and feelings. Emulating the spirit of nature and salvaging the self from societal impositions and influences enable one to appreciate the wonders of the world here and now.

Zen aesthetics thus calls for a vision of the harmonious relationship man can have with nature. A Zen-inspired haiku, like a Zen painting, seldom deals with dreams, fantasies, or concepts of heaven; it is strictly concerned with the portrayal of nature—mountains, trees, birds, waterfalls, and the like. For the Zen artist, nature is a mirror of the enlightened self; one must see and hear things as they really are by making one's consciousness pure and clear. What the haiku poet perceives has little to do with true or false, gain or loss, good or evil, war or peace, life or death. Zen is thus a way of self-discipline and self-reliance. Its emphasis on self is derived from the prophetic admonishment Gautama Buddha is said to have given to his disciples: "Seek within, you are the Buddha." Not only is Zen's self-enlightenment analogous to Daniels's, but the outlook of life Wright's protagonist achieves at the end of the story is not as negative and annihilative as that of a nihilist.

The ambivalence between nihilism and Zen in Daniels's character is also related to the racial theme of the story. The essential difference between the two philosophies is that whereas nihilism advocates the meaninglessness of all things and the destruction of all values, Zen teaches the value of achieving a purity without undue thought and excessive emotion—the human weaknesses that lead to desire, selfishness, and materialism. Although Daniels is sympathetic to the nihilistic spirit prevalent in the 1940s, as is Meursault, Wright is also convinced that these human weaknesses are the very causes of racial prejudice and oppression. And the ambivalence in Daniels's perception is reflected in the structure of the story as well. On the surface, Wright is concerned throughout with Daniels's universal guilt, but, underneath, Wright buttresses his dialectics with the fact that a man like Daniels is indeed a victim of racism.

To the follower of Zen, all human strivings and conflicts keep one from knowing oneself, from realizing one's true nature. To Daniels, forgetting the past and alienating himself from the activities of the world become a form of self-reliance. His "cave" is similar to the cave Plato talks about in *The Republic*, a place where a truth is discovered that makes it difficult for the seer to return to the external world. It is ironic that by blinding himself to the facts of society above, he seizes upon a new vision of life. Living in his cave teaches him how chaotic and meaningless life on earth really is. As if in a comic relief, he decorates his residence with jewels hung on electric wires and hundred-dollar bills pasted on the walls to show himself how worthless and meaningless they look. To the people living in the world above, human life is orderly and meaningful, but to Daniels it is filled with greed, hatred, and violence. Because he has acquired a new way of looking at human life, he becomes anxious "to go somewhere and say something to somebody" (*EM*, 75). This is why he seeks out the policemen who had earlier condemned him. The "something" he is happy to share with others remains unstated, but this understatement at the final scene as elsewhere in the story further heightens the effect of the narrative.

Daniels's achievement of enlightenment, then, makes "The Man Who Lived Underground" a unique racial discourse among Wright's works.

Unlike *Uncle Tom's Children* and *Native Son*, examples of naturalistic protest fiction, this novella thrives upon symbolism and metaphor. As a result, Wright's social protest is understated and at times muted, yet his voice is conveyed as strongly as in his previous books. The narrative style of this story is reminiscent of what Ezra Pound said about an intensive art. In expounding his theory of vorticism, Pound argued that a writer should be "concerned with the relative intensity, or relative significance, of different sorts of expression. . . . They are more dynamic. I do not mean they are more emphatic, or that they are yelled louder."[14]

Pound's statement about vorticism also echoes in Zen aesthetics. Yone Noguchi, a Japanese Zen-inspired poet and critic who influenced Pound and other modernist writers, made a modest proposal for English writers. "I think," Noguchi wrote, "it is time for them to live more of the passive side of Life and Nature, so as to make the meaning of the whole of them perfect and clear, to value the beauty of inaction as to emphasise action, to think of Death so as to make Life more attractive." To the Japanese mind, an intensive art can be created not from action but from inaction. Noguchi observed that the larger part of life "is builded upon the unreality by the strength of which the reality becomes intensified; when we sing of the beauty of night, that is to glorify, through the attitude of reverse, in the way of silence, the vigour and wonder of the day."[15] Stylistically, then, "The Man Who Lived Underground" also has an affinity with Zen-inspired writing.

The strength of "The Man Who Lived Underground" thus comes from a subtle fusing of various intentions. It is the problem of race that prompts the story to unfold, and as the story develops, it becomes an allegory that expresses in turn a universal theme. That is, Wright's intention is to show that just as a black man is victimized by white racism, an individual regardless of race falls prey to materialism. In the mid-1940s, Wright, disenchanted with Communism, became interested in existentialism, a literary zeitgeist developed by French writers such as Camus, Sartre, and de Beauvoir. Wright's intention in "The Man Who Lived Underground" was to mold his version of existentialism on racism

14. Ezra Pound, "Vorticism," 468. For a recent discussion of the influence of Japanese poetry on Pound's aesthetics, see Yoshinobu Hakutani, "Ezra Pound, Yone Noguchi, and Imagism."
15. Yone Noguchi, *The Spirit of Japanese Poetry*, 24–25.

in American society. In this allegorical story, therefore, Wright succeeds in making his racial and universal themes intensify each other.

3

Despite the impressive allegory developed in "The Man Who Lived Underground" and the poignant portrait of a black youth in "The Man Who Was Almost a Man," *Eight Men* received a decidedly less positive response from critics than did *Uncle Tom's Children*. Saunders Redding dismissed *Eight Men* as the work of a declining author.[16] Although all the stories in the collection indicated Wright's distress with his rootlessness, Redding theorized that his long exile somehow lightened "his anguish," which was "the living substance of his best books." For Redding, even the most impressive story, "The Man Who Lived Underground," as mentioned earlier, seemed only a Gothic tale. In a similar vein, Richard Gilman found the stories inept, "dismayingly stale and dated," and said that Wright's attempts at humor, tragedy, and pathos "all fail." *Eight Men,* however, pleased Irving Howe for its signs of the author's continuous experimentation despite uneven results. Howe found in "Big Black Good Man" "a strong feeling for the compactness of the story as a form. . . . When the language is scraggly or leaden there is a sharply articulated pattern or event."[17]

There is a distinct change of tone in *Eight Men* in comparison with *Uncle Tom's Children*. The earlier racial hatred is replaced by racial understanding in a story such as "Big Black Good Man." Moreover, Daniels's adventures in "The Man Who Lived Underground" may suggest Wright's own feelings after ten years in the Communist underground. In any event, Wright thrived on naturalism, for when he moved from his naturalistic style in *Uncle Tom's Children* to a more subtle technique in *Eight Men,* as Howe has pointed out, he was not as impressive a writer as he was in *Native Son* and *Black Boy.*

The critics' lessened enthusiasm about *Eight Men* can be explained in another way. "The Man Who Saw the Flood," the fourth story in the

16. Review of *Eight Men,* in Reilly, 345–47.
17. Gilman, "The Immediate Misfortunes of Widespread Literacy," in Reilly, 352–53; Howe, "Richard Wright: A Word of Farewell," in Reilly, 349–52.

collection, written in the 1930s, reflects the hard times black farmers faced in the South. Since the theme and style of the story are reminiscent of those of "Down by the Riverside," one can hardly detect a new development in Wright's artistry. "The Man Who Saw the Flood" portrays a family of three stranded by a flood (just as Mann's family in "Down by the Riverside" was trapped by a flood) and then threatened by a white store owner because of their overdue debt. "The Man Who Saw the Flood" is thus a purely naturalistic story in which black people are victims not only of a natural disaster but also of racial oppression.

Like *Black Boy*, this story is replete with images of desolation and destitute:

> The cabin had two colors; near the bottom it was a solid yellow; at the top it was the familiar gray. It looked weird, as though its ghost were standing beside it. . . . A dresser sat cater-cornered, its drawers and sides bulging like a bloated corpse. The bed, with the mattress still on it, was like a giant casket forged of mud. Two smashed chairs lay in a corner, as though huddled together for protection. (*EM*, 112)

Although racism is not a major issue in "The Man Who Saw the Flood," as it is not in "The Man Who Was Almost a Man," this brief story nonetheless amply demonstrates that the economic disadvantage black farmers suffer is caused by society, not by nature. While despair and hopelessness dominate "Down by the Riverside," stoicism and perseverance inspire the fighting spirit of the victims in "The Man Who Saw the Flood" as they do in *12 Million Black Voices*.

In contrast to "The Man Who Was Almost a Man" and "The Man Who Saw the Flood," both written in the 1930s, the stories in *Eight Men* written in the 1940s focus on an urban environment in describing the alienation of black people. Saul Saunders in "The Man Who Killed a Shadow" remains an invisible man, and the central figure in "The Man Who Went to Chicago" works in the basement of a hospital. Because of the characters' outsider or underground status in society, both stories somewhat resemble "The Man Who Lived Underground."

As "The Man Who Saw the Flood" is a repetition of "Down by the Riverside," an earlier story about the racial and economic oppression black people suffered in the South, the stories of the 1940s also present themes developed in Wright's earlier fiction. "The Man Who Killed a

Shadow" treats the psychology of fear in a black man.[18] Saul Saunders, encountering in a public library a white seductress who falsely "cries rape," as Bigger Thomas faces Mary Dalton in her bedroom, kills her for fear of being discovered. The world in which Saul was born is separated from the white world, in Wright's words, "by a million psychological miles. So, from the very beginning, Saul looking timidly out from his black world, saw the shadowy outlines of a white world that was unreal to him and not his own" (*EM*, 193–94). In the real white world, when a white man is tempted by a sexually starved white woman like Maybelle Eva Houseman, Saul's temptress, he would naturally be induced to have sexual relations with her. But the unnaturalness of the relationship between Saul and Maybelle has a direct corollary in the distance between the two worlds in which they lived. The thickness of the racial wall separating the two individuals indicates how deeply the fear of miscegenation is ingrained in Saul's psyche. "His world," Wright describes, "was now full of all the shadows he had ever feared. He was in the worse trouble that a black man could imagine" (*EM*, 201–2). If he were a white man, his action would be called hideous and atrocious. But, to him, Maybelle is an agent of death. To survive, he must destroy the woman, the shadowy figure that has threatened him all his life. Although Saul is convicted of premeditated murder by a grand jury, as is Bigger, whether or not Saul is guilty of killing Maybelle is moot. For Wright's ultimate intention was to bring home the verdict that white racism is the cause of Maybelle's death.

"The Man Who Went to Chicago," another story with an urban setting that Wright wrote in the 1940s, is concerned with the same psychological fear Saul Saunders suffers. This story, anthologized as "Early Days in Chicago" in the 1945 collection *Cross Section*, is based on Wright's own experience: he was employed first in a Jewish delicatessen, where he saw a white woman cook spit in the food she prepared, and later in a hospital, where he observed a scientifically unreliable experiment being conducted in the name of science. At the outset of the story Wright's observation of the white world is ironic. On the surface, northerners are less prejudiced than southerners, as Wright shows in *12 Million Black Voices*. When Wright worked in a restaurant with a white waitress, she tried to press her body against his, "an incident that had never happened

18. "The Man Who Killed a Shadow" was originally published as "L'homme qui une ombre" in French in *Les Lettres Françaises* (October 4, 1946), 1–10.

to me before in my life, an incident charged with the memory of dread. But she was not conscious of my blackness or of what her actions would have meant in the South" (*EM*, 219). The irony of the situation rests in the fact that while there appeared to be less racism in the North, a black man like Wright who had suffered from white racism in the South continued to suffer from a psychological fear of racism. In retrospect, Wright says:

> Slowly I began to forge in the depths of my mind a mechanism that repressed all the dreams and desires that the Chicago streets, the newspapers, the movies were evoking in me. . . . And, slowly, it was upon exactly that nothingness that my mind began to dwell, that constant sense of wanting without having, of being hated without reason. A dim notion of what life meant to a Negro in America was coming to consciousness in me, not in terms of external events, lynchings, Jim Crowism, and the endless brutalities, but in terms of crossed-up feeling, of emotional tension. (*EM*, 214–15)

This silent suffering finds its expression in one of the most inhumane episodes in Wright's work. When he worked as an assistant to a young Jewish doctor in a hospital, he was ordered to cut out the vocal cords of young dogs sent from the city pound so that their howls would not disturb the hospital patients. As the voiceless dogs awoke, Wright painfully saw them "lift their heads to the ceiling and gape in a soundless wail. The sight became lodged in my imagination as a symbol of silent suffering" (*EM*, 239). The mistreatment of the dogs is reminiscent of the drudgery of the mule on the white man's farm in "The Man Who Was Almost a Man." In *Black Boy*, one may recall, Wright describes an incident in which his supervisor at a company instigated animosity between Wright and a black boy working for another company so that they would try to stab each other. Instead Wright agreed to have a boxing match to avert a tragedy. Such an experience convinced him that white men not only treated black boys as servants but also considered them entertainers. It was great pleasure for white men to watch black boys fight as if they were dogs or cocks (*BB*, 207–8).

"The Man Who Went to Chicago" ends with a bizarre episode in which a fight erupts between two black hospital workers who destroy cages that hold experimental rats, mice, guinea pigs, and rabbits. In trying to put the animals back in their proper cages the workers misplace them, but the scientists will not know about the rearrangement of the experimental animals. Wright thinks about reporting the disaster to the director, but doing so would jeopardize the two fellow workers' employment and possibly his own. Because the director does not treat him as a human being, he feels no moral responsibility to support the director's cause. "The hospital," Wright observes, "kept us four Negroes as though we were close kin to the animals we tended, huddled together down in the underworld corridors of the hospital, separated by a vast psychological distance from the significant processes of the rest of the hospital—just as America had kept us locked in the dark underworld of American life for three hundred years—and we had made our own code of ethics, values, loyalty" (*EM*, 250).

In contrast to the short stories written in the forties, those of the fifties are marked by experimentation in theme and style. These stories are still concerned with white racism, but this subject matter is kept in the background. Consequently, the naturalistic protest mode that characterized Wright's earlier fiction is replaced with a form of satire and irony. Two of the short stories have their settings abroad while the third focuses on white men rather than black men in dealing with racial issues. "Big Black Good Man," originally published in French in *La Parisienne* (1958), treats humorously the inferiority complex of a Danish hotel clerk confronted by a huge black sailor who asks for a room, a bottle of whiskey, and a woman companion. "Man of All Work," written in 1957 but first published in *Eight Men*, describes an unhappily married white man who is shocked after he makes amatory advances to a maid who turns out to be a black man in disguise. "Man, God Ain't Like That," also previously unpublished, portrays a white American painter, John, who adopts a native African boy, Babu, as his servant. Babu privately conducts a secret ritual of making sacrifices to his Ashanti ancestors but publicly sings Christian hymns. Impressed by white civilization, he reasons that white men must have killed Christ to create such a civilization and that he now must kill John, his master, whom he regards as a Christ figure.

What the three stories have in common is Wright's use of comic irony and humor. In "Big Black Good Man," Olaf, the Danish hotel clerk, frightened when he encounters a huge, fierce-looking black man, feels physically threatened as the guest tries to touch Olaf's neck. It turns out that he merely wants to measure the size of Olaf's neck so that he can buy six beautiful shirts that fit him as a token of his gratitude for having been provided with a female companion for the six nights he spent in the hotel during the previous year. This ironic event brings out tears in Olaf, who appreciates the black man's thoughtfulness. The sailor, in turn, laughs and as he leaves the hotel says, "Daddy-O, drop dead" (*EM*, 109).

Irony and humor, however, are not the only elements that Wright uses to dramatize human loyalty and kindness. For Wright earlier in the story pays attention to what is innate in males regardless of race. Having a great deal of sympathy with human needs, Olaf reflects: "But he liked sailors. They reminded him of his youth, and there was something so direct, simple, and childlike about them. They always said straight out what they wanted, and what they wanted was almost always women and whisky . . . 'Well, there's no harm in that . . . Nothing could be more natural,' Olaf sighed" (*EM*, 95).

Although Wright's short stories of the 1950s are marked by what Edward Margolies calls "a lessening of the fierce tensions that had characterized his fiction up until this time,"[19] his expression of irony and humor in "Man of All Work" is directly related to the racial tensions in American life. Early in the story Carl argues to his wife that white people would not notice his sexual identity since, he says, "we all look alike to white people. . . . You'd take one look at me and take me for a woman because I'm wearing a dress" (*EM*, 124). Such a dialogue, however trivial it may sound, reveals a serious racial problem: white people always treat black women as domestics and black men as laborers. "Man of All Work" also alludes to a volatile racial issue in America. Fairchild, learning the maid's sexual identity, tries to concoct a lie that Carl, who wore a woman's dress, was trying to rape Fairchild's wife. "Ha! *See?*" Fairchild says. "Then I detected 'im. I shot 'im in self-defense, shot 'im to protect my honor, my home. . . . I was protecting white womanhood from a nigger rapist impersonating a woman!" (*EM*, 154).

"Man, God Ain't Like That" is the least accomplished piece of fiction in *Eight Men*. While the plot of the story consists of a series of obscure, bizarre incidents, the elements of irony and humor added from time to time sound gratuitous. As Saunders Redding has noted, "it takes more than dialogues to establish a compelling motive for ritual murder, and to explain the failure of the police to solve it, and to drive home the obscure point of it all—if there is a point."[20] Although Wright's intention

19. Margolies, *Art of Richard Wright,* 74.
20. Review of *Eight Men,* in Reilly, 346

is not clear, the story can be read as an allegory about the misunderstanding between Westerners and Africans. Westerners, represented by the American artist John and his wife, regard Africans, represented by Babu, as primitives who serve their colonial masters. Africans, in return, worship Westerners, who might rescue them from their tribal culture. Babu's mission in Paris, therefore, is to seek out the white God, but he fails because "Babu walk white-man streets and look at white man. All white man look alike" (*EM*, 188), an ironic twist of racial stereotype that is similar to regarding all black women as domestics in "Man of All Work." It is also ironic that the Paris police, trying to apprehend suspects, dismiss Babu since he looks like "a staunch Christian" (*EM*, 192) who would not have killed another Christian.

Despite Wright's attempt to deal with white racism from an ironic and comic point of view, his later short stories greatly suffer from a comparison with those in *Uncle Tom's Children*. As social satire, however, the later stories succeed in shifting his vantage point from social oppression to psychological malady. In these stories, white oppressors are pitied as much as are black victims. Because Fairchild in "Man of All Work" is dominated by his wife, he tries to recover his virility in drinks and black maids. Because Olaf in "Big Black Good Man" finds himself old and lonesome, he envies the black sailor's libidinousness. While *Uncle Tom's Children* is permeated with inhumane violence and death, most of the stories in *Eight Men*, full of life and humanity, deplore racial issues with subtlety and poignancy.

11

The Long Dream as Racial
and Sexual Discourse

When *The Long Dream*, Wright's last novel, written in exile in France, appeared in 1958, two years before his death, it encountered largely negative reviews in America. Despite his efforts to portray black people's bitter experiences in the Deep South, as he did so successfully in *Uncle Tom's Children* and *Black Boy, The Long Dream*, some readers felt, betrayed a distinct decline in his creative power. Saunders Redding, who had earlier detected a danger inherent in Wright's exile, observed that in *The Long Dream* Wright "has cut the emotional umbilical cord through which his art was fed, and all that remains for it to feed is the memory, fading, of righteous love and anger." Nick Aaron Ford, another black critic, concurred with Redding that Wright had lost touch with his native soil and the swiftly changing racial current in the United States. Agreeing with Redding and Ford, Maxwell Geismar remarked that while *Uncle Tom's Children, Native Son,* and *Black Boy* are "solid, bitter, savage, almost terrifying fictional studies of the Negro mind," *The Long Dream* turns out to be "a surrealistic fantasy of paranoid and suicidal impulses, veiled in political terminology."[1]

The lack of depth some critics deplored was appreciated as socially authentic by others. Such reviewers as Redding and Ford considered the novel merely repetitious of what Wright had shown before, while others deemed his racial discourse as developing and continuing in relevance. One reviewer argued that the novel presents "a social document

1. Redding, "The Way It Was," in Reilly, 329; Ford, "A Long Way from Home," in Reilly, 335–36; Geismar, "Growing Up in Fear's Grip," in Reilly, 333.

of unusual worth" with its catalog of lynching, police brutality, and race riots in a southern town. Writing in *Best Sellers,* another reviewer found a value in Wright's depiction of black characters as amoral and as "interested in practically nothing but irregular but frequent sexual relations." This reviewer, however, cautioned that such an idiosyncrasy of black people "is in reality blamed on the white people." Still another reader compared *The Long Dream* with *Native Son* for the way in which it treats race problems directly, rather than by analogy, as well as with well-established social novels like *An American Tragedy* and *The Grapes of Wrath.*[2]

What is implicit in much of the criticism *The Long Dream* has received is the perception that, even though it thrives on authentic details, it lacks artistic merit in its structure and characterization. Most critics have accepted Wright's racial views in it as realistic and convincing but found the ending of the book abrupt because Wright allows Fishbelly, despite his emerging manhood, to remove himself from the African American world, go to jail, and then flee to France in search of freedom and equality. What seems lacking at the crucial point in Fishbelly's development is the mental and physical toughness in battling against racism and achieving independence that is shown by Wright's other heroes like Bigger Thomas and Cross Damon. Edward Margolies takes a highly sympathetic attitude toward *The Long Dream* and provides a discerning analysis in *The Art of Richard Wright.* But, arguing that any dream must be related to an authentic environment, he concludes that "Fishbelly's removal from that environment somehow alloys the dream." Similarly, Katherine Spandel interprets the novel in terms of Wright's own life. Spandel's observation is valuable, since she cogently relates the hero's quest to what actually happened to Wright. She, however, notes: "As early as his childhood Wright could find little love in his own people, and he surely found little in whites. It is not surprising, then, although it is disappointing, that Wright leaves his last hero literally up in the air."[3]

To reassess *The Long Dream* would require a new approach, not to its social and cultural backgrounds, which are history and legend, but to Wright's construction of a unique discourse. It was most important for

2. Roy Ottley, "Wright's New Novel Isn't for Squeamish," in Reilly, 327; Paul Kiniery, review of *The Long Dream,* in Reilly, 332; Charles Shapiro, "A Slow Burn in the South," in Reilly, 334.

3. Margolies, *Art of Richard Wright,* 166; Spandel, *"The Long Dream."*

Wright to express what he actually felt as a black youth growing up in the Deep South. This subjectivity is what earlier critics overlooked, but it enabled Wright to develop the theme of miscegenation as a personally felt experience for Fishbelly, rather than as the background for character as it was used earlier in *Native Son*. For *The Long Dream*, then, Wright constructed a twofold discourse: racial reality and self-portrait. The dual discourse is unified on the strength of a sexual theme, for the taboo of interracial sex is the product of sociohistorical environment and personal desire.

1

Although the title suggests that *The Long Dream* is concerned with an unrealistic quality Wright finds in Fishbelly's life, the book is based on solid facts and believable events. Many of its episodes draw upon the life of the young Wright as it is portrayed in *Black Boy*. Both Fishbelly and Wright at an early age discover that their fathers are having extramarital affairs. Rejecting their home environment at a crucial point in their development, both seek an entirely new environment, Fishbelly moving to another country and Wright going to the North. Although Fishbelly and Wright do not actually see lynching and castration, they both hear about events that give their sexual initiation a traumatic impact. Fishbelly, in fact, witnesses the castrated body of his friend in his father's undertaking parlor.

In some aspects *The Long Dream* differs from *Black Boy*: Fishbelly tries to become a rich businessman like his father but gives up that ambition in favor of seeking his own dreams, whereas Wright, a talented, precocious youth, tries to survive the racial oppression in the South but leaves there with an ambition to become a writer. The most important difference between the two books is Wright's treatment of miscegenation, and this issue underlies Fishbelly's initiation into manhood. In *Black Boy*, Wright's chief interest lies in the self-creation of an intellectual, and the discourse closely reflects the workings of a mind focused on the cultural, social, and political issues of the period. By contrast, *The Long Dream* deals with the self-creation of manhood by an adolescent, and much of its writing is controlled by Fishbelly's sexual instincts. Fishbelly is determined to cross "the line that the white world had dared him to cross under the threat of death" (*LD*, 165). Because the prerequisite to his manhood is freedom to have sexual relations with a white woman, this taboo imposed by the white world emerges as the central problem in his life. *The Long Dream* thus becomes a discourse of miscegenation in which the white woman is used as a sign. At crucial moments in the discourse, the narrative voice conveys the anger, fear, and frustration Fishbelly and other black boys feel, as well as the psychological wounds they suffer because of the taboo.

Thematically, *The Long Dream* focuses on Fishbelly's creation of himself through sexual initiation. Not only does the initiation mold his character, but the confrontation between the forces that buttress the sexual taboo and those that try to destroy it governs the structure of the novel. As the story begins, Fishbelly and his pals are enjoying pastoral scenes in the warm South similar to those in *Black Boy* and "Big Boy Leaves Home." In contrast to these works, however, *The Long Dream* features a protagonist who is not overjoyed with such an environment. Behind the tranquil surface of a southern town lurks an unwritten law prohibiting black men from consorting with white women. Since this novel is replete with the social and political details, some of which are swiftly provided, Wright's concentration on the psychological and overtly sexual implications of the taboo unifies the story. The unity is far more important to the effect of the story than to the racial views expressed by the characters, for the contentions of the protagonist and those of the white world are not only in direct opposition but irreconcilable. On the one hand, his achievement of manhood is expressed in terms of a long dream; on the other, his violation of the taboo brings a death penalty meted out in the most inhuman means.

Wright's dialectic of freedom and oppression in *The Long Dream* is not as simple as it appears. In effect, Fishbelly's personal freedom is realized, preserved, and fulfilled because of social oppression. Tyree Tucker, Fishbelly's father, is adamantly opposed to the manhood his son desires and continues to dream about. In Wright's other books, such as *Black Boy*, *Native Son*, and *The Outsider*, the protagonist's father is nonexistent or disappears, whereas Tyree plays a dominant role in attempting to shape his son's future. But in the process a generational rift arises between father and son. Tyree, obsequious as he is, uses the white world for his materialistic gains and is used by the corrupted white politicians and officials. Fishbelly, a talented and sexually awakened youth, loves the white world, as his father does, but is also enchanted with white woman, with whom Tyree persistently warns him not to associate. Wright is showing here the differences between the two characters in their relationships to society. Because Fishbelly is young and idealistic, he has little control over his social environment.

The narrative structure of *The Long Dream* is as complex as is Wright's characterization. Wright tells the story through the gradual progress Fishbelly makes from a racially well-protected childhood to the threshold of manhood and from a safe but confined black community in the white world to France, a less racist white society. From another point of view, the story is twofold. One aspect of its development focuses on a series of social, economic, and political events relating to Tyree's business activities. Racism always plays a crucial role in these events, which involve corruption and intrigue. The other aspect deals with Fishbelly's life. While Wright's description of the racial turmoil constitutes the surface structure of the novel, to borrow a linguistic terminology, the deep structure consists of Fishbelly's initiation into manhood, which Wright portrays in personal, psychological, and sexual terms. Fishbelly, indeed, is an innocent, shy black boy in the beginning, but in the end he is on the way to being a robust cosmopolitan, as Wright himself became when he went to Paris.

Although Fishbelly's manhood is the central theme, the surface structure of the novel is dominated by various ideas and impressions about racism in general. Some of the racial views expressed in the book are Wright's own, but most of them derive not only from historical facts but also from the prevailing sentiments held by black and white people living in the Deep South in the 1930s and 1940s. Many of the incidents and episodes in *The Long Dream*, as in Wright's other works, are based on his experiences. The lynching of Chris derives from Wright's observation of such an incident when he worked as a bellboy, as told in *Black Boy*. Pastor Ragland's funeral sermon for the victims of the Grove fire, as Michel Fabre shows in *The Unfinished Quest of Richard Wright*, derives from Wright's hearing of such sermons. The fire at the Grove that has forty-two black victims in the novel is based on the nightclub fire in Natchez, Mississippi, that killed 215 people, many of them black teenagers.[4] Wright is often perceived as a protest novelist because of the powerful statements he made in his earlier novels, views that are

---

4. Fabre, *Unfinished Quest*, 48; Henry F. Winslow, "Nightmare Experiences," in Reilly, 337.

solidly based on facts. In the *Long Dream* he expresses the same ideas, but he does so from the perspectives of various individuals. Even among the black characters, Tyree and Fishbelly express their racial views not only as men representative of two generations but as men with different outlooks on sexuality and love. Chief of Police Cantley, even though he is a confirmed racist who condones police brutality, is capable of placing himself in black people's shoes.

The first part of the novel, as the title "Daydreams and Nightmares . . ." suggests, is mostly concerned with Fishbelly's sexual initiation, which continues to have its development in the second part, called "Days and Nights. . . ." The second part is filled with episodes that express the racial views of Clintonville's residents. This middle section of the novel opens with an expression of the frustrations felt by Maybelle, a black girl, who is jealous of Gladys, Fishbelly's near-white girlfriend. Maybelle screams in a rage: "Go to hell, you white-looking bitch! . . . I ain't blind! I know they made their goddam choice! They want *white* meat! But you sluts ain't *white!* You *niggers* like me! But you the nearest thing that they can git that *looks* white!" (*LD*, 177). Ironically, Maybelle is not the only spurned woman; Gladys's father, a white man, also refuses to see his daughter. Though Gladys is courted by Fishbelly, her problems seem insoluble. Wright explains her problems through his narrative voice:

> A white man had a black woman; that black woman gave birth to a near-white bastard girl child; and, because it was known that that near-white bastard girl child had had a white father, black men ran after her. And that near-white bastard girl child, in turn, would have a bastard baby that could ask protection of neither whites nor blacks. Such a girl could find men, but rarely a husband. (*LD*, 184)

As narrator, Wright also interprets the social views expressed in the novel. Some of the ideas are shared with black intellectuals residing in Clintonville, but others, which are of his own making, are expressed through the narrative voice. When Fishbelly goes around the town to collect rent, he meets those who are eager to express their views on life, which are directly related to black life. Miss Hanson, a retired schoolteacher "living alone in one disinfectant-reeking room on a government pension," responds to Fishbelly's call with a sense of humor: " 'Good morning, Miss Hanson,' he would greet her. 'I'll take the rent, if you don't mind.' 'I do mind, but there it is,' Miss Hanson would cackle." His encounter with her, however, reveals how concerned some people are about Tyree's operation of a brothel. She makes it a ritual to wash her coins with a solution of disinfectant and snare her dollar bills with tweezers. "That's one thing I don't understand about people," she explains. "They bathe, brush their teeth, wear nice clothes, want clean food, and then they touch money all day long, money that's been in the hands of even those nigger whores on Bowman Street, with all their venereal diseases. *Think of it!* Mr. Tucker, money carries *germs!* Doesn't your common sense tell you that?" (*LD,* 202–3). She also chides him, reminding him that he is putting the cigarette in his mouth with the same fingers he has used to give her change.

Miss Hanson's comments on money serve the idea of a dual narrative. On the one hand, they contribute to Wright's discourse on race because Tyree's business of running a house of prostitution is intertwined with the racial bigotry rampant in the town. On the other, the well-respected retired schoolteacher's commentary on money makes Wright's discourse on sex a satire on Fishbelly's initiation into manhood. In effect, this talk of sex becomes an indispensable thread to the narrative of Fishbelly's growth and development. His education, moreover, reaches its apogee immediately after the episode with Miss Hanson, when on another day his friend Sam's father gives him a lecture on having pride in his black heritage: "The white man's done conquered us 'cause he's made us 'shamed of our hair, our skin, our noses—'shamed of Africa. There was a time when the black man was high up! Read, Fish. . . . Did you know that the Egyptians was *black*? Did you know an English king had a *black* wife? Did you know that Beethoven had *black* blood in 'im? Read, Fish" (*LD,* 204).

Despite his rapid physical growth, his affluent family life prevents him from gaining insight into racial oppression. He is not aware of corruption, let alone injustice, among the town officials, nor does he recognize that his father is a successful businessman only because he subserviently cooperates with white people with power. What is worse, Tyree exploits the black people by owning illicit establishments and rental property. It is Tyree who pampers Fishbelly and hinders him from becoming a man of honor and vision. Only the narrative voice suggests that black men like Tyree and Dr. Bruce, a physician, are not really superior to their oppressors. Precocious though he is, Fishbelly has not yet grown up enough to be able to listen to such a voice.

In the middle of the story Wright provides an ironic view that corruption is the only common ground where black and white people can meet; otherwise, they do not want to share their lives in any way, an observation that the young Wright made while growing up in the Deep South. Throughout the novel, especially in part 2, "Days and Nights . . . ," Wright takes pains to show that the white people who fear the social progress the black people will make if given a chance know that the only way to prevent it from happening is to keep them intimidated and poor. The authenticity of the racial views expressed in *The Long Dream* can be demonstrated by *Black Boy* and *Uncle Tom's Children*, but the unique quality of this discourse is Wright's judicious treatment of white characters. While some of the black people, such as Tyree and Dr. Bruce, the leaders of the black community, are not even worth saving, some of the white people are morally superior. Harvey McWilliams, a white lawyer, for example, is a staunch supporter of human values, the pillar of fairness and decency for Clintonville. Fighting against any form of injustice and exploitation, he opposes prostitution whether its victims are black or white. It is understandable that his defense of Tyree's interest is halfhearted and thus unsuccessful. Despite a moral weakness on his part, Tyree tries to defend his position:

> "But the white man took the bribes," Tyree argued. "There ain't no law but *white* law. . . . You say it's against the law to take bribes, but the white man takes 'em."
> "And now you don't want the white man to squeeze your money out of you?" McWilliams asked.
> "Why should only we suffer and go to jail?" Dr. Bruce asked.
> "That's a fair question," McWilliams said, nodding. "But don't you realize that you were wrong in what you did?"
> "There was nothing else to do," Tyree spoke testily.
> "That's no defense in a court of law," McWilliams told him.
> (*LD*, 288–89)

Though unwilling to compromise his principles, McWilliams nonetheless sympathizes with Tyree in his point of view that white corruption causes black corruption and that therein lies injustice.

Just as McWilliams is portrayed as an individual who can feel sympathy for his fellow human beings, Wright in *The Long Dream* creates other characters, white or black, endowed not only with intelligence but also with compassion. Fishbelly differs from Tyree because Fishbelly can sympathize with a white motorist lying on the roadside seriously injured in an accident and calling for help. Even though the suffering man insults him—saying, "G-goddammit, q-quick, nigger!"—Fishbelly does not shirk his duty in trying to save the man's life (*LD*, 143). Chief of Police Cantley, the chief culprit of the corruption, exerts his power in oppressing the black people. To the black world he is a symbol of intimidation and disrespect. But Wright does not make him a Ku Klux Klansman; instead Cantley is portrayed as a man at times capable of compassion and understanding. Frustrated by Fishbelly's refusal to hand him the canceled checks that would acquit him, Cantley screams:

> Goddamn you, you black sonafabitch! I wish to hell I could *believe* you! . . . But you *can't* tell me the truth! . . . Hell, no! You can't speak what you feel! . . . I swear to God, I don't know what we can do with you niggers. . . . We make you scared of us, and then we ask you to tell us the truth. And you *can't!* Goddammit, you *can't!* (*LD*, 366)

However despicable Cantley may appear to the black people, he is nevertheless capable of understanding their plight and point of view.

2

As Fishbelly grows in stature in the third and final part of the novel, called "Waking Dream . . . ," he challenges Cantley and surpasses him in wisdom and action. Cantley tells Fishbelly: "You're one of these new kind of niggers. I don't understand you" (*LD*, 365). Now that Tyree is dead, Fishbelly attempts to create the self by severing himself from his father's image of an ideal son. All his life he has been compelled to follow Tyree's footsteps in business matters, but in his heart he has despised Tyree for cringing when he talks to white people, for keeping a mistress and making his mother unhappy, and for getting rich by running a brothel. As he grows older he realizes that by bribing the police Tyree receives for burial the corpses of black men, victims of police brutality. At an earlier age, described in the first part of the book, Fishbelly receives a lesson from his father: "I make money by gitting *black* dreams ready for burial. . . . A black man's a dream, son, a dream that can't come true. Dream, Fish. But be careful what you dream. Dream only what can happen" (*LD*, 80). It is ironic that, by cooperating with corrupt officials and politicians, Tyree is destroying Fishbelly's dream of becoming a man of courage and integrity. Ironically as well, Tyree warns Fishbelly: "Don't force your dreams, son; if you do, you'll die" (*LD,* 80). By pursuing his own version of the dream of success, Tyree finds himself killed at the hands of the corrupted police.

Some critics regard Wright's portrayal of Tyree as far superior to that of Fishbelly. Edward Margolies observes: "The most singular achievement of this section is not, however, Wright's facility in moving Fishbelly from a subjective world to an external world—but rather the very remarkable portrait of Tyree. Indeed, though it is obviously not Wright's intention, it is Tyree who runs away with the novel—and it is Tyree one remembers most vividly after one has finished the novel." Katherine Fishburn notes: "The most significant scenes in Part II are those where Tyree plays his role as 'nigger,' since the acting is witnessed by Fish who is amazed at Tyree's versatility in exploiting the white man's preconceived notions of blacks."[5] Tyree is an impressive character in the middle section, where Fishbelly is initiated into manhood, because Tyree's racial view is diametrically opposed to Fishbelly's. Wright depicts the actions and skills with which Tyree asserts himself in realizing his dream of material success. As a result, Wright succeeds in creating a formidable character in the father against whom Fishbelly must and does rebel in order to realize his own dream of manhood. Thematically, then, Tyree in this part of the story is playing the crucial role of a foil. The most significant achievement of this novel, however, is Wright's ability to make dialogue and narration realistic and free of the Marxist language in *Uncle Tom's Children* and of the existentialist statements in *The Outsider.* Although Granville Hicks maintains in his review of *The Long Dream* that the novel is overly melodramatic because Wright "displays a preoccupation with scenes of violence that can be understood but cannot be fully defended,"[6] Wright's portrayal can be defended just as Zola's realistic descriptions of the lives of miners and their children in *Germinal* can be defended.

The interactions between father and son that take place in the middle part of the novel determine the kind of manhood Fishbelly eventually achieves. Because his feelings about racism in general and miscegenation in particular cannot be freely expressed, they are realized in his

5. Margolies, *Art of Richard Wright,* 158; Fishburn, *Richard Wright's Hero,* 36.
6. "The Power of Richard Wright," in Reilly, 324.

dreams. One might argue that what Wright considers realism in *The Long Dream*, especially in the middle section, is a surface realism, as Fishbelly, Granville Hicks says, "is not merely alienated from the culture in which he has been born; he is alienated from reality."[7] But the narrative of part 2, "Days and Nights . . . ," consists of two layers. What appears to be a surface realism is filled with a series of racial incidents that directly influence Tyree's business activities. The clashes that occur between black and white citizens result from prevailing social, economic, and political views and have little to do with the desires, fears, and doubts Fishbelly keeps within him. As the surface structure of the story thrives on the social details, the deep structure is immersed in his personal life. Though he is deeply involved in the social, economic, and political activities relating to his father's business, he is more concerned about his sexual initiation into manhood than worried about school or society. In fact, he brings Tyree, not himself, to grief when he fails to pass his examinations at school because of his affair with a near-white girl.

While much of the action in *The Long Dream* is described in terms of racial oppression, Fishbelly's development is portrayed in a sequence of dreams. He begins to dream about sexual relations with white girls after Chris, his best friend, accepts a white girl's sexual advances and is caught sleeping with her in a hotel. Chris consequently is lynched, castrated, and killed. Fishbelly's dreams, focused on such a traumatic experience, begin early in the novel. They continue through the second part and constitute the undercurrent of the story while the racial theme is developed on the surface. Part 3, "Waking Dream . . . ," which deals with the denouement of Fishbelly's manhood, unites the themes of sex and race, as developed earlier, into the final action of the story, his flight to Paris.

The crucial dimension in Wright's work as a whole is the development of a social and personal discourse in telling a story. *Native Son* reads not merely as a protest novel but as a powerful narrative that dramatizes the polarities between oppression and rebellion as they affect Bigger. *Black Boy* is eloquently focused on the young Wright's rejection of the South and his escape to the North. While Wright treats the problem of miscegenation throughout his writing, he makes a concentrated effort to probe this issue in *The Long Dream*. As a result, this novel succeeds

7. Ibid., 325.

in dramatizing the polarities between Mississippi and France, America and Europe, that dominate and determine the protagonist's eventual expatriation. From the age of six, when he becomes curious about sex as it relates to his parents, to the age of eighteen, when he leaves home, Fishbelly gradually comes to the realization that he cannot call himself a human being until he has the freedom of sexual relationship with a woman regardless of her skin color. Hence miscegenation underlies and incites Fishbelly's battle in achieving manhood.

How seriously Wright intended to deal with this problem in *The Long Dream* is suggested by what he says about it in *Black Boy*. It is true that *Black Boy* is not focused on the hero's sexual initiation. In *Black Boy*, sex, like religion, tends to victimize rather than develop an adolescent. The only woman to whom the young Wright is sexually attracted is a church elder's wife. His desires, however, are converted into "a concrete religious symbol," depicted in grotesque and physical expressions instead of pleasant and spiritual images: "a black imp with two horns; . . . a scaly, naked body; wet, sticky fingers; moist sensual lips; and lascivious eyes" (*BB*, 125). Such a description indeed debases his attitude toward human sexuality. Even though Wright is not concerned about the hero's sexual awakening in *Black Boy*, he lists twenty-one topics of taboo, of which the first four are directly related to miscegenation. It is beyond dispute that miscegenation occupied the mind of the young Wright as he came of age in the Deep South. While *Black Boy* merely intimates that white men do not mind black men's talking about sex as long as it is not interracial, *The Long Dream* powerfully demonstrates this fact. Wright thus intended to show in *The Long Dream* that the fear of miscegenation is the root of white racism.

Tyree is fearful that allowing Fishbelly to have white female companionship will ensure his son's death. As Tyree can believe that miscegenation leads to the black man's death, so can Fishbelly; but Fishbelly, discreet as he is, cannot help dreaming of having a white girlfriend. When he witnesses "the cruel crucifixion of Chris," he is warned by what Wright calls "A harsh challenge: *You are nothing because you are black, and proof of your being nothing is that if you touch a white woman, you'll be killed!*" (*LD*, 165). Despite this warning, as Wright portrays Fishbelly's state of mind at the end of part 1,

> he knew deep in his heart that there would be no peace in his
> blood until he had defiantly violated the line that the white

world had dared him to cross under the threat of death. He
walked beside Tyree, verbally agreeing with him, but he was
being magnetically pulled toward another and a more dangerous goal. A mandate more powerful than his conscious will
was luring him on, subsuming the deepest layers of his being.
(*LD*, 165)

Only through violating this inhuman white law can he justify his existence and hence achieve manhood.

Earlier in the story Fishbelly was ashamed of having Tyree as his
father, for he realized, Wright says, "that no white man would ever need
to threaten Tyree with castration; Tyree was already castrated" (*LD*, 151).
Fishbelly has already been threatened by the police with a knife when
he is caught watching white women, and now he loses his confidence
in Tyree's ability to instruct him on sexual initiation. "A woman's just
a woman," Tyree tells his son in earnest, "and the dumbest thing on
earth for a man to do is to git into trouble about one. When you had one,
you done had 'em all. And don't git no screwy ideas about their color.
I had 'em white as snow and black as tar and they all the same. The
white ones feel just like the black ones. There ain't a bit of difference,
'less you make one, and that's crazy" (*LD*, 158). Despite Tyree's sincere
effort to educate his son, Fishbelly is not entirely convinced of Tyree's
argument. For he has observed that Gladys, who is "willowy and almost
white in color," is more popular among the black boys than Maybelle,
who is "short, fat, jet black" (*LD*, 176). Interesting, however, Gladys is
described as being more attractive than Maybelle since she is slender
while Maybelle is short and fat.

However, the most important reason for Fishbelly's disagreement
with his father is not that Fishbelly is sexually more attracted to a white
woman than to a black woman, but that he feels that in a free, democratic
society he has the right to associate with the women of his choice. His
state of mind is reminiscent of Cross Damon's relationship with Eva,
the wife of a Communist, in *The Outsider*. Cross falls in love with the
white woman despite, and because of, the fact that it is taboo for a
black man to desire a white woman. The problem of miscegenation
Fishbelly faces is also similar to that confronted by Bigger Thomas,
for the image of forbidden sexual relations is central to Fishbelly's
dream as it is to Bigger's tragedy. As Wright shows in this novel, an
interracial sexual relationship, however natural and spontaneous, is
suppressed and condemned as socially unacceptable. Since a black man

like Fishbelly can only dream about such an experience, it has assumed the status of myth in American culture.

The scene of miscegenation Wright describes in *The Long Dream,* as in *Native Son,* has the status of myth, not only because Fishbelly and his friends dream about this experience, but also because such an experience evokes the historical fact that slave owners took advantage of black women for sex. Fishbelly and his friends, on the contrary, never exploit white women. "Long Black Song," as discussed previously, deals with a sexual encounter between a black woman, the wife of a farmer, and a white man, a phonograph salesman. In contrast to *The Long Dream,* the short story features an interracial sexual relationship in which man and woman exploit each other for their own emotional and physical needs.

By contrast, Wright portrays the interracial sexual scenes in *The Long Dream* with genuinely human sentiments that come from the hearts of the individuals concerned rather than with social and economic motives that get in the way. Fishbelly in his dreams and Chris in reality involve themselves with white women in purely personal relationships, just as does Bigger, who watches a white woman in a movie and has a sexual encounter with Mary Dalton. As noted before, that the sexual feelings Bigger and Mary express are mutual is shown by the original portrayal of the scene, which Wright deleted from the galleys in fear of censorship. For Bigger, not only is "the gay woman" as first visualized in the movie and later realized in his own life a symbol of success and power, but she also becomes a symbol of the fulfillment of his youthful dreams and desires. *The Long Dream,* then, incorporates into this symbol a symbol of human right and equality.

Within the racist context of the novel, Fishbelly's dreams become even more idealistic and romantic. In direct opposition to the sensibility born and nurtured in Fishbelly, Wright reconstructs with subtlety and care a racist discourse in which a black youth like Chris dares to violate the taboo at the risk of his life. When Bigger is captured, the newspaper account of him reflects the warning that white women must be protected from black men. The *Chicago Tribune* prints a lengthy article in which the reporter describes him as "a beast utterly untouched by the softening influences of modern civilization" (*NS,* 260). In *The Long Dream,* written two decades later, Wright does not have to use a journalistic technique to intimate the sexual taboo. Instead he portrays a scene in which Chris's body is mutilated and his sexual organ is severed, a scene in which many of the white women flock together in curiosity. Not only is such a scene based upon facts of lynching in the South, but it also places the hero of *The Long Dream* in a dilemma of life or death not faced in *Native Son*.

3

The final section of *The Long Dream*, entitled "Waking Dream . . . ," shows not only that Fishbelly's desire for white women remains a dream that cannot be fulfilled in Mississippi, but also that he is between a dream that has turned into a nightmare and still another dream that he has yet to experience. Unlike Bigger and Cross, he does not have to resort to violence and killing to justify his existence. Much like Melville's Bartleby, he prefers not to live in the world that dictates his way of life. Fishbelly is neither an erudite existentialist like Cross nor a defiant rebel like Bigger, but he is endowed with intelligence and common sense. At the funeral for the victims of the Grove fire, the Reverend Ragland delivers a moving sermon in which he says in part: "The men who run this town can be white as snow, but *we* know who's boss! GAWD'S THE BOSS! And He's more powerful than the president, the governor, the mayor, the chief of police" (*LD*, 348). The sermon sounds cogent to the black congregation, but Fishbelly is not convinced that God has the power to overrule the segregationists or help him realize his dreams. What Wright is demonstrating here is the fact that the segregationists maintained their unjust power during the 1920s, when he grew up in the South, and still did so as strongly three decades later, when he wrote *The Long Dream*.

The only way to resolve Fishbelly's dilemma at the end of the novel is for Wright to let his hero leave the very environment that has long suppressed Fishbelly's yearning for manhood and self-creation. On the surface, Fishbelly has wavered between accepting Tyree's advice, thereby acquiescing to white power, and rebelling against his father. Deep in his heart, however, he feels compelled to act on his own instincts in search of a new life. Once Tyree dies, not only is Fishbelly forced to charter his own course in creating the self, but he is also overwhelmed by his true feelings about himself as an adult. He now envisions a new world in which he can live like a human being. The reader might think that Fishbelly is expressing Wright's ideas instead of his own,[8] but Fishbelly's decision clearly results from an agonizing battle he has waged against society, a confrontation between his dreams and the forces of racial oppression. Only through Fishbelly's ordeal and dream is Wright able to define Fishbelly's ideals; in the process Wright's ideas and Fishbelly's feelings become intertwined. In defining the word *consciousness* as "the experience of thought," William James wrote that consciousness is "inseparable from the world of things of which we speak of being conscious of."[9] Fishbelly's consciousness is indeed the product of his experience, not of Wright's.

Throughout Fishbelly's adolescent life, society and his parents, especially Tyree, have indoctrinated him with racial separation and inequality. He has constantly been warned not to stare at a white woman, a symbol of the Blessed Virgin that Wright associates, in *Pagan Spain*, with "the purity of white womanhood" the Ku Klux Klansmen try to protect in the South. Wright observes: "These hooded penitents had been protecting the Virgin, and in the Old American South hooded Ku Kluxers had been protecting 'the purity of white womanhood.' . . . Some underlying reality more powerful than the glittering Virgin or southern white women had gripped these undeniably primitive minds. They were following some ancient pattern of behavior and were justifying their actions in terms that had nothing whatever to do with that pattern" (*PS*, 237). Yet Fishbelly finds himself falsely charged with raping a white girl and put in jail. It is in jail that he receives a letter from Zeke, his army friend stationed in France. "France ain't no heaven," Zeke writes, "but folks don't kill you for crazy things. These white folks just more like real human beings than them crackers back there in Mississippi" (*LD*, 398). Such a report, optimistic as it is, convinces Fishbelly that there is another world where he will be able to realize his dreams. Although expatriation implies the denunciation of one's country, Fishbelly's determination to go to France smacks of the twin traits of the American national character: individual freedom and the pursuit of happiness, as guaranteed in the Constitution.

An interesting aspect of Fishbelly's new dream is how such a dream is perceived by different characters in the book. Chief of Police Cantley,

---

8. Granville Hicks, for example, writes: "One ought to feel, as I do not, that the ideas Fish expresses are his ideas and not Richard Wright's" (ibid., 324).

9. See *William James: A Comprehensive Edition*, ed. John J. McDermott, 184–93.

who has recognized a generation gap between Fishbelly and Tyree, attempts to dissuade Fishbelly from pursuing his dream by saying emphatically, "Those French are dirty. . . . You're better off here, Fish" (*LD*, 400). Commenting on the letters Fishbelly has received from his friends in France, Chief Murphy appears less opinionated about France than Cantley and says, "Sounds like they don't like our Mississippi" (*LD*, 400). What Murphy says is an ironic understatement because it does not simply signal that Fishbelly's friends were unhappy living in Mississippi, but it really means that history condemns racism in America, whether it is in the South or in the North. Less concerned about Fishbelly's new dream than about his present plight in jail, his mother can only say: "Pray, son. . . . Gawd'll deliver you" (*LD*, 395). The religious attitude of Fishbelly's mother is reminiscent of that of the black mothers Wright deplores in *Black Boy*, *Native Son*, and *The Outsider*. For Fishbelly, then, the most exciting account of the new world is provided by Zeke, who writes him frequently. In one letter he writes in part:

> Man, we are stationed at Orleans, not far from Paris. It rains here most of the time, but we got good old cognac to keep us warm. . . . Both me and Tony's learning a little French and we get to Paris almost every weekend. Man, Paris is cool. Paris is crazy. These frogs over here even know about rock and roll. And what they don't know about jazz you can put in a thimble. Man, you ought to see these French cats go. These frenchies can jitterbug from way back. . . . Man, these blond chicks will go to bed with a guy who's black as the ace of spades and laugh and call it Black Market. Man, it's mad. You know what I mean. (*LD*, 383–84)

Toward the end of the novel Wright carefully incorporates a more serious discourse on race. In his last letter Zeke argues: "If somebody would prove to me that God's white, I don't think I would ever go to church no more. God just can't be like these goddamned white folks" (*LD*, 398). If this were said by Fishbelly, it would not sound true, for he has not acquired a perspective Zeke has by being able to juxtapose American life to French life. Wright's achievement in the final section of the novel is the creation of a unified vision in which Zeke's informed point of view and Fishbelly's new dream intensify each other. This new vision, moreover, is buttressed by an existentialist view Wright has earlier stated in characterizing Fishbelly as an emerging hero. When Fishbelly is asked by McWilliams, his lawyer, whether he supports Cantley or Tyree, whom Cantley has killed, he becomes confused, but

Wright replies on his behalf: " 'Yessir,' he confessed finally, realizing for the first time that he did not know whose side he was on. He was on nobody's side. He was for himself because he felt he had to be. He was black" (*LD*, 357).

Fishbelly's new vision of life reaches its culmination as he flies to Paris. On the plane from Memphis to New York, he lets a blond air hostess strap his seat belt as he watches her golden hair and white skin. On the plane from New York to Paris he nervously sits among the white passengers for over two hours, but finally he is attracted to a young white woman with dark brown hair sitting just two feet ahead of him. Imagining "the exciting, hidden geography of her body," he wonders why this woman, a simple image of the forbidden fruit, had caused "his deepest fears of death." "The woman," Wright says, "was as unreal and remote as had been that bleeding white man he had left to die under that overturned Oldsmobile on that far-off summer day when fear had robbed the world of its human meaning" (*LD*, 405). But all this brooding ceases, for he feels for the first time in his life that he is treated as an equal.

One might read the story, as does Earle V. Bryant, as saying that Fishbelly's sexual initiation through a white woman is "an absolute prerequisite for his survival in the white world" and that his quest is unfulfilled. Bryant's first observation proves true, but his second depends on the reader's point of view. The problem with the second judgment lies in his reading of Fishbelly's flight to Paris as a sign of his ultimate failure in sexual initiation. Fishbelly at the end of the novel, Bryant says, "is a man riddled with self-loathing, consumed by disgust for his own race, and paralyzed with dread of a racist white society." Surely this is not Wright's portrayal of Fishbelly on the plane, nor is it Zeke's and Fishbelly's imagined portrayal of Fishbelly in France. "As Fish sees it," Bryant further remarks, "white women *are* decidedly different from—indeed, even better than—black ones."[10] The difference between white and black women is obvious, but it remains only a sign or, to borrow a linguistic term, a "surface structure." What is signified, the deep structure, in Fishbelly's mind is the notion that white women and black women should be equal provided their counterparts, white men and black men, are treated equally.

10. "Sexual Initiation and Survival in Richard Wright's *The Long Dream*," 430–31, 428.

The last scene on the plane, furthermore, creates irony for the novel. For the first time in his life, Fishbelly meets a northerner, an Italian American who is on his way to Italy to pay homage to his father's birthplace. Ironically, the Italian American recalls in conversation with Fishbelly that his father used to talk to him about America "like a man describing a beautiful woman" and that his father called America his "Wonderful Romance." "That man's father," Wright says, "had come to America and had found a dream; he had been born in America and had found a nightmare" (*LD*, 406–7). It is also ironic that, when the Italian American inquires about life in Mississippi, Fishbelly, too embarrassed to tell the truth, only says, "We live just like anybody else" (*LD*, 406).

However persistent his self-consciousness may be, Fishbelly is now able to convert the feelings he has gained on the plane into "the bud of a new possible life that was pressing ardently but timidly against the shell of the old to shatter it and be free" (*LD*, 410). He thus leaves America behind him, brooding that a man's worth as a sexual being should be determined by any quality other than the color of his skin. This rationale is buttressed by Zeke's experience with French girls, to whom Zeke is more attractive than a Frenchman, just as, to Eva Blount in *The Outsider*, Cross Damon is more attractive than her white husband. Bryant's reading that white women to Fishbelly are "indeed, even better than" black women may be true on the surface of the narrative, but it does not tell what Fishbelly is dreaming or Wright was thinking.

As the conversion of his feelings about himself occurs, the theme of sexual initiation is united with that of racial relationship. To Fishbelly, leaving Mississippi for Paris means leaving a society where sex and race are intertwined as if black people were less than human. Though he is fully aware that Paris is no heaven, as Zeke had told him, he is now convinced that the French will not be obsessed with miscegenation as southerners are. His mother would like to have him back, but he will not go home. Nor will Huck Finn, as Mark Twain had shown half a century earlier, because Aunt Sally was going to adopt him and civilize him, and he couldn't stand it. He said, "I been there before."[11] Unlike many of the American expatriates in Europe in the 1920s, Richard Wright did not come back to America.

---

11. Twain, *Adventures of Huckleberry Finn*, 288.

12

Nature, Haiku, and "This Other World"

1

In 1960, less than a year before his death, Wright selected, under the title "This Other World: Projections in the Haiku Manner," 817 out of the about four thousand haiku he had composed since the summer of the previous year.[1] His motive for writing so many haiku in the final years of his life is not entirely known, but he told Margrit de Sablonière, his Dutch translator and friend: "During my illness I experimented with the Japanese form of poetry called haiku; I wrote some 4,000 of them and am now sifting them out to see if they are any good."[2] It is also known that a young South African who loved haiku described the form to Wright, who in turn borrowed from him the four volumes of *Haiku* by R. H. Blyth, a well-detailed study of the genre and a commentary on the works of classic and some modern Japanese haiku poets.[3]

A reading of the haiku in "This Other World," as well as the rest of his haiku, indicates that Wright, turning away from the moral, intellectual, social, and political problems dealt with in his prose work, found in nature his latent poetic sensibility. Above all, his fine pieces of poetry

1. The manuscript consists of a title page and eighty-two pages, page 1 containing the first seven haiku and each of the other pages ten. The manuscript, dated 1960, is deposited among the Wright collection in the Beinecke Rare Book and Manuscript Library, Yale University, New Haven, Connecticut. I have numbered each of the haiku consecutively 1 through 817. Subsequent references will appear parenthetically in the text as "OW," using these numbers.
2. See Fabre, *Unfinished Quest*, 505.
3. See R. H. Blyth, *Haiku* and *A History of Haiku*.

show, as do classic Japanese haiku, the unity and harmony of all things, the sensibility that man and nature are one and inseparable. In his prose work, despite the social and racial conflicts described, he had an insatiable desire to find peace and harmony in society. Bigger Thomas's muted protest before execution and Cross Damon's last message to his fellow human beings as he lies dying are meant to unite division in human life. Only when Fred Daniels in "The Man Who Lived Underground" achieves Zen-like enlightenment, his peace of mind with the world, is he shot dead by police. It is in another country that Fishbelly Tucker's quest for manhood, his dream of happiness and love, can be fulfilled. Although Wright wanted to belong to two cultures, American and African, as *Black Power* demonstrates, he was at times torn between the two worlds and remained an exile in Europe. His haiku, on the other hand, poignantly express a desire to transcend social and racial differences and a need to find union and harmony with nature. While his prose exhibits a predilection for a rational world created by human beings out of their narcissistic image of themselves, the humanism expressed in his haiku goes beyond a fellowship of human beings. It means an awareness of what human beings share with all living things. The human images in his haiku represent life at its deepest level.

The genesis of Wright's poetic sensibility is clearly stated in "Blueprint for Negro Writing," even though his theory is Marxist and hence political rather than literary. An African American writer's perspective, Wright defines, "is that part of a poem, novel, or play which a writer never puts directly upon paper. It is that fixed point in intellectual space where a writer stands to view the struggles, hopes, and sufferings of his people."[4] Wright established this vantage point in *Black Boy*, a nonfictional, autobiographical prose work. Yet he consciously created a poetic vision through and against which racial conflict could be depicted. The first chapter contains a long series of images from nature:

> There was the delight I caught in seeing long straight rows of red and green vegetables stretching away in the sun to the bright horizon.
> There was the faint, cool kiss of sensuality when dew came on to my cheeks and shins as I ran down the wet green garden paths in the early morning.

4. "Blueprint for Negro Writing," 45.

There was the vague sense of the infinite as I looked down upon the yellow, dreaming waters of the Mississippi River from the verdant bluffs of Natchez.

There were the echoes of nostalgia I heard in the crying strings of wild geese winging south against a bleak, autumn sky.

There was the tantalizing melancholy in the tingling scent of burning hickory wood.

There was the teasing and impossible desire to imitate the petty pride of sparrows wallowing and flouncing in the red dust of country roads.

There was the yearning for identification loosed in me by the sight of a solitary ant carrying a burden upon a mysterious journey.

There was the disdain that filled me as I tortured a delicate, blue-pink crawfish that huddled fearfully in the mudsill of a rusty tin can. . . .

There was the languor I felt when I heard green leaves rustling with a rainlike sound. . . .

There was the experience of feeling death without dying that came from watching a chicken leap about blindly after its neck had been snapped by a quick twist of my father's wrist. . . .

There was the thirst I had when I watched clear, sweet juice trickle from sugar cane being crushed. . . .

There was the speechless astonishment of seeing a hog stabbed through the heart, dipped into boiling water, scraped, split open, gutted, and strung up gaping and bloody.

There was the love I had for the mute regality of tall, moss-clad oaks. . . .

There was the saliva that formed in my mouth whenever I smelt clay dust potted with fresh rain.

There was the cloudy notion of hunger when I breathed the odor of new-cut, bleeding grass.

And there was the quiet terror that suffused my senses when vast hazes of gold washed earthward from star-heavy skies on silent nights. (*BB*, 14–15)

Two kinds of natural images are intermingled. On the one hand, those representing harmony and tranquillity in nature are presented as simple descriptions: "rows of red and green vegetables," "dew . . . on to my cheeks and shins," "wild geese winging south," "the tingling scent of burning hickory wood," "green leaves rustling with a rainlike sound," "the mute regality of tall, moss-clad oaks," "clay dust potted with fresh rain," "vast hazes of gold." On the other hand, those representing stressful and violent events in nature relate to human conflict and violence:

"the petty pride of sparrows," "a solitary ant carrying a burden," "a [tortured] delicate, blue-pink crawfish," "a chicken [leaping] about blindly after its neck [is snapped]," "sugar cane being crushed," "a hog stabbed through the heart," and "the odor of new-cut, bleeding grass." What Wright calls a writer's perspective is not only a juxtaposition of the images of harmony with those of conflict, but also a use of images of conflict and violence in nature to allude to those same elements in society. In fact, one of Wright's haiku, "Don't they make you sad, / Those wild geese winging southward, / O lonely scarecrow?" ("OW," 581), originates from a passage quoted above: "There were the echoes of nostalgia I heard in the crying strings of wild geese winging south against a bleak, autumn sky."

Another series of poetic images is included in the second chapter of *Black Boy* in the aftermath of a beating the young Wright has sustained after his bath for telling Granny, "When you get through, kiss back there" (*BB*, 49). Unlike the first series, this one predominantly consists of images from nature that generate feelings of joy and happiness, a sense of harmony between man and nature. "The days and hours," Wright recalls, "began to speak now with a clear tongue. Each experience had a sharp meaning of its own" (*BB*, 53). Of the eighteen sentences beginning with "There was," fourteen of them feature images of nature, harmony, and joy: "the breathlessly anxious fun of chasing and catching flitting fireflies"; "the drenching hospitality in the pervading smell of sweet magnolias"; "the aura of limitless freedom distilled from the rolling sweep of tall green grass"; "the feeling of impersonal plenty when I saw a boll of cotton"; "the pitying chuckle . . . when I watched a fat duck waddle across the back yard"; "the suspense I felt when I heard the taut, sharp song of a yellow-black bee hovering . . . above a white rose"; "the drugged, sleepy feeling that came from sipping glasses of milk"; "the slow, fresh, saliva-stimulating smell of cooking cotton seeds"; "the excitement of fishing in muddy country creeks with my grandpa on cloudy days"; "the puckery taste . . . when I ate my first half-ripe persimmon"; "the greedy joy in the tangy taste of wild hickory nuts"; "picking blackberries . . . with my fingers and lips stained black with sweet berry juice"; "the relish of eating my first fried fish sandwich"; "the long, slow, drowsy days and nights of drizzling rain" (*BB*, 53–55).

Even the two sentences that contain images of unfriendly nature basically differ from those in the first series that contain images of society and conflict. The second series includes the following: "There was the fear and awe I felt when Grandpa took me to a sawmill to watch the giant whirring steel blades whine and scream as they bit into wet green logs. . . . There was the morning when I thought I would fall dead from fear after I had stepped with my bare feet upon a bright little green garden snake" (*BB*, 54–55). But in these passages his feelings of anxiety have little to do with nature itself, since nature is not to blame for such feelings. Indeed, the poetic passages in *Black Boy* signify Wright's incipient interest in the exaltation of nature and the usefulness of natural images for his poetic sensibility.

The primacy of the spirit of nature over the strife of man is further pronounced in his later work, especially *Black Power*. In "Blueprint," one of the theoretical principles calls for the African American writer to explore universal humanism, what is common among all cultures. "Every iota of gain in human thought and sensibility," Wright argues, "should be ready grist for his mill, no matter how far-fetched they may seem in their immediate implications."[5] After a journey into the Ashanti kingdom in West Africa in 1953, when he was forty-five, he wrote in *Black Power:*

> The truth is that the question of how much of Africa has survived in the New World is misnamed when termed "African survivals." The African attitude toward life springs from a natural and poetic grasp of existence and all the emotional implications that such an attitude carries; it is clear, then, that what the anthropologists have been trying to explain are not "African survivals" at all—they are but the retention of basic and primal attitudes toward life. (*BP*, 266)

Wright's exploration of the Ashanti convinced him that the defense of African culture meant renewal of Africans' faith in themselves. He realized for the first time that African culture was buttressed by universal human values, such as awe of nature, family kinship and love, faith in religion, and honor, that had made the African survival possible. This primal outlook on life that he witnessed in Africa had a singular influence on his poetic vision.

Before discussing Ashanti culture, he quotes a passage from Edmund Husserl's *Ideas* that suggests that the world of nature is preeminent over the scientific vision of that world, that intuition is preeminent over

5. Ibid.

knowledge in the search for truth. This relationship of human beings to their world is somewhat remindful of Emerson, who emphasizes the preeminence of the spiritual and transcendental over the material and empirical. As Emerson urges his readers to realize their world rather than to attain material things, Wright defines the primal vision in African culture as the preeminence of spirit over matter.

Similarly, Wright's interpretation of African philosophy recalls a teaching in Zen Buddhism. Unlike the other sects of Buddhism, Zen teaches that every individual possesses Buddhahood and all he or she must do is realize it. One must purge one's mind and heart of any materialistic thoughts or feelings and appreciate the wonder of the world here and now. Zen is a way of self-discipline and self-reliance. Its emphasis on self is derived from the prophetic admonishment Gautama Buddha is said to have given to his disciples: "Seek within, you are the Buddha." Zen's emphasis on self-enlightenment is indeed analogous to Emersonian transcendentalism, in which an individual is taught to discipline the self and look within, for divinity resides not only in nature but also in human beings.

But there are differences between Zen and Emerson. Fascinated by the mysticism of the East, Emerson adapted to his own poetical use many allusions to Eastern religions. From time to time, however, one is surprised to find in his essays an aversion to Buddhism. This "remorseless Buddhism," he wrote in his *Journals,* "lies all around, every enterprise, every sentiment, has its ruin in this horrid Infinite which circles us and awaits on dropping into it." Although such a disparaging remark may betray the young Emerson's unfamiliarity with the religion, as Frederic Ives Carpenter has suggested, this passage may also indicate Emerson's aversion to the concept of nirvana. For Emerson, the association of this Buddhistic enlightenment with an undisciplined state of oblivion to the self and the world is uncongenial to his stoicism and self-reliance.[6] *Satori* in Zen is an enlightenment that transcends time and place and even the consciousness of self. The African primal outlook upon existence, in which a person's consciousness, as Wright explains, corresponds to the spirit of nature, has a closer resemblance to the concept of enlightenment in Zen than it does to Emersonian transcendentalism. To the African mind and to Zen, divinity exists in nature only if the person is intuitively

6. See Emerson, *Journals of Ralph Waldo Emerson, 1820–1872,* 318; Carpenter, *Emerson and Asia,* 150.

conscious of divinity in the self. To Emerson and Whitman, for example, God exists in nature regardless of whether the person is capable of such intuition.

Just as, in Zen, a tree contains satori only when the viewer can see it through his or her enlightened eyes, Wright saw in African life a closer relationship between human beings and nature than between human beings and their social and political environment:

> Africa, with its high rain forest, with its stifling heat and lush vegetation, might well be mankind's queerest laboratory. Here instinct ruled and flowered without being concerned with the nature of the physical structure of the world; man lived without too much effort; there was nothing to distract him from concentrating upon the currents and countercurrents of his heart. He was thus free to project out of himself what he thought he was. Man has lived here in a waking dream, and, to some extent, he still lives here in that dream. (*BP*, 159)

Wright thus created an image of the noble black man: Africa evokes in one "a total attitude toward life, calling into question the basic assumptions of existence," just as Zen teaches one a way of life completely independent of what one has been socially and politically conditioned to lead. As if echoing the enlightenment of Zen, Wright says: "Africa is the world of man; if you are wild, Africa's wild; if you are empty, so's Africa" (*BP*, 159).

Wright's discussion of the African concept of life is also suggestive of Zen's emphasis on transcending the dualism of life and death. Just as Zen master Dogen taught that life and death are beyond human control and not separate, the funeral service Wright saw in an Ashanti tribe showed him that "the 'dead' live side by side with the living; they eat, breathe, laugh, hate, love, and continue doing in the world of ghostly shadows exactly what they had been doing in the world of flesh and blood" (*BP*, 213), a portrayal of life and death reminiscent of Philip Freneau's "Indian Burial."

Wright was moreover fascinated by the African reverence for non-human beings, a primal African attitude that corresponds to Buddhist belief. He thus observed:

> The pre-Christian African was impressed with the littleness of himself and he walked the earth warily, lest he disturb the presence of invisible gods. When he wanted to disrupt the terrible

majesty of the ocean in order to fish, he first made sacrifices to its crashing and rolling waves; he dared not cut down a tree without first propitiating its spirit so that it would not haunt him; he loved his fragile life and he was convinced that the tree loved its life also. (*BP*, 261–62)

The concept of unity, continuity, and infinity underlying life and death is what the Akan religion and Buddhism share. Interviewed by *L'Express* in 1955 shortly after the publication of *Black Power*, Wright was asked, "Why do you write?" He responded, "The accident of race and color has placed me on both sides: the Western World and its enemies. If my writing has any aim, it is to try to reveal that which is human on both sides, to affirm the essential unity of man on earth."[7] When Wright was among the Ashanti, he was not conscious of an affinity between the two religions, but as he later read Blyth's explanation of Zen and its influence upon haiku, he found both religious philosophies fundamentally alike. Indeed, his reading of the African mind conforms to both religions in their common belief that mankind is not at the center of the universe. It is this revelatory and emulating relationship between nature and human beings that makes the African primal outlook upon life akin to Zen Buddhism.

2

Like transcendentalists such as Emerson and Whitman, Japanese haiku poets were inspired by nature, especially its beautiful scenes and seasonal changes.[8] Although the exact origin of haiku is not clear, the close relationship haiku has with nature suggests the ways in which the ancient Japanese lived on their islands. Where they came from is unknown, but they must have adapted their living to the ways of nature. Many were farmers; others were hunters, fishermen, and warriors. While they often confronted nature, they always tried to live in harmony with it: Buddhism and Shintoism constantly taught them that the soul existed in them as well as in nature, the animate and the inanimate alike, and

7. See "Richard Wright: I Curse the Day When for the First Time I Heard the Word 'Politics,' " in *Conversations with Richard Wright*, 163.
8. See Hakutani, "Emerson, Whitman, and Zen Buddhism."

that nature must be preserved as much as possible. Interestingly, haiku traditionally avoided such subjects as earthquakes, floods, illnesses, and eroticism—ugly aspects of nature. Instead haiku poets were attracted to such objects as flowers, trees, birds, sunsets, the moon, and genuine love. Those who earned their livelihood by labor had to battle with the negative aspects of nature, but noblemen, priests, writers, singers, and artists found beauty and pleasure in natural phenomena. Since the latter group of people had the time to idealize or romanticize nature and impose a philosophy on it, they became an elite group of Japanese culture. Basho (1644–1694) was an essayist, Buson (1715–1783) was a painter, and Issa (1762–1826) was a Buddhist priest, and each of them was also an accomplished haiku poet.

The genesis of haiku can be seen in the *waka*, or Japanese song, the oldest verse form of thirty-one syllables in five lines (5-7-5-7-7). As an amusement at the court one person would compose the first three lines of a *waka* and another person was challenged to provide the last two lines to complete the verse. The haiku form, a verse of seventeen syllables arranged 5-7-5, with such exceptions as 5-7-6 and 5-8-5, thus corresponds to the first three lines of the *waka*. *Hyakunin Isshu* (One hundred poems by one hundred poets), a *waka* anthology compiled in 1235 by Fujiwara no Sadaiye, contains haikulike verses, such as Sadaiye's "Chiru Hana wo" (The Falling Blossoms):

> Chiru hana wo   The falling blossoms:
> Oikakete yuku   Look at them, it is the storm
> Arashi kana   That is chasing them.[9]

The focus of this verse is the poet's observation of a natural object, the falling blossoms. To a beautiful picture Sadaiye adds his feeling about this phenomenon: it looks as though a storm is pursuing the falling flower petals.

This seventeen-syllable verse form was preserved by noblemen, courtiers, and high-ranked samurai for more than two centuries after the publication of *Hyakunin Isshu*. Around the beginning of the sixteenth century, however, the verse form became popular among the poets. It constituted a dominant element of another popular verse form called

9. The translations of this verse and other Japanese poems quoted in this chapter, unless otherwise noted, are by Yoshinobu Hakutani.

renga, or linked song. A *renga* consisted of a continuous chain of verses of fourteen (7-7) and seventeen (5-7-5) syllables, each independently composed, but connected as one poem. The first collection of *renga, Chikuba Kyogin Shu,* contains over two hundred *tsukeku* (adding verses) linked with the first verses of another poet. As the title of this *renga* collection suggests, the salient characteristic of *renga* was a display of ingenuity and coarse humor. *Chikuba Kyogin Shu* also collected twenty *hokku* (starting verses). Because the *hokku* was considered the most important verse of a *renga* series, it was usually composed by the senior poet attending a *renga* session. The fact that this collection included fewer *hokku* in proportion to *tsukeku* indicates the poets' interest in the comic nature of the *renga.*[10]

By the 1680s, when Matsuo Basho wrote the first version of his celebrated poem on the frog jumping into the old pond, *haikai,* an older poetic genre from which haiku evolved, had become a highly stylized expression of poetic vision. Basho's poem was totally different from most of the *haikai* poems written by his predecessors: it was the creation of a new perception and not merely an ingenious play on words. As most scholars observe, the changes and innovations brought about in *haikai* poetry were not accomplished by a single poet.[11] Basho and his contemporaries attempted to create the serious *haikai,* the verse form known in modern times as haiku. The haiku, then, was a unique poetic genre that was short but could offer more than wit or humor: a haiku late in the seventeenth century became a crystallized expression of one's vision and sensibility.

To explain Basho's art of haiku, Yone Noguchi, a noted bilingual poet and critic, quoted "Furu Ike ya" ("The Old Pond"):

> Furu ike ya   The old pond!
> Kawazu tobi komu   A frog leapt into—
> Mizu no oto   List, the water sound![12]

10. Donald Keene, *World within Walls: Japanese Literature of the Pre-Modern Era, 1600–1868,* 13.

11. A group of poets including Ito Shintoku (1634–1698) and Ikenishi Gonsui (1650–1722) of the Teitoku school, and Uejima Onitsura (1661–1738), Konishi Raizan (1654–1716), and Shiinomoto Saimaro (1656–1738) of the Danrin school, each contributed to refining Basho's style (ibid., 56–70). A detailed historical account of *haikai* poetry is given in ibid., 337–55.

12. The translation of this haiku is by Noguchi, in *Selected English Writings of Yone Noguchi: An East-West Literary Assimilation,* 2:73–74.

One may think a frog an absurd poetic subject, but Basho focused his vision on a scene of desolation, an image of nature. The pond was perhaps situated on the premises of an ancient temple whose silence was suddenly broken by a frog plunging into the deep water. As Noguchi conceived the experience, Basho, a Zen Buddhist, was "supposed to awaken into enlightenment now when he heard the voice bursting out of voicelessness, and the conception that life and death were mere change of condition was deepened into faith."[13] Basho was not suggesting that the tranquillity of the pond meant death or that the frog symbolized life. He was describing the sensation of hearing the sound bursting out of soundlessness. A haiku is not a representation of goodness, truth, or beauty; there is nothing particularly good, true, or beautiful about a frog's leaping into the water.

It seems as though Basho, in writing the poem, carried nature within him and brought himself to the deepest level of nature where all sounds lapse into the world of silence and infinity. Although his vision is based upon reality, it transcends time and space. What a Zen poet like Basho is showing is that man can do enough naturally, enjoy doing it, and achieve his peace of mind. This fusion of man and nature is called spontaneity in Zen. The best haiku, because of their linguistic limitations, are inwardly extensive and outwardly infinite. A severe constraint imposed on one aspect of haiku must be balanced by a spontaneous, boundless freedom on the other.

From a Zen point of view, such a vision is devoid of intellectualism and emotionalism. Since Zen is the most important philosophical tradition influencing Japanese haiku, the haiku poet aims at understanding the spirit of nature. Basho thus recognizes little division between man and nature, the subjective and the objective; he is never concerned with the problems of good and evil. The satori that the Zen poet seeks is defined as the state of *mu*, nothingness, which is absolutely free of any thought or emotion; it is so completely free that such a state corresponds to that of nature. For a Zen-inspired poet, nature is a mirror of the enlightened self; one must see and hear things as they really are by making one's consciousness pure and clear. Classic haiku poets like Basho, Buson, and Issa avoided expressions of good and evil, love and hate, individual feeling and collective myth; their haiku indeed

13. Ibid., 74.

shun such sentiments altogether. Their poetry is strictly concerned with the portrayal of nature—mountains, trees, flowers, birds, waterfalls, nights, days, seasons. For the Japanese haiku poet, nature reflects the enlightened self; the poet must always make his or her consciousness pure, natural, and unemotional. "Japanese poets," Noguchi wrote, "go to Nature to make life more meaningful, sing of flowers and birds to make humanity more intensive."[14]

The haiku poet may aim not only at expressing sensation but also at generalizing and hence depersonalizing it. This characteristic can be shown even by one of Basho's lesser-known haiku:

> Hiya hiya to   How cool it is,
> Kabe wo fumaete   Putting the feet on the wall:
> Hirune kana[15]   An afternoon nap.

Basho was interested in expressing how his feet, anyone's feet, would feel when placed on a wall in the house on a warm summer afternoon. His subject was none other than this direct sensation. He did not want to convey any emotion, any thought, any beauty; there remained only poetry, only nature.

Because of their brevity and condensation, haiku seldom provide details. The haiku poet delineates only an outline or a highly selective image, and the reader must complete the vision. Above all, a classic haiku, as opposed to a modern one, is required to include a clear reference to one of the four seasons. In Basho's "The Old Pond," said to be written in the spring of 1686, a seasonal reference to spring is made by the frog in the second line: the plunging of a single frog into the deep water suddenly breaks the deadly quiet. Although the frog traditionally is a *kigo*, a seasonal reference, to spring, Yone Noguchi interprets "The Old Pond" as an autumnal haiku: "the Japanese mind turns it into high poetry (it is said that Basho the author instantly awoke to a knowledge of the true road his own poetry should tread with this frog poem; it has been regarded in some quarters as a thing almost sacred although its dignity is a little fallen of late) . . . because it draws at once a picture of an autumnal desolation reigning on an ancient temple pond."[16] As a

14. Ibid., 69.
15. The original is quoted from Harold G. Henderson, *An Introduction to Haiku*, 49.
16. *Selected English Writings of Noguchi*, 2:74.

result, the poet's perception of the infinitely quiet universe is intensified. It is also imperative that a haiku be primarily concerned with nature; if a haiku deals with man's life, that life must be viewed in the context of nature rather than of society.

The predilection to portray man's life in association with nature means that the poet is more interested in genuinely human sentiments than in moral, ethical, or political problems. That haiku thrives upon the affinity between man and nature can be illustrated by this famous haiku by Kaga no Chiyo (1703–1775), a foremost woman poet in her age:

Asagao ni   A morning glory
Tsurube torarete   Has taken the well bucket:
Morai mizu[17]   I'll borrow water.

Since a fresh, beautiful morning glory has grown on her well bucket overnight, Chiyo does not mind going to her neighbor to borrow water. Not only does her action show a desire to preserve nature, but the poem also conveys a natural and tender feeling for nature. A classic haiku, while it shuns human-centered emotions, thrives upon such a nature-centered feeling as Chiyo's. Nor can this sensibility be explained by logic or reason. Longer poems are often filled with intellectualized or moralized reasoning, but haiku avoid such language.

Because the haiku is limited in its length, it must achieve its effect through an internal unity and harmony. Feelings of unity and harmony, indicative of Zen philosophy, are motivated by a desire to perceive every instant in nature and life: an intuition that nothing is alone, nothing is out of the ordinary. One of Basho's later haiku displays this sense of unity and relatedness:

Aki fukaki   Autumn is deepening:
Tonari wa nani wo What does the neighbor do
Suru hito zo[18]   For a living?

Although a serious poet, Basho was enormously interested in the com-monplace and in common people. As autumn approaches winter and he nears the end of his life, he takes a deeper interest in his fellow human

---

17. The original is quoted from Fujio Akimoto, *Haiku Nyumon*, 23.

18. The original is quoted from Noichi Imoto, *Basho: Sono Jinsei to Geijutsu*, 231.

beings. His observations of the season and his neighbor, a total stranger, are separate, yet they intensify each other. His vision, as it is unified, evokes a deeply felt sentiment. In haiku, two entirely different things are joined in sameness: spirit and matter, present and future, doer and deed, word and thing, meaning and sensation. Basho's oft-quoted "A Crow" depicts a crow perching on a withered branch, a moment of reality:

> Kare eda ni   A crow
> Karasu no tomari taruya   Perched on a withered tree
> Aki no kure[19]   In the autumn evening.

This image of the crow is followed by the coming of an autumn nightfall, a feeling of future. Present and future, thing and feeling, man and nature, each defining the other, are thus unified.

The unity of sentiment in haiku is further intensified by the poet's expression of the senses. Basho's "Sunset on the Sea," for instance, shows the unity and relatedness of the senses:

> Umi kurete   Sunset on the sea:
> Kamo no koe   The voices of the ducks
> Honoka ni shiroshi[20]   Are faintly white.

The voices of the ducks under the darkened sky are delineated both as white and as faint. Interestingly, the chilled wind after dark evokes the whiteness associated with coldness. The voices of the ducks and the whiteness of the waves refer to two entirely different senses, but, each reinforcing the other, the images create a unified sensation. This transference of the senses may occur between color and mood, as shown in a haiku by Usuda Aro, a contemporary Japanese poet:

> Tsuma araba   Were my wife alive,
> Tozomou asagao   I thought, and saw a morning glory:
> Akaki saku[21]   It has blossomed red.

19. The original is quoted from ibid., 86. The English version is quoted from Blyth, *History of Haiku*, 2:xxix. The middle line in a later version of the poem reads: "Karasu no tomari keri" (Henderson, *Introduction to Haiku*, 18). The earlier version has a syllabic measure of 5-10-5 while the later one has 5-9-5, both unusual patterns.
20. The original is quoted from Imoto, *Basho*, 117.
21. The original is quoted from Akimoto, *Haiku Nyumon*, 200.

The first line conveys a feeling of loneliness, but the red morning glory reminds him of a happy life they spent when she was living. The redness—rather than the whiteness or blueness—of the flower is transferred to the feeling of happiness and love. The transference of the senses, in turn, arouses a sense of balance and harmony. His recollection of their happy marriage, a feeling evoked by the red flower, compensates for the death of his wife, a reality.

Well-wrought haiku thrive upon the fusion of man and nature and upon the intensity of love and beauty this fusion creates. A haiku by Takarai Kikaku (1661–1707), Basho's first disciple and one of the most innovative poets, is exemplary:

> Meigetsu ya   The harvest moon:
> Tatami no ue ni   Lo, on the tatami mats
> Matsu no kage[22]   The shape of a pine.

The beauty of the moonlight here is not only humanized by the light shining on the man-made object but also intensified by the shadows of a pine tree that fall upon the mats. The beauty of the shadow reflected on the man-made object is far more luminous than the light itself, for the intricate pattern of an ageless pine tree as it stamps the dustless mats intensifies the beauty of the moonlight. Not only does such a scene unify an image of man and an image of nature, but it also shows that man and nature do interact.

3

As the haiku has developed over the centuries, certain aesthetic principles have been established. To define and illustrate them is difficult since they refer to subtle perceptions and complex states of mind in the creation of poetry. Above all, these principles are governed by the Japanese national character as it developed over the centuries, and they do not necessarily mean the same today as they did in the seventeenth century. Discussion of these terms, furthermore, proves difficult simply

---

22. The original is quoted from "*Meigetsu | ya | tatami-no | ue | ni | matsu-no-kage*" (Henderson, *Introduction to Haiku*, 58).

because poetic theory does not always correspond to what poets actually write. It has also been true that the aesthetic principles of the haiku are often applied to other genres of Japanese art such as Noh drama, flower arrangement, and the tea ceremony.

One of the most delicate principles of Eastern art is called "yugen." Originally *yugen* in Japanese art was an element of style pervasive in the language of Noh. It was also a philosophical principle that originated in Zen metaphysics. In Zen, as noted earlier, every individual possesses Buddhahood and must realize it. *Yugen,* as applied to art, designates the mysterious and dark, what underlies the surface. The mode of expression is subtle as opposed to obvious, suggestive rather than declarative. In reference to the works of Zeami, the author of many of the extant Noh plays, Arthur Waley expounds this difficult term:

> It is applied to the natural grace of a boy's movements, to the gentle restraint of a nobleman's speech and bearing. "When notes fall sweetly and flutter delicately to the ear," that is the *yūgen* of music. The symbol of *yūgen* is "a white bird with a flower in its beak." "To watch the sun sink behind a flower-clad hill, to wander on and on in a huge forest with no thought of return, to stand upon the shore and gaze after a boat that goes hid by far-off islands, to ponder on the journey of wild-geese seen and lost among the clouds"—such are the gates to *yūgen.*[23]

Such scenes convey a feeling of satisfaction and release, as does the catharsis of a Greek play, but *yugen* differs from catharsis because it has little to do with the emotional stress caused by tragedy. *Yugen* functions in art as a means by which man can comprehend the course of nature. Although *yugen* seems allied with a sense of resignation, it has a far different effect upon the human psyche. A certain type of Noh play like *Takasago* celebrates the order of the universe ruled by heaven. The mode of perception in the play may be compared to that of a pine tree with its evergreen needles, the predominant representation on the stage. The style of *yugen* can express either happiness or sorrow. Cherry blossoms, however beautiful they may be, must fade away; love between man and woman is inevitably followed by sorrow.

This mystery and inexplicability, which surround the order of the universe, had a strong appeal to a classic haiku poet like Basho. His "The

23. *The No Plays of Japan,* 21–22.

Old Pond," as discussed earlier, shows that while the poet describes a natural phenomenon realistically, he conveys his instant perception that nature is infinitely deep and absolutely silent. Such attributes of nature are not ostensibly stated; they are hidden. The tranquillity of the old pond with which the poet was struck remained in the background. He did not write "The rest is quiet"; instead he wrote "The sound of water." The concluding image was given as a contrast to the background enveloped in quiet. Basho's mode of experience is suggestive rather than descriptive, hidden and reserved rather than overt and demonstrative. *Yugen* has all the connotations of modesty, concealment, depth, and darkness. In Zen painting, woods and bays, as well as houses and boats, are hidden; hence these objects suggest infinity and profundity. Detail and refinement, which would mean limitation and temporariness of life, destroy the sense of permanence and eternity.

Another frequently used term in Japanese poetics is *sabi*. This word, a noun, derives from the verb *sabiru*, to rust, implying that what is described is aged. Buddha's portrait hung in Zen temples, as the Chinese painter Liang Kai's *Buddha Leaving the Mountains* suggests, exhibits the Buddha as an old man in contrast to the young figure typically shown in other temples.[24] Zen's Buddha looks emaciated, his environment barren: his body, his tattered clothes, the aged tree standing nearby, the pieces of dry wood strewn around—all indicate that they have passed the prime of their life and function. In this kind of portrait the old man with a thin body is nearer to his soul as the old tree with its skin and leaves fallen is nearer to the very origin and essence of nature.

Sabi is traditionally associated with loneliness. Aesthetically, however, this mode of sensibility smacks of grace rather than splendor; it suggests quiet beauty as opposed to robust beauty. Basho's "A Crow," quoted earlier, best illustrates this principle. Loneliness, suggested by a single crow on a branch of an old tree, is reinforced by the elements of time indicated by nightfall and autumn. The picture is drawn with little detail and the overall mood is created by a simple, graceful description of fact. Furthermore, parts of the picture are delineated, by implication, in dark colors: the crow is black, the branch dark brown, the background dusky. The kind of beauty associated with the loneliness in Basho's poem is in marked contrast to the robust beauty depicted in a poem by Mukai Kyorai (1651–1704), Basho's disciple:

24. See Max Loehr, *The Great Paintings of China*, 216.

Hana mori ya	The guardians
Shiroki kashira wo	Of the cherry blossoms
Tsuki awase	Lay their white heads together.[25]

The tradition of haiku established in the seventeenth century produced eminent poets like Buson and Issa in the eighteenth century, but a revolt against this tradition took place toward the end of the nineteenth century under the banner of a young poet, Masaoka Shiki (1867–1902). On the one hand, Basho's followers, instead of becoming innovators, as was their master, resorted to an artificiality reminiscent of the comic *renga*. On the other hand, Issa, when he died, left no disciples. The Meiji restoration (1868) called for changes in all aspects of Japanese culture, and Shiki became a leader in the literary revolution. He launched an attack on the tradition by publishing a controversial essay, "Criticism of Basho." In response to a haiku by Hattori Ransetsu (1654–1707), Basho's disciple, Shiki composed his own. Ransetsu's haiku had been written two centuries earlier:

Ki giku shira giku	Yellow and white chrysanthemums:
Sono hoka no na wa	What other possible names?
Naku-mogana	None can be thought of.

To Ransetsu's poem, Shiki responded with this one:

Ki giku shira giku	Yellow and white chrysanthemums:
Hito moto wa aka mo	But at least another one—
Aramahoshi[26]	I want a red one.

Shiki advised his followers to compose haiku to please themselves. To Shiki, some of the conventional poems lacked direct, spontaneous expressions: a traditional haiku poet in his adherence to old rules of grammar and devices such as *kireji* (cutting word) resorted to artificial twisting of words and phrases.

A modernist challenge Shiki gave to the art of haiku, however, kept intact such aesthetic principles as *yugen* and *sabi*. Classic poets like

25. Blyth, *History of Haiku,* 2:vii.
26. The originals of both haiku are quoted from Henderson, *Introduction to Haiku,* 160.

Basho and Issa, who adhered to such principles, were also devout Buddhists. By contrast, Shiki, while abiding by the aesthetic principles, was regarded as an agnostic: his philosophy of life is demonstrated in this haiku:

Aki kaze ya	The wind in autumn
Ware ni kami nashi	As for me, there are no gods,
Hotoke nashi[27]	There are no Buddhas.

Although his direct references to the divinities of Japanese culture smack of a modernist style, the predominant image created by "the wind in autumn," a conventional *kigo* (seasonal word), suggests a deep-seated sense of loneliness and coldness. Shiki's mode of expression in this haiku is based upon *sabi*.

Some well-known haiku poets in the twentieth century also preserve the sensibility of *sabi*. The predicament of a patient described in this haiku by Ishida Hakyo arouses *sabi*:

Byo shitsu ni	In the hospital room
Su bako tsukuredo	I have built a nest box but
Tsubame kozu[28]	Swallows never appear.

Not only do the first and third lines indicate loneliness, but the patient's will to live suggested by the second line also evokes a poignant sensibility. To a modern poet like Hakyo, the twin problems of humanity are loneliness and boredom. He sees the same problems existing in nature, as this haiku by him illustrates:

Ori no washi	The caged eagle;
Sabishiku nareba	When lonely
Hautsu ka mo	He flaps his wings.[29]

The feeling of *sabi* is also aroused by the private world of the poet, the situation others cannot envision, as this haiku by Nakamura Kusatao, another modernist, shows:

27. The original is quoted from ibid., 164.
28. The original is quoted from Akimoto, *Haiku Nyumon*, 222.
29. Blyth, *History of Haiku*, 2:347.

Ka no koe no	At the faint voices
Hisoka naru toki	Of the flying mosquitoes
Kui ni keri[30]	I felt my remorse.

Closely related to *sabi* is a poetic sensibility called *wabi*. Traditionally *wabi* has been defined in sharp antithesis to a folk or plebeian saying, "Hana yori dango" (Rice dumplings are preferred to flowers). Some poets are inspired by the sentiment that human beings desire beauty more than food, a sentiment lacking in animals and other nonhuman beings. *Wabi* thus refers to the uniquely human perception of beauty stemmed from poverty. *Wabi* is often regarded as religious, as the saying "Blessed are the poor" suggests, but the spiritual aspect of *wabi* is based upon an aesthetic rather than a moral sensibility.

This mode of expression is often attributed to Basho, who did not come from a well-to-do family. Basho's life as an artist was that of a wandering bard, as recorded in his celebrated diaries and travelogues, the most famous of which is *Oku no Hoso Michi* (The narrow road of Oku). *Nozarashi Kiko* (A travel account of my exposure in the fields), one of Basho's earlier books of essays, opens with this revealing passage with two haiku:

> When I set out on my journey of a thousand leagues I packed no provisions for the road. I clung to the staff of that pilgrim of old who, it is said, "entered the realm of nothingness under the moon after midnight." The voice of the wind sounded cold somehow as I left my tumbledown hut on the river in the eighth moon of the Year of the Rat, 1684.

Nozarashi wo	Bones exposed in a field—
Kokoro ni kaze no	At the thought, how the wind
Shimu mi ka na	Bites into my flesh.

Aki too tose	Autumn—this makes ten years;
Kaette Edo wo	Now I really mean Edo
Sasu kokyoo	When I speak of "home."[31]

The first haiku conveys a sense of *wabi* because the image of his bones suggests poverty and eternity. Although Basho has fallen of fatigue

---

30. The original is quoted from ibid., 2:322.
31. Quoted and translated by Keene, *World within Walls,* 81.

and hardship on his journey, he has reached a higher state of mind. The expression of *wabi* in this verse is characterized by the feelings of agedness, leanness, and coldness. Basho's attachment to art rather than to provision on his travel is shown in this haiku:

> Michinobe no   Upon the roadside
> Mukuge wa uma ni   Grew mallow flowers: my horse
> Kuwarekeri   Has eaten them all.[32]

Rikyu (1521–1591), the famed artist of the tea ceremony, wrote that food that is enough to sustain the body and a roof that does not leak are sufficient for man's life. For Basho, however, an empty stomach was necessary to create poetry. Among Basho's disciples, Rotsu (1651?–1739?), the beggar poet, is well known for having come into Basho's legacy of *wabi*. This haiku by Rotsu best demonstrates his state of mind:

> Toridomo mo   The water-birds too
> Neitte iru ka   Are asleep
> Yogo no umi   On the lake of Yogo?[33]

Rotsu portrays a scene with no sight or sound of birds on the desolate lake. The withered reeds rustle from time to time in the chilly wind. It is only Rotsu the beggar and artist who is awake and is able to capture the beauty of the lake.

The sensibilities of *yugen, sabi,* and *wabi* all derive from the ways in which Japanese poets have seen nature over the centuries. Although the philosophy of Zen, on which the aesthetics of a poet like Basho is based, shuns emotion and intellect altogether, haiku is nonetheless concerned with one's feeling and thought. If haiku conveys the poet's feeling, that feeling must have been aroused by nature. That the art of haiku comes from man's affinity with nature is best explained by Basho in his travelogue *Oi no Kobumi* (Manuscript in my knapsack):

> One and the same thing runs through the waka of Saigyō, the renga of Sōgi, the paintings of Sesshū, the tea ceremony of Rikyū. What is common to all these arts is their following nature and making a friend of the four seasons. Nothing the artist sees but is flowers, nothing he thinks of but is the moon. When what a

32. The original is quoted from ibid., 81.
33. See Blyth, *History of Haiku*, 2:viii–ix.

man sees is not flowers, he is no better than a barbarian. When what he thinks in his heart is not the moon, he belongs to the same species as the birds and beasts. I say, free yourselves from the barbarian, remove yourself from the birds and beasts; follow nature and return to nature![34]

Basho not only had great confidence in his art but he also believed that, though the form of haiku differs from that of any other art, the essence of haiku remains the same.

4

In trying his hand at haiku, Wright initially modeled his work after classic Japanese poets such as Moritake (1472–1549), Basho, Kikaku, Buson, and Issa. Two of the haiku in "This Other World"—"Off the Cherry Tree" ("OW," 626) and "A Leaf Chases Wind" ("OW," 669)— have a thematic resemblance to Moritake's famous *hokku*:

> Rakka eda ni   Fallen petals
> Kaeru to mireba   Seemed to return to the branch,—
> Kochō kana   A butterfly![35]

Both of Wright's haiku, "Off the Cherry Tree" and "A Leaf Chases Wind," create an illusion similar to that in Moritake's poem. In "Off the Cherry Tree" a twig with its red blossom flies into the sun as if a bird flew off the cherry tree. Likewise "A Leaf Chases Wind" captures a scene in which a leaf seems to be chasing wind and shaking a pine tree rather than the other way around. (A literal translation of Moritake's first two lines would be, "A fallen flower appears to come back to its branch.")

Interestingly enough, it is this *hokku* by Moritake that influenced Ezra Pound's composition of the famous metro poem, "The apparition of these faces in the crowd: / Petals, on a wet, black bough." Pound acknowledged for the first time in his career his indebtedness to the spirit of Japanese poetry in general and the art of haiku in particular. In the

---

34. Quoted and translated by Keene, *World within Walls*, 93.
35. The third line in Moritake's *hokku*, "Kochō kana," has five syllables since the long *o* consists of two syllables in Japanese. The original and the translation are quoted from Blyth, *History of Haiku*, 2:56.

"Vorticism" essay, he quoted Moritake's *hokku* just before discussing his famous "In a Station of the Metro," often regarded as the first published haiku written in English.[36] According to Margaret Walker, Wright was fascinated by the American Imagists, including Pound, but Pound was not likely the original source of Wright's interest in haiku.[37]

Another pair of Wright's haiku in "This Other World"—"In the Silent Forest" ("OW," 316) and "A Thin Waterfall" ("OW," 569)—in their style and content are reminiscent of two of Basho's most celebrated haiku. Wright's "In the Silent Forest" echoes Basho's "It's Deadly Quiet":

> It's deadly quiet:
> Piercing into the rocks
> Is the shrill of cicada.

As Basho expresses the awe of quietude, Wright juxtaposes silence in the forest to the sound of a woodpecker. Similarly, Wright's "A Thin Waterfall" is akin to Basho's "A Crow," quoted earlier. Basho, as noted earlier, focuses upon a single crow perching on a branch of an old tree,[38] as does Wright upon a thin waterfall. In both haiku, the scene is drawn with little detail and the mood is provided by a simple, reserved description of fact. As parts of the scene are painted in dark colors, so is the background. Both haiku create the kind of beauty associated with the aesthetic sensibility of *sabi* that suggests loneliness and quietude as opposed to overexcitement and loudness.

It is legend that Basho inspired more disciples than did any other haiku poet and that Kikaku is regarded as Basho's most innovative disciple. Two of Wright's unpublished haiku, "Beads of Quicksilver" ("OW," 106) and "A Pale Winter Moon" ("OW," 671), bear some resemblance to Kikaku's "The Harvest Moon," quoted earlier, since both poets emphasize an interaction between man and nature in the creation of beauty. In Kikaku's haiku, as pointed out earlier, the beauty of the harvest moon is intensified by the tatami mats, man-made objects, on which the shape of a pine tree is reflected as if it were a beautifully

36. Pound, "Vorticism." For the influence of haiku on Pound's imagism, see Hakutani, "Ezra Pound, Yone Noguchi, and Imagism."

37. *Richard Wright: Daemonic Genius*, 313.

38. A literal translation of Basho's "A Crow" (the original given earlier) is "On a withered branch / A crow is perching: / Sunset in autumn." In Blyth's translation (*History of Haiku*, 2:xxix), "A crow" is in the first line instead of the second.

drawn painting. In Wright's first poem, an element of nature, "Beads of quicksilver," is reinforced by a man-made object, "a black umbrella." In "A Pale Winter Moon," while the second line portrays the loneliness of a doll, a pale winter moon, a beauty of nature, is intensified by the presence of a man-made object.

"This Other World" includes a number of haiku that depict seasonal, climatic changes in nature, as do those by classic Japanese haiku poets. Wright's published "I Would Like a Bell" ("OW," 13), for instance, is comparable to Buson's well-known "On the Hanging Bell" in the simple depiction of a spring scene:

> I would like a bell
> Tolling in this soft twilight
> Over willow trees.

> On the hanging bell
> Has perched and is fast asleep,
> It's a butterfly.

Buson was well known in his time as an accomplished painter, and many of his haiku reflect his singular attention to color and its intensification. Wright's unpublished "A Butterfly Makes" ("OW," 82), for example, is reminiscent of Buson's "Also Stepping on":

> Also stepping on
> The mountain pheasant's tail is
> The spring setting sun.

For a seasonal reference to spring, Buson links an image of the bird with a spring sunset, because both are highly colored. As a painter he is also interested in an ambiguous impression the scene he has drawn gives him; it is not clear whether the setting sun is treading on the pheasant's tail or the tail on the setting sun. In any event, Buson has made both pictures beautiful to look at, just as Wright in his haiku draws pictures of a butterfly and the sunshine, themselves highly colorful and bright, which in turn intensify each other.

Although some of Wright's haiku in "This Other World" read like *senryu*, humorous, often graceless poems related to haiku in form, rather than like genuine haiku, a great majority of them are serious compositions in accordance with the basic principles and requirements of haiku.

Many of his pieces show that one of his chief aims as a haiku poet is to create beauty in his perception of nature. These haiku illustrate his attempts to express newly perceived sensations in his close contact with nature. "The Path in the Woods" ("OW," 76), portraying a scene of spring where insects live in their natural environment, creates an image of beauty. Similarly, "After the Parade" ("OW," 262) expresses the pleasant sensation that the snow, a representation of nature, has absorbed the flags, a representation of society. And "I Wonder How Long" ("OW," 662) expresses a surprising awareness that nature perpetually creates beauty whether man notices or not.

In "On the Pond's Green Scum" ("OW," 84), "Spring Dawn Is Glinting" ("OW," 177), and "On a Bayonet" ("OW," 477), for example, the beauties of nature are intensified by contrast. "On the Pond's Green Scum" is a haiku of balance and harmony, which is characteristic of some classic and modern haiku. Not only does a yellow butterfly, an image of beauty, counterbalance the pond's green scum, an image of ugliness, but the entire scene becomes beautiful because of two yellow butterflies, perhaps a couple, instead of one. In "Spring Dawn Is Glinting" it looks as though the beauty of nature is toning down the ugly aspects of human life. Similarly, in "On a Bayonet," the beauty of a spring moon at dawn mitigates the turmoil and suffering in human life.

Some of Wright's haiku, such as "The First Day of Spring" ("OW," 173) and "A Blindman's Eyebrows" ("OW," 241), as do some Japanese haiku, intensify an image of beauty through a sense of paradox. "The First Day of Spring" depicts the arrival of spring with winter lingering on the mountains. The bright sun intensifies the beauty of snow; as a paradox, the poem extols winter while celebrating spring. In "A Blindman's Eyebrows," the autumn fog, while keeping the living from seeing, creates beads of light, a beautiful image, for a man who unfortunately cannot see.

Because Wright was deeply concerned with the creation of beauty in his haiku, he quite consciously used such aesthetic modes of expression as *yugen, sabi,* and *wabi.* Haiku criticism has traditionally apotheosized Basho's "The Old Pond," the frog poem, for his manner of *yugen,* of describing what is hidden and hence mysterious. Interestingly enough, Wright's haiku "The Fog's Density" ("OW," 318) and "Above Corn Tassels" ("OW," 798) both focus on a frog's croaking, which sounds mysterious. In both poems the object depicted is hidden by a hazy mist as the croaking underscores a scene of mystery and nebulosity. In Wright's "Faint in Summer Haze" ("OW," 388), green hills are hidden and nebulous because of a haze and clouds of flies.

Many of Wright's haiku also suggest the feeling typical of *yugen* that nothing in nature or human life remains the same and nothing is immortal. In "A Falling Petal" ("OW," 83) the common destiny of a falling petal and a floating petal exhibits inevitable change in nature, as do the color and odor of a rose in "How Could This Rose Die?" ("OW," 650). Similarly, in "Under the First Snow" ("OW," 657), the color and sound of yellow leaves recall this change in nature.

Many of Wright's haiku are also composed in the manner of *sabi*, expressing loneliness, as does this published haiku by Wright:

> An autumn sunset:
> A buzzard sails slowly past,
>   Not flapping its wings. ("OW," 141)

Both "The Road Is Empty" ("OW," 136) and "An Autumn Sunset," quoted above, express loneliness, as does Basho's famous "A Crow," with a reference to autumn. In Wright's unpublished "Yellow Petals Gone" ("OW," 125), the third line, "a drizzling rain," makes a clear reference to autumn, as do the other two pieces, and the second line, describing the sunflower with its yellow petals fallen off, reinforces a vision of loneliness. In "The Road Is Empty" and "An Autumn Sunset," one empty road leading into hills and a single buzzard sailing slowly in the open sky without flapping its wings, respectively, convey loneliness and isolation.

Wright's "Don't They Make You Sad" ("OW," 581), "From the Rainy Dark" ("OW," 584), and "O Cat with Gray Eyes" ("OW," 594) also exhibit modes of expression characteristic of *sabi* and *yugen*. As pointed out earlier, the middle line of "Don't They Make You Sad" originates from a passage in *Black Boy*. These three poems, with their dark backgrounds, all express feelings of loneliness as well as of mysteriousness.

Some contemporary Japanese haiku, though characterized by the sensibility of *sabi*, convey a sense of balance and harmony in human life. Such a mode of expression is also characteristic of some of Wright's haiku. In "While Convalescing" ("OW," 224), a feeling of happiness suggested by red roses compensates for the loneliness suggested by convalescing, as the color of the flowers compensates for the absence of smell. In "Leaving the Doctor" ("OW," 243), a feeling of isolation and loneliness, a modernist theme, is balanced by the presence of the doctor just as night is by day and sadness by happiness. Likewise, "In a Bar's Doorway" ("OW," 405) depicts a scene in which spring wind counterbalances loneliness in human life.

As the sensibility of *sabi* produces an effect of balance and harmony, so does that of *wabi*, "the 'beauty' of poverty";[39] it is a reflection of self-discipline and self-reliance in Zen Buddhism. The sensibility of *wabi* also has an affinity with Emerson in his belief in the primacy of nature over materialism. Many haiku in "This Other World" are characteristic of *wabi*, as this published haiku by Wright indicates:

> Merciful autumn
> Tones down the shabby curtains
> Of my rented room. ("OW," 174)

Rotsu's haiku "The water-birds too / Are asleep / On the lake of Yogo?" depicts, as discussed earlier, the experience of a poet in which he could capture the beauty of the lake, a natural beauty only the beggar and artist saw. In the same way Wright's haiku, while describing his poverty and isolation, intimates the transcendence of materialism and the creation of beauty. The beauties of nature—as represented by one more winter in "In This Rented Room" ("OW," 412), one buzzing fly in "This Tenement Room" ("OW," 421), the moonlight in "I Am Paying Rent" ("OW," 459), and the autumn sun in "My Decrepit Barn" ("OW," 695)—not only compensate for one's plight of existence but fulfill the ultimate goal of an artist.

5

While emulating the techniques of classic haiku poets, Wright also composed his own haiku by focusing on the spirit of nature. The great majority of his haiku constitute various representations of nature, as well as concise expressions of what nature means to human life. Many of his pieces simply express unity in nature in poignant contrast with

39. Ibid., 2:viii.

disunity in society. As the unpublished "An Apple Blossom" ("OW," 78), "Would Not Green Peppers" ("OW," 527), and "From a Cotton Field" ("OW," 725) show, the poet's vision has little to do with human life. "An Apple Blossom" describes not only a sense of unity and harmony between bees and flowers, but also an interaction between them that creates a beautiful scene of nature. "Would Not Green Peppers," as do many of Wright's haiku on nature, finds unity in the world of nature with a sense of humor. In "From a Cotton Field," as in the other two haiku, nature exists in its own unity and harmony.

Some of the haiku included toward the end of "This Other World," such as "From the Cherry Tree" ("OW," 730), "In Deep Deference" ("OW," 791), and "A Tolling Church Bell" ("OW," 795), provide images of unity both in nature and between man and nature. Because these poems depict the relationship not only between natural objects but also between man and nature, the mode of expression is not as simple as that in the three haiku described above. In "From the Cherry Tree," as a simple image created in the first two lines signals unity of man and nature, a metaphor in the third line alludes to unity of the living and the nonliving. "In Deep Deference" shows the unity that exists between the living and the nonliving on the basis of an interaction of the senses occurring between the softness of snowflakes and the gentleness of birds' cheeping. In showing an affinity between natural and human sounds, this haiku conveys an intuition that nature itself performs a concert. In "A Tolling Church Bell," the tolling of a church bell and the moonlight above, an interaction between man and nature, sound and sight, create a spell over a rat, part of nature.

A number of haiku in Wright's selection focus their poetic vision on man's union with nature. In some of these pieces, Wright offers simple, direct scenes in which man and nature exist in harmony, in contrast with those complex, intriguing scenes in society where man is always at strife. "Seen from a Hilltop" ("OW," 42) finds unity in man and nature: a man, a mule, a rain, a meadow, and a hill. "In the Winter Dusk" ("OW," 377), like "Seen from a Hilltop," is a direct description of a scene in which a girl lives in harmony with nature. It is not clear whether a girl leads a cow or a cow her: creating such an ambiguous image intensifies the unity and harmony between them. In "After the Sermon" ("OW," 541), the seasonal reference is ambiguous, but Wright finds unity and an analogy between man and nature, "the preacher's voice" and "the caws of crows."

As Wright's finely composed haiku show, the manner of expression relies on an interaction and transference of the senses. In "The Cathedral Bell" ("OW," 220), the interaction between the bell and the spring moon reflected on the river points to man's union with nature. Similarly, "From a Tenement" ("OW," 253) creates an interaction between the sound of a trumpet and mists. In "From a Green Hilltop" ("OW," 428), a transference of the senses between the tolling of a cathedral bell and the blue sky creates a harmonious picture of man and nature. In "Putting Out the Light" ("OW," 539), the union of man with nature suggested by a transference between the light and the sound of sleet intensifies the natural phenomenon.

Whether perceiving nature for its own sake or in its relation to man, Wright's haiku thrive upon subtle interactions of the senses captured in seventeen syllables. For instance, in this published haiku the poet seems to detach himself from a natural scene:

> The spring lingers on
> In the scent of a damp log
> Rotting in the sun. ("OW," 47)

The feeling of the warm sun, the scent of a damp log, the sight and silence of an outdoor scene—all coalesce into an image of spring. In the process the overall image evolves from the separate visual images of the sun, of the log, and of the atmosphere. The three images of sight, moreover, are intertwined with the images of warmth from the sun and the rotting log, as well as with the image of smell from the log, all five images interacting with one another. In another finely wrought haiku, Wright portrays man's relationship with nature in terms of art:

> From across the lake,
> Past the black winter trees,
> Faint sounds of a flute. ("OW," 571)

Unlike "The Spring Lingers On," this haiku admits a human involvement in the scene: someone is playing the flute as the poet listens from the other side of the lake. Through a transference of the senses between the faint sounds of a flute and the black winter trees, an interaction of man and nature takes place. As the sound of man and the sight of nature affect each other, Wright has created beautiful images of man as well as of nature.

Traditionally, the haiku in its portrayal of man's association with nature often conveys a kind of enlightenment, a new way of looking at man and nature. In some of his haiku, Wright follows this tradition. "A Wilting Jonquil" ("OW," 720) teaches the poet a lesson that nature out of its environment cannot exhibit its beauty. In "Lines of Winter Rain" ("OW," 722), the poet learns that only when an interaction between man and nature occurs can natural beauty be savored.

This revelatory tradition derived from Zen philosophy, which underlies much of the thirteenth-century Chinese art by such painters as Liang Kai and Mu-chi[40] and much of the Japanese traditions of flower arrangement, tea ceremony, and haiku. Several of the pieces Wright selected and included toward the end of "This Other World" reflect his interest in Zen. For example, in "As My Anger Ebbs" ("OW," 721) Wright tries to attain a state of mind called *mu*, nothingness, in Zen by controlling his emotion. This state of nothingness is not synonymous with a state of void, but leads to what Wright calls in *Black Power* "a total attitude toward life" (*BP*, 159). "So violent and fickle," he writes, "was nature that [the African] could not delude himself into feeling that he, a mere man, was at the center of the universe" (*BP*, 262). In this haiku, as Wright relieves himself of anger, he begins to see the stars "grow bright again" and "the wind" return. Only when he attains a state of nothingness and "a total attitude toward life" can he perceive nature with his enlightened senses.

Similarly, in "Why Did This Spring Wood" ("OW," 809), Wright echoes questions posed by a Zen master: why nature remains silent and what nature is. A student of Zen, Wright in the haiku learns that he must attain *mu*, a state of nothingness that is absolutely free of any human-centered thought or emotion, of human selfishness and egoism. He also learns that this enlightenment is so completely free that such a consciousness corresponds to that of nature. Here he tries to give an admonition, as he does in many of his other haiku, that only by paying nature the utmost attention can human beings truly see themselves.

The four thousand haiku Wright wrote at the end of his life were a reflection of changes that had occurred during his career as a writer. But, more important, the new point of view and the new mode of expression

---

40. See Loehr, *The Great Painters of China*, 215–25.

he acquired in writing haiku suggest that Wright was convinced more than ever that materialism and its corollary, greed, were the twin culprits of racial conflict. Just as his fiction and nonfiction directly present this conviction, his haiku as racial discourse indirectly express the same conviction.

Bibliography

This bibliography contains only those items cited in the text. A date in brackets indicates the year in which a work was originally published.

Works by Wright

"Almos' a Man." *Harper's Bazaar* 74 (January 1940): 40–41.

American Hunger. New York: Harper and Row, 1979 [1977].

"Big Boy Leaves Home." In *The New Caravan,* edited by Alfred Kreymborg et al., 124–58. New York: Norton, 1936.

Black Boy: A Record of Childhood and Youth. New York: Harper and Row, 1966 [1945].

Black Power: A Record of Reactions in a Land of Pathos. New York: Harper, 1954.

"Blueprint for Negro Writing." In *Richard Wright Reader,* edited by Ellen Wright and Michel Fabre, 36–49. New York: Harper and Row, 1978. [First published in *New Challenge* 2 (fall 1937): 53–65.]

"Bright and Morning Star." *New Masses* 27 (May 10, 1938): 97–99, 116–22, 124.

The Color Curtain: A Report on the Bandung Conference. Cleveland: World, 1956.

Conversations with Richard Wright. Edited by Keneth Kinnamon and Michel Fabre. Jackson: University Press of Mississippi, 1993.

"Early Days in Chicago." In *Cross Section: A Collection of New American Writing,* edited by Edwin Seaver, 306–42. New York: L. B. Fischer, 1945.

Eight Men. Cleveland: World, 1961.

"Fire and Cloud." *Story Magazine* 12 (March 1938): 9–41.

"The Handiest Truth to Me to Plow Up Was in My Own Hand." *P. M. Magazine,* April 4, 1945, 3.

"I Tried to Be a Communist." *Atlantic Monthly,* August 1944, 61–70; September 1944, 48–56.

Lawd Today. New York: Walker, 1963.

The Long Dream. New York: Harper and Row, 1987 [1958].
"The Man Who Lived Underground." In *Cross Section: A Collection of New American Writing,* edited by Edwin Seaver, 58–102. New York: L. B. Fischer, 1945.
Native Son. New York: Harper and Row, 1966 [1940].
The Outsider. New York: Harper and Row, 1965 [1953].
Pagan Spain. New York: Harper, 1957.
Richard Wright: Early Works. Edited by Arnold Rampersad. New York: Library of America, 1991.
Richard Wright: Later Works. Edited by Arnold Rampersad. New York: Library of America, 1991.
Richard Wright Reader. Edited by Ellen Wright and Michel Fabre. New York: Harper and Row, 1978.
"Silt." *New Masses* 24 (August 24, 1937): 19–20.
"This Other World: Projections in the Haiku Manner." Ms. New Haven: Beinecke Rare Book and Manuscript Library, Yale University, 1960.
12 Million Black Voices. New York: Viking, 1941.
Uncle Tom's Children. New York: Harper and Row, 1965 [1940].
White Man, Listen! Garden City, N.Y.: Doubleday / Anchor, 1964 [1957].

Works by Others

Aaron, Daniel. "Richard Wright and the Communist Party." *New Letters* 38 (winter 1971): 170–81.
Adams, J. Donald. "Speaking of Books." *New York Times Book Review,* February 16 and April 6, 1958.
Akimoto, Fujio. *Haiku Nyumon.* Tokyo: Kodansha, 1971.
Altschuler, Melvin. "An Important, but Exasperating Book." *Washington Post,* March 22, 1953.
Atkinson, Michael. "Richard Wright's 'Big Boy Leaves Home' and a Tale from Ovid: A Metamorphosis Transformed." *Studies in Short Fiction* 24 (summer 1987): 251–61.
Auchincloss, Louis. "Introduction" In *Sister Carrie,* by Theodore Dreiser, v–xi. Columbus: Charles Merrill, 1969 [1900].
Baker, Houston A., Jr. "On Knowing Our Place." In *Richard Wright: Critical Perspectives Past and Present,* edited by Henry Gates Jr. and K. A. Appiah, 200–225. New York: Amistad, 1993.
———. "Racial Wisdom and Richard Wright's *Native Son.*" In *Long Black Song,* 50–59. Charlottesville: University of Virginia Press, 1972.
———. *Workings of the Spirit: The Poetics of Afro-American Women's Writing.* Chicago: University of Chicago Press, 1991.

Bakish, David. *Richard Wright*. New York: Frederick Unger, 1973.

Baldwin, James. "Everybody's Protest Novel." *Partisan Review* 16 (June 1949): 578–85.

———. "Many Thousands Gone." *Partisan Review* 18 (November–December 1951): 665–80. [Reprinted in Baldwin's *Notes of a Native Son* (New York: Bantam Books, 1968), 18–36.]

———. *Nobody Knows My Name*. New York: Dial Press, 1961.

———. *Notes of a Native Son*. New York: Bantam Books, 1968 [1955].

———. "The Survival of Richard Wright." *Reporter* 24 (March 16, 1961): 52–55. [Reprinted as "Eight Men" in Baldwin's *Nobody Knows My Name* (New York: Dial Press, 1961), 146–52.]

Baraka, Amiri. *Home: Social Essays*. New York: Morrow, 1966.

———. "The Myth of a 'Negro Literature.'" *Saturday Review* 46 (April 20, 1963): 19–21, 40.

Blyth, R. H. *Haiku*. 4 vols. Tokyo: Hokuseido, 1949.

———. *A History of Haiku*. 2 vols. Tokyo: Hokuseido, 1963, 1964.

Blythe, Hal, and Charlie Sweet. "'Yo Mama Don Wear No Drawers': Suspended Sexuality in 'Big Boy Leaves Home.'" *Notes on Mississippi Writers* 21 (1989): 31–36.

Bone, Robert. *Richard Wright*. Minneapolis: University of Minnesota Press, 1969.

Bontemps, Arna. Review of *The Outsider*. *Saturday Review* 36 (March 28, 1953): 15–16.

Brignano, Russell C. *Richard Wright: An Introduction to the Man and His Works*. Pittsburgh: University of Pittsburgh Press, 1970.

Brown, Lloyd. "Outside and Low." *Masses and Mainstream* 6 (May 1953): 62–64.

Brown, Sterling A. "Insight, Courage, and Craftsmanship." *Opportunity* 18 (June 1940): 185–86.

Bryant, Earl V. "Sexual Initiation and Survival in Richard Wright's *The Long Dream*." In *Richard Wright: Critical Perspectives Past and Present*, edited by Henry Louis Gates Jr. and K. A. Appiah, 424–32. New York: Amistad, 1993. [First published in *Southern Quarterly* 21 (spring 1983): 57–66.]

Burrison, William. "Another Look at *Lawd Today*: Richard Wright's Tricky Apprenticeship." *CLA Journal* 29 (June 1986): 424–41.

Butler, Robert. *Native Son: The Emergence of a New Black Hero*. Boston: Twayne, 1991.

Camus, Albert. *Lyrical and Critical Essays*. Edited by Philip Thody. Translated by Ellen C. Kennedy. New York: Knopf, 1968.

———. *The Stranger*. Translated by Stuart Gilbert. New York: Vintage Books, 1946 [1942].

Cappetti, Carla. "Sociology of an Existence: Wright and the Chicago School." *MELUS* 12 (summer 1985): 25–43.

Carpenter, Frederic Ives. *Emerson and Asia.* Cambridge: Harvard University Press, 1930.

Castro, Américo. *The Structure of Spanish History.* Princeton: Princeton University Press, 1954.

Cayton, Horace R. "Discrimination—America: Frightened Children of Frightened Parents." *Twice-a-Year* 12–13 (1945): 262–69.

Chase, Richard. *The American Novel and Its Tradition.* New York: Doubleday, 1957.

Cleaver, Eldridge. *Soul on Ice.* New York: McGraw-Hill, 1968.

Cobb, Nina Kressner. "Richard Wright and the Third World." In *Critical Essays on Richard Wright,* edited by Yoshinobu Hakutani, 228–39. Boston: G. K. Hall, 1982.

Cowley, Malcolm. "The Case of Bigger Thomas." *New Republic* 102 (March 18, 1940): 382–83.

Crane, Stephen. *Great Short Works of Stephen Crane.* New York: Harper, 1958.

Danquah, J. B. *The Akan Doctrine of God: A Fragment of Gold Coast Ethics and Religion.* London: Frank Cass, 1968 [1944].

Davis, Benjamin, Jr. Review of *Native Son. Sunday Worker,* April 14, 1940, section 2, pp. 4, 6.

———. "Some Impressions of *Black Boy*." *Daily Worker,* April 1, 1945, 9.

Delmar, P. Jay. "Charles W. Chesnutt's 'The Web of Circumstance' and Richard Wright's 'Long Black Song': The Tragedy of Property." *Studies in Short Fiction* 17 (spring 1980): 178–79.

de Luppe, Robert. *Albert Camus.* Paris: Temps Present, 1951.

Dreiser, Helen. *My Life with Dreiser.* Cleveland: World, 1951.

Dreiser, Theodore. *An American Tragedy.* New York: New American Library, 1964 [1925].

———. *A Book about Myself.* New York: Boni and Liveright, 1923.

———. *Dawn.* New York: Liveright, 1931.

———. "An Interview." *New York Times,* January 15, 1901.

———. "A Monarch of Metal Workers—Andrew Carnegie." In *Selected Magazine Articles of Theodore Dreiser: Life and Art in the American 1890s,* edited by Yoshinobu Hakutani, 1:158–69. Cranbury, N.J.: Associated University Presses, 1985, 1987. [First published as "A Monarch of Metal Workers," *Success* 2 (June 3, 1899): 453–54.]

———. "Nigger Jeff." In *Free and Other Stories,* 76–111. New York: Boni and Liveright, 1918. [First published in *Ainslee's* 8 (November 1901): 366–75.]

————. *Selected Magazine Articles of Theodore Dreiser: Life and Art in the American 1890s.* Edited by Yoshinobu Hakutani. 2 vols. Cranbury, N.J.: Associated University Presses, 1985, 1987.

————. *Sister Carrie.* New York: Doubleday, Page and Co., 1900.

————. "Some Aspects of Our National Character." In *Hey Rub-a-Dub Dub,* 24–59. New York: Boni and Liveright, 1920.

Du Bois, W. E. B. "Richard Wright Looks Back." *New York Herald Tribune Book Review,* March 4, 1945, 2.

Durdin, Tillman. Review of *The Color Curtain. New York Times Book Review,* September 26, 1954.

Ellison, Ralph. *Invisible Man.* New York: Random House, 1952.

————. "Richard Wright's Blues." *Antioch Review* 5 (June 1945): 198–211.

Embree, Edwin R. "Richard Wright: Native Son." In *13 Against the Odds,* 25–46. New York: Viking, 1944.

Emerson, Ralph Waldo. "Give All to Love." In *The Poems of Ralph Waldo Emerson,* edited by Louis Untermeyer, 65. New York: Heritage, 1945.

————. *Journals of Ralph Waldo Emerson, 1821–1872.* Vol. 1. Edited by E. W. Emerson and W. E. Forbes. Boston: Houghton Mifflin, 1911.

Fabre, Michel. "Richard Wright: Beyond Naturalism?" In *American Literary Naturalism: A Reassessment,* edited by Yoshinobu Hakutani and Lewis Fried, 136–53. Heidelberg: Carl Winter Universitätsverlag, 1975.

————. "Richard Wright, French Existentialism, and *The Outsider.*" In *Critical Essays on Richard Wright,* edited by Yoshinobu Hakutani, 182–98. Boston: G. K. Hall, 1982.

————. "Richard Wright: The Man Who Lived Underground." *Studies in the Novel* 3 (summer 1971): 165–79.

————. *The Unfinished Quest of Richard Wright.* New York: William Morrow, 1973.

Fadiman, Clifton. "A Black 'American Tragedy.' " *New Yorker* 16 (March 2, 1940): 52–53.

Fanon, Frantz. *The Wretched of the Earth.* Translated by Constance Farrington. New York: Grove, 1968 [1961].

Farrell, James T. *The League of Frightened Philistines.* New York: Vanguard, 1945.

————. "Lynch Patterns." *Partisan Review* 4 (May 1938): 57–58.

Faulkner, William. "Letter to Richard Wright." In *Richard Wright: Impressions and Perspectives,* edited by David Ray and Robert M. Farnsworth, 143. Ann Arbor: University of Michigan Press, 1973.

Felgar, Robert. *Richard Wright.* Boston: Twayne, 1980.

Feuerlicht, Ignace. "Camus's *L'Étranger* Reconsidered." *PMLA* 78 (December 1963): 606–21.

Fishburn, Katherine. *Richard Wright's Hero: The Faces of a Rebel-Victim.* Metuchen, N.J.: Scarecrow, 1977.

Ford, Nick Aaron. "The Fire Next Time? A Critical Survey of Belles Lettres by and about Negroes Published in 1963." *Phylon* 25 (summer 1964): 123–34.

———. "A Long Way from Home." *Phylon* 19 (winter 1958): 435–36.

Freud, Sigmund. *The Basic Writings of Sigmund Freud.* Edited and translated by A. A. Brill. New York: Modern Library, 1938.

Gannett, Lewis. "*Lawd Today* by Richard Wright." *New York Herald Tribune Books,* May 5, 1963, 10.

Gayle, Addison. *Richard Wright: Ordeal of a Native Son.* Garden City, N.Y.: Anchor Press/Doubleday, 1980.

Geismar, Maxwell. "Growing Up in Fear's Grip." *New York Tribune Book Review,* November 16, 1958, 10.

Gibson, Donald B. "Richard Wright: Aspects of His Afro-American Literary Relations." In *Critical Essays on Richard Wright,* edited by Yoshinobu Hakutani, 82–90. Boston: G. K. Hall, 1982.

Gilman, Richard. "The Immediate Misfortunes of Widespread Literacy." *Commonweal* 28 (April 1961): 130–31.

Glicksberg, Charles I. "Existentialism in *The Outsider.*" *Four Quarters* 7 (January 1958): 17–26.

———. "The God of Fiction." *Colorado Quarterly* 7 (autumn 1958): 207–20.

Green, Gerald. "Back to Bigger." *Kenyon Review* 28 (September 1966): 521–39.

Hakutani, Yoshinobu. "Creation of the Self in Richard Wright's *Black Boy.*" *Black American Literature Forum* 19 (summer 1985): 70–75.

———. "Emerson, Whitman, and Zen Buddhism." *Midwest Quarterly* 31 (summer 1990): 433–48.

———. "Ezra Pound, Yone Noguchi, and Imagism." *Modern Philology* 90 (August 1992): 46–69.

———. "Father and Son: A Conversation with Isamu Noguchi." *Journal of Modern Literature* 42 (summer 1990): 13–33.

———. "*Native Son* and *An American Tragedy:* Two Different Interpretations of Crime and Guilt." *Centennial Review* 23 (spring 1979): 208–26.

———. "Richard Wright's Experiment in Naturalism and Satire: *Lawd Today.*" *Studies in American Fiction* 14 (autumn 1986): 165–78.

———. "Richard Wright's *The Outsider* and Albert Camus's *The Stranger.*" *Mississippi Quarterly* 42 (fall 1989): 365–78.

——. "Yone Noguchi's Poetry: From Whitman to Zen." *Comparative Literature Studies* 22 (spring 1985): 67–79.

Hakutani, Yoshinobu, ed. *Critical Essays on Richard Wright*. Boston: G. K. Hall, 1982.

Hemingway, Ernest. *The Sun Also Rises*. New York: Charles Scribner's Sons, 1926.

Henderson, Harold G. *An Introduction to Haiku*. New York: Doubleday / Anchor, 1958.

Hicks, Granville. "Dreiser to Farrell to Wright." *Saturday Review* 46 (March 30, 1963): 37–38.

——. "The Power of Richard Wright." *Saturday Review* 41 (October 18, 1958): 13, 65.

Howe, Irving. "Black Boys and Native Sons." In Howe's *A World More Attractive*, 98–110. New York: Horizon, 1963. [First published in *Dissent* 10 (autumn 1963): 353–68.]

——. "Richard Wright: A Word of Farewell." *New Republic* 144 (February 13, 1961): 17–18.

——. *A World More Attractive*. New York: Horizon, 1963.

Hurston, Zora Neale. "Stories of Conflict." *Saturday Review of Literature* 17 (April 2, 1938): 32.

Imoto, Noichi. *Basho: Sono Jinsei to Geijitsu*. Tokyo: Kodansha, 1968

Jacks, Peter. "A Tragic Novel of Negro Life in America—Richard Wright's Powerful 'Native Son' Brings to Mind Theodore Dreiser's 'American Tragedy.' " *New York Times Book Review*, March 3, 1940, 2, 20.

Jackson, Blyden. "Richard Wright: Black Boy from America's Black Belt and Urban Ghettos." *CLA Journal* 12 (June 1969): 287–309.

——. "Richard Wright in a Moment of Truth." In *Modern American Fiction: Form and Function*, edited by Thomas Daniel Young, 170–83. Baton Rouge: Louisiana State University Press, 1989.

JanMohamed, Abdul. "Negating the Negation as a Form of Affirmation in Minority Discourse: The Construction of Richard Wright as Subject." *Cultural Critique* 7 (fall 1987): 245–66.

Johnson, Barbara. "The Re(a)d and the Black." In *Modern Critical Interpretations: Richard Wright's "Native Son,"* edited by Harold Bloom, 115–23. New York: Chelsea, 1988.

Joyce, Joyce Ann. "The Figurative Web of *Native Son*." In *Richard Wright: Critical Perspectives Past and Present*, edited by Henry Gates Jr. and K. A. Appiah, 171–87. New York: Amistad, 1993.

——. *Richard Wright's Art of Tragedy*. Iowa City: University of Iowa Press, 1986.

Kearns, Edward. "The 'Fate' Section of *Native Son.*" *Contemporary Literature* 12 (spring 1971): 146–55.

Keene, Donald. *World within Walls: Japanese Literature of the Pre-Modern Era, 1600–1868.* New York: Grove Press, 1976.

Kim, Kichung. "Wright, the Protest Novel, and Baldwin's Faith." *CLA Journal* 17 (March 1974): 387–96.

Kiniery, Paul. Review of *The Long Dream. Best Sellers* 18 (November 1, 1958): 296–97.

Kinnamon, Keneth. *The Emergence of Richard Wright.* Urbana: University of Illinois Press, 1972.

———. "How *Native Son* Was Born." In *Writing the American Classics,* edited by James Barbour and Tom Quirk, 209–34. Chapel Hill: University of North Carolina Press, 1990.

———. "*Lawd Today:* Richard Wright's Apprentice Novel." *Studies in Black Literature* 2 (summer 1971): 16–18.

———. "*Native Son:* The Personal, Social, and Political Background." *Phylon* 30 (spring 1969): 66–72.

———. "The Pastoral Impulse in Richard Wright." *Midcontinent American Studies Journal* 10 (spring 1969): 41–47.

Kinnamon, Keneth, ed. *New Essays on Native Son.* Cambridge: Cambridge University Press, 1990.

Klotman, Phyllis R. "Moral Distancing as a Rhetorical Technique in *Native Son:* A Note on 'Fate.'" *CLA Journal* 18 (December 1974): 284–91

Kurebayashi, Kodo. *Introduction to Dogen Zen.* Tokyo: Taiho Rinkaku, 1984.

Learned, Barry. "U.S. Lets Negro Explain Race Ills, Wright Declares." In *Conversations with Richard Wright,* edited by Keneth Kinnamon and Michel Fabre, 184–86. Jackson: University Press of Mississippi, 1993. [First published in *American Weekend,* January 24, 1959.]

Leary, Lewis. "*Lawd Today:* Notes on Richard Wright's First/Last Novel." *CLA Journal* 15 (June 1972): 411–20.

Leibowitz, Herbert. "'Arise, Ye Pris'ners of Starvation': Richard Wright's *Black Boy* and *American Hunger.*" In *Richard Wright: Critical Perspectives Past and Present,* edited by Henry Louis Gates Jr. and K. A. Appiah, 328–58. New York: Amistad, 1993.

Loehr, Max. *The Great Paintings of China.* New York: Harper and Row, 1980.

Logue, Ellen. "Review of *The Color Curtain.*" *Books on Trial* 14 (1956): 351.

McCall, Dan. *The Example of Richard Wright.* New York: Harcourt, 1969.

McDermott, John J., ed. *William James: A Comprehensive Edition.* New York: Random House, 1967.

Margolies, Edward. *The Art of Richard Wright*. Carbondale: Southern Illinois University Press, 1969.

―――. "The Short Stories: *Uncle Tom's Children; Eight Men*." In *Critical Essays on Richard Wright*, edited by Yoshinobu Hakutani, 128–50. Boston: G. K. Hall, 1982.

Matthiessen, F. O. *Dreiser*. New York: William Sloane, 1951

Melville, Herman. *Moby-Dick*. Edited by Charles Feidelson Jr. Indianapolis: Bobbs-Merrill, 1964.

Meyerowitz, Eva L. R. *The Sacred State of the Akan*. London: Faber and Faber, 1951.

Miller, Eugene E. *Voices of a Native Son: The Poetics of Richard Wright*. Jackson: University of Mississippi Press, 1990.

Moore, Gerian Steve. "Richard Wright's *American Hunger*." *CLA Journal* 21 (September 1977): 79–89.

Moore, Jack B. " 'No Street Number in Accra': Richard Wright's African Cities." In *The City in African-American Literature*, edited by Yoshinobu Hakutani and Robert Butler, 64–78. Cranbury, N.J.: Associated University Presses, 1995.

Murphy, Beatrice M. Review of *Black Boy*. *Pulse* 3 (April 1945): 32–33.

Nagel, James. "Images of 'Vision' in *Native Son*." *University Review* 36 (December 1969): 109–15.

Noguchi, Yone. *Selected English Writings of Yone Noguchi: An East-West Literary Assimilation*. Edited by Yoshinobu Hakutani. 2 vols. Cranbury, N.J.: Associated University Presses, 1990, 1992.

―――. *The Spirit of Japanese Poetry*. London: John Murray, 1914.

Norris, Frank. *The Octopus*. Garden City, N.Y.: Doubleday, 1956 [1901].

Ottley, Roy. "Wright's New Novel Isn't for Squeamish." *Chicago Sunday Tribune Magazine of Books*, October 26, 1958, 3.

Parker, Hershel. "The Lowdown on *Pudd'nhead Wilson*: Jack-leg Novelist, Unreadable Text, Sense-Making Critics, and Basic Issues in Aesthetics." *Resources for American Literary Study* 11 (autumn 1981): 215–40.

Pizer, Donald. "Theodore Dreiser's 'Nigger Jeff': The Development of an Aesthetic." *American Literature* 41 (November 1969): 331–41.

Pound, Ezra. "Vorticism." *Fortnightly Review* 573, n.s. (September 1914): 461–71.

Prescott, Orville. Review of *The Outsider*. *New York Times*, March 10, 1953, 29.

Purdy, Stropher B. "*An American Tragedy* and *L'Étranger*." *Comparative Literature* 19 (summer 1967): 252–68.

Redding, Saunders. "The Alien Land of Richard Wright." In *Soon, One Morning*, edited by Herbert Hill, 50–59. New York: Knopf, 1963.

———. Review of *Eight Men*. *New York Herald Tribune Book Review*, January 22, 1961, 33.

———. Review of *The Outsider*. *Baltimore Afro-American*, May 19, 1953, 15–16.

———. "The Way It Was." *New York Times Book Review*, October 26, 1958: 4, 38.

Reilly, John M. "Richard Wright and the Art of Non-Fiction: Stepping Out on the Stage of the World." *Callaloo* 9 (summer 1986): 507–20.

———. "The Self-Creation of the Intellectual: *American Hunger* and *Black Power*." In *Critical Essays on Richard Wright*, edited by Yoshinobu Hakutani, 213–27. Boston: G. K. Hall, 1982.

———. "Self-Portraits by Richard Wright." *Colorado Quarterly* 22 (summer 1971): 31–45.

Reilly, John M., ed. *Richard Wright: The Critical Reception*. New York: Burt Franklin, 1978.

Rhea, James N. Review of *The Outsider*. *Providence Sunday Journal*, March 22, 1953.

Richter, F. K. Review of *Black Boy*. *Negro Story* 1 (May–June 1945): 93–95. [Reprinted in *Richard Wright: The Critical Reception*, edited by John M. Reilly, 170–71. New York: Burt Franklin, 1978.]

Said, Edward. *Culture and Imperialism*. New York: Knopf, 1993.

Shapiro, Charles. "A Slow Burn in the South." *New Republic* 139 (November 24, 1958): 17–18.

Shorer, Mark. *Sinclair Lewis: An American Life*. New York: McGraw-Hill, 1961.

Siegel, Paul N. "The Conclusion of Richard Wright's *Native Son*." *PMLA* 89 (May 1974): 517–23.

Smith, Valerie. *Self-Discovery and Authority in Afro-American Narrative*. Cambridge: Harvard University Press, 1987.

Snelling, Paula. "Import of Bandung." *Progressive* 19 (June 1956): 39–40.

Soitos, Stephen. "Black Orpheus Refused: A Study of Richard Wright's *The Man Who Lived Underground*." In *Richard Wright: Myths and Realities*, edited by C. James Trotman, 15–25. New York: Garland, 1988.

Spandel, Katherine. "*The Long Dream*." *New Letters* 38 (winter 1971): 88–96.

Standley, Fred L. "' . . . Farther and Farther Apart': Richard Wright and James Baldwin." In *Critical Essays on Richard Wright*, edited by Yoshinobu Hakutani, 91–103. Boston: G. K. Hall, 1982.

Stephenson, Mary Ellen. "Spain Gets Bitter Barbs from Visitor." In *Richard Wright: The Critical Reception*, edited by John M. Reilly, 307.

New York: Burt Franklin, 1978. [First published in *Richmond News Leader,* August 28, 1957.]

Swanberg, W. A. *Dreiser.* New York: Charles Scribner's Sons, 1965.

Tanner, Laura E. "Uncovering the Magical Disguise of Language: The Narrative Presence in Richard Wright's *Native Son.*" In *Richard Wright: Critical Perspectives Past and Present,* edited by Henry Gates Jr. and K. A. Appiah, 132–48. New York: Amistad, 1993.

Tate, Claudia C. "Christian Existentialism in Richard Wright's *The Outsider.*" *CLA Journal* 25 (June 1982): 371–95.

Tener, Robert. "The Where, the When, the What: A Study of Richard Wright's Haiku." In *Critical Essays on Richard Wright,* edited by Yoshinobu Hakutani, 273–98. Boston: G. K. Hall, 1982.

Thaddeus, Janice. "The Metamorphosis of Richard Wright's *Black Boy.*" *American Literature* 57 (May 1985): 199–214.

Twain, Mark. *Adventures of Huckleberry Finn.* Boston: Houghton Mifflin, 1962 [1884].

———. *The Love Letters of Mark Twain.* Edited by Dixon Wecter. New York: Harper, 1949.

———. *"Pudd'nhead Wilson" and "Those Extraordinary Twins."* Edited by Sidney E. Berger. New York: Norton, 1980.

Vivas, Eliseo. "Dreiser, an Inconsistent Mechanist." In *The Stature of Theodore Dreiser,* edited by Alfred Kazin and Charles Shapiro, 237–45. Bloomington: Indiana University Press, 1955.

Waley, Arthur. *The No Plays of Japan.* New York: Grove Press, 1920.

Walker, Margaret. "Richard Wright." *New Letters* 38 (winter 1971), 198–99.

———. *Richard Wright: Daemonic Genius.* New York: Warner Books, 1988.

Webb, Constance. *Richard Wright: A Biography.* New York: Putnam, 1968.

Webb, Tracy. "The Role of Water Imagery in *Uncle Tom's Children.*" *Modern Fiction Studies* 34 (spring 1988): 5–16.

Williams, John A. *The Most Native of Sons: A Biography of Richard Wright.* Garden City, N.Y.: Doubleday, 1970.

Winslow, Henry F. "Nightmare Experiences." *Crisis* 66 (February 1959): 120–22.

Zola, Émile. "The Experimental Novel." In *Documents of Modern Literary Realism,* edited by George J. Becker, 162–96. Princeton: Princeton University Press, 1963.

Index